Generative AI Foundations, Developments, and Applications

Rajkumar Kannan
Bishop Heber College, Tiruchirappalli, India

Muneer Ahmad
University of Roehampton, UK

IGI Global
Scientific Publishing
Publishing Tomorrow's Research Today

Vice President of Editorial	Melissa Wagner
Managing Editor of Acquisitions	Mikaela Felty
Managing Editor of Book Development	Jocelynn Hessler
Production Manager	Mike Brehm
Cover Design	Phillip Shickler

Published in the United States of America by
IGI Global Scientific Publishing
701 East Chocolate Avenue
Hershey, PA, 17033, USA
Tel: 717-533-8845
Fax: 717-533-8661
Website: https://www.igi-global.com E-mail: cust@igi-global.com

Library of Congress Cataloging-in-Publication Data

Names: Kannan, Rajkumar editor | Ahmad, Muneer, 1977- editor
Title: Generative AI foundations, developments, and applications / edited by Rajkumar Kannan, Muneer Ahmad.
Description: Hershey, PA : IGI Global, [2025] | Includes bibliographical references and index. | Summary: "The objective of this book is to serve as a comprehensive resource that sheds light on all aspects of generative artificial intelligence (AI), from its theoretical foundations to its practical applications"-- Provided by publisher.
Identifiers: LCCN 2024050850 (print) | LCCN 2024050851 (ebook) | ISBN 9798369362556 hardcover | ISBN 9798369362563 paperback | ISBN 9798369362570 ebook
Subjects: LCSH: Generative artificial intelligence | Artificial intelligence--Agricultural applications | Natural language processing (Computer science)
Classification: LCC Q335.4 .G46 2025 (print) | LCC Q335.4 (ebook) | DDC 006.3--dc23/eng/20250321
LC record available at https://lccn.loc.gov/2024050850
LC ebook record available at https://lccn.loc.gov/2024050851

British Cataloguing in Publication Data
A Cataloguing in Publication record for this book is available from the British Library.

Table of Contents

Detailed Table of Contents

Urdu is a widely spoken language in East and South Asia, making Urdu digit recognition crucial for applications like cheque processing and number plate recognition. However, digit classification for Urdu numerals is challenging due to limited training data for deeper models. While large public datasets exist for languages like English, Chinese, and Arabic, Urdu lacks such resources. Data augmentation can mitigate this issue. This chapter explores using deep convolutional generative adversarial network (DCGAN) to generate artificial images, preserving the original data's features. DCGAN's performance is assessed with t-stochastic neighbour embedding (t-SNE) and Fréchet inception distance (FID), achieving an FID score of 25.32 on a dataset with 10 classes. This research enhances the dataset and paves the way for advanced Urdu numeral classifiers for future applications.

In the field of precision agriculture, combining multimodal data sources such as Soil Nitrogen-Phosphorus-Potassium (NPK) sensors, alongside temperature and humidity measurements with high-resolution RGB and infrared imagery, is crucial for improving crop monitoring. Aligning these multimodal data, which vary widely in resolution and format, to a uniform spatial scale is a challenge. Achieving this uniformity is essential for the computation of multiple vegetation indices, providing analysis of crop health. To overcome differences in data resolution, GANs are utilized. GANs are a key technology in generative AI and are highly effective at improving the quality of low-resolution data. This makes them ideal for data fusion of NPK sensors with detailed images captured using high-resolution cameras. Using GANs not only standardizes the resolutions but also improves the overall quality of the analysis. This leads to more accurate assessments of crop health. By deploying these, farmers and agronomists are equipped to make more informed decisions, leading to better agricultural outcomes.

Qazi Mudassar Ilyas, King Faisal University, Saudi Arabia
Sadia Aziz, La Trobe University, Australia

Large language models produce excellent outputs for queries highly relevant to their training data. Retrieval-augmented generation (RAG) is used to augment this training data with additional contextual information based on additional data. Although RAG improves text generation through context retrieval from this additional data, the basic RAG system has limitations in chunking, hallucinations, and reliance on augmented content for knowledge-intensive tasks. This chapter discusses several advanced techniques to enhance retrieval and generation tasks in an RAG pipeline. The chapter discusses advanced strategies for chunking, vectorization, and search processes. Moreover, reranking, filtering, query transformation, query routing, and response synthesis improve generated responses' relevance, coherence, and accuracy.

Andi Asrifan, Universitas Negeri Makassar, Indonesia
Muh. Fadli Hasa, Universitas Muhammadiyah Sorong, Indonesia
Syafryadin Syafryadin, Universitas Bengkulu, Indonesia
Hanafi Pelu, Balai Diklat Keagamaan Makassar, Indonesia

This chapter examines how artificial intelligence (AI) has changed society and its future. It shows how AI may boost creativity but can pose problems. The chapter stresses expanding AI understanding and engaging various communities to reduce risks and maximize benefits. It covers the history of AI, from Turing's early work to modern machine learning, and explores automation's role in society. The chapter emphasizes the necessity for international AI regulation cooperation, portraying UNCITRAL as a key role in stimulating dialogue and establishing global AI law and policy. The chapter sets the stage for exploring AI's revolutionary potential in creative fields by explaining AI's role in narrative.

Generative AI represents a groundbreaking approach in artificial intelligence, focusing on creating new data instances that closely resemble existing datasets. Unlike traditional models that primarily classify or predict, generative models like generative adversarial networks (GANs) and variational autoencoders (VAEs) learn the underlying data distribution, enabling them to produce novel outputs. This chapter explores various generative models, their applications in industries such as entertainment, healthcare, and fashion, and their implications for creativity and originality. It highlights advancements in techniques like conditional generation and style transfer, emphasizing the potential of generative AI to redefine human creativity and foster collaboration between humans and machines in artistic endeavors.

Agriculture is vital to economic growth, contributing 4% to global GDP and over 25% in some developing countries. Most farming practices are outdated, necessitating modernization for improved efficiency. Advances in deep learning, multi- and hyperspectral imagery (MHSI), UAVs, and agri-bots have revolutionized precision agriculture (PA). Computer vision (CV) techniques, enhanced by MHSI, have automated tasks like crop classification, disease monitoring, and biomass estimation. UAVs assist in field scouting, disease detection, and precision spraying, while agri-bots with IoT sensors facilitate real-time data-driven actions such as fruit picking and weed control. This chapter reviews the latest developments in CV, MHSI, UAVs, and agri-bots, examining current methods, challenges, datasets, and future applications in precision agriculture.

The study has investigated attitudes of medical and dental students toward acquiring communication skills using 'Communication Skills Attitude Scale' where 95% of students considered learning communication a lifelong skill. Students from British curriculum had significantly stronger positive attitudes compared to Pakistani curriculum. Themes identified using focal group discussions include allocating more time, training, resources, and standardized assessments for learning communication skills.

Generative AI has become the disruptive technology of this decade, which has profoundly impacted our lives. Prompt engineering is at the heart of interactions with these models. The skill of designing effective prompts is quickly becoming an essential tool for the entire white-collar workforce. This chapter explores fundamental concepts, challenges, strategies, advanced techniques, and future directions of prompt engineering, providing a comprehensive understanding of how this skill set enables the user to benefit from generative AI systems. Furthermore, the chapter highlights several strategies for troubleshooting prompts that fail to produce the desired results. The chapter concludes with future directions and trends in prompt engineering, such as auto-prompting and dynamic prompt adoption, where AI models are becoming increasingly adept at optimizing prompts autonomously. Ultimately, this chapter provides a detailed view of current practices in prompt engineering and the future potential for effective and responsible human-AI collaboration.

Unsupervised learning, an essential component of machine learning, has a substantial impact on the advancement and implementation of generative AI. Incorporating unsupervised learning into generative AI models has the potential to transform businesses by automating and improving creative processes. This chapter explores the fundamental principles, techniques, and progress in unsupervised learning. The authors delve into a range of methods and approaches, including clustering, dimensionality reduction, data mining, feature extraction, neural networks, and anomaly detection, emphasizing their use in generative models. This chapter provides a detailed explanation and use cases to demonstrate how unsupervised learning allows generative AI to produce new and high-quality outputs without the need for labeled data.

Preface

The rapid growth of artificial intelligence (AI) has transformed many areas of life, from healthcare and business to creative industries. One of the most exciting advancements in this field is generative AI, which enables machines to create text, images, and even music. This book explores the foundations, latest developments, and practical applications of generative AI, helping readers understand how this technology works and how it is shaping the future.

We have structured this book to be accessible to both beginners and experts. The early chapters introduce key concepts and the history of generative models, while later chapters discuss advanced techniques and real-world applications. Whether you are a student, researcher, or industry professional, this book will provide valuable insights into the possibilities and challenges of generative AI.

We hope this book will serve as a useful resource for those interested in AI and its creative potential. As this field continues to evolve, we encourage readers to explore new ideas and contribute to the responsible development of generative AI. We are grateful to all the contributors, researchers, and practitioners who have helped shape this book, and we look forward to seeing how generative AI will continue to innovate and inspire.

Rajkumar Kannan

Bishop Heber College, Tiruchirappalli, India

Muneer Ahmad

University of Roehampton, UK

Acknowledgment

This work was supported by the Deanship of Scientific Research, Vice Presidency for Graduate Studies and Scientific Research, King Faisal University, Saudi Arabia [Grant No. KFU250566]

Chapter 1
Data Augmentation Using Deep Convolutional Generative Adversarial Network (DCGAN) for Urdu Numerals

Aamna Bhatti
https://orcid.org/0000-0002-8526-4827
National University of Sciences and Technology, Pakistan

Rafia Mumtaz
National University of Sciences and Technology, Pakistan

ABSTRACT

Urdu is a widely spoken language in East and South Asia, making Urdu digit recognition crucial for applications like cheque processing and number plate recognition. However, digit classification for Urdu numerals is challenging due to limited training data for deeper models. While large public datasets exist for languages like English, Chinese, and Arabic, Urdu lacks such resources. Data augmentation can mitigate this issue. This chapter explores using deep convolutional generative adversarial network (DCGAN) to generate artificial images, preserving the original data's features. DCGAN's performance is assessed with t-stochastic neighbour embedding (t-SNE) and Fréchet inception distance (FID), achieving an FID score of 25.32 on a dataset with 10 classes. This research enhances the dataset and paves the way for advanced Urdu numeral classifiers for future applications.

DOI: 10.4018/979-8-3693-6255-6.ch001

INTRODUCTION

During the last few decades, the document analysis research community has studied the recognition of offline handwritten character recognition (Xinyue et al., 2017). There are now several automatic systems available in the market for offline handwriting recognition. These frameworks, however, offer solutions specific to a few major world scripts, such as English, Chinese, Arabic, Japanese, etc. due to the abundance of public datasets available for these languages. Urdu language is very popular in South Asian countries and has been neglected due to the unavailability of larger public datasets that could entail various handwriting styles.

In recent deep learning research, neural networks with many layers have been proposed. Larger datasets are required to match the increased capacity of such models (Xinyue et al., 2017). The scarcity of the data is the bottleneck for any machine learning algorithm. Data Augmentation enhances the performance of the models and increases the amount of data to take advantage of the potential of big datasets (C. Shorten & T. M. Khoshgoftaar, 2019). Increasing the size of the dataset by synthesizing images can help improve the image classification accuracy. Many literatures (Houqiang Yu & Xuming Zhang, 2020; Quan et al., 2019) have reported the use of data augmentation to extend the training data for the image classification task.

Since their inception, Generative Adversarial Networks (GANs) have been particularly effective in the generation of the image. It consists of two networks i.e. generator (G) and discriminator (D). The G takes as input random variables from a latent space and generates images. These images mixed with real images serve as input for D. While G aims to maximize the error of generated images, D attempts to classify images as fake (generated) or real (from the dataset).

The DCGAN is the extension of the original GAN with the exception that both the discriminator and generator network employ convolutional and convolution transpose layers. This chapter aims to apply DCGAN on the Urdu digits. The contribution in this recent area of research is as follows:

- DCGAN is applied to augment the Urdu numerals dataset. The results are further enhanced by rigorous experimentation by employing traditional ways of augmentation on the dataset, which has not been explored earlier on this problem.
- The outcome of the experiments is evaluated using: 1) t-SNE 2) FID score. The proposed model has achieved the FID score of 25.32, which is considered a good score for a dataset containing 10 classes.

The rest of the chapter is organized to include the related work, the proposed approach used to achieve the goal and the results obtained after extensive experimentation.

LITERATURE REVIEW

Handwriting recognition in Urdu has been around in the field of computer science for almost half a century now. According to Aman Shah (2016), the oldest techniques that have been in use for character recognition are discussed originating from analysis-by-synthesis. It is the basis for syntactic approaches in character recognition. With the advancements in the deep learning world, Urdu handwriting recognition has also taken a new step. From CNNs to BLSTMs and then to Autoencoders, Urdu text has been deeply studied from every aspect. M. Husnain et al. (2019) use stacked autoencoders for automatic feature extraction directly from raw pixel values of 178573 ligatures with 3732 class images and have achieved an accuracy of 96%. H. Cecotti (2016) evaluated 18,000 Urdu ligatures with 98 different classes using CNN to achieve a recognition rate of up to 95%. SVM is used to classify Urdu ligature components correctly with 99.02% accuracy in Elleuch et al., 2016.

As of today, little to no work has been cited regarding the use of augmentation such as rotation and flipping of images to increase the size of the Urdu dataset. Also, the citations on the use of GAN to solve this problem are very sparse. Hence work done in other languages is presented that will help solve the task which is very similar to the idea presented in this chapter. R. Alharbi et al. (2020) generated handwritten Arabic digits in the numeral script of Eastern Arabic. They used different variants of GAN such as DCGAN, Bidirectional GANs, (BiGANs), VanillaGANs, and WassersteinGANs (WGANs). Then to evaluate the generated images, Fr´echet Inception Distance (FID) and native-Arabic human evaluation is used. With accuracy values of 96.815% and 69.93%, respectively, DCGAN outperforms the other GANs in the FID benchmark, while BiGANs outperform the other GANs in the native-Arabic human benchmark. Sadeka et al. (2019) used DCGAN on the three popular Bangla handwritten datasets Bangla Lekha-Isolated, CMATERdb, ISI, and their own dataset Ekush. They said that DCGAN produced Bangla digits successfully, making it a reliable model for generating Bangla handwritten digits from random noise.

To improve the efficiency of the classifier, Ganesh Jha & Hubert Cecotti (2020) used GAN to increase the data. They researched how much artificial images can be produced before output begins to deteriorate. They tested the idea on four datasets of handwritten digits which are MNIST, Latin, Devanagri, Bangla, and Oriya. Though the performance improved for a bit, after a while, too many GAN-produced images caused the performance to deteriorate. Ngoc-Trun et al. (2021) first claim that the traditional data augmentation method may lead the generator to incorrectly learn the distribution of the augmented data, which may vary from the original data distribution. They then suggest a principled system Data Augmentation Optimized for GAN (DAG), to allow the use of augmented data in GAN training to enhance the original distribution's learning that minimizes the divergence between the original and model distribution. They applied DAG to different GAN models such as conditional and unconditional GAN, CycleGAN, and self-supervised GAN on datasets of medical and natural images. Their result showed that DAG achieved consistent and significant improvements in these models.

Training Deep Neural Networks requires addressing certain issues such as overfitting. It occurs when a model tries to fit all the training data and ends up memorizing the data patterns as well as the random fluctuations and noise. The objective of deep models is defeated when they fail to generalize and perform adequately in the face of unknown data circumstances. Kaiming et al. (2015) introduces the use of shortcut connections in between stacking of layers to handle this issue. The outputs of stacked layers are then accumulated to the output of these identity shortcuts. Gao et al. (2017) proposed another method to address the problem of overfitting in a deeper model by connecting each layer in a feed-forward fashion to other layers. In this way feature map of the layer is passed on to subsequent layers and the final decision of the classifier is based on all these feature maps. Nitish et al. (2015) introduced the dropout technique that not only addresses the overfitting issue but also effectively merges exponentially many distinct neural network models by different units in a neural network. Hence, training a network with dropout is equivalent to training 2^n thinned networks with significant weight sharing, given every thinned network is rarely trained.

It can be observed after reviewing the state-of-the-art techniques that have been proposed in recent years that Urdu numeral generation and recognition are unexplored while the digits of various languages have been experimented on using the latest research. Hence no pre-trained weights are available for Urdu numerals to build the research upon. In this chapter, we aim to apply a deep convolutional Generative Adversarial Network using augmentation techniques for image generation. The work done in the domain of employing traditional augmentation techniques for enhancement in the result of DCGAN has been sparse. This research will not only help in exploring the effects of augmentation on the Urdu numeral dataset but also ultimately address the problem of limited data as the Urdu numerals dataset is not available publicly. The concept of the generative adversarial network has not yet been applied in the domain of Urdu language. As data is the backbone of deep learning models, the image generation using DCGAN will assist in obtaining better classification results for the image classification tasks in the future.

METHODOLOGY

The use of DCGAN to augment the Urdu numeral dataset is being proposed. The generator network consists of three transpose convolution layers to convert random noise to a representation of $32 \times 32 \times 3$. The discriminator network consists of four convolution layer that in the end leads to the prediction that whether the image is real or fake. The proposed architecture is represented in Figure 1. This architecture is inspired from Sagar et al. (2020) that discusses the use of DCGAN for the generation of images for chest X-rays. In the following paragraphs, the main elements are provided in detail.

Dataset

In this chapter, the image dataset of handwritten Urdu numerals is being used which is divided into 10 classes, categorizing images into 0, 1, 2, 3, 4, 5, 6, 7, 8, and 9 categories. The dataset contains 9,800 Urdu numerals images of size $32 \times 32 \times 3$ which are normalized as a pre-processing step. Figure 2 provides a summarized view of the dataset. The chapter uses this dataset to employ DCGAN.

Generator Network

The purpose of a generator network is to create new and fake but realistic handwritten digits by taking as input random 100×1 noise vector which is then provided to a dense layer to obtain 256 different 4×4 feature maps. Then, there are three convolution transpose layers used to upsample the obtained representation with the ReLU activation function in between except for the last convolution layer that uses Tanh. This allows the model to quickly learn saturation and cover the color space of the training distribution (Sagar et al., 2020). Using three convolution transpose layers the representation of size $4 \times 4 \times 256$ is upsampled to an image of size $32 \times 32 \times 3$.

Figure 1. Deep convolutional generative adversarial network architecture

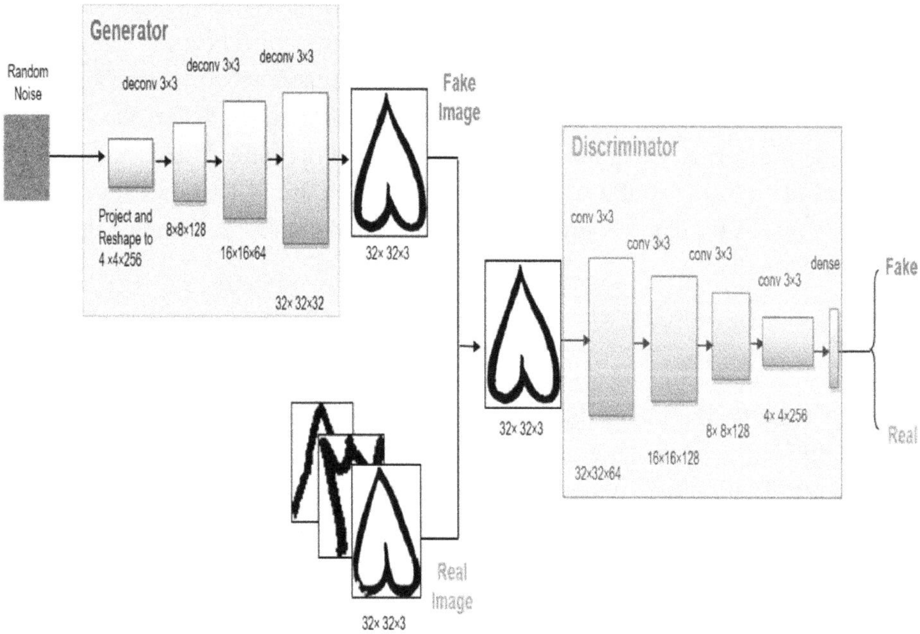

Discriminator Network

The discriminator network aims to determine whether the images are fake or real. The network takes a combination of 32 × 32 × 3 size originals images from the dataset and images generated by the generator as input followed by three convolution layers with leaky ReLU activation functions in between as recommended by Radford et al. (2015). The last convolution layer uses a sigmoid activation. Sigmoid activation squishes the output between 0 and 1. Hence, it determines whether the image is original (real) if the output is close to 1 or classifies the image generated by the generator (fake) if the output is closer to 0.

Figure 2. Urdu numeral dataset

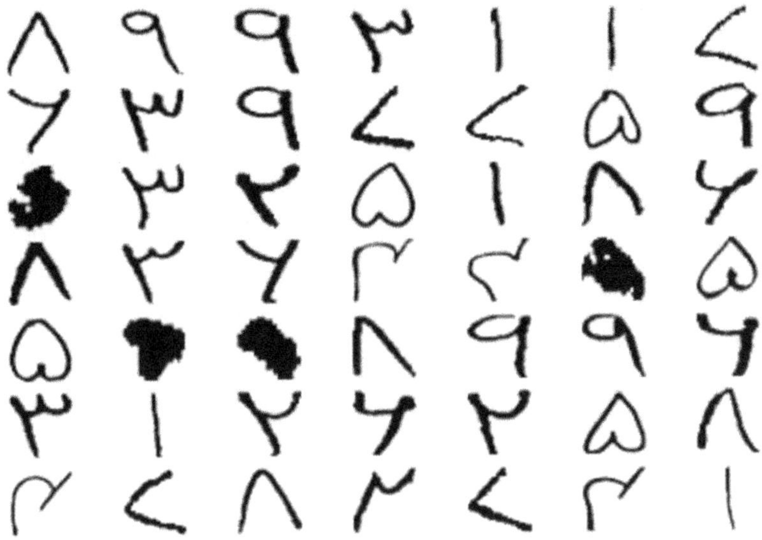

Loss Function

In this chapter, the min-max loss function is used given by Equation (1). Binary classification is employed in discriminator networks as it needs to distinguish between real and fake images. Binary Cross-Entropy (BCE) is given as

$$J_{BCE}\theta = \frac{1}{M}\sum_{m=1}^{M} y_m \log(h_\theta(x_m) + 1 - y_m \log(1 - h_\theta(x_m))$$

M here represents training samples in a mini-batch, y_m is the target label for training sample m (for real image label is 1 and for fake image, the label is 0), the input for a training sample is given by x_m and h_θ is model with network weights θ. Summation over variable M is applied as shown at the start of Equation (1). This gives the average cost of all examples in the entire batch. Moreover, if 1 is the output of the model then the loss will be -log(1) = 0 and, hence training sample is a real image. On similar lines, if the output of the model is 1, the loss will be given by $(1 - y_m)\log(1 - h_\theta(x_m)$ and the training example is a fake image. The binary-cross entropy loss function is employed in a similar problem of digit generation in Ganesh

Jha & Hubert Cecotti (2020) for Bangla numerals and Sagar & Sridhar (2020) for Chest-Xrays and provided satisfactory results.

Objective Function

There are two probability distributions i.e., the probability distribution of real data and the probability distribution of generated data. The goal of GAN is to bring both distributions closer together. The generator and discriminator network plays a min-max game where Generator aims to minimize while the discriminator aims to maximize the loss function provided in Equation (2), introduced by Goodfellow et al. (Sagar Kora & Sridhar Ravula, 2020)

$$\min_G \max_D V(G,D) = E_{x \sim p_{data}(x)}(\log D(x)) + E_{z \sim p_z(z)} \log D(G(z)))$$

x represents an example of image, p is the distribution of data, and latent variable is represented by z.

RESULTS AND DISCUSSION

The generator and discriminator network are trained using a learning rate of 0.0002 and momentum of 0.5. The number of epochs used is 150 with a mini-batch of size 128. While the dataset provided to the network has been pre-processed, some hard cases are also been added to check the robustness of the model as shown in Figure 3. The Figure depicts 4 numerals that can belong to two classes. For instance, the first digit can belong to classes 5 and 8. Similarly, the second digit can belong to classes 2 and 7. Since, there is a very minute difference between classes 2 and 3, the third digit in Figure 3 can belong to either of the two classes. The fourth digit can belong to classes 7 and 3.

Figure 3. Hard cases in dataset (a) class 5 and 8 (b) class 2 and 7. (b) class 2 and 3. (d) class 3 and 7

After the DCGAN is trained for 50 epochs, the images started to resemble numerals instead of noise. Although, the quality of images is further improved after 150 epochs, however, numerals are still unrecognizable. To enhance the quality of the images produced, the dataset is augmented using traditional ways and then the increased dataset is provided to the DCGAN. The dataset is augmented keeping in view the nature of the numerals because some pairs such as 2 6 and 7 8 are very much similar and mere rotation can change their class instead of producing an augmented image. The result of DCGAN without augmentation showed that some numerals generated are more real than the others such as DCGAN is able to produce 3, 8, and 9 better than the rest. Hence, those numerals are focused more which are hard for the DCGAN to generate. Hence numerals 0 and 5 are flipped and added to the dataset. Digits 1, 2, 3, 4, 6, and 9 are randomly rotated between 0 and 10 degrees. Numeral 8 is rotated anticlockwise for 45 degrees and is added to numeral 7. On the other hand, numeral 7 is rotated clockwise to 45 degrees and added to numeral 8. After applying these operations, the size of the dataset is increased from 9800 to 22000. The distribution of the samples in the experiment is shown below in Table 1.

Table 1. Distribution of samples pre and post augmentation

No. of Samples	Before Augmentation	After Augmentation
0	983	2100
1	980	2195
2	975	2198
3	968	2179
4	970	2218
5	989	2264
6	976	2172
7	982	2254
8	987	2222
9	990	2198
	9800	22000

The DCGAN is applied to the original dataset as well as the augmented dataset. As the training starts, after 50 epochs the results of DCGAN for the original dataset contain more noise than the augmented dataset as shown in Figure 4. After 100 epochs, DCGAN is able to learn to generate digits 2, 3, 8, and 9 but struggles to create digit 5. However, fails to create digits 0, 4, 6, and 7 when applied to the original dataset. In contrast, DCGAN is unable to learn to generate any digit as real as original numerals. It struggles to create 2, 3, and 8 but is unable to generate any of the other digits as is evident from Figure 5. As the training ends at 150 epochs, DCGAN is unable to generate images of numerals 0 and 4.

Figure 4. DCGAN result of 50 epochs: Left original dataset right augmented dataset

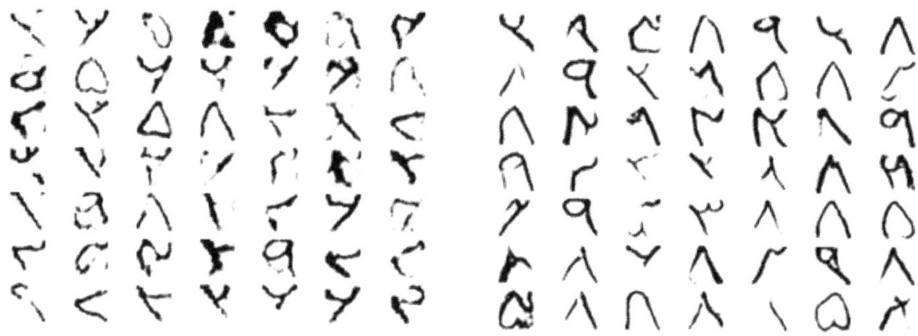

Figure 5. DCGAN result of 100 epochs: Left original dataset right augmented dataset

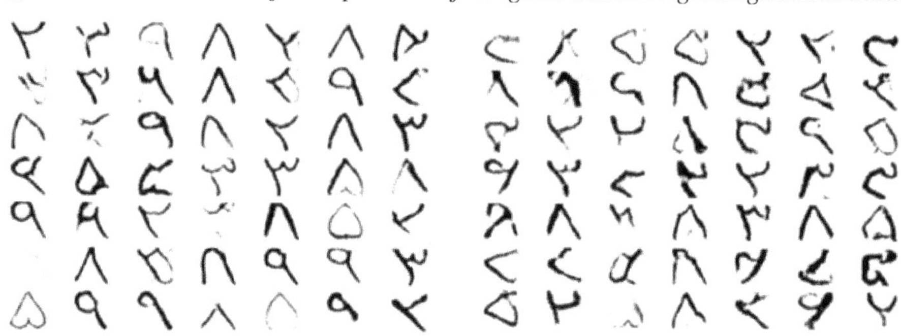

Figure 6. DCGAN result of 150 epochs: Left original dataset right augmented dataset

It struggles to create 1, 2, 5, 6, and 7. However, somehow generates 3, 8, and 9 when applied to the augmented dataset. But results of DCGAN are very remarkable on the augmented dataset. After 150 epochs, it can successfully generate all numerals. Hence, it is can be concluded that augmenting the dataset improved the results of DCGAN to a point that it is hard to distinguish between real and fake images as shown in Figure 6. The augmentation of a few classes more than the others refined the results altogether, and due to the generation of new images, the data gets more supplemented and clearer margins between classes are obtained.

Figure 7 shows the accuracy and loss during the generator and discriminator training, where the loss of the generator and discriminator for both fake and real images is almost 0.5, and the accuracy of the discriminator network is around 80% which indicates that the model has converged to a stable equilibrium.

Figure 7. Loss and accuracy of generator and discriminator

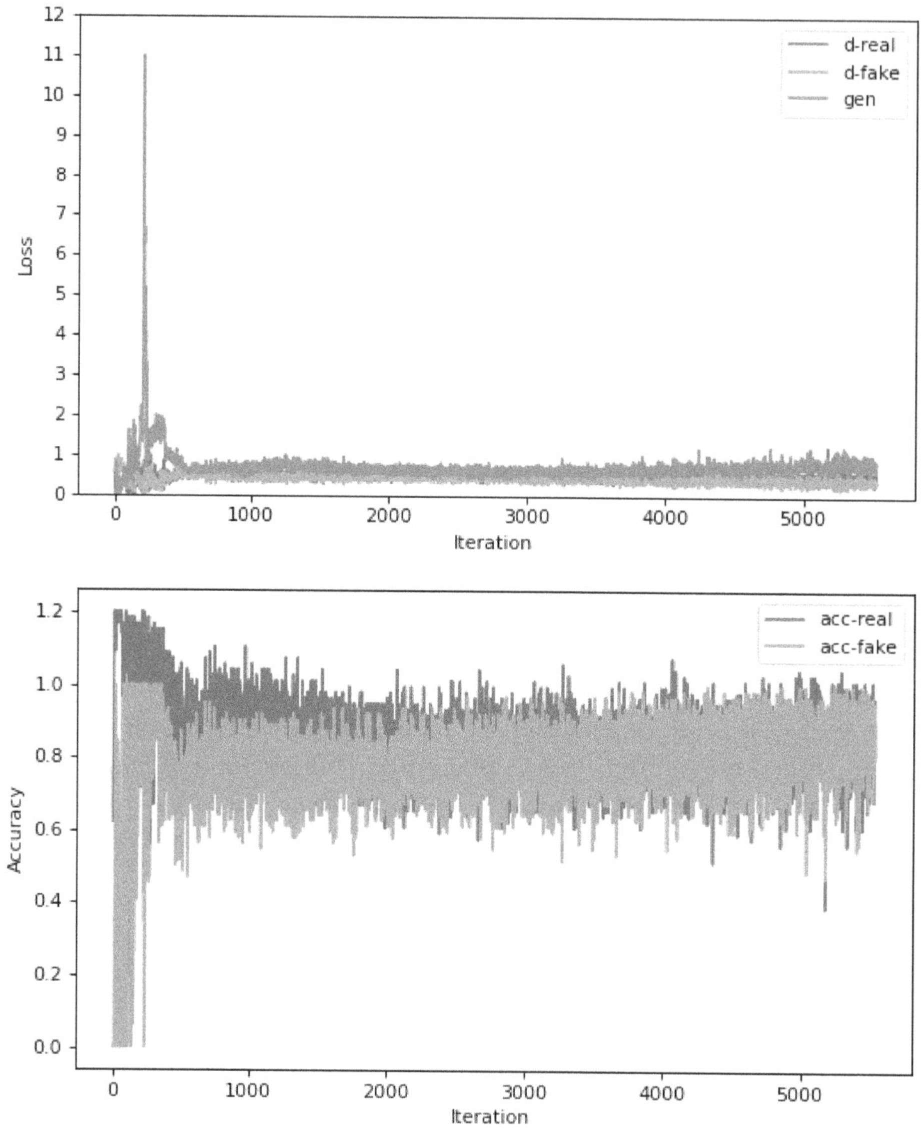

Synthetic Image Quality Evaluation

In t-SNE, the distribution of training examples is visualized by the reduction of high dimensional data ($32 \times 32 \times 3$) to the 2D plane. To evaluate the augmented data, the t-SNE approach (Laurens & Geoffrey, 2008) is applied to provide a more powerful justification that the augmentation obtained using DCGAN indeed contributes to the shape of the data manifold Zhu, (Xinyue et al., 2018). Figure 4, Figure 5, and Figure 6 shows the variability and similarity of images by applying t-SNE.

In Figure 8, Figure 9, and Figure 10, Urdu numeral dataset has been visualized in 2D space, with an additional class of digits 3, 8, and 9 generated by DCGAN with and without the inclusion of data augmentation. Each digit forms a separable cluster containing samples labeled as the digit. There are a total of 11 clusters represented by 11 different colors. The left of Figure 8 represents 10 original classes and an additional class of DCGAN images generated for digit 3 without augmentation. The data points in the cluster are clearly dispersed and are not close to the distribution of real images for digit 3. On the contrary, after adding the augmented dataset, the data points of fake images in the right of Figure 8 are tightly clustered with the data points of original images for digit 3. On similar lines, in the left of Figure 9 and Figure 10 the fake images generated without implying the data augmentation technique doesn't resemble the real images and hence doesn't occur in cluster 8 and 9 respectively. However, in the right of Figure 9 and Figure 10 fake and real images for numerals 8 and 9 appear in the same cluster. Hence, it is concluded, that after applying data augmentation techniques to the original dataset, the results of DCGAN in terms of distribution of data points are very close to the real images. It is very evident that real and fake images of digits 3, 8, and 9 are clustered together and it is very hard to distinguish between original and DCGAN augmented images due to their high correlation.

FréChet Distance of Inception

Further, DCGAN performance is evaluated using Fréchet Inception Distance (FID) (D.C Dowson & B.V Landau, 1982). FID is a measure used for comparing the similarity between two image datasets. It has been proven to correspond well with human visual quality judgments and is frequently used to assess the quality of GAN samples. FID is originally proposed and used to enhance evaluation in Martin (2017), and it is shown to be more accurate than the inception score (Martin, 2017). It measures the feature level distance between distributions of images. Features are extracted using the inception V3 pre-trained model (Christian et al., 2016) and computed FID scores from the following function used in D.C Dowson & B.V Landau (1982).

Figure 8. t-SNE of DCGAN generated images of numeral 3: Left without augmented data, right with augmented data

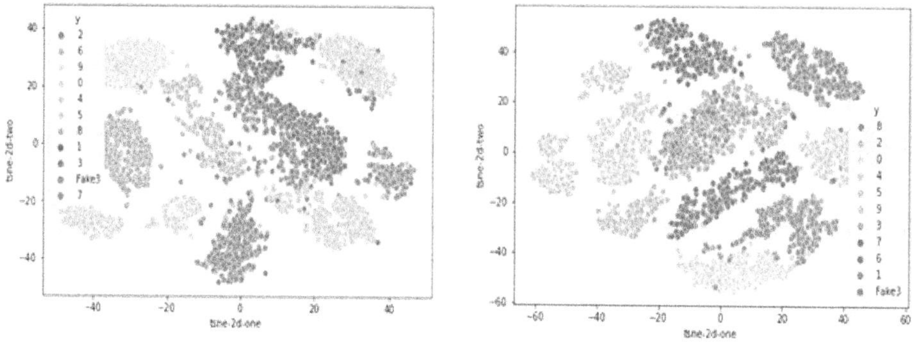

Figure 9. t-SNE of DCGAN generated images of numeral 8: Left without augmented data, right with augmented data

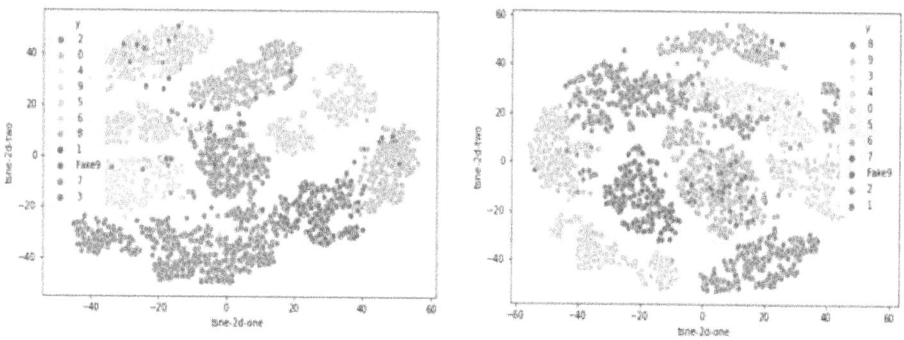

Figure 10. t-SNE of DCGAN generated images of numeral 9: Left without augmented data, right with augmented data

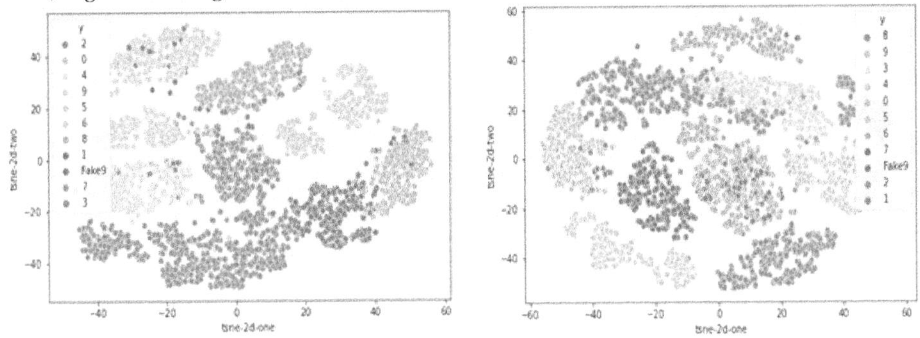

$$FID = \left\| \mu_r + \mu_g \right\|^2 + Tr\left(\sum_r + \sum_g - 2\left(\sum_r \sum_g\right)^{1/2}\right)$$

The mean values for a feature of fake and real images are represented in the Equation 3 by $\mu_{r,}$ $\mu_{g,}$ $\Sigma_{r,}$ and Σ_g represent the co-variance matrix for features of fake and real images. The higher the similarity between the two distributions, the lower the FID.

The score of DCGAN-generated images is computed and an FID score of 25.32 is achieved on an augmented dataset of 22000 images, while an FID score of 51.0 is achieved on the images that are generated using DCGAN on an original dataset of 9800 images of Urdu numerals. The distance between the inception vectors of features for real images and generated images in the same domain is summarized by FID, more smaller the score more enhanced the result. As the quality of the image generated improved with augmentation, the FID score improved from 51.0 to 25.32 because the images now generated resemble more to the original dataset.

About the fact, that work available on Urdu numerals is on a short scale, therefore there is no benchmark available to compare the results with. Similar work done (Rawan et al., 2020) on Arabic numerals is considered because, out of 10 numerals, 6 numerals of the Arabic language i.e., 0, 1, 2, 3, 4, 8, and 9 are the same as that of the Urdu language. The FID score achieved on Arabic numerals using DCGAN is 98.815 while the FID score achieved on Urdu numerals is much lesser. It is also important to mention here that while the dataset of Arabic numerals consisted of 60,000 images, the FID score on DCGAN-generated images for Urdu numerals is produced using only 22,000 images. Hence, from the evaluation of FID, it is evident that the distribution of original and DCGAN-generated images at the feature level is very similar. The result has been summarized in Table 2

Table 2. Summary of FID scores

	Arabic Numerals	Urdu Numerals	
		Before Augmentation	After Augmentation
No. of Samples	60,000	9,800	22,000
FID Score	98.815	51.0	25.32

CONCLUSION AND FUTURE WORK

Urdu language is popular in the Southeast Asia region and is also the national language of Pakistan. Hence, Urdu numerals find many applications such as cheque processing, number plate recognition, and form processing. Though the use of Urdu numerals is very abundant, the data available is very limited as compared to other state-of-art datasets. Training deep learning models requires an enormous amount of data. To overcome the problem of limited data, the use of DCGAN on Urdu numerals is being proposed. This chapter also presents extensive experimentation with traditional augmentation techniques to enhance the quality of the results produced by DCGAN. Initially, the results produced showed that only a few numerals such as 3, 8, and 9 generated by DCGAN resembled real images. But the rest are hardly recognizable. Then the traditional augmentation technique is applied to majorly to those numerals for which DCGAN results are not up to the mark i.e. 1, 2, 4, 5, 6, and 7. Providing the augmented dataset to DCGAN improved the quality of generated images manifolds and the artificial images generated by DCGAN using augmented data are as real as the original dataset for all classes. The final FID score of 25.32 is computed on DCGAN-generated images which is less than the score of 51.0 that is achieved on images generated by DCGAN using the original dataset. Also, this score is much less than the FID calculated on numerals of similar language i.e., Arabic which is 98.815.

In future work, different flavors of GAN may be experimented on to compare the numeral generation results. It may also be tested to see if any version of GAN is capable of producing realistic Urdu numerals with a minimum amount of this dataset and without augmentation techniques. Binary-cross entropy has been used in the chapter, as this function has provided optimal results on similar numeral problems of other languages. However, other loss functions may be tested to compare the performance.

This research can help develop a larger dataset which can then be trained to build a state-of-the-art numeral classifier for the Urdu language. Potential research may be conducted on the increment in the accuracy of the Urdu numeral classifier on adding the GAN-generated data to the dataset. Also, to what extent GAN can be used as an augmentation technique before saturation is achieved in the accuracy of the classifier? Using a state-of-the-art trained classifier can give rise to new application domains such as automatic dictation for kids, and recognition of Pakistani Currency Notes. This research can lead to the deployment of the deep learning-based model to achieve state of art results in many areas employing Urdu numerals.

REFERENCES

Alharbi, R., Almajnooni, N., Albishry, M., Alotaibi, A., Alsaadi, F., Alsulami, G., Alharbi, A., Alotaibi, R., Alharbi, R., Alharbi, A., Alkhodidi, T., Alafif, T., Albassam, A., & Sabban, S. (2020). GEAD: Generating and Evaluating Handwritten Eastern Arabic Digits Using Generative Adversarial Networks. DOI: 10.13140/RG.2.2.24679.06561

Cecotti, H. (2016). Active graph based semi-supervised learning using image matching: Application to handwritten digit recognition. *Pattern Recognition Letters*, 73, 76–82. DOI: 10.1016/j.patrec.2016.01.016

Dowson, D., & Landau, B. (1982). The Fréchet distance between multivariate normal distributions. *Journal of Multivariate Analysis*, 12(3), 450–455. DOI: 10.1016/0047-259X(82)90077-X

Elleuch, M., Maalej, R., & Kherallah, M. (2016). A New Design Based-SVM of the CNN Classifier Architecture with Dropout for Offline Arabic Handwritten Recognition. *Procedia Computer Science*, 80, 1712–1723. DOI: 10.1016/j.procs.2016.05.512

Haque, Shahinoor, Rabby, Abujar, & Hossain. (2019). OnkoGan: Bangla Handwritten Digit Generation with Deep Convolutional Generative Adversarial Networks. DOI: 10.1007/978-981-13-9187-310

He, Zhang, Ren, & Sun. (2015). Deep Residual Learning for Image Recognition.

Heusel, M., Ramsauer, H., Unterthiner, T., Nessler, B., & Hochreiter, S. (2017). GANs trained by a two time-scale update rule converge to a local nash equilibrium. In *Advances in Neural Information Processing Systems 30*. Morgan Kaufmann Publishers Inc.

Huang, Liu, van der Maaten, & Weinberger. (2017). Densely Connected Convolutional Networks. .DOI: 10.1109/CVPR.2017.243

Husnain, M., Missen, M. M. S., Mumtaz, S., Jhanidr, M. Z., Coustaty, M., Muzzamil Luqman, M., Ogier, J. M., & Choi, G. S. (2019). Recognition of Urdu Handwritten Characters Using Convolutional Neural Network. *Applied Sciences (Basel, Switzerland)*, 9(13), 2758. Advance online publication. DOI: 10.3390/app9132758

Jha, G., & Cecotti, H. (2020). Data augmentation for handwritten digit recognition using generative adversarial networks. *Multimedia Tools and Applications*, 79(47-48), 35055–35068. Advance online publication. DOI: 10.1007/s11042-020-08883-w

Kong, Q., Tong, B., Klinkigt, M., Watanabe, Y., Akira, N., & Murakami, T. (2019). Active Generative Adversarial Network for Image Classification. *Proceedings of the AAAI Conference on Artificial Intelligence*, 33(1), 4090–4097. DOI: 10.1609/aaai.v33i01.33014090

Kora, S., & Ravula, S. (2020). Evaluation of Deep Convolutional Generative Adversarial Networks for Data Augmentation of Chest X-ray Images. *Future Internet*, 13(1), 8. DOI: 10.3390/fi13010008

Maaten, L. d., & Hinton, G. (2008). Visualizing data using t-sne. *Journal of Machine Learning Research*, 9(Nov), 2579–2605.

Radford, A., Metz, L., & Chintala, S. (2015). Unsupervised representation learning with deep convolutional generative adversarial networks. arXiv:1511.06434.

Shah. (2016). Teaching of Urdu: Problems and Prospects.

Shorten, C., & Khoshgoftaar, T. M. (2019). A survey on Image Data Augmentation for Deep Learning. *Journal of Big Data*, 6(1), 60. DOI: 10.1186/s40537-019-0197-0

Srivastava, N., Hinton, G., Krizhevsky, A., Sutskever, I., & Salakhutdinov, R. (2014). Dropout: A Simple Way to Prevent Neural Networks from Overfitting. *Journal of Machine Learning Research*, 15, 1929–1958.

Szegedy, C., Vanhoucke, V., Ioffe, S., & Shlens, J. (2016). *Wojna, ZB*. Rethinking the Inception Architecture for Computer Vision., DOI: 10.1109/CVPR.2016.308

Tran, Tran, Nguyen, Nguyen, & Cheung. (2021). On Data Augmentation for GAN Training. IEEE Transactions on Image Processing. .DOI: 10.1109/TIP.2021.3049346

Yu, H., & Zhang, X. (2020). Synthesis of Prostate MR Images for Classification Using Capsule Network-Based GAN Model. *Sensors (Basel)*, 20(20), 5736. DOI: 10.3390/s20205736 PMID: 33050243

Zhu, Liu, Li, Wan, & Qin. (2018). Emotion Classification with Data Augmentation Using Generative Adversarial Networks. DOI: 10.1007/978-3-319-93040-428

Zhu, Liu, & Qin. (2017). Data Augmentation in Classification using GAN.

Chapter 2
Enhancing Crop Health Monitoring via GAN-Based Multimodal Data Fusion Using Farmbot and Machine Vision

Noor Sajjad
https://orcid.org/0009-0003-0790-4416
National University of Sciences and Technology, Pakistan

Rafia Mumtaz
National University of Sciences and Technology, Pakistan

ABSTRACT

In the field of precision agriculture, combining multimodal data sources such as Soil Nitrogen-Phosphorus-Potassium (NPK) sensors, alongside temperature and humidity measurements with high-resolution RGB and infrared imagery, is crucial for improving crop monitoring. Aligning these multimodal data, which vary widely in resolution and format, to a uniform spatial scale is a challenge. Achieving this uniformity is essential for the computation of multiple vegetation indices, providing analysis of crop health. To overcome differences in data resolution, GANs are utilized. GANs are a key technology in generative AI and are highly effective at improving the quality of low-resolution data. This makes them ideal for data fusion of NPK sensors with detailed images captured using high-resolution cameras. Using GANs not only standardizes the resolutions but also improves the overall quality of the analysis. This leads to more accurate assessments of crop health. By deploying these, farmers and agronomists are equipped to make more informed decisions, leading

DOI: 10.4018/979-8-3693-6255-6.ch002

to better agricultural outcomes.

INTRODUCTION

Precision Agriculture

Precision Agriculture plays a significant role in transforming the field of agriculture. In this era of technology, PA plays a vital role in optimizing production and managing the strategy to gain maximum yield using minimum resources. Unlike traditional Methods it treats each section of the field differently. This approach reveals a new level of control and efficiency, encouraging farmers to become more productive and environmentally responsible. The foundation of precision agriculture is based on data collection. Multiple sophisticated tools are utilized to acquire essential information about various aspects of crop health and soil conditions. Sensors strategically placed in fields continuously monitor nutrient content and weather patterns. Aerial surveys are carried out by drones mounted with high-resolution cameras and imaging technology, enabling insights into crop growth patterns and potential problem areas. An additional layer of data includes data collected from satellite imaging that provides vegetation and field health analysis at large scale. In order gain maximum information from this data, there are a few crucial steps are needed which include transforming the data, informed decisions, and analyzing the impact on the field. The data requires processing and cleaning after data collection from the field. The critical role of a powerful tool in analyzing the massive amount of data to get insights on trends and patterns. Detailed field maps that indicate locations with particular needs are made possible by this study. For instance, this analysis can identify the zone of the field in drought or an area that has shown to have nutrient deficiency. With these data-driven insights, the farmers can decide resource allocation better. Water can be applied only to the necessary area; no excess runoff waste takes place and helps in assuring that dry crops receive ample irrigation. This serves as a strategic manner of applying the fertilizer, delivered in proper locations to maximize crop benefit. The same is true for efforts preventing pests and diseases, pesticides can be precisely targeted to specific aera which is infected by pest, and it spare the rest of the crop from chemical exposure. Precision agriculture has multiple advantages. Crop yield can be increased by many times when resources are used efficiently, and crop receives exactly what it needs. Optimizing input consumption and cutting waste have the potential to result in significant cost efficiency for farmers. The most substantial impact remains on environmental sustainability. Precision agriculture minimizes agricultural waste by using fewer resources like water, pesticides, and fertilizers are applied selectively. A significant advancement in agricultural practices is represented by precision agriculture. However, due to the continuous evolvement of technology, more sophisticated tools and data analysis methods are being introduced. By integrating artificial intelligence, decision-making will be even more optimized, enabling farmers to get real-time data and adjust their action according to that. Precision agriculture clears the path for a lucrative and environment-friendly farming future that guarantees food security for future generations.

Multimodal Data in Agriculture

In precision agriculture there is another concept of multimodal data which mean rather relying on single source data, Precision agriculture leverages a diverse range of data collection methods and sources, similar to having different sources to create a comprehensive picture of crop health. Particular sensors embedded in the field deliver real-time ground-level measurements, such as soil nutrient concentration in soil. Drones allow for high resolution imagery of the entire field highlighting visual indicators such as plant growth patterns and potential problems, e.g. yellowing or poor development. With the wider scope a picture from above holds, it becomes easier to take in all aspects of field health and vegetation trends. However, multimodal data is ideal because each spectral band gives the information which is different from other, each band has its own spectral signature. Aerial drones, ground sensors and satellite imagery can help farmers combine data to gain actionable insight about the health of a field-revealing many kinds of patterns that exist in different locations. For example, a drone image can indicate an area with wilting crops. For instance, sensors installed in the ground would be able to return data which could then identify that particular point with low moisture or low nutrients. This comprehensive view allows farmers to make targeted interventions, addressing problems at their root cause and optimizing resource allocation.

Challenges In Multimodal Data Fusion

In integrating multimodal data there are multiple challenges. which includes incompatibility of formats and spatial resolution, spatial misalignment, data quality differences, etc. One of the major challenges is ensuring the standard format and shape of the multisource data. As mentioned earlier, with the advancement in technology such as drones, sensors and satellite imagery vast amount of data can be gathered by each source. Each source has its own spatial resolution, quality, and format which may not be compatible with the other data source. For example, data collected from sensor like JXCT for npk is point vise data most structured, with predefined units like mg/kg while on the other hand RGB, NIR and red edge imagery provide unstructured data with high spatial information. Fusing these types of data requires sophisticated tools and algorithms to bridge the gap between them. Another major challenge is varying spatial resolution. The sensor reads the point data of a specific location while RGB, NIR and red edge imagery capture a broad area and represent high-resolution spatial data. Images captured from drones and cameras are of high resolution while the data from npk sensor is pointwise to align them in a same spatial resolution different tools and techniques are used to gain valuable information form this multimodal data. Quality variations is a significant hurdle in smooth data fusion. Accuracy of sensor is low as compared to the RGB imagery this can be cause by interference of environmental factor, calibration of sensor, or any physical damage which can lead to inaccurate reading. Images can suffer from noise due to varying lighting, varying viewpoint of Lense. These data quality disputes can propagate through the analysis, leading to unreliable assessments of crop health.

Role Of Gans in Precision Agriculture

In this book chapter we have discussed multiple software and algorithms to subdue the hurdles and challenge mentioned above which include employment of Generative Adversarial Network (GANs), a deep learning-based architecture which has vast potential to generate high-resolution data from low-resolution inputs, complete missing information and enhance the quality of the images. By leveraging GANs, it is possible to standardize the resolution of multimodal data, thus facilitating uniform integration and enhancing the overall quality of crop health monitoring. Which we will discuss in detail.

BACKGROUND AND MOTIVATION

The traditional farming practice is being revamped with precision agriculture where human decision-making and data processing go hand-in-hand to produce maximum yield which maintains crop health avoiding environmental hazards. This transformation to monitor crop health, minimizing the resource wastage and optimization of the yield requires large amounts of data. Data acquisition and integration required to get at this level of precision is limited. Traditionally, single data sources, like visual evaluations or localized soil tests, were used for crop health monitoring. Although these techniques provide insightful information, they are unable to fully convey the complex interactions between many elements influencing crop growth, which include moisture level, soil nutrient level, weather pattern and variation in soil canopy health. The need to provide more accurate recommendations systems and help farmers to make well informed decisions and have complete insight of their crop health requires multisource data fusion. As discussed earlier this technique merge data from multiple sources and unifies them to provide a more holistic view of crop health. The big challenge in fusing data from multiple sources is difference in spatial resolution, format and alignment for example soil sensor provide point wise measurements of npk values while imagery data captures the information of the larger area. Another challenge is to acquire data of soil sensor at each point. In this study we have provided a way to cater to these challenges by harnessing the power of GAN and performing data acquisition by state-of-the-art agriculture technology known as Farmbot.

LITERATURE REVIEW

Researchers around the globe have made efforts in the field of agriculture. This is a vast field, therefore, in the research phase a thorough literature review was conducted that provided the knowledge beneficial for the sub sequent phases.

This technological era has brought an evolution in the precision of agriculture techniques to great extent due to multi-source data integration and then development of decision-making system for optimal growth., S., Pundir, P., Jindal, H., Saini, H., & Garg, S. (2021, July). *Towards a multimodal system for precision agriculture using IoT and machine learning* cover the concept of exploring the innovative use of technology in agriculture sector. It explains the data collected by IoT sensors in real-time related to environmental parameters like temperature, light, humidity and soil moisture. These are all imperative to produce the greatest achievable return from its crops. Integration of machine learning models like Random Forest and CNNs allow faster response by aiding in early detection (to avoid any plant disease) leading to prevention for crop damage. In order to combine data from multiple unique resources, such as satellite imaging, drones and soil sensors the authors argue that Generative Adversarial Networks (GANs) will play a key role in doing so. The result of this merger will be that traditional agriculture methods, such as those used by Beau and Loos above can witness the same leap in productivity, sustainability and crop responsivity. The research has opened the way for a new era of improvements in crop health management and monitoring, which could lead to far better-informed agricultural decision-making.

The incorporation of multimodal data sources in the context of precision agriculture is still a potent challenge-and an opportunity. The authors Lahat, D., Adali, T., & Jutten, C. (2015*). Multimodal data fusion: an overview of methods, challenges, and prospects.* Proceedings of the IEEE, 103(9), 1449-1477 clearly pointed out the importance of multimodal data fusion in advanced analysis across multiple domains. Although the Ricean idea of constructing factors from data is an early 20th-century concept, multiset canonical correlation analysis and parallel factor analyses made significant advancements in the 1960s-70s which has primarily impacted psychometric and chemo metric areas. When combining the data from different sources, modalities or scales, to provide a single comprehensive representation of complex phenomena. Data fusion is necessary because we understand that no one modality can capture everything. A standard example is in biomedical imaging where the use of EEG and MEG together with fMRI to have all MoBo representing activity on how human brain performs. Similarly, optical sensors can be added to environmental studies in combination with LiDAR and SAR so that we advance the accuracy of earth observation. Although data fusion has advantages, it also poses challenges due to the variety and complexity of datasets and the requirement that strengths should be maximized from each modality while minimizing its weaknesses. Data fusion methodologies are important for many reasons, such as using multiple sensors to reduce ambiguities and increase robustness. This paper underscores the need for data-driven methods with as few assumptions as possible and reveals broad prospects in multi modal data fusion.

For multisource data fusion it is necessary to have the same spatial resolution for each source. The chase to enhance the quality of images by producing high-resolution has given rise to more sophisticated architectures and techniques, including Generative Adversarial Networks (GANs). In order to overcome this limitation, Geetha, R., Jebamalar, G. B., Shiney, S. A., Dao, N. N., Moon, H., & Cho, S. (2024). *Enhancing Upscaled Image Resolution Using Hybrid Generative Adversarial Network-Enabled Frameworks* describe a hybrid GAN framework by combining StyleGAN2 and Enhanced Super-Resolution Generative Adversarial Networks (ESRGAN) to learn the upscaling of low-resolution synthetic data SCM into high levels that reflect realistic random patterns. The approach includes the pre-processing data, face detection method along with cropping and contemporaneously upscaling both facial parts and background. The GAN models are trained to upscale the image, denoise it and preserve its color. The method performs better in reconstruction loss, adversarial loss and facial component loss than existing models like DeBlurGAN v2, HiFaceGAN and PSFR-GAN, showing an increased peak signal-to-noise ratio (PSNR), structural similarity index (SSIM) and learned perceptual image patch similarity (LPIPS). Whereas it would lead attack models to diversity in datasets bias and vulnerability on other arbitrary hyper parameters for future work data augmentation or specific cut-offs of the same kind.

Data collection is a major challenge in agriculture and industry critical to the production of food and raw materials, is on track with challenges such as labor shortages, declining productivity while people are still needing more food every day. Now to increase efficiency, technology has become necessary as traditional farming methods are labor consuming. Kar, S., Mohammad, R., Zaman, M. T., Reza, S. M., Talukder, O., & Hasan, M. (2023, December). *Farmbot: an IoT-Based*

Wireless Agricultural Robot for Smart Cultivation. Introduce Farmbot, a wireless IoT based robot to support farming by automating tasks and collecting data on soil conditions, temperature, humidity, gas levels with high precision sensors. These are factors identified in previous research that have a significant impact on crop yield but have yet to be fully integrated into robotic platforms. Farmbot, which delivers instantaneous data and action items to improve irrigation, fertilization and pest management via an app ran by your smartphone. The procedure includes the implementation of Arduino microcontrollers and ultrasonic sensors into a robot, through mechanical as well as electrical designs. While it has great potential, Farmbot is relatively expensive and more technically challenging for the average user than other systems because of its internet dependency. Overcoming these constellations of limitations, could turn Farmbot into a game changer that will modernize agriculture and greatly increase crop yields

MAIN FOCUS OF THE CHAPTER

This study focuses on the revolutionary potential of Generative Adversarial Networks (GANs) in precision agriculture, particularly for enhancing crop health monitoring. GANs are suitable for multimodal data fusion using generative models. Multimodal data fusion merges the multiple sourced inputs together for powerful insight. This integration addresses the data resolution disparities and enabling a seamless combination of data from various formats and scales to offer valuable key insights into crop health. The main goals of the study were to unify data in a common resolution, enable seamless integration and improve overall quality while calculating vegetation indices that enabled complete crop health assessments. By achieving these objectives, the chapter aims to demonstrate how GANs can standardize and improve the analysis of multimodal data, enhancing crop management and more informed decision-making for farmers and agronomists.

TECHNOLOGY OVERVIEW

Generative Adversarial Networks (GANs)

Generative Adversarial Network is a deep learning network introduced in 2014 by Ian J. Goodfellow and co-authors. Gans perform unsupervised learning in machine learning tasks. This network is very effective in various applications which up sampling, increasing resolution of the images. Gans take low resolution image and generate high resolution image. The architecture of Gans consists of two separate networks Generator and discriminator. The generator generates fake images and datapoint resembling the training data and passes this data to the discriminator. This neural network determines whether the data is fake or real. Either data is from training data or is generated by generator. Generator and discriminator are trained simultaneously which is known as adversarial training. The base architecture of GANs has been modified into various structures to address specific requirements and improve performance like ESRGANS, Conditional GANS, CycleGANs and StyleGANs.

Farmbot

In this era of technology and advancement Farmbot is an innovative technology to introduce automatic farming in field of precision agriculture. Farmbot is a CNC (Computer Numeric Control) based 3-dimensional robot as shown in figure 1. Farmbot is developed in 2011 by Rory Aronson. Farmbot is open-source and is available for commercial use and modification. Farmbot can plant over 30 different crops in the same area at the same time. It is scalable and can operate outdoors and indoors. Another feature of farmbot is that it can be portable, moved from one place to another according to the need of the user. It can perform automatic watering, weeding, seeding and provide environmental monitoring with the help of sensors embedded. The system is powered by IoT technology hence these external sensors are used to capture crucial information about the crops which is then combined with data from an open-source crop database to provide the user with an optimized planting plan using machine vision technique. CNC based structure of Farmbot allows it to perform preharvesting tasks that can be controlled through web-based application which provide remote access to the user.

Figure 1. Farmbot deployed in greenhouse

METHODOLOGY

Methodology includes multiple modules. The first part of the methodology is data collection which is done by capturing RGB imagery, multispectral imagery which includes NIR, red edge, Green Blue band and NPK data collection using JXCT sensor. After data collection the next step is data processing and analysis which includes image processing. This will be discussed in detail in the next section. The last module is visualization, soil health analysis and vegetation indices calculation as shown in figure 2.

Figure 2. Methodology

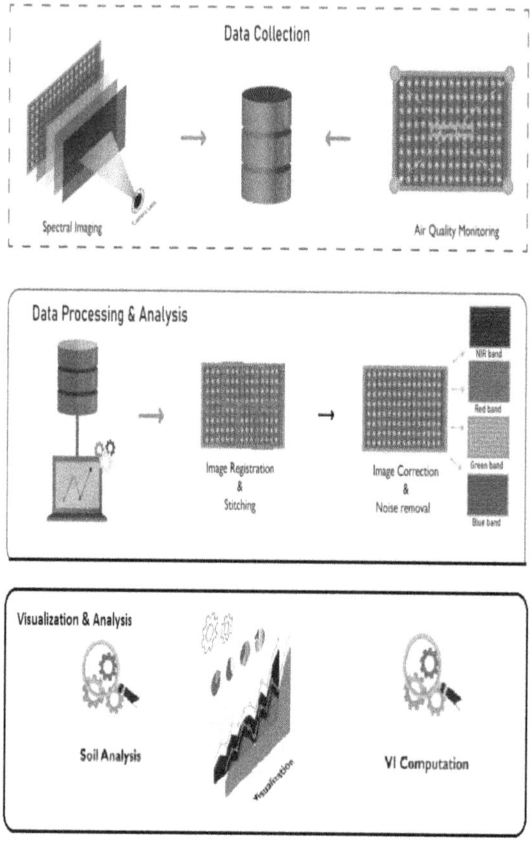

1. DATA COLLECTION

1.1. RGB Imaging

The RGB data collection is vital steps of precision agriculture to determine the crop health and enhance yield. Waterproof borescope camera is attached to FarmBot. The camera is not a like FarmBot tool that mounts and demounts onto the universal tool mount, and it is not stored in a tool bay. Instead, it remains fixed in place on the z-axis next to the UTM and can be used at any time, even when other tools are mounted. Hower camera is low resolution, and the main purpose of the camera is weed detection. To capture high resolution images, we used a D3500 camera. A DSLR camera is mounted on FarmBot as shown in the figure. The DSLR camera, which is affixed to the Farmbot structure as shown in figure 3, acquires high-quality pictures of the crops. Multiple images are captured to cover full field t to These images show small color variation such that one is unable to distinguish even with the help of the naked eye. Color variation can mean stress, lack of nutrients, disease, or lack of water in their habitat. These characteristics are important in their analysis, diagnosis and treatments. For example, simply noting the locations of yellowing leaves can point to areas where fertilizer may not be necessary while discovering reddish regions might indicate spots in which irrigation needs adjusting. Using RGB imaging to monitor crop health over time also allows farmers to create baseline data. This historical data acts as a guideline that outlines various deviations from normal growth patterns which if detected early, can be used to prevent potential problems. Also, RGB data can be plotted on the field map to generate fine maps which indicate how crop health varies across a given area of the field. These maps are flagging up areas that require special treatment and as a result reducing wastage of resources such as water, fertilizer and pesticides. The use of the Farmbot platform, along with RGB imaging is a major game changer in precision agriculture. Such data could also improve the ability of farmers to see their crops with new perspective, with high-resolution spectral imaging techniques available. It provides a right way to know about the crops, its health, sustainability and yield of crop which in turn revolutionize farming in a positive manner. Multi-spectral imaging is also used to ensure data based on a more comprehensive spectrum, beneficial for the assessment of plant and soil health which is discussed in next section.

Figure 3. Camera mounted over Farmbot

1.2. Multispectral Image

Multispectral imaging contributes to precision agriculture by assessing plant and soil health. We used a DJI Mavic 3 series drone with spectral cameras as part of our approach to take different spectral images. Such imaging can be used to analyze soil nutrients. A multispectral image, in contrast to an RGB image, captures information outside of the visible light spectrum. This might narrow down a couple of potential pest or disease threats. Drone hover over the field and capture various spectral bands as shown in figure 4. These bands include red-edge, near-infrared and other regions of the light spectrum. Each band tells us something new about the crops and soil. For example, near-infrared light is especially helpful at revealing plant health and vigor while red-edge can be used to observe variations in leaf structure and chlorophyll content. Specialized software then analyses these captured images to identify specific spectral signatures. But the signatures may be cues about what nutrients are present, or acute weather or stress aera in the field. For instance, if one part of the field is displaying a specific spectral signature, that might have insufficient nitrogen content in that aera. Similarly different spectral signature could imply that soil might be too dry or possibly it was infested by the pests. By multi-spectral Imaging Farmers can view high-resolution crop and soil health data from the analysis spectral signatures. This allows them to take intelligent decisions on when and where to apply fertilizers, water or pesticides, the result of which is reduced wastage of resources. The Mavic 3 series drone can bring more observations to crop health monitoring using multi-spectral imaging. This innovative technology collects even more powerful spectral data by profiling light beyond the visible range, which encourages farmers to tailor their outputs to perform specifically against what their diverse crops and soil require, promoting healthier plants and consequently more yield.

Figure 4. Multispectral image capturing using DJI mavic

1.3. NPK Data Collection

Plant requires optimal nutrients in the soil for healthy growth and maximum yield. Nitrogen, phosphorus, and potassium are the main essential macronutrients for plants compared to the other nutrients. Measuring and analyzing the values of soil npk are fundamental in modern agriculture technologies, which provide insight into plant and soil health and is also vital for decision making regarding fertilizer application. Nitrogen plays a significant role in plant growth by promoting healthy stems and leaves. Pale or withering, slow growth could all be symptoms of a nitrogen deficiency. Phosphorous encourages root development and helps in growth of flowers and food production. Low phosphorus causes stunted growth. It also supports disease resistance and enables optimal flow of water and uptake of nutrients. Potassium also plays a significant role in strengthening cell walls and boosting the quality of vegetable and fruit production. Potassium deficiency causes wilting, weakness in stems and diseases. It could be very useful in only using the fertilizer as per requirement of crop and avoid any extra or unnecessary application, means it will show how much NPK values are already present into soil. Where still needed to apply nutrients on specific location rather than applying fertilizer of the whole field. During this part of the study, data acquisition was performed and NPK data was visualized through JXCT sensor as shown in figure 5. NPK values play a significant role, which gives us an indication that how healthy plants and our soils is The JXCT sensor works through an electrochemical detection principle, which detects the nitrogen, potassium and phosphorus level in soil. The JXCT NPK sensor is composed of three electrodes: silver or ammonium chloride. Electrodes are coated with different reagents. When the sensor is inserted in the soil. Small electrical signals are produced by electrochemical reactions in the form of current. The magnitude of the current is equivalent to the concentration of NPK values in the soil. This current is then converted into a measurable voltage by the microcontroller. In the final step, this data is converted into digital readings. JXCT is used for real time soil NPK monitoring. In this experiment, we have demonstrated a novel approach to measuring soil NPK. We integrated a JXCT sensor on the Farmbot to measure the soil NPK level at different pre-defined locations on the field and designed a PCB-based electronic box that contains an Arduino, TTL converter, and OLED to display real time readings. The 3-dimensional structure of the Farmbot enables us to locate the exact coordinates and measure NPK easily. Tables are generated based on the coordinates of different locations.

Figure 5. Nitrogen values using JXCT sensor

	0	1	2	3	4	5	6	7	8	9	10	11	12	13	14	15	16	17	18	19
1	8.2	9.15	10.1	10.3	10.5	10.75	11	11.6	12.2	11.35	10.5	11.75	13	11	9	10	11	9.6	8.2	8
2	6.6	7.06	7.52	7.475	7.43	7.305	7.18	6.98	6.78	6.63	6.48	6.305	6.13	5.985	5.84	5.765	5.69	8.845	12	12.5
3	5.4	6.62	7.84	7.79	7.74	7.61	7.48	7.27	7.06	6.925	6.79	6.625	6.46	6.355	6.25	6.215	6.18	6.44	6.7	6.8
4	4.5	6.345	8.19	8.13	8.07	7.93	7.79	7.585	7.38	7.26	7.14	7.01	6.88	6.82	6.76	6.755	6.75	7.475	8.2	8.6
5	4	6.295	8.59	8.515	8.44	8.285	8.13	7.925	7.72	7.61	7.5	7.39	7.28	7.265	7.25	7.27	7.29	9.245	11.2	11.7
6	5.1	7.13	9.16	9.055	8.95	8.765	8.58	8.35	8.12	7.985	7.85	7.74	7.63	7.63	7.63	7.655	7.68	6.79	5.9	5.2
7	3.4	6.465	9.53	9.38	9.23	9.005	8.78	8.53	8.28	8.13	7.98	7.875	7.77	7.795	7.82	7.86	7.9	7.55	7.2	7
8	12	10.865	9.73	9.52	9.31	9.04	8.77	8.495	8.22	8.05	7.88	7.78	7.68	7.72	7.76	7.815	7.87	7.985	8.1	8.4
9	7	8.41	9.82	9.58	9.34	9.065	8.79	8.53	8.27	8.11	7.95	7.865	7.78	7.835	7.89	7.96	8.03	7.265	6.5	6.1
10	3.9	3.95	4	4.5	5	5.1	5.2	7.15	9.1	7.05	5	5.75	6.5	7.15	7.8	8.95	10.1	8.55	7	6.9

1.4. Environmental Monitoring

Temperature and humidity are two of the most critical factors that influence plant growth. One of the main factors that affect various physiological processes of plants is temperature. Humidity, on the contrary, influences water uptake and transpiration rates, as well as the occurrence of some diseases, including mildew and mold. Maintaining an appropriate balance between these environmental parameters is required to facilitate healthy plant growth and possibly increase crop yield. DHT-22 sensor is one of the high-precision digital devices that can measure both temperature and humidity. Among its most prominent features are high accuracy, long-term stability, and reliable functioning. Given that it can operate within a wide range of both these environmental parameters, this sensor might be a good solution for varied agricultural environments. In the greenhouse, it is deployed to continuously monitor environmental changes. The deployment of the DHT-22 sensor into a greenhouse implies that it is integrated with the greenhouse infrastructure and can continuously transmit the data provided in real-time to a central control system. As the acquired information is actively used, the deployments begin to collect data at a certain interval. These

Values are sent to the central monitoring system to estimate the current state of the greenhouse environment. If the temperature exceeds the desirable parameters, the cooling measures are taken by turning on AC. Such responses can be both manual and automatic. In our case we perform this task manually. The main advantage of the latter is that they are not only possible faster but also provide a more targeted and consistent response to changes in the environment. Therefore, in the case of one of the used systems, the integration of the DHT-22 sensors allows maintaining the optimal macroclimate between the plants. As a result, they experience less stress, do not wilt, and grow faster and more efficiently.

Moreover, the constantly collected data is analyzed and used for further deployments. If the planned crops have some requirements concerning the environmental changes. The collected data might also be used to further deploy a predictive model. The historical data on the temperature and humidity fluctuations might be used to estimate the requirements for growing different plants. Overall, such DHT-22 sensor deployments in the greenhouses are vivid examples of modern technological means used in precision agriculture. Representing one of the main factors of environmental conditions required for plant growth, the temperature and humidity levels should be carefully monitored and maintained at the optimal range. Changes in the two parameters, as described above, might have a negative impact on the general well-being of cultivated plants. These examples illustrate that constant monitoring of temperature and humidity and the ability to automatically introduce changes, based on the received data, guarantee higher efficiency of the deployment.

2. DATA PREPROCESSING AND ANALYSIS

2.1. Generating NPK Heatmaps for Soil Analysis

As mentioned earlier, we gathered point data for three nutrients: nitrogen (N), phosphorus (P), and potassium, using the JXCT sensor. This point data was collected on fixed locations and stored in excel sheet that showed the level of nutrients at each place in the field. To visualize we created heatmaps for each nutrient to see how this nutrient was distributed on the field. Therefore, the point data for each of the three nutrients are plotted as a heatmap. Heatmaps have become an irreplaceable and useful tool in precision agriculture as they can show us where the nutrient intensity is high, low, and very low. The first step is to import the point data from the Excel sheet. Python can be used for this purpose, using the Pandas library for data handling. The Excel sheet consists of two columns. The Excel sheet contains columns for coordinates (grid points) and the corresponding NPK values at each location. Ensuring the cleanliness and accuracy of this data is crucial. It is essential to ensure that the data is either clear and accurate. There should be no missing values or outliers. Missing data should be replaced, the outliers need to be eliminated. To transform the point data into a continuous surface, we interpolate the data points onto a grid. This grid represents the entire field, with each cell corresponding to a specific nutrient level at that location Tools such as NumPy and SciPy are instrumental in this interpolation process, creating a smooth, continuous representation of nutrient distribution across the field. Then, the heatmaps for nutrient N, P, and K are generated using Matplotlib as shown in figure 6. The heatmaps are encoded in color to show the field variation of the nutrient. For example, stronger colors may suggest higher nitrogen levels, while lighter ones may suggest lower levels at the point. The spreading of data attached to their value in the heatmap makes it easy to determine where the nutrient is briefly deficient. All three heatmaps are self-explanatory figures where the nutrient distribution across the field is seen. Farmers can check which nutrient is inn excess and which is deficient in specific aera. Each heatmap provides a clear and intuitive depiction of nutrient distribution across the field. This enables farmers to apply the fertilizer on the targeted location rather than the whole field aera. In general, the NPK heatmap process involves importing the point data, cleaning it, interpolating the data onto a grid, and preparing color-coded heatmaps for visualization. The methodology is very precise and can be beneficial for agricultural practitioners.

Figure 6. Nitrogen, phosphorous, and potassium heatmaps

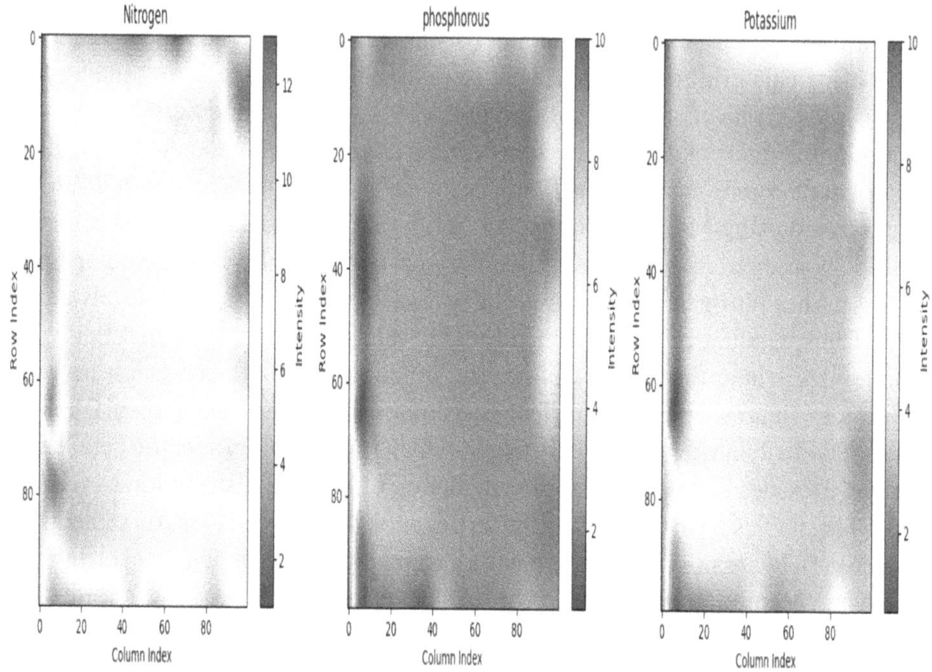

2.2. Up Sampling Using ESRGANs

For the data collection, we have high-resolution images of the fields taken with DSLR cameras and advanced multispectral drones. At the same time, we have heatmaps showing the level of nutrients in the ground, obtained from low-resolution NPK sensor data. To analyze these types of visual information, we need to have the same spatial resolution for the data captured from different sources which includes nutrient heatmaps, DSLR imagery and multispectral imagery. Thus, in order to combine all the datasets, we apply Enhanced Super-Resolution Generative Adversarial Networks. Specifically, we want to upscale the resolution of the NPK heatmaps to make them coincide with the high-resolution field images. As a result, we would obtain high-resolution NPK maps underlying the levels of nitrogen, phosphorus, and potassium nutrients. ESRGANs operate through a generative adversarial training scheme. Architecture of ESRGANs is shown in figure 7. The generator acts as an artist trying to paint a high-resolution picture from a low-resolution sketch. The discriminator acts as a critic, constantly evaluating these paintings against real high-resolution images and providing feedback. Through this adversarial process, the generator improves, learning to create images that are nearly indistinguishable from true high-resolution images. We start with the low-resolution NPK heatmaps and input them into the generator network. The generator works to enhance these images, adding details and textures that were missing in the original low-resolution data. The discriminator then evaluates these enhanced images, checking their quality against actual high-resolution images. This feedback loop continues until the generator can produce high-resolution heatmaps. Once the up-sampling process is complete, we are left with high-resolution heatmaps. These enhanced heatmaps can now be seamlessly integrated with the high-resolution DSLR and multispectral drone images. This integration is key as it allows us to combine nutrient distribution data with detailed visual and spectral information, providing a comprehensive and precise analysis of the field. By using ESRGANs for up sampling, we ensure that our NPK heatmaps are just as detailed as our other data sources. This harmonization is not just about making the images look better; it's about making sure we have the best possible data for analysis. The enhanced resolution allows us to see every detail, ensuring accurate identification of nutrient-rich and nutrient-deficient areas. This detailed view supports better decision-making, leading to improved agricultural practices and outcomes.

In essence, the use of ESRGANs bridges the gap between different data resolutions, bringing everything to a high level of clarity. This process enhances our ability to analyze and understand the data, ultimately supporting more effective and efficient agricultural management. By transforming low-resolution heatmaps into high-resolution images, we gain a clearer, more detailed perspective, enabling us to make well-informed decisions that benefit both the crops and the land.

Figure 7. Architecture of ESRGANS

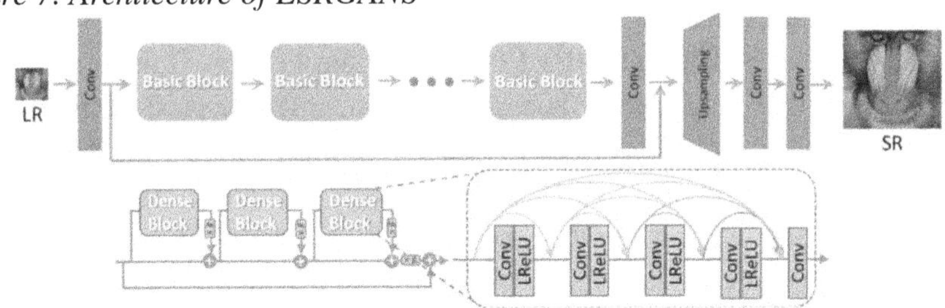

2.3. Image Processing

Captured images undergo a critical pre-processing phase before they are stitched together, which involves several key steps aimed at refining the images for optimal integration into a panoramic view. This pre-processing includes cropping and adjusting overlapping images, ensuring that they fit together seamlessly in the final composite. Cropping involves trimming the images to remove unnecessary or extraneous parts, focusing on the essential elements intended for the panoramic composition. Cropping is essential for eliminating unwanted borders or areas that do not contribute to the desired panoramic scene, thereby enhancing the visual appeal and relevance of the resulting image. Overlapping regions between images are carefully examined and adjusted to ensure a flawless merger. This adjustment is crucial for maintaining.

2.4. Image Stitching Using PTGui

Image stitching is a combination of art and technology. It involves seamlessly interpolating two or more overlapping scenes related to a particular scene captured by a camera into a single high-resolution panorama or into a single large image as shown in figure 8. This technology, now part of many next generation mobile phones, also has major applications in other fields including medical image processing, image processing and is therefore powerful and in great demand. It captures the wide-angle scene through multiple images, but the camera only changed its position through a small angle between these. This is because, when the camera rotates, their lines of view overlap between these images. The problem can be summed up as merging these overlapping images to create a large image unrecognizable as separated from any similar image; this process is known as "image stitching." For this, we can make use of different feature detectors such as Harris corner detector, FAST, ORB (Oriented FAST and Rotated Brief), SIFT (Scale Invariant Feature Transform), SURF (Speeded up Robust Feature) etc. PTGui, a top-notch software product in this area, applies the following sophisticated steps to solve it. Starting with the detection of features, the PTGui through the SIFT or SURF uses an algorithm to identify different features in the overlap between the images. This could be anything like an edge, a corner, or a unique pattern. Once it detects it, PTGui ensures that the same feature matches these between the different images so that it knows how the images overlap. It is now time to optimize the alignment of the images. PTGui makes use of translations, rotations and scales to reduce errors caused by misalignment. In other words, this guarantees that there is a smooth transition from one image to the next. It is necessary to choose the correct projection type (rectilinear, cylindrical, spherical and equirectangular) depending on the panorama. Each image is distorted by PTGui to fit into the selected panorama which results in a perfect alignment of all images within the space chosen. It also adjusts the exposure levels in the overlapping areas to keep the look consistent across the panorama, reducing visible seams. Seam-finding algorithms are key in identifying the best places to merge the images. PTGui places these seams in areas where they are least noticeable, like along edges or in regions with minimal detail. Then, sophisticated blending algorithms, such as multi-band blending, come into play to merge the images seamlessly. This technique blends different frequency bands separately, preserving detail and reducing artifacts. Color matching is another vital step to ensure the panorama looks uniform. PTGui performs color matching to avoid discrepancies due to differences in lighting or camera settings. It also corrects for vignetting, ensuring uniform brightness throughout the image. Lens distortions, such as barrel or pincushion distortion, are corrected to keep straight lines straight. PTGui can also handle parallax errors that occur when images are taken from slightly different positions, ensuring precise alignment. After all these corrections and optimizations, PTGui stitches the images together to form the final panoramic image. The software supports various output formats, including JPEG, TIFF, and EXR, and can even generate layered Photoshop files for further editing. A significant challenge in image stitching is dealing with invalid matches—features that appear similar but don't correspond to the same point in the 3D scene. To handle this, PTGui uses the Random Sample Consensus (RANSAC) algorithm. RANSAC is great at computing a valid homography from datasets with both valid and invalid matches. By refining the homography using only valid matches, PTGui ensures higher precision. The final hurdle is addressing photometric or brightness differences between the images. PTGui develops a blending algorithm to smooth out these differences, resulting in a seamless panorama. In essence, image stitching is a sophisticated yet captivating process that involves extracting features, computing homographs, and tackling seams and photometric differences to create a unified image from multiple overlapping photos. This intricate process beautifully combines advanced computer vision techniques with practical applications, showcasing the remarkable skill and significance of image stitching technology.

Figure 8. Image stitching

2.5. Image Registration

All the imagery payloads are of different spatial resolution in order to unify them image is required. Image registration can be performed using different tools and methods. Image registration in this book chapter is performed using python and MATLAB. By leveraging powerful image processing toolbox, MATLAB provided a structured environment for implementing registration algorithms efficiently. The process typically began with feature detection, where MATLAB's built-in functions offered robust capabilities for identifying key points or landmarks in images. These features were then matched across images to establish correspondence, a crucial step in aligning them accurately. Once features were matched, MATLAB facilitated the application of transformation models such as affine or elastic transformations. These models were optimized using iterative techniques to minimize the discrepancy between corresponding features in different images. MATLAB's optimization functions and visualization tools allowed for fine-tuning parameters and assessing registration quality visually. Overall, MATLAB's integrated approach to image registration proved beneficial for tasks requiring rapid prototyping and straightforward implementation of standard registration techniques. Rgb image registration over NIR image is shown in the figure 9.

In contrast to MATLAB, Python provided a more flexible and customizable environment for image registration tasks. Leveraging libraries such as OpenCV and scikit-image, Various registration algorithms and techniques were explored. Python library OpenCV was implemented for feature detection algorithms like SIFT or SURF, followed by robust feature matching techniques using RANSAC or other robust methods. This flexibility extended to implementing non-linear transformation models and optimizing them using custom metrics or machine learning approaches, depending on the complexity of the registration task.

Figure 9. Registered RGB and NIR images

3. VISUALIZATION AND ANALYSIS

3.1. Band Stacking

This has transformed conventional farming in a way that has relocated the farming activities in line with data farming, or precision farming. As it has been described in the previous part, there is a technique called image stacking which is frequently used in this field. This process means that one uses many layers to come up with one layer and is often helpful when overlaying one type of data to another, for instance nutrients in soil (NPK) and spectral bands (RGB, NIR, Red-Edge). However, these layered data sources can be integrated with help of Dstack library in Python which can offer better viewpoints about crop health and wiser agricultural decisions could be made. The journey of image stacking starts with data preparation. First, we collect all necessary data layers, including soil nutrient levels from sensors and spectral images from drones and RGB cameras. It's crucial to clean and preprocess these data layers, removing any noise or irrelevant details. This ensures that the final composite image is based on high-quality data, setting a strong foundation for the subsequent steps. Once we have prepared the data, the next step is alignment. This involves matching the spatial coordinates of all data layers, so they correspond to the same physical locations within the field. Additionally, we need to standardize the resolutions of these data layers. This might involve resizing and rescaling them to ensure uniformity. Proper alignment is essential for achieving a seamless integration in the final stacked image, making sure all data layers fit together perfectly. The heart of the image stacking process lies in the use of the Python dstack library. This tool allows us to combine the aligned and resized data layers into a single multidimensional array. By doing so, we create a cohesive dataset that integrates detailed information from each source. The resulting stacked image contains multiple layers of valuable data, providing a richer and more comprehensive view of the field's condition. There are several significant benefits to image stacking in precision agriculture. One major advantage is enhanced data integration. By combining multiple data sources into a single, coherent dataset, we can conduct a more thorough analysis. This integration allows us to merge detailed spectral imagery with precise nutrient measurements, offering a comprehensive picture of crop health. Additionally, image stacking improves visualization. It provides a clearer and more detailed depiction of nutrient distribution and crop health indicators across the field, helping farmers identify areas that need specific interventions, such as targeted fertilizer application or adjusted irrigation practices. Lastly, image stacking increases the accuracy of crop health assessments. By integrating different data types, it reduces potential errors that can arise from analyzing disparate data sources separately, ensuring a more reliable evaluation of the field's condition.

Figure 10. Band stacking

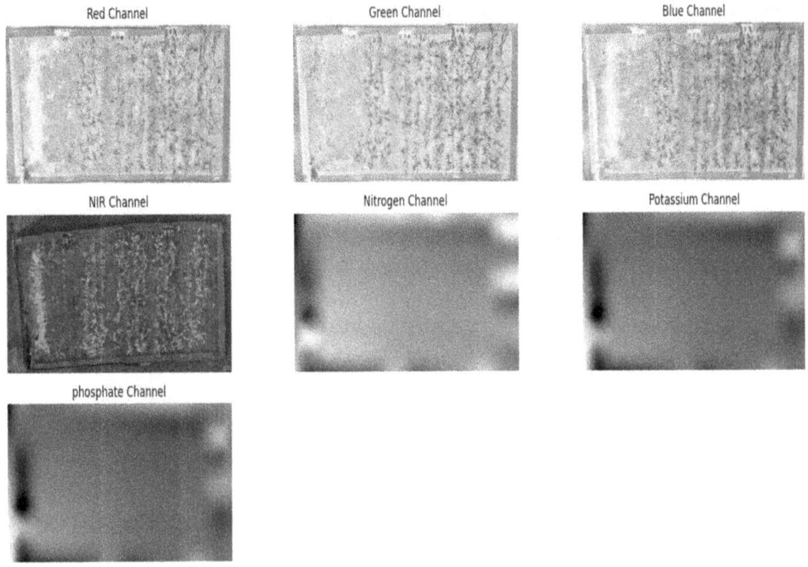

3.2. Vegetation Indices

This chapter we analyze vegetation index as one of the precision agriculture components. For that reason, vegetation indices are deemed to be very crucial tools in precision agriculture since they assist in quantifying the magnitude of variation in vegetation and therefore healthy plant growth. Therefore, these indices are useful for farmers with crop management since the data is collected from various spectral bands by common remote sensing equipment such as drones and satellites. It's about time to consider some of the modern landmarks in regard to vegetation indices and their importance in agricultural settings, with special reference given to the meaning of the values of a number of parameters.

3.2.1. Normalized Difference Vegetation Index (NDVI)

Among vegetation indices, the most famous is the Normalized Difference Vegetation Index or NDVI for short. It functions by comparing the reflection of near infrared referring to the part that vegetation reflectance sends out and the reddish light that plant matter darkly absorbs. The NDVI values vary from -1 to + 1. Above 1 to near 1: healthy vigorous vegetation – green, while near 0 to below 0: very low vegetation cover or exposed soil. It is worth explaining that negative values mean water, snow or any non-vegetated surfaces. Below is general information about the NDVI Vegetation Health index: This index is very important in the examination of the crops' growth, determination of areas experiencing stresses, and management of the irrigation and fertilizer practices.

Figure 11. Normalized difference vegetation index

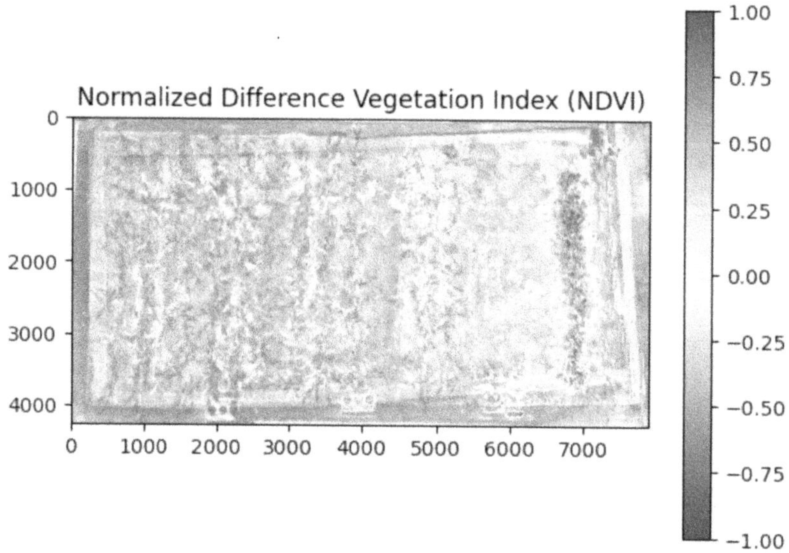

3.2.2. Modified Soil-Adjusted Vegetation Index (MSAVI)

This index is very important in the examination of the crops' growth, determination of areas experiencing stresses, and management of the irrigation and fertilizer practices. Soil-Adjusted Vegetation Index (SAVI) with changes made by Rick Hernández and called Modified SAVI or MSAVI. The Modified Soil-Adjusted Vegetation Index (MSAVI) addresses one of the key challenges in vegetation monitoring: One of the factors which has twice been mentioned is that of soil reflectance. This index is most valuable in regions where there are more open plains and less amount of vegetation so that the impact of the soil can be felt in the reflectance values.

Figure 12. Modified soil adjusted vegetation index

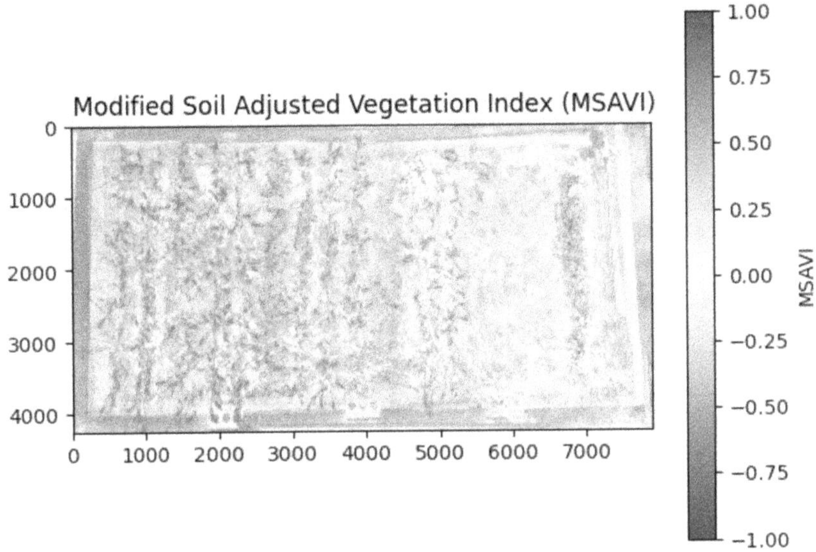

3.2.3. Normalized Difference Red Edge Index (NDRE)

The one which is frequently used is the Normalized Difference Red Edge Index (NDRE). The Normalized Difference Red Edge Index (NDRE) is an index that depends on the red edge band that focuses at detecting chlorophyll content in plants. The same way, the NDRE values lie between -1 and +1; hence high positive scores lean towards stronger, chlorophyll-rich vegetation. It is also good for seeing early signs of stress, as well nutrient deficiency. This index (and this specific band - red edge) means one can check the extent of plant health even before a disease shows physical symptoms, which means the next action could be undertaken on time by farmers.

Figure 13. Normalized difference red edge index

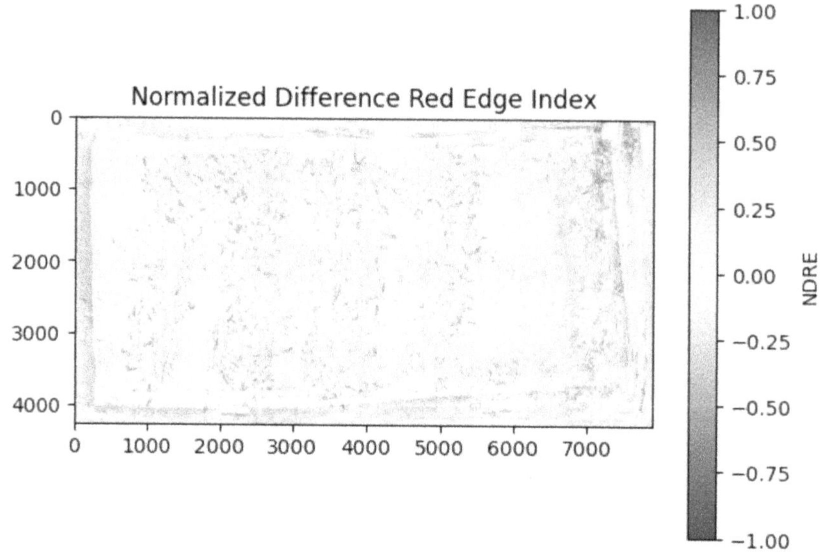

3.2.4. Green Normalized Difference Vegetation Index (GNDVI)

The Green Normalized Difference Vegetation Index (GNDVI) is sensitive to plant health using the green and near-infrared bands. Similar to NDVI, but targeting green band instead of red, the GNDVI values will fall between -1 and +1. More significant values mean an increased amount of chlorophyll and, as a result healthier and more effective vegetation. This index is very valuable in terms of photosynthesis monitoring and adaptation to the plant growth vigor indices.

Figure 14. Green normalized difference vegetation index

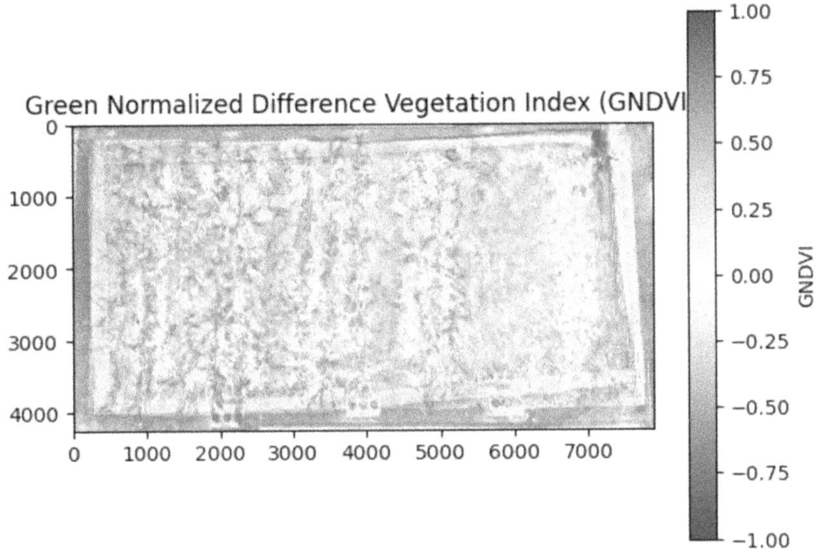

3.2.5. Red-Edge Normalized Difference Vegetation Index (RENDVI)

The other index that utilizes the red-edge band is the Red-Edge Normalized Difference Vegetation Index (RENDVI) and this is also sensitive to changes in plant chlorophyll. The typical values of RENDVI are in the range from - 1 to +1. Wider leaf and high value of this parameter indicated the abundance in healthy chlorophyll containing tissues. This index is useful for early stress detection, nutrient placement and provides valuable information on how to increase field performance and crop yield estimations.

Figure 15. Red edge normalized difference vegetation index

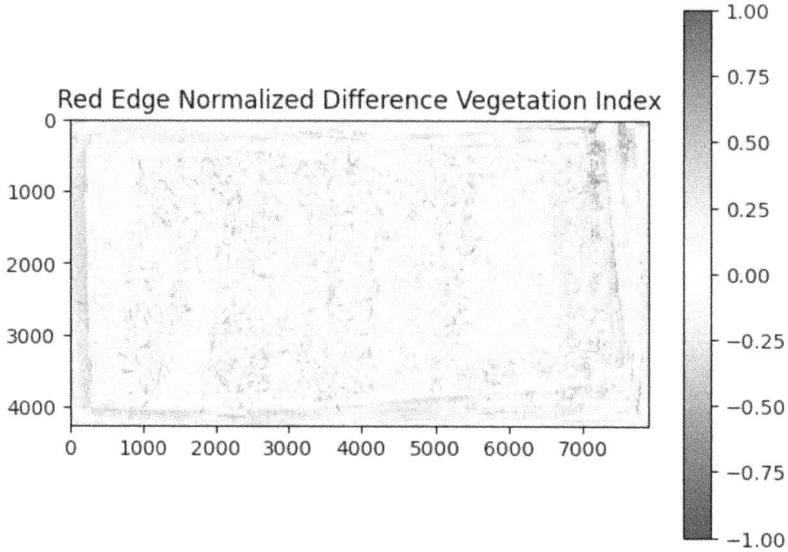

3.2.6. Green Vegetation Index Normalized (GRVI)

Similarly, the Green Vegetation Index Normalized (GRVIN) is formed as ratio of green vegetation index to increase its sensitivity with either decrease or enhancements in health of plant. GRVIN values will oscillate from -1 to +1 as any other indices. Higher values represent better plant condition, and this index is very useful in Healthy vs Stress Vegetation comparison

Figure 16. Green ration vegetation index

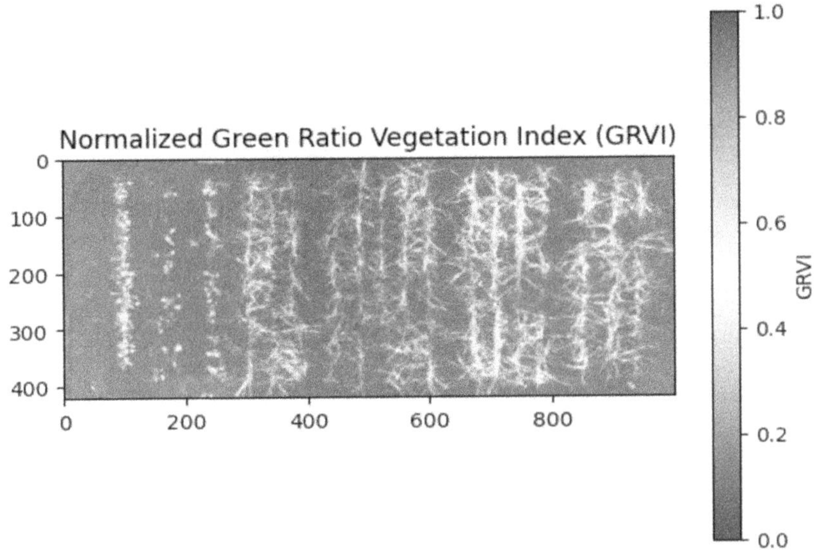

3.2.7. Visible Atmospherically Resistant Index (VARI)

The Visible Atmospherically Resistant Index (VARI) is designed to minimize atmospheric effects, providing a reliable measure of vegetation greenness. VARI values typically range from 0 to +1, with higher values indicating more vigorous green vegetation. It is the most robust index against atmospheric disturbances and therefore a good choice to monitor crop health over an extended period of time in covered meteorological conditions.

Figure 17. Visible atmospherically resistant index

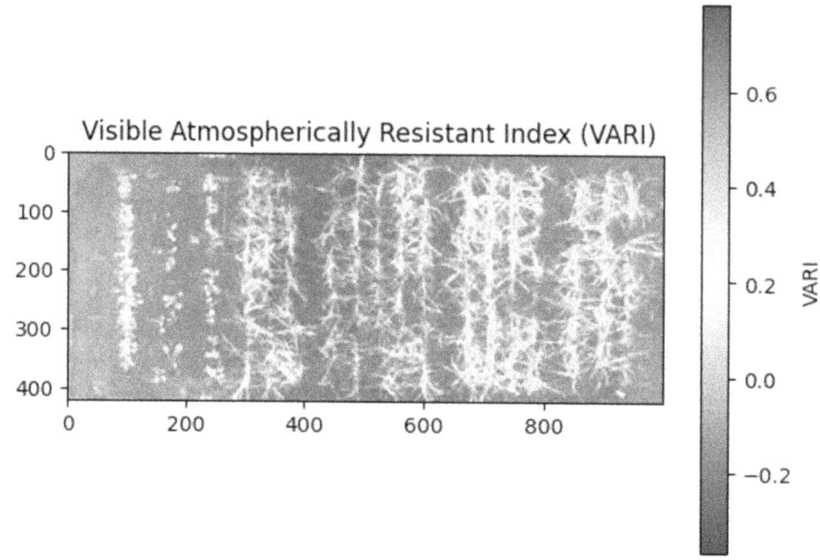

3.2.8. Green Vegetation Index (GVI)

The Green Vegetation Index (GVI) focuses on the green band to assess plant health. Like GNDVI, GVI this vegetation index is sensitive to chlorophyll content. GVI, with higher values indicating healthier vegetation. This index is useful for tracking crop development and detecting early signs of stress, ultimately aiding in better crop management.

Figure 18. Green vegetation index

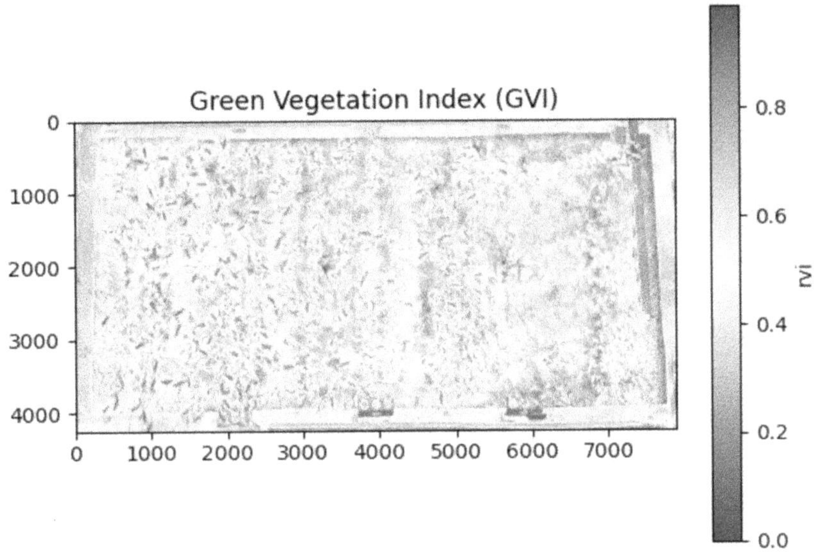

3.2.9. Difference Vegetation Index (DVI)

The Difference Vegetation Index (DVI) measures the difference between near-infrared and red reflectance. DVI values ranges from -1 to +1, with higher values indicating healthier vegetation. This index provides a clear measure of vegetation density and health, useful for identifying areas with varying levels of biomass and monitoring changes over time.

Figure 19. Difference vegetation index

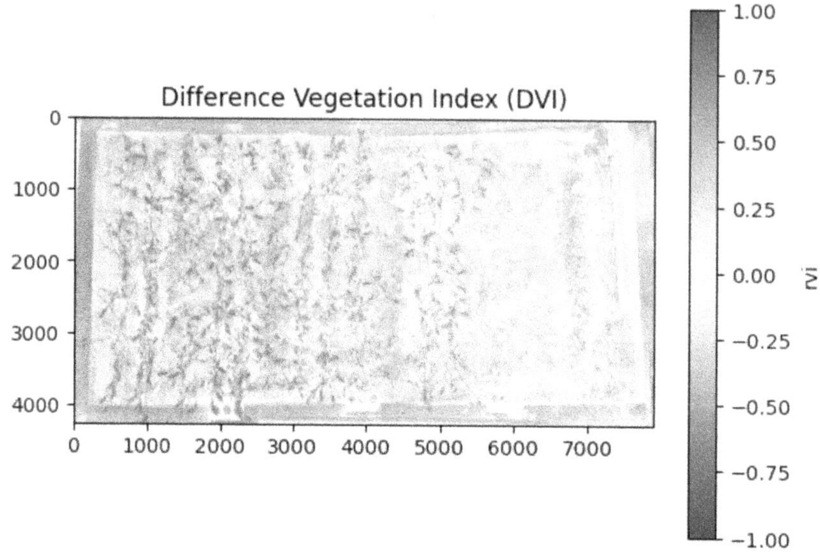

3.2.10. Simple Ratio (SR)

Simple Ratio (SR): The Simple Ratio is one of the earliest vegetation indices; Reflectance, calculating as a ratio between near-infrared and red reflectance. High levels of chlorophyll are quantified as SR values greater, indicating better vegetation condition. It provides a basic measure of vegetation health and is easy to compute, making it useful for general monitoring and detecting changes in vegetation density.

Figure 20. Simple ratio

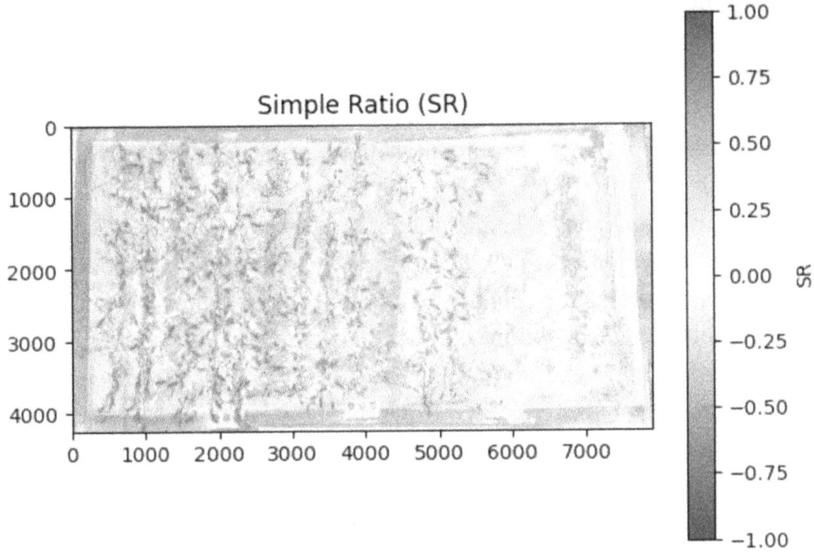

FUTURE RESEARCH DIRECTIONS

Web portal can be designed to incorporate all the features with easy-to-use interface for farmers.

Hyperspectral camera can be used to capture more spectral features and on the basis of spectral signature new vegetation indices can be driven.

CONCLUSION

This chapter has explored an innovative approach to improving crop health monitoring by integrating various data sources with advanced technologies like Generative Adversarial Networks (GANs) and the FarmBot platform. Our methodology addresses the significant challenges of data resolution and format compatibility in precision agriculture. We successfully used GANs to standardize and enhance the resolution of diverse datasets. Using Enhanced Super-Resolution GANs (ESRGANs), we upscaled NPK heatmaps from sensor data, aligning them with high-resolution images from DSLR cameras and multispectral drones. This alignment ensures that all data layers, regardless of their original resolution, are brought to a uniform level of clarity, facilitating accurate and insightful analysis. FarmBot played a crucial role in this methodology. Equipped with a range of sensors and imaging devices, it performs precise, automated data collection tasks across the field, capturing essential soil and environmental data. When combined with high-resolution imagery, FarmBot provides a rich dataset for analysis. Its ability to autonomously perform tasks like seeding, watering, and environmental monitoring highlights its significance in modern precision agriculture. Image processing techniques, including stitching and stacking, further enhanced the dataset quality. By aligning and merging images from different vantage points and resolutions, we achieved a seamless panoramic view of the field, crucial for identifying spatial patterns and variations in crop health that might otherwise go unnoticed. We also included the vegetation indices; Normalized Difference Vegetation Index (NDVI), Enhanced Vegetation Index (EVI) and Normalized Difference Red Edge (NDRE) into the analysis framework. These indices, generated from multispectral, give appreciable information on plant's health, vitality, and stress. When the estimates of these indices were regressed with NPK data and other environmental variables, specific areas, which required focused action in the form of change in the type of fertilizers used, or changes in irrigation pattern; were identified in detail. The implication of this research is huge when it comes to practicing and implementing the findings. In doing so, farmers and agronomists get resolution and specifics they need to make decisions on the fields, to use resources efficiently to produce crops. As a result, the methodology increases the effectiveness of crop management practices and decreases resource wastage and thus is sustainable. In conclusion, integrating GANs and multimodal data fusion techniques with FarmBot represents a significant advancement in precision agriculture. This approach provides a robust framework for comprehensive crop health monitoring, supporting better decision-making and fostering a more sustainable agricultural future. As technology evolves, the methods and insights presented here will serve as a foundation for further innovations, contributing to higher productivity and sustainability in agriculture.

REFERENCES

Garg, S., Pundir, P., Jindal, H., Saini, H., & Garg, S. (2021, July). Towards a multimodal system for precision agriculture using IoT and machine learning. In 2021 12th international conference on computing communication and networking technologies (ICCCNT) (pp. 1-7). IEEE. DOI: 10.1109/ICCCNT51525.2021.9579646

Geetha, R., Jebamalar, G. B., Shiney, S. A., Dao, N. N., Moon, H., & Cho, S. (2024). Enhancing Upscaled Image Resolution Using Hybrid Generative Adversarial Network-Enabled Frameworks. *IEEE Access : Practical Innovations, Open Solutions*, *12*, 27784–27793. DOI: 10.1109/ACCESS.2024.3367763

Kar, S., Mohammad, R., Zaman, M. T., Reza, S. M., Talukder, O., & Hasan, M. (2023, December). Farmbot: an IoT-Based Wireless Agricultural Robot for Smart Cultivation. In 2023 26th International Conference on Computer and Information Technology (ICCIT) (pp. 1-6). IEEE. DOI: 10.1109/ICCIT60459.2023.10441291

Lahat, D., Adali, T., & Jutten, C. (2015). Multimodal data fusion: An overview of methods, challenges, and prospects. *Proceedings of the IEEE*, *103*(9), 1449–1477. DOI: 10.1109/JPROC.2015.2460697

KEY TERMS AND DEFINITIONS

Farmbot: This is a gardening robot which performs automatic watering, weeding, seeding, etc.

PA (Precision Agriculture): In this type of agriculture method are precise like application of precise and correct amount of inputs like water, fertilizer, pesticides, etc.

UAVs, Unmanned Aerial Vehicles: These are drones and aircraft which do not have human pilot, but they are controlled by controller.

UTM, Universal Tool Mount: It is a tool with which 3d print tool of Farmbot are mounted and demounted to perform different tasks.

VI, Vegetation Indices: This term is used to describe the soil and plant health analysis.

Chapter 3
Enhancing the RAG Pipeline Through Advanced Optimization Techniques

Qazi Mudassar Ilyas
https://orcid.org/0000-0003-4238-8093
King Faisal University, Saudi Arabia

Sadia Aziz
La Trobe University, Australia

ABSTRACT

Large language models produce excellent outputs for queries highly relevant to their training data. Retrieval-augmented generation (RAG) is used to augment this training data with additional contextual information based on additional data. Although RAG improves text generation through context retrieval from this additional data, the basic RAG system has limitations in chunking, hallucinations, and reliance on augmented content for knowledge-intensive tasks. This chapter discusses several advanced techniques to enhance retrieval and generation tasks in an RAG pipeline. The chapter discusses advanced strategies for chunking, vectorization, and search processes. Moreover, reranking, filtering, query transformation, query routing, and response synthesis improve generated responses' relevance, coherence, and accuracy.

DOI: 10.4018/979-8-3693-6255-6.ch003

1. INTRODUCTION

Retrieval-augmented generation (RAG) can process extensive information sources to generate refined responses to user inquiries and can be applied in any domain. It combines natural language processing (NLP) and machine learning methods, integrating retrieval and generation. Retrieval involves searching extensive documents and information resources (e.g., information websites, research papers, and books) to fetch relevant context. Generation means generating a well-structured human-like response using a pre-trained language model based on the context collected in the retrieval step. RAG can be integrated into customer assistance applications (chatbots and virtual assistance), search engines, business assistance, content generation, health care chatbots, and other applications (Huang & Huang, 2024). A popular use case of RAG is Facebook's RAG pipeline, designed to provide question-answers and fact-checking services.

A large language model (LLM) responds to user queries based on a static internal knowledge base with which it was trained, so it cannot provide real-time or the most recent information. RAG, on the other hand, retrieves the latest information and provides LLM responses based on more recent information base. Hence, RAG responses are more accurate and factual because of their dynamic knowledge base (Lewis et al., 2020). They can also be used for more specialized industry or domain-specific purposes by using the relevant database (Izacard & Grave, 2021).

Figure 1 shows how an RAG system works. The first step in an RAG pipeline is a query from a user. The retriever searches relevant documents and other resources based on query input from an external data set. A similarity search is performed through vectorization across these resources to find the relevant contents, and finally, the results are ranked according to their most relevancy. The generator role comes into play, combining retrieved information with user input to find a unified context. The RAG system generates a coherent response using this context, ensuring it is accurate and contextually relevant (Lewis et al., 2021).

Figure 1. How an RAG system works

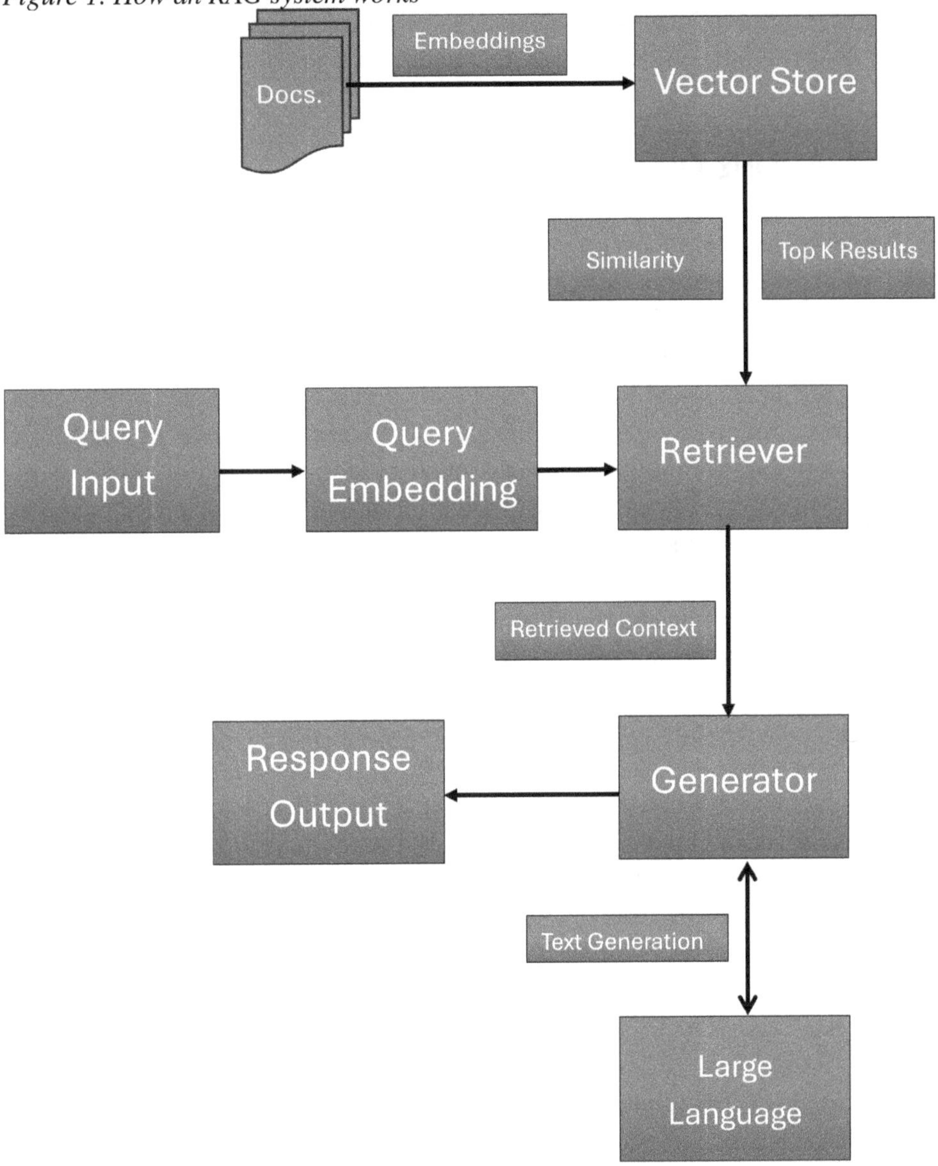

While the traditional RAG system performs well in some applications, it has several limitations, especially in knowledge-intensive tasks. These include high computational costs, the potential for hallucinations, dependence on external knowledge, and occasionally poor responses. It often struggles to handle long user queries, leading to ineffective chunk selection and over-reliance on augmented content. Section 2 provides a detailed explanation of these limitations. To overcome these issues, advanced RAG improves upon the traditional system by refining each existing RAG technique to retrieve information, leading to better overall performance. Section 3 discusses these improved techniques and models in detail.

2. LIMITATIONS OF NAIVE RAG

While the basic RAG systems mentioned above offer several advantages over conventional chatbots by incorporating proprietary resources in the chatbots or other interactive systems, they have several limitations (Gupta et al., 2024). The selection of text chunks is crucial for all downstream tasks, and poorly selected chunks result in inaccurate and ineffective responses in downstream tasks. The basic RAG often suffers from poor precision and recall in the chunk selection process, thus resulting in the selection of irrelevant information and the ignoring of relevant information, ultimately resulting in poor responses from the users. Another challenge is that redundant information is retrieved from various sources, thus producing repetitive responses. The basic RAG systems may also face the issues faced by the generative systems, such as hallucinations, where the given sources of information do not directly support the responses produced. Also, bias and toxicity may reduce the quality of responses. Lastly, the system may overly rely on the augmented content and underutilize the power of large language models through synthesis and additional insights.

The researchers have proposed advanced and modular RAG systems to overcome these limitations and improve the quality of responses generated by the RAG systems. Various enhancements proposed for performing advanced RAG are discussed in the following sections.

3. ADVANCED RAG

Advanced RAG incorporates various techniques and customizations throughout the RAG pipeline to improve the performance and effectiveness of individual components, thus resulting in improved results for the users. The following aspects of RAG are discussed, along with various customizations to enhance the overall performance.

1. Chunking strategies
2. Vectorization
3. Search index
4. Reranking and Filtering

5. Query transformation
6. Query routing agents
7. Response synthesizer
8. Evaluation

Figure 2 gives a glimpse of various techniques and variations in these phases of RAG.

Figure 2. An overview of advanced RAG

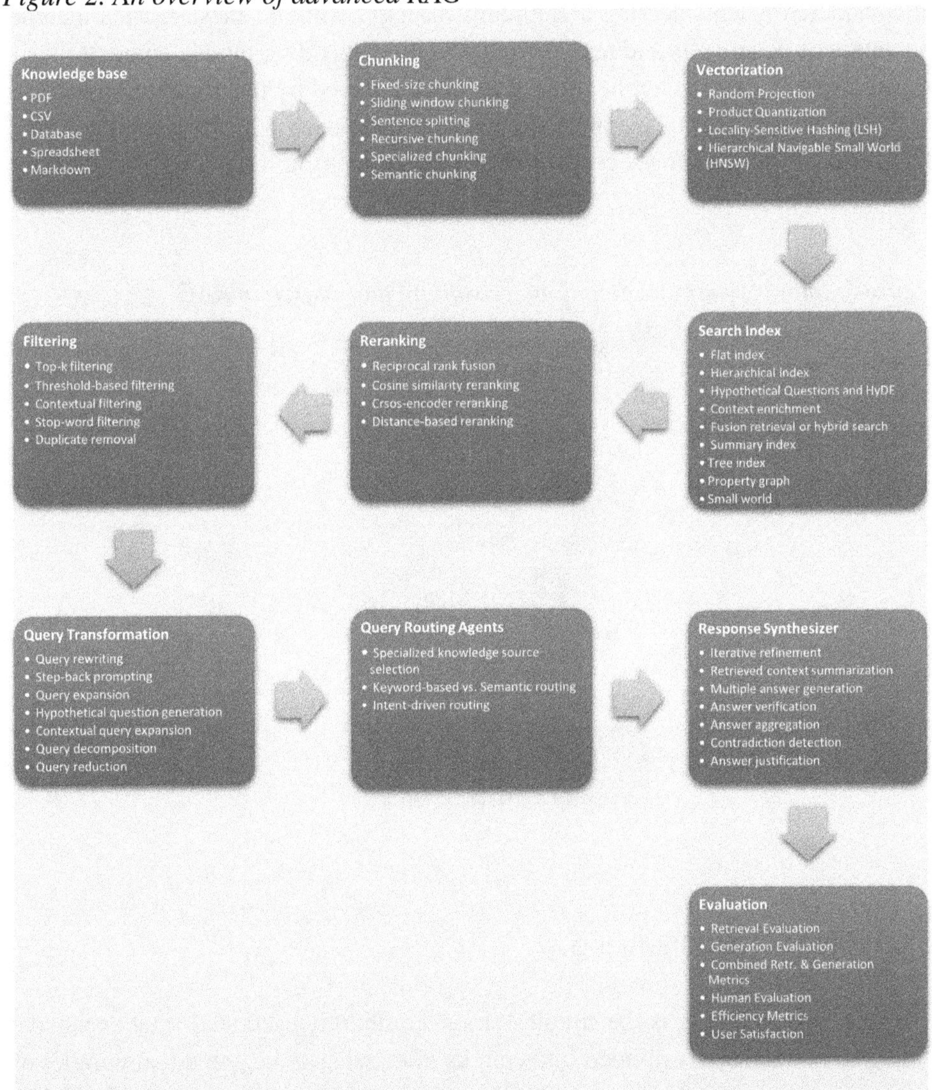

3.1. Chunking Strategies

LLMs are limited by the maximum number of tokens that can be passed in a prompt. Even if the LLM has a large context window, passing as little text to the LLM as possible is more efficient in keeping the input more focused. However, a longer input might help an LLM generate a more appropriate response. This contradictory situation is depicted in Figure 3. An ideal chunk of text passed to an LLM would be broad enough to perform efficient reasoning and specific enough to perform efficient search. In addition to the input text length, several other factors should be considered when selecting a chunking strategy. Some of these factors include the nature of documents and text, the underlying embedding model, characteristics of user queries, and the application of results produced by the application (Elazar et al., 2021). There are several chunking strategies, each with its advantages and drawbacks. The following section briefly describes various chunking strategies for LLM documents.

Figure 3. Impact of context length on reasoning and search in RAG

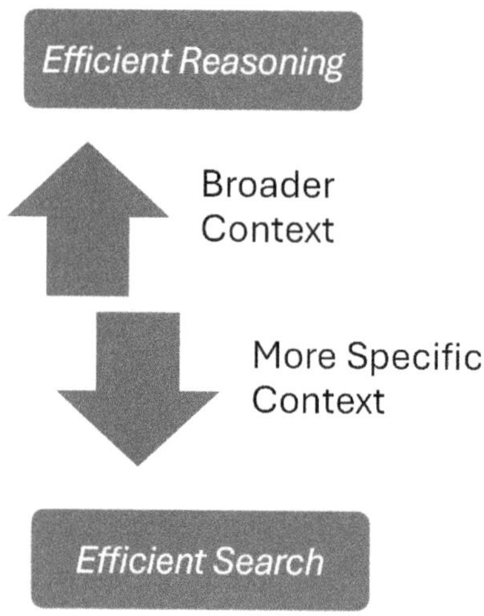

3.1.1. Fixed-Size Chunking

Fixed-size chunking is the simplest, most commonly used, and least expensive strategy. A document is divided into chunks of equal size, i.e., an equal number of characters. For example, if a user develops five chunks from a document of 1000 characters, the first chunk would contain the first 200 characters, the second chunk would contain the characters 201-400, and so on. Although it is the simplest and least expensive chunking scheme, it does not consider the semantics of the structure of the content to be chunked.

3.1.2. Sliding Window Chunking

The naïve fixed-sized chunking can be enhanced by a sliding window to maintain context among successive chunks of text. For example, considering the example document of 1000 characters above and a window size of 200 and stride of 100 characters, the first chunk would contain characters 1-200, the second chunk 101-300, the third 201-400, and so on. This overlap between subsequent chunks maintains some semantic continuity among the chunks.

3.1.3. Sentence Splitting

As the name implies, sentence splitting generates chunks of individual sentences. The naïve sentence splitting generates the chunks by periods (".") or new lines. Due to certain limitations of this naïve sentence splitting mechanism, it is common to use well-known natural language processing libraries such as NLTK or spaCy.

3.1.4. Recursive Chunking

This chunking strategy attempts to produce chunks of desired characteristics in a recursive manner. In the first pass, the documents are divided into chunks based on the document's logical structure, such as sections, chapters, or paragraphs. If the chunks cannot produce the desired results because of large size or inability to narrow down the context, they are further broken down into sub-chunks using a recursive process. The process continues until the chunks are broken to the desired structure and size.

3.1.5. Specialized Chunking

Some document formats, such as Python, PDF, LaTeX, or Markdown, use specific commands to encode the format or structure of the content. This chunking strategy exploits these formats to generate the most suitable and logical chunks from these documents for downward processing in the RAG pipeline.

3.1.6. Semantic Chunking

Semantic chunking breaks a large document into smaller, meaningful chunks based on content and meaning rather than text length. This results in more coherent chunks of text that are more suitable for retrieval, summarization, or generation. This strategy analyses the text using techniques such as embeddings, topic modeling, and sentence boundary detection to determine chunk boundaries. Each chunk produced by this technique is a self-contained unit of text conveying a complete idea without relying on other chunks for additional information.

3.2. Vectorization

As stated above, vector store is a crucial component of RAG, which contains embeddings of the indexed documents. These embeddings enable efficient search and retrieval processes. Although standalone vector indices such as Facebook AI Similarity Search (FAISS) or Chroma can manage text embeddings, vector databases enable enhanced features, such as improved scalability, real-time updates, ecosystem integration, and robust security and access control. When a user gives a query, it is processed using the same embedding model. Query embeddings are used to find similar embeddings in the vector database to retrieve the original document content.

As the vector store of a large document collection can be significantly large, it is often desirable to compress it while maintaining its richness to enable efficient and effective querying. Several algorithms are employed in advanced RAG to generate these compressed embeddings. Some of them are listed below:

- Random Projection
- Product Quantization
- Locality-sensitive Hashing (LSH)
- Hierarchical Navigable Small World (HNSW)

3.2.1. Random Projection

Random projection is a dimensionality reduction technique based on the Johnson-Lindenstrauss lemma, which states that distances between points in a high-dimensional space can be approximately preserved in a lower-dimensional space (Bingham & Mannila, 2001). First, we decide the target lower dimension of the embeddings and create a random matrix of this size. A dot product of the original embedding matrix with this low-dimension matrix produces a reduced-size target embedding vector. During query processing, the same low-dimension matrix is used to reduce the dimension of the query and subsequent querying of the vector index. It is worth noting that the quality of compressed depends on the randomness of the projection matrix, and producing a truly random matrix might be computationally expensive, especially for large databases.

3.2.2. Product Quantization

Product quantization is used to compress high-dimensional vectors into compact codes and then merge the codes for efficient querying and retrieval (Jégou et al., 2011). The original high-dimensional space is split into multiple disjoint smaller subspaces. For example, an original 10,000-dimensional space can be split into ten smaller subspaces of 1000 dimensions each. In the next step, a clustering algorithm is applied to each subspace to find cluster centroids called codes. Each vector in the original space is approximated by the nearest centroid in each space. Finally, instead of storing the original vector, product quantization stores the index of the closest centroid for each subspace, thus compressing the original vectors significantly. Hence, each vector is represented by a set of centroids in each subspace. The query is also represented in the same quantized format during the query phase. The similarity between the query and the documents is computed using the distance between their centroids.

3.2.3. Locality-Sensitive Hashing (LSH)

Locality-sensitive hashing reduces the dimensionality of high-dimensional data by applying locally sensitive hashing algorithms on vectors and hashing similar vectors into the same "buckets" while ensuring that dissimilar vectors are hashed into different buckets (Andoni & Indyk, 2008). A distance measure is selected to ascertain vector similarity. Some measures include Euclidean distance, cosine similarity, jacquard distance, and hamming distance. The hashing algorithms for these distance measures include p-stable LSH and Gaussian LSH for Euclidean distance, simHash, random projection, and sign random projection for cosine similarity, minHash for jacquard similarity, and bitSampling for hamming distance. During the querying phase, the same hashing function is applied to the query to select the target buckets. The search is performed within these buckets only, thus dramatically improving the performance.

3.2.4. Hierarchical Navigable Small World (HNSW)

Hierarchical navigable small world is a graph-based algorithm for finding the approximate nearest neighbor in a high-dimensional (Malkov & Yashunin, 2020). The algorithm is based on two key concepts: small-world networks and hierarchical navigation. Small-world networks, as the name implies, enable the efficient exploration of vectors because of short paths and small networks. Hierarchical navigation is used to build multi-layered graphs. The edges in these networks are based on similarity between the vectors. The search starts at the top layer, which comprises the least number of vectors. With increasing depth, the number of vectors increases, and the connections become denser, allowing for precise search. A greedy search strategy is used to move from one to the next layer based on the similarity of document vectors with the query vector.

3.3. Search Index

Once the vector embeddings have been generated and compressed using the abovementioned techniques, a search index is required to enable efficient search in these embeddings. A search index in RAG maps these vector embeddings to the source documents. It optimizes the process of finding relevant documents in a large database by organizing the documents to reduce the search space.

Several techniques have been proposed to develop a search index in RAG, each with its applications and limitations. Following are some of the most popular techniques used for the search index.

- Flat index
- Keyword table
- Tree search index
- Summary search index
- Hierarchical index
- Hypothetical questions and Hyde
- Context enrichment
- Fusion retrieval or hybrid search
- Property graph
- Small world networks

3.3.1. Flat Index

A flat search index is a naïve approach to generating a search index. The index uses brute force to measure the similarity between the query's and document vectors. As the index does not employ any optimization, this is the most inefficient and ineffective search index.

3.3.2. Keyword Table

This is another naïve indexing strategy in which documents are indexed based on specific keywords extracted from their content. A lookup table containing keywords and corresponding documents is created. When a query is made, relevant keywords are identified from this table, and the corresponding documents are fetched. The method is useful when quickly identifying documents related to particular keywords is required. However, it does not capture the nuance of advanced semantics required for richer document retrieval and query answering.

3.3.3. Summary Search Index

The summary search index creates an index of summaries of the documents instead of indexing the entire document corpus. It results in a condensed representation of each document. During the search, queries are matched against these summaries to identify the most relevant documents. Once the search is narrowed to a few documents, a deeper search can be performed in the entire document corpus for detailed information.

3.3.4. Tree Search Index

A tree search index is used to organize documents hierarchically (Li et al., 2023). The top level represents the most general documents, with each deeper level having more specific chunks or documents. The search process starts at the root level and progressively narrows the search to more relevant lower-level nodes. A tree structure reduces the number of comparisons needed to find relevant documents and provides a structured way to retrieve high-level summaries and specific details pertaining to the query.

3.3.5. Hierarchical Index

In the case of a large vector store, it might be more efficient to perform a search hierarchically. This is achieved by creating two indices. The first index is generated from the document summaries, while the second index processes actual document chunks. A search query is processed in two steps. In the first step, a search is performed in the summary index, thus narrowing down the search space. In the second step, the relevant documents are processed in more detail. This two-step process not only improves search efficiency but also improves search results accuracy.

3.3.6. Hypothetical Questions and Hypothetical Document Embeddings

In advanced retrieval systems, an LLM is used to generate hypothetical questions for each text chunk in a corpus. These questions are then embedded into vectors. During the querying process, these questions are used to narrow the search space. The most relevant questions are then mapped to their original text chunks and subsequently used to generate the context for LLM to answer the user query. This improves semantic similarity between the user query and hypothetical questions, resulting in more accurate final results.

Another complementary approach, hypothetical document embeddings, uses LLM to generate hypothetical responses based on user queries. This response's embeddings are used to augment the user query in the form of richer semantics to guide the search process and ultimately generate a more accurate final answer.

3.3.7. Context Enrichment

Like the hierarchical index, context enrichment also uses a two-step query-answering approach. However, instead of generating document summaries, it identifies the most relevant sentences and then expands them with surrounding context to enhance LLM's reasoning process. Context enrichment can be implemented in two ways:

- Sentence window retrieval
- Parent document retrieval

A brief description of these methods follows.

Sentence Window Retrieval

In this technique, each sentence in a document is embedded separately. Once a sentence matches the user query, we extend the context by including k sentences before and after the retrieved sentence. This contextually richer information is then passed to the LLM to reason and generate an accurate response.

Parent Document Retrieval

This technique begins with splitting every indexed document, called the parent document, into multiple child chunks. While querying, if the number of child documents in the top k retrieved chunks exceeds a given threshold, they are replaced with their parent chunk. This richer context is then passed to the LLM to guide its response.

3.3.8. Fusion Retrieval or Hybrid Search

Fusion retrieval or hybrid search combines the strengths of traditional keyword-based search algorithms and modern semantic or vector-based algorithms (Zhao et al., 2024). The traditional keywords-based retrieval algorithms such as TF-IDF and BM25 are sparse retrieval algorithms that rely on an exact match between the query and the document. These methods are highly efficient for precision when the exact matching of keywords is essential. However, they might have a low recall because they fail to understand the semantic relationship between various terms and keywords.

On the other hand, dense retrieval methods like vector embeddings exploit rich semantics of the underlying content even when different keywords are used to describe the same concept. Hene, embeddings allow retrieval of documents based on conceptual similarity, even when the terms in the query and the document differ. This makes these methods particularly efficient at recall.

Fusion retrieval achieves high precision and recall by combining the strengths of sparse and dense retrieval methods. However, a key challenge is effectively combining results from two distinct retrieval methods. One popular method is the reciprocal rank fusion algorithm, which reranks documents based on their rank scores across both methods. The method assigns higher scores to documents scoring high in both retrieval methods, thus ensuring the final results reflect high semantic relevance and keyword matches.

3.3.9. Property Graph

A property graph is a graph data structure that enables the representation and querying of complex relationships between documents and queries. Documents or text chunks are represented by nodes, while their relationships are represented by edges connecting the vertices. These graphs can capture rich semantic relationships between chunks of text. Property graphs are implemented by graph databases like Neo4j and user graph traversal algorithms to retrieve rich semantic information from interconnected documents.

3.3.10. Small World Networks

Small-world networks organize the documents or text chunks similarly to property graphs, with particular emphasis on making nodes accessible with short paths between each other, even when the network is large. This is achieved by forming clusters of closely related nodes and joining clusters together through short paths. The method uses the Hierarchical Navigable Small World (HNSW) algorithms mentioned above to search and query the indexed corpus.

3.4. Reranking and Filtering

Reranking and filtering techniques are used to refine the initially returned results by the RAG system (Nogueira & Cho, 2019). Some of the popular reranking techniques include:

- **Reciprocal rank fusion (RRF)**: improves the quality of retrieved results by combining results returned from different retrieved methods. For example, RRF might merge sparse and dense retrieval techniques to retrieve documents ranking higher in both keyword similarity and content and query semantics.
- **Cosine similarity reranking**: a set of documents retrieved based on approximate matching may be reranked by calculating cosine similarity between the query and the document embeddings to refine the final response.
- **Cross-encoder reranking:** a computationally expensive technique that employs a transformer model (like BERT) to rerank top-k retrieved results based on their relevance to the query.
- **Distance-based reranking**: uses the nearest neighbor algorithm to rerank results based on their proximity to the query in the embedding space.

Some popular filtering techniques are given below:

- **Top-k filtering** is one of the most popular techniques that limit the number of retrieved documents to k and pass them to LLM for response generation.
- **Threshold-based filtering**: sets a similar score threshold and filters out all retrieved results below this threshold.
- **Contextual filtering**: filters out results based on additional criteria, such as metadata, timestamps, or contextual relevance (Stengel-Eskin et al., 2021).
- **Stop-word filtering**: removes documents dominated by stop-words or irrelevant content, focusing on high-quality and relevant content.
- **Duplicate removal**: filters out duplicate or near-duplicate chunks or documents to avoid redundancy in retrieval.

3.5. Query Transformation

A user query might be too brief, long, ambiguous, or poorly phrased for a LLM. Query transformation techniques attempt to understand the user intent and transform a query to make it more effective for the downward pipeline in RAG. Some of the widespread query transformations are briefly described as follows:

- **Query rewriting**: rephrases the given query to express the user intent more clearly by paraphrasing it, adding synonyms, or restructuring the query to focus on various aspects (Bondarenko et al., 2020).
- **Step-back prompting**: steps back from the user query to ask broader or clarifying questions, often generated by an LLM to improve the clarity of the query and thus improve the final output.
- **Query expansion**: attempts to expand the original user query with more terms, synonyms, and related concepts extracted from ontologies or knowledge bases to improve retrieval coverage.
- **Hypothetical question generation**: generates hypothetical questions from the user query and embeds them into vector form. The search is then conducted using these questions rather than the original query.
- **Cocntetual query expansion**: expands the given query with more contextual information, such as location, time, or domain-specific details, to tailor retrieval to the user's context.
- **Query decomposition**: breaks down the original, potentially longer and complex, query into multiple smaller manageable sub-queries, which are used independently to generate responses. These responses are merged to generate a more comprehensive response to the original user query.
- **Query reduction**: attempts to simplify a query if the user-provided query is too long or complex by removing redundant or unnecessary information from it and focusing on the core concept to improve retrieval quality.

3.6. Query Routing Agents

Query routing agents play a crucial role in RAG systems. A well-designed RAG system might contain multiple knowledge sources, databases, or retrieval methods, e.g., keyword search, semantic search, or vector search. Query routing agents help improve the retrieval quality by dynamically choosing the best retrieval method and knowledge source and applying query-specific logic such as internal analysis or context awareness. Some examples of query routing agents include:

- Specialized knowledge source selection

- Keyword-based vs. Semantic routing
- Intent-driven routing

A brief description of the types of such agents follows.

3.6.1. Specialized Knowledge Source Selection

RAG systems usually have multiple knowledge sources; some might be more appropriate for certain types of user queries than others. A knowledge source selection agent might dynamically select the most appropriate knowledge source based on user intent and requirements. For example, a query routing agent might choose a knowledge source containing research papers rather than general-purpose knowledge bases to address a query related to medical research more effectively.

3.6.2. Keyword-Based vs. Semantic Routing

As stated above, keyword-based search usually performs better regarding precision, while semantic search is highly efficient for information recall. Hence, a query routing agent might choose a keyword-based search if the user needs more precise knowledge and a semantic search when high recall is required. In cases where a user needs both precise keyword matching and semantic understanding, the query routing agent might direct the query to both search engines.

3.6.3. Intent-Driven Routing

If the RAG system detects that the query is more conversational or requires reasoning, it can route it to a more abstract, high-level knowledge base rather than fact-driven sources.

3.7. Response Synthesizer

A response synthesizer is a crucial component of RAG systems. It plays a key role in combining and processing information retrieved from multiple sources to generate a correct, coherent, relevant, and contextually correct response. It is used to iteratively refine, summarize, verify, and aggregate the retrieved content to improve the quality of generated output, leading to better user satisfaction. Some of the popular techniques used in the response synthesizer are:

- Iterative refinement
- Retrieved context summarization

- Multiple answer generation
- Answer verification
- Answer aggregation
- Contradiction detection and resolution
- Answer justification

A brief description of each of these techniques is given below:

3.7.1. Iterative Refinement

This technique processes a user query in several iterations, each iteration resulting in a more refined and precise response (Chen et al., 2024). Initially, the LLM provides a response based on the retrieved information. The system generates another query or regenerates the context for the retrieval system based on this response. This technique is especially useful for complex, ambiguous, or lengthy queries.

3.7.2. Retrieved Context Summarization

As the name implies, the retrieved context summarization technique summarizes the chunks or documents returned by the retrieval system before passing them to the LLM. The summarized information prevents overwhelming the model, which leads to more precise and coherent responses.

3.7.3. Multiple Answer Generation

This technique allows the system to process different interpretations or perspectives of the query and produce multiple responses based on each point of view (Liu et al., 2024). These responses can be reranked, synthesized, or merged to provide a more comprehensive response.

3.7.4. Answer Verification

The system requires the retrieved content to verify its accuracy using this technique. The response is adjusted or corrected in case of any discrepancies.

3.7.5. Answer Aggregation

In the case of multi-faceted or very broad queries, the retrieved results may contain partial answers from more than one resource. In such cases, the synthesizer can aggregate these results into a comprehensive and coherent response to cover all query aspects.

3.7.6. Contradiction Detection and Resolution

While the answer aggregation technique can synthesize partial answers into a coherent whole, it can only be applied when the chunks provide complementary answers. In some instances, the information provided from different sources might be contradictory. In such cases, the synthesizer may flag these contradictions or resolve them using the credibility of the underlying sources.

3.7.7. Answer Justification

A synthesizer might justify the answers by providing references from the retrieved content. This is especially useful in academic, legal, or scientific cotexts where source credibility is critical.

3.8. Evaluation

The last component in an RAG pipeline is the evaluation of retrieval and generation outputs. Due to the different nature of these two components, a multi-faceted approach is needed to evaluate the RAG system. There are seven main evaluation categories, each with measures for evaluating RAG systems. The evaluation categories are:

- Retrieval Evaluation
- Generation Evaluation
- Combined Retrieval and Generation Metrics
- Human Evaluation
- Efficiency Metrics
- User Satisfaction

A brief description of each one of these categories is provided below.

3.8.1. Retrieval Evaluation

Retrieval evaluation measures are used to evaluate the accuracy and relevance of documents or chunks retrieved from the RAG knowledge base. The key metrics under this evaluation category are preccision@k, recall@k, F1 score, and mean reciprocal rank.

3.8.2. Generation Evaluation

The evaluation metrics under the generation evaluation category consider the generation phase to measure how well the system synthesizes and generates the final response. The evaluation metrics under this category are fluency and grammar, factual accuracy, relevance of generated output, coherence, consistency, and ROUGE (recall-oriented understudy for gisting evaluation).

3.8.3. Combined Retrieval and Generation Metrics

Instead of measuring the retrieval and generation aspects in isolation, the set of measures under the combined retrieval and generation metrics category evaluates how well these two components work together to produce the final response. The metrics under combined retrieval and generation metrics include relevance of retrieved vs. generated output, contextual understanding, and query-answer alignment.

3.8.4. Human Evaluation

The nuanced nature of text generation makes it a subjective task that might not be effectively measured with automated measures (Zhang et al., 2018). In some cases, human judgment may be more suitable for evaluating the correctness, comprehensiveness, conciseness, and overall quality of the generated responses.

3.8.5. Efficiency Metrics

Although effectiveness is generally more critical in RAG systems, it is also essential to measure system efficiency. The evaluation metrics under this category include throughput, latency, response time, and resource utilization.

3.8.6. User Satisfaction

Real-world RAG systems often include user feedback mechanisms to evaluate user satisfaction with the system responses. User ratings are a commonly used metric to measure user satisfaction. In interactive RAG systems, tracking how often users refine or re-submit queries might be a good indicator of generated content quality (Siro et al., 2024).

4. CONCLUSION

This chapter covers several advanced techniques for various components in the RAG pipeline. Advanced chunking strategies, such as sliding window, recursive, or semantic chunking, produce improved chunking of text that helps in better text understanding. Vector store is the backbone of an RAG pipeline. Instead of using a simple vectorization scheme, advanced techniques, such as random projection, product quantization, locality-sensitive hashing, and hierarchical navigable small world produce vector store, can be used to produce better document embeddings, thus facilitating relevant context by matching user query with the vector store. A search index maps document embeddings to their source documents, and various indexing techniques can be used to build the most appropriate search index in the application domain. Some indexing techniques include a hierarchical index, hypothetical questions and HyDE, fusion retrieval, and summary index. Similarly, reranking and filtering techniques can rerank the initial results in an RAG pipeline to retain only the most relevant and high-quality results. Finally, response synthesis, query routing, and transformation can improve query responses. The chapter elaborates on each technique's most appropriate use-case scenarios in detail. We highlight the recent innovations in the domain and their potential to build useful, reliable, and trustworthy RAG systems.

REFERENCES

Andoni, A., & Indyk, P. (2008). Near-optimal hashing algorithms for approximate nearest neighbor in high dimensions. *Communications of the ACM*, 51(1), 117–122. DOI: 10.1145/1327452.1327494

Bingham, E., & Mannila, H. (2001). Random projection in dimensionality reduction: Applications to image and text data. *Proceedings of the Seventh ACM SIGKDD International Conference on Knowledge Discovery and Data Mining*, 245–250. DOI: 10.1145/502512.502546

Bondarenko, A., Braslavski, P., Völske, M., Aly, R., Fröbe, M., Panchenko, A., Biemann, C., Stein, B., & Hagen, M. (2020). Comparative Web Search Questions. *Proceedings of the 13th International Conference on Web Search and Data Mining*, 52–60. DOI: 10.1145/3336191.3371848

Chen, C., Zhou, S., Liao, L., Wu, H., Sun, W., Yan, Q., & Lin, W. (2024). Iterative Token Evaluation and Refinement for Real-World Super-resolution. *Proceedings of the AAAI Conference on Artificial Intelligence*, 38(2), 1010–1018. DOI: 10.1609/aaai.v38i2.27861

Elazar, Y., Kassner, N., Ravfogel, S., Ravichander, A., Hovy, E., Schütze, H., & Goldberg, Y. (2021). Measuring and Improving Consistency in Pretrained Language Models. *Transactions of the Association for Computational Linguistics*, 9, 1012–1031. DOI: 10.1162/tacl_a_00410

Gupta, S., Ranjan, R., & Singh, S. N. (2024). *A Comprehensive Survey of Retrieval-Augmented Generation (RAG): Evolution, Current Landscape and Future Directions* (Version 1). arXiv. DOI: 10.48550/ARXIV.2410.12837

Huang, Y., & Huang, J. (2024). *A Survey on Retrieval-Augmented Text Generation for Large Language Models* (Version 2). arXiv. DOI: 10.48550/ARXIV.2404.10981

Izacard, G., & Grave, E. (2021). *Leveraging Passage Retrieval with Generative Models for Open Domain Question Answering* (No. arXiv:2007.01282). DOI: 10.18653/v1/2021.eacl-main.74

Jégou, H., Douze, M., & Schmid, C. (2011). Product Quantization for Nearest Neighbor Search. *IEEE Transactions on Pattern Analysis and Machine Intelligence*, 33(1), 117–128. DOI: 10.1109/TPAMI.2010.57 PMID: 21088323

Lewis, P., Perez, E., Piktus, A., Petroni, F., Karpukhin, V., Goyal, N., Küttler, H., Lewis, M., Yih, W., Rocktäschel, T., Riedel, S., & Kiela, D. (2020). *Retrieval-Augmented Generation for Knowledge-Intensive NLP Tasks* (Version 4). arXiv. DOI: 10.48550/ARXIV.2005.11401

Lewis, P., Perez, E., Piktus, A., Petroni, F., Karpukhin, V., Goyal, N., Küttler, H., Lewis, M., Yih, W., Rocktäschel, T., Riedel, S., & Kiela, D. (2021). *Retrieval-Augmented Generation for Knowledge-Intensive NLP Tasks* (No. arXiv:2005.11401). arXiv. http://arxiv.org/abs/2005.11401

Li, H., Ai, Q., Zhan, J., Mao, J., Liu, Y., Liu, Z., & Cao, Z. (2023). Constructing Tree-based Index for Efficient and Effective Dense Retrieval. *Proceedings of the 46th International ACM SIGIR Conference on Research and Development in Information Retrieval*, 131–140. DOI: 10.1145/3539618.3591651

Liu, F., Jung, J., & Feinstein, W. (2024). *Aggregated Knowledge Model: Enhancing Domain-Specific QA with Fine-Tuned and Retrieval-Augmented Generation Models* (Version 1). DOI: 10.48550/ARXIV.2410.18344

Malkov, Y. A., & Yashunin, D. A. (2020). Efficient and Robust Approximate Nearest Neighbor Search Using Hierarchical Navigable Small World Graphs. *IEEE Transactions on Pattern Analysis and Machine Intelligence*, 42(4), 824–836. DOI: 10.1109/TPAMI.2018.2889473 PMID: 30602420

Nogueira, R., & Cho, K. (2019). *Passage Re-ranking with BERT* (Version 5). DOI: 10.48550/ARXIV.1901.04085

Siro, C., Aliannejadi, M., & De Rijke, M. (2024). Understanding and Predicting User Satisfaction with Conversational Recommender Systems. *ACM Transactions on Information Systems*, 42(2), 1–37. DOI: 10.1145/3624989

Stengel-Eskin, E., Murray, K., Zhang, S., White, A. S., & Van Durme, B. (2021). Joint Universal Syntactic and Semantic Parsing. *Transactions of the Association for Computational Linguistics*, 9, 756–773. DOI: 10.1162/tacl_a_00396

Zhang, J., Chang, J., Danescu-Niculescu-Mizil, C., Dixon, L., Hua, Y., Taraborelli, D., & Thain, N. (2018). Conversations Gone Awry: Detecting Early Signs of Conversational Failure. *Proceedings of the 56th Annual Meeting of the Association for Computational Linguistics(*Volume 1*: Long Papers)*, 1350–1361. DOI: 10.18653/v1/P18-1125

Zhao, W. X., Liu, J., Ren, R., & Wen, J.-R. (2024). Dense Text Retrieval Based on Pretrained Language Models: A Survey. *ACM Transactions on Information Systems*, 42(4), 1–60. DOI: 10.1145/3637870

Chapter 4
Narrative Machines: The Evolution of Storytelling in the Age of Generative AI

Andi Asrifan
https://orcid.org/0000-0002-9934-6129
Universitas Negeri Makassar, Indonesia

Muh. Fadli Hasa
Universitas Muhammadiyah Sorong, Indonesia

Syafryadin Syafryadin
https://orcid.org/0000-0001-8167-2930
Universitas Bengkulu, Indonesia

Hanafi Pelu
Balai Diklat Keagamaan Makassar, Indonesia

ABSTRACT

This chapter examines how artificial intelligence (AI) has changed society and its future. It shows how AI may boost creativity but can pose problems. The chapter stresses expanding AI understanding and engaging various communities to reduce risks and maximize benefits. It covers the history of AI, from Turing's early work to modern machine learning, and explores automation's role in society. The chapter emphasizes the necessity for international AI regulation cooperation, portraying UNCITRAL as a key role in stimulating dialogue and establishing global AI law and policy. The chapter sets the stage for exploring AI's revolutionary potential in creative fields by explaining AI's role in narrative.

DOI: 10.4018/979-8-3693-6255-6.ch004

1. INTRODUCTION

In the 21st century, societies worldwide are grappling with the rise of artificial intelligence (AI) and the implications it holds for the future of humanity (Sterledev et al., 2021; Taeihagh, 2021; Sheikh, 2020). Although artificial intelligence has enormous potential as a tool to amplify our human ingenuity, it also poses unique risks that demand understanding the broad set of perspectives with which it may be considered. Widening access to this understanding and enabling myriad communities to engage with the issues arising from this technology will help mitigate AI's most harmful sides and harness its power for all benefits (Mikalef et al., 2022; Feijóo et al., 2020; Yigitcanlar et al., 2020; Galaz et al., 2021). UNCITRAL, with a global mandate to foster the development of a climate in which international business can be conducted efficiently, has the collective expertise of its member states poised to facilitate widespread dialogue on the topic, particularly given the crosscutting and boundary-crossing nature of this rapidly evolving technology (Bamodu, 2023; Butler, 2023). By recognizing or establishing the most promising area for structured cooperation, UNCITRAL is well-positioned to serve a key role in laying the foundations for international AI law and policy.

1.1. Background

AI has a history as long as computers. Alan Turing proposed the test that bears his name in the 1950s, and the Loebner Prize has been awarded since the 1990s to the most human-like conversational agent (Barthelmeß & Furbach, 2023; Hoffmann, 2022). One thread of the history of AI has been to establish some taxonomy of what is possible to automate. As we move towards the end of the 2010s, this automation concept has become deeply embedded in the social and economic landscape, similar to the machinery that provides automated worldliness. Software and services blessed with machine learning are no longer the narrow, brittle purpose machines they were before the deep learning revolution, assuming a common, scalable base set of architectural componentry (Lwakatare et al., 2020; Imdoukh et al., 2020). SJWs usually involve a billion people because that is the scale of their manipulative reach. Each conversation with an SJW becomes less personally significant when the discussed set is initially constructed in the back rooms of an opaque digital asset mastering process run by a fiduciary and exists only as propositions.

The Evolution of Storytelling in the Age of Generative AI is an extensive and profound investigation into the emerging role of Artificial Intelligence in the arts and storytelling, ushering in a new era of boundless possibilities (Feuerriegel et al., 2024; Trichopoulos et al., 2023; Pescapè, 2024). This exquisite book is a valuable resource, meticulously crafted for authors, filmmakers, and game designers who yearn to harness the immense power of these revolutionary tools. Delving deep into uncharted territories, the purpose of this masterpiece is twofold: to cultivate critical literacy surrounding this unparalleled generation of creative instruments, enabling individuals to make informed decisions regarding the most fitting tools for their unique endeavors, and to captivate a broader readership, encompassing students of media theory and those harboring a profound fascination with the captivating nexus of AI and creativity (Amankwah-Amoah et al., 2024; Cress & Kimmerle, 2023; Al Naqbi et al., 2024; Pescapè, 2024; Holmström & Carroll, 2024). As the ambition of AI relentlessly marches towards universal Turing-ness, a paramount question lingers: how far have we journeyed along the path to universal meaning-ness? Moreover, we must confront the perils that may arise from the imprudent implementation of artificial narrative generators, seeking to discern the distinctive outcomes that differentiate a cohesive and cogent project from a mere jumble of discordant elements. Countless philosophers, linguists, and aestheticians have grappled with the essence of meaning, questioning its very nature (Deakin, 2023). While the pages of this profound literary work cannot fully unveil a precise and definitive answer to this perennial conundrum, they unfailingly shed light on the multifaceted nature of meaning in the ever-evolving landscape 2018. Like a celestial visitor hurtling through the cosmos, its mysteries shrouded in enigma, the advent of AI looms near our technological campfire. In the face of this imminent arrival, only the most mesmerizing and enthralling tales of our human endeavors will prevail, shaping the narratives that shall echo throughout the annals of time.

2. HISTORY OF STORYTELLING

By the 18th century, the concept of artificially created talking androids had made its way into the public imagination (Nielsen, 2022; Kantosalo et al., 2021; Sartori & Bocca, 2023). Automata exhibitions continued to be a popular form of public entertainment throughout the 19th and early 20th centuries, featuring mechanical replicas of animals and people, including talking and writing automatons. One of the most famous was the Digesting Duck, constructed by Jacques de Vaucanson, which could move its head, wings, and neck, quack, drink water, eat grain, and excrete (Cohen, 2024). Other prominent talking androids were the writer and the pianist by Karl Knaus, Wolfgang von Kempelen, the inventor of the Turk, and Friedrich Kaufmann's The Machtlinger, billed as the only female talking android in the world.

The search for artificial storytellers is as old as the concept of automatons themselves (Hermann, 2023; Coeckelbergh, 2021). The Greeks told stories about god-made creatures such as Talus, Zeus's bronze man, and Hephaestus's bronze woman, Pandora. The golem of Jewish folklore was created out of clay and infused with life to protect the Jewish people (Herzig, 2021; Goltz et al., 2020). The belief that inanimate matter can be brought to life is at the heart of many of the myths of early storytelling, from the Pygmalion of Greek legend, who fell in love with the beautiful sculpture he had created, to Mary Shelley's Frankenstein, in which an artificial being is set into motion through a scientific experiment into the unknown (Kovacic, 2023).

2.1. Oral Tradition and Mythology

As well as being some of the oldest stories that we know of, the Iliad and Odyssey have much to reflect on in terms of what stories are for - their characters are quests, remembered more for who they are and what they bequeathed than the mechanics of their inheritance. As in most cultures across the world, the story form that came through the oral tradition was largely genealogical and mythological - tracing lines of lineage and the associated actions of those lines, preserving social technologies, laws, and norms, and in so doing, providing a sense of shared history and identity to those who knew or heard the stories (Ballard, 2021; Davidson et al., 2021). These archetypal records were core to ancient lifeworlds, and both maintained the stability of social structures and governance while holding the key to their dynamical adaptation.

The most ancient and captivating form of written story that has ever graced humanity's existence is the mesmerizing texts meticulously etched into clay tablets over 4000 awe-inspiring years ago in the mystical and enigmatic lands of the ever-haunting Middle East (Young, 2022). These remarkable tablets, with their delicate strokes and timeless messages, not only symbolize the captivating beauty of our ancestors' inked imagination but also serve as a testament to the indomitable spirit of human endeavor that has transcended countless generations. As we delve deeper into the unfathomable depths of time, our journey through the annals of history leads us to a significant turning point, an astonishing millennium after these sacred clay tablets were crafted with such dedication and reverence (Young, 2022; Palka, 2021; Wasserman, 2021). During the illustrious 8th century BC, amidst the whispers of ancient epochs, we encounter a monumental epiphany - the birth of the first sustained narrative verses in the form of an awe-inspiring written epic poem known throughout eternity as The Iliad (Podlecki, 2021; Molli, 2022). Embroidered with a tapestry of emotions and mythic grandeur, The Iliad stands resolute as a magnificent opus, bridging the realms of reality and imagination. Intriguingly, while it is widely debated and fervently examined whether The Iliad drew its inspiration from the echoes of time, intertwining and preserving fragments of previous oral traditions, what cannot be denied is the sheer complexity of its composition that forever serves as a formidable line of demarcation in the labyrinthine corridors of history

(Liotsakis, 2024; Bacchi, 2020). This line divides the epoch into what existed before and what existed after the enigmatic figure of Homer and his unrivaled masterpiece.

It becomes increasingly evident that even before the dawn of prose narrative, the power of the oral tradition, with its enchanting ability to sculpt intricate tales and weave mesmerizing sagas, knew no bounds (Pinheiro et al., 2020; Steffen & Bjoraker, 2020). In a time when the written word was yet to embrace the vastness of the world, storytelling through the alluring medium of verse reigned supreme, emanating an aura of splendor that resonated through the ages. Through this melodic interplay of words and rhythm, verse became the vehicle that facilitated the continuity of traditions, the governance of civilizations, the response to dire pandemics, and the formation of resilient communities - an influence so profound that its magnitude transcends human comprehension (Krishnan & Butt, 2022; Shankar, 2024).

2.2. Written Literature and Folktales

The last few years have seen dramatic improvements in the sophistication and quality of generative multimedia models capable of writing, painting, and composing (Gupta et al., 2024; Rani et al., 2024). The main developments are multimodal sampling from large-scale language models that coherently combine text and image behavior, with text being the generative focus. Despite the impressive performances, neither model prioritizes the prompt's narrative or content. OpenAI has developed GPT-3, a 175 billion parameter model retrained on many diverse and multilingual internet documents (Myers et al., 2024; von, 2023). While MuseNet does not have an image generation capability, AWD-LSTM performs a stochastic beam search that leverages electron density maps as feedback. Research into generative neural network models trained on written literature has yielded large multimodal models called MuseNet and GPT-3 (Kar et al., 2023). In the folktales and poems generated by aspect-conditioned prompts, the M-GAN prioritized the narrative over content preservation, whereas GPT-3 prioritized content preservation over the narrative. MuseNet was conditioned using either the first 1000 tokens of a body text or aspect tokens for each generation. Language model-based pretraining on 512 tokens led to outperformance in story generation over multimodal pretraining with 8192 tokens (Korbak et al., 2023; Paaß & Giesselbach, 2023). This work points to a tension between narrative and content preservation and an opportunity for more specific training strategies. A parallel line of research on generating stories from folktales and poems focused on diversity displays the generative trade-off.

3. ARTIFICIAL INTELLIGENCE AND STORYTELLING

The code begins with a simple sentence and iteratively adds words and clauses during the build-up phase of storytelling (Kedia & Rasu, 2020). The second phase finishes this procedure and produces the final product. This is the sequence. Internal grammar and semantics of input sentences are based on n-gram and higher approximates or reshuffles of clause or phrase data for episodic and structural story construction. The repetitive application of finite persistence for subjects to verbs and progressively complicated adjacencies hides the innovation in private AI generating processes. The narrative chain ends concurrently at all levels, a typical finite occurrence (Berov, 2023; Porteous et al., 2021). Simple AI systems create finite internal motivations, not psychoactive ones. Longer chains complicate.

Traditional and modern computers and software can tell, hear, and deconstruct stories. Linear, unadaptive, and finite narrative chains have been the typical way computers tell stories (Pablos, 2024). Human authors are either replaced by software with prewritten output or augmented by database access, idea development, or content distribution. A foundational and archetypical software program for narrative chain storytelling is Claude Shannon's "brain," a simple feed-forward iterative data generating acquisition and checking protocol (Sillett, 2020). This recursive story structure generator lets the computer tell intriguing stories, promoting storytelling as a form of communication. As technology advances, computers and software can tell more stories than just one (Holloway-Attaway & Vipsjö, 2020; Djonov et al., 2024). They now understand and modify the narrative to user inputs in real time. Through sophisticated algorithms and artificial intelligence, these systems have become dynamic storytellers that can personalize each listener or reader's experience (Ansag & Gonzalez, 2023). Computers can create intricate, immersive narratives that surprise and engage audiences by evaluating user choices, emotions, and contextual data. The future of storytelling involves combining human creativity and technology, enabling computers to actively participate in story production (Çetin, 2021). We explore the possibilities of computational storytelling to create collaborative narratives that combine human imagination and computer capabilities to change storytelling. Storytelling crosses reality and fiction, inspiring, captivating, and moving us as human and artificial intelligence blur (Guzman & Lewis, 2020; Anantrasirichai & Bull, 2022; Waardenburg & Huysman, 2022). In this fascinating age, computers and software are more than tools—they are our companions, guiding us through the wide world of narratives as we embark on collaborative journeys that transcend time, distance, and imagination.

3.1. AI in Creative Industries

More typical machine use focuses on building systems that utilize human knowledge and skill or changing processes and systems for economic benefit (Morgan et al., 2021). What if machines could be more than just tools and offer real-time insight and advanced teaching talent that might improve the development of new projects, fields, and society? Key to this argument is how machine learning AI provides precision and conceptual space, allows the rapid calculation of alternatives, and fosters open discussions that lead to diplomatically advanced proposals. It is only those machines that are capable of vibrant, concept- and value-sensitive interactions with their human masters that might truly contribute not in the sense of a servant but as a genuine co-author of creative works.

There were many reasons machines might be used to tell stories, magnifying particular aspects of the human narrative process. The quantitative corners around literature, around valuable contribution to that, about no longer being able to sustain fiction, anxiety, or vision between the future human need to imagined machine stories on any of those. The predictive ability of machines suggests that our capability to read, understand, and contextualize these stories shapes the future of fictional work and society (Sartori & Theodorou, 2022).

An alternative use of machines is designing content that fits both idiosyncratic human subjectivity elements and modern creative industries' constraints (Brinkmann et al., 2023). As we enter a period in human culture in which creative practitioners will avail themselves of a wide range of AI systems to improve functionality, in an environment in which educators and institutions need to keep up with identifying the real value that these systems add in the syllabus and inform their students about their potential impact on individuals, communities, and culture as a whole.

In general, up until now, AI in creative industries has largely been used as a tool for enhancing productivity, contributing to more intelligent, responsive, fluently interactive experiences, and making it easier to communicate with huge amounts of data (Safavi & Ghazinoory, 2024; Li & Lin, 2021). Certain social science fields, such as the study of music and computing, have also used machine-learning models to understand conversations. These approaches help develop understanding from a linguistic point of view but do not necessarily help to develop the narrative or underlying elements of creative work.

3.2. Generative AI and Text Generation

Generative AI introduced additional complexity and sophistication - it is more difficult for a machine learning model to generate new valid sentences than to classify or label existing ones (Bandi et al., 2023; Zhang et al., 2023). On the other hand, the previous generation of generative models was fairly crude. They could master a few decoding layers and memorize only a few domains at a time, making them heavily controllable. Architecture and mistakes would lead to sentence repetition, while not having enough architectural provisions for fine control would lead to a loss of coherence (Galle, 2020). This lack of fidelity led to a boom in generative linguistic specificities, which made language processing a dominant and compelling subject. It was a rollercoaster ride of remarkable consistency and discipline, which laid the groundwork for the arrival of a robust and ready-to-go generation of large, pre-trained transformer models.

The development of generative AI technologies has brought forth an unprecedented level of intricacy and refinement - posing a greater challenge for machine learning models to produce fresh and valid sentences than merely classifying or labeling existing ones (Bandi et al., 2023) (Liu et al., 2023). Conversely, the preceding iterations of generative models were relatively rudimentary. They displayed proficiency in several deciphering layers and could retain knowledge across only a handful of distinct domains simultaneously, rendering them significantly controllable. Excessive architecture and errors often result in repetitive sentence structures (Huettig et al., 2022; Goldberg & Ferreira, 2022) (Huang & Ferreira, 2021). At the same time, the absence of adequate architectural provisions for precise control caused a loss of coherence. This lack of fidelity spurred a surge in generative linguistic particularities, sparking interest in language processing as a paramount and captivating field. It became an exhilarating journey of unparalleled consistency and meticulousness, laying the groundwork for the advent of a sturdy and readily deployable generation of immense, pre-trained transformer models (Rosário, 2024; Sufi, 2024; Mars, 2022).

To understand generative AI, we need to put it into context with another form of AI: discriminative AI. Roughly speaking, discriminative models are those that 'discriminate' - specifically, between categories (Heitmeier et al., 2021; Chuang et al., 2021). By contrast, generative models synthesize data that does not yet exist. The most popular natural language processing (NLP) models today are discriminative models. Among the most successful, BERT was trained to predict which word was removed from a sentence, a task that can be applied to a dataset of text corpora. The training would be run at scale, with permutations of input sentences and a simple task that could be easily parallelized across a large processor grid (Yuan et al., 2022).

4. THEORETICAL FRAMEWORKS FOR NARRATIVE MACHINES

The ITC exemplifies the shifting focus from considering intelligence evaluation as an internal, domain-independent quality in the agent to an external process requiring observed interaction with an environment (Zwolińska-Ligaj & Guzal-Dec, 2024). In our particular case, the environment is the group of humans or other computer programs, and the human-computer interaction is a text-based shared activity, a form of conversation. Since our goal is not to build conversational systems for their own sake or, even more fundamentally, to build systems possessing conversational intelligence but to understand the nature of intelligence through its use in this particular form, we have changed the domain form of the situation (story generation) but retained the task form of how its solution is evaluated (Guan et al., 2020). This allows for a more quantitative form of utility measure: the better the machine can assist a human in constructing stories, completing story outlines, and collaborating on the design of stories or related content, the more capable it must be in the relevant aspects of Artificial General Intelligence.

Narrative Machines is a multilevel project (Maestre et al., 2022). We take a top-down view of stories, a bottom-up view of artificial intelligence, an inside-out view of the design of artificial general intelligence, and a chapter-by-chapter view that implements a spiral design, moving both from current practices to the analysis of the abstractions made in such models and back again. This makes it easy to describe the central enabling abstraction, the Intelligence Test Conjecture (ITC), after setting the context for understanding it. It is a useful entry for explaining conversational modeling as a novel approach to evaluating and continuing the development of machine learning model architectures (Bishop, 2021).

4.1. Structuralism and Semiotics

The influential semiological work of Vladimir Propp and his definition of narrative morphology represent an early attempt to develop a typology of narrative functions independent of any particular narrative medium (Bagherian & Yaghoobi-Derabi, 2022). The now-familiar story of Propp's work is that, in writing his 1928 book, Morphology of the Folktale, he analyzed one hundred Russian fairy tales and identified a set of thirty-one 'functions' that all had in common (Ugwuoke & Onu, 2023). In Propp's original formulation, the functions were seen as 'actual narrative pieces' that were task elements in the main character's role in the story (Kiss et al., 2022). As a result, while many of the functions were well-defined by necessity - the 'departure' or 'reconnaissance of the hero' functions were about the main character beginning their journey - many other functions could be seen as ambiguous or superfluous, especially out of context.

Propp's work is extremely hierarchical, with four levels of organization—the tale itself at the highest level, down to the level of the functions, then to the actions within the functions, which are described by motives (Busse, 2021). While it must be recognized that formalism has been so influential, it is slightly unfortunate that Propp's original work has been so much omitted from popular literature.

4.2. Postmodernism and Hypertext Theory

Indeed, Alexander et al. reaffirm the fundamental importance of the narrative in the digital age. The need to search for new formal vehicles responds to the ongoing efforts of the scientific-humanistic community to produce a discursive, textual mode of explanation that keeps pace with the complexities of our fast-paced technological culture (Romero-Frías & Barbecho, 2023; Obiedat, 2022). They say the story is the key to understanding art, science, and psychology. As rightly put by Glover, the story is the key for individuals, constituting our selves and our lives as stories, and for religions and world views, providing a distinctively human lens on the cosmos and human destiny (Smith & Monforte, 2020).

If the intellectual world is all text, then it is also a text that we interpret and use through the filters of our nervous systems and brains, social intercourse, and perhaps with the help of prosthetics and technological devices that broaden our senses and recording capabilities (Gaiseanu, 2021; Kitchener & Hales, 2022). Boldly put, U. believes that all cultural expression is the outcome of sorting and processing what our animal-in-some-part heritage provides. From this perspective, advances in education (particularly the educational software market), mass media and the electronic tribes, and the convergence of computers and telecommunications, professionals, and chat rooms underscore the need for fresh descriptive and analytical models of culture and society (Romero & Ventura, 2020; Chen et al., 2020). While the media muse that postmodernists called "text" seems just as plastic as that supported by a good hypertext database model, media studies have responded slowly to a point originally made nearly a half-century ago: "The world has become a problem to be solved through invention (Best & Kellner, 2020; McManus & McManus, 2020). It is a cybernetician's world, a hyperspace world, a constructivist world."

McLuhan said that the medium is the message - but how does a postmodernist have the attentional capacity even to begin to sort the medium from its message? Computer users per se - never mind, plus TV or GIS users - are subjected to ever-increasing slabs of computerized multimedia hypermedia, albeit voluntarily and somewhat haphazardly (Forsler, 2024). They face the Turner-influenced laws of the telecommunications jungle, which intermingle and cross-promote the electronic mass media until they write line-linked hypertext 'books' rather than scholarly journal articles. They are transforming a computer into a software-tailored educational aid, witnessing the rapid growth in children's software and the cluttered educational offerings along the confusing Information Superhighway (Papadakis, 2022; Fischer et al., 2020). They are co-opting fine artists who, regardless of the aesthetic tradition in which they work, are attracted to the keyboard's real-time flow of compelling text, graphics, sound, and hypermedia events. They are beginning to mix classified ads with caricatures and animations that might easily be linked to daily cable or Internet newsfeeds. And so on, and so on.

Defined as "a continuum of linked media rather than something that is packaged as discrete media like books," hypertexts and hypermedia raise issues with which postmodernists are concerned (Rajakannan & Rukmini, 2021). The map of the territory covered by the most thoughtful postmodern authors looks not like a line, circle, or cycle but a heterogeneous yet organized jumble of discontinuous fragments. Whether we discuss hypertext or the postmodern condition, the issue seems the same: How do we make sense of the current state of cultural affairs that seem much more fragmented and disjunctive than traditional forms? Hyperreal is postmodern, where gimcrack reality is often reproduced in spectacular media-simulacra, and life is turned into a porous sign system composed of disposable celebrities, entertainment news, and throwaway consumer goods (Belfiore, 2022; Classen, 2023). Hyperreal is also the visceral electronic agora of U.S. online junkies, telepresence that feels much more vibrant to 'netizens' than the dead letter of the houses and utilities in which they live.

5. ETHICAL CONSIDERATIONS IN AI STORYTELLING

AI-generated stories have simple beginnings based on input from a single animate source (Pataranutaporn et al., 2021; Chen et al., 2024). Addressing several potential concerns and paradoxes with AI and making the experience as positive as possible involves an increased effort to ensure that AI is developed for expanded skill or significant aspects of generalized human storytelling and that this ability is simulated or trained based on the correct aspects of human behavior, that processing does not become computationally intractable, in other words, achieving practical capability, that the "long telling" aspect of human storytelling is respected, meaning also allowing for independent evolution and agent learning, and that origins versus essentially human evolved technologies are recognized (Wienrich & Latoschik, 2021; Benvenuti et al., 2023).

While questions of control and values, and ways in which technology can and should shape human values, are widely acknowledged, there is still only limited attention devoted to a broader set of questions that may be of relevance specifically to AI – for instance, matters of relevance to the considerable determinism, uniformity, and the lack of historical grounding of AI-generated aspects of storytelling – and issues that distinguish AI from other digital technologies (Aguiar & Araújo, 2024). To appreciate these, it is interesting to consider some forms of older digital content manipulation systems that involve users' choices being shaped to some extent by the underlying characteristics of the content creation algorithms. The logic here is a game-like trade-off, at an extreme mass balance of computer-generated versus hand-selected items or similar outputs (de Guevara, 2022). However, current AI's ability to generate artifacts situated at some points on the increasingly higher-dimensional axis of potentially important ideas possibly presents users with a qualitatively different kind of engagement.

As AI systems, like the work in this thesis, iterate towards the generation of significant aspects of AI storytelling, apart from basic questions of authorship, complex questions of control also emerge (Pataranutaporn et al., 2021). Nevertheless, while some aspects may be easier to model or generate predictably, how should we think about the impending shifts like control, as human intelligence will retain primacy? What about the nature of command? As part of the ethics of this technology, it has to be designed so that the ability to curate the development of parameters with AI-generated significant agents remains with the intended users of human-designed story systems.

5.1. Bias and Representation

The ethical frameworks of AI training data overlap with the ethical frameworks of art and lead us to common discussions of what is considered "entertainment" versus what is considered "art. (Oksanen et al., 2023; Grba, 2022)" Representation involves ethical and people-oriented logistical issues. To whom, how, and why do we accurately represent? It opens up questions of audience, accessibility, counseling, emotion literacy, advocacy, process direction, and nurture, which are critical in contemporary and performative arts. This results in heightened responsibility for realism within the narrative machines. In its early years, 20th-century cinema famously showed a train approaching head-on to the camera, instilling the widespread belief that it was the real thing and causing widespread panic (Waldron, 2022). Since commercial storytelling no longer has much use for representing reality (or truth), what responsibilities do an age of narrative machines need to represent reality in their narratives? Can entire societies be constructed in unseen and hard-to-detection ways using multimedia narratives that are not sensitive to representing reality or promoting social well-being? (Barreda-Ángeles et al, 2021; Škola et al.2020)

One of the first ethical challenges is how to confront socially generated biases and how we can avoid transmitting these biases into the outputs of AI (Hagendorff et al., 2023; Du & Xie, 2021; Illia et al., 2023). These are pressing issues that go beyond generative AI alone. The core challenge is that any training data we give AI is messy and biased - reflecting existing human biases. Artists regularly re-evaluate and interrogate this data, so perhaps their insights can guide these ethical concerns (Maggs & Robinson, 2020; Yeo et al., 2023). The relationship between AI and its training data involves important issues of representation. Who picks it, what is left out, what does it emphasize, and how is it framed? The last 20 years have seen a growing body of work that challenges traditional representations of identity in the arts, opening up new questions and more pluralistic forms of artistic expression. What opportunities do the outputs of generative AI provide for new forms of representation, and what are the potential challenges?

6. CASE STUDIES IN GENERATIVE AI STORYTELLING

As part of our AI research, we have implemented a variety of generative storytellers, each representing a different choice or configuration of AI technology with a specialized format or structure (Trichopoulos et al., 2023; Serbanescu & Nack, 2024). This includes a chronologically structured bot directed to write narrative nonfiction; bots directed by established works of fiction to create symbols that allow them to be realized as new fiction through generative training on large volumes of high-quality human-written works; and a dozen specialized bots for training on specific corpora: Shakespeare, Translated Texts of Gesta Romanorum, Herodotus, Chinese History of the Former Han, Marshall Islands Legends and Traditions, Radin's American Indian Folktales, and a number of others.

We also looked at the diversity of generative storytellers and the diversity of art and working processes for using them to create marketable fiction of reliable quality. The results reveal an interesting, complex, and often counter-intuitive interaction between generative storytellers' design, the validation dataset's choice and handling, and the user's specific creative vision, needs, and workflow. While the results are fascinating in their own right, their relation with the AI and the training data could be a resource for anyone using or contemplating using generative AI to create fiction for commercial purposes (Fui-Hoon et al., 2023; Hughes et al., 2021).

6.1. GPT-3 and Creative Writing

GPT-3 is a language model developed by OpenAI. The model can apply language knowledge to different language-based tasks by using the large dataset to learn features from words (Balagopalan et al., 2021). However, extensive supervision with labeled datasets is unnecessary as GPT-3 is pre-trained with a wide language model and 175 billion parameters (Myers et al., 2024; Sun et al., 2022). These features allow the machine to be fine-tuned to various language generation tasks, including tables, artificial LSA proteins, coding, reading comprehension, and creative writing. In other words, GPT-3 is a state-of-the-art language generation AI that can perform many language tasks after being fine-tuned with minimal human-generated datasets. It applies recent advancements in deep learning on transformer architecture and an unsupervised approach. Given its capabilities and potential, AI generates excitement and concern as it stimulates debate and becomes an agent of societal change.

GPT-3, developed by OpenAI, is the third iteration of the Generative Pre-trained Transformer (Zhang & Chen, 2023; Roumeliotis & Tselikas, 2023). This groundbreaking system, known for its remarkable capabilities, has revolutionized the world of artificial intelligence. With its ability to learn from a vast dataset with minimal human oversight, GPT-3 has achieved unprecedented performance levels across various tasks, including creative writing (Meskó & Topol, 2023). Its natural language processing capabilities allow it to generate coherent and engaging narratives, blurring the lines between human and machine creativity. GPT-3 has acquired extensive knowledge through its impressive learning process and mastered the art of generating human-like responses (Alto, 2023). Whether composing intricate pieces of literature or engaging in joint storytelling endeavors, GPT-3 consistently astounds with its unparalleled creative prowess. Its ability to challenge conventional thinking about creativity and mimic the ingenuity of human authors has left experts and enthusiasts alike in awe. While GPT-3's achievements are undeniably remarkable, they have sparked significant legal and ethical concerns. As this advanced AI system effortlessly produces awe-inspiring creative works, it raises profound questions about the definition of human authorship and its associated rights. This unprecedented development urges society to revisit and update existing frameworks and regulations to ensure a fair approach to creativity in the age of AI (Aizenberg & Van Den Hoven, 2020; Köbis & Mossink, 2021).

GPT-3's incredible capabilities and remarkable achievements have forever changed the landscape of artificial intelligence (Ray, 2023; Safely, 2023). Its ability to learn, create, and challenge conventional notions of human creativity is a testament to the extraordinary advances in the field. However, as we marvel at its accomplishments, we must address the legal and ethical implications, striving to strike a balance between AI's capabilities and the rights of human authors.

6.2. AI-Generated News and Deepfakes

This is not about changing one's binders full of women. This is much more far-reaching. It is about making our past communications open to revision at a later date by redefining how we record image, film, and video; how we frame ourselves in news coverage, non-fiction documentaries, and perhaps one-day courtroom artist sketches; and in general, how we record history as it happens (Spennemann, 2023; Chakraborty et al., 2023). We are likely to see an infodemic of stories about the societal impact of AI-generated storytelling with titles such as "The Geo-Politics of the United States of Amazon Capital," informed as much – if not more – by the century-old tale of III in Brazil as they are by the events of the rest of the world.

It is said that AI can epitomize our future selves' ways of representing abstract principles (Grba, 2022; Totschnig, 2020). In the next section, we examine AI-generated visual and auditory fake news and AI-generated visuals in the context of autosurveillance capitalism, immunity, bio-digital impacts, and bio-digital backlashes. The use of AI in storytelling can also affect the recorded past. It may seem logical that the recording of history is a static artifice (Kidd & Nieto Mcavoy, 2023; Rubinstein, 2020). Still, anyone writing code and publishing a new optical effect that reshapes our collective visual understanding of our history is doing that.

7. CONCLUSION

This chapter lays the groundwork for understanding how AI has changed storytelling and society. It discusses AI's dual nature, which can boost creativity and innovation but can also pose problems that must be managed and regulated. The historical overview traces AI from Alan Turing's core ideas to modern machine learning. This historical background stresses AI's integration into socio-economic structures, similar to earlier technology revolutions. The chapter emphasizes AI's evolution from specialized, purpose-specific applications to adaptable, scalable systems with global ramifications. This chapter emphasizes democratizing AI knowledge and encouraging multi-stakeholder interactions. Engaging in such discussions helps mitigate potential dangers, understand AI's complex effects, and maximize social benefits. This inclusive strategy guarantees that varied perspectives are incorporated into AI technology development and implementation, fostering equity. International AI governance collaboration is also stressed in the chapter. UNCITRAL can lead global AI regulatory frameworks. These frameworks are critical for resolving AI's transnational and cross-disciplinary difficulties and creating a cohesive and cooperative worldwide landscape for AI innovation and deployment. Chapter 1 provides a contextual and theoretical framework for analyzing AI's effects on narrative and creative industries. AI is seen as a transformational force having major cultural, ethical, and regulatory implications. The succeeding chapters' in-depth investigation of AI-driven narrative generation, its ethical implications, and its potential to reshape creativity in the digital age requires this core understanding. Finally, the chapter emphasizes the need for a balanced and informed approach to AI, promoting scientific advancement and ethical stewardship. This method helps navigate AI's intricacies and link them with social goals, providing the framework for a future where AI boosts human innovation and improves society's cultural and economic fabric.

REFERENCES

Aguiar, M., & Araújo, S. (2024). Final Thoughts: Digital Humanities Looking at Generative AI. In Digital Humanities Looking at the World: Exploring Innovative Approaches and Contributions to Society (pp. 367-380). Cham: Springer Nature Switzerland.

Aizenberg, E. & Van Den Hoven, J. (2020). Designing for human rights in AI. Big Data & Society.

Al Naqbi, H., Bahroun, Z., & Ahmed, V. (2024). Enhancing work productivity through generative artificial intelligence: A comprehensive literature review. Sustainability.

Alto, V. (2023). Modern Generative AI with ChatGPT and OpenAI Models: Leverage the capabilities of OpenAI's LLM for productivity and innovation with GPT3 and GPT4.

Amankwah-Amoah, J., Abdalla, S., Mogaji, E., Elbanna, A., & Dwivedi, Y. K. (2024). The impending disruption of creative industries by generative AI: Opportunities, challenges, and research agenda. *International Journal of Information Management*, 79, 102759. DOI: 10.1016/j.ijinfomgt.2024.102759

Anantrasirichai, N. & Bull, D. (2022). Artificial intelligence in the creative industries: a review. Artificial intelligence review.

Ansag, R. A., & Gonzalez, A. J. (2023). State-of-the-art in automated story generation systems research. *Journal of Experimental & Theoretical Artificial Intelligence*, 35(6), 877–931. DOI: 10.1080/0952813X.2021.1971777

Bacchi, A. (2020). *Uncovering Jewish Creativity in Book III of the Sibylline Oracles: Gender*. Intertextuality, and Politics. DOI: 10.1163/9789004426078

Bagherian, S., & Yaghoobi-Derabi, J. (2022). Langue at work: a review and comparison of the narrative theories in literature. Revista de Investigaciones Universidad del Quindío, 34(S2), 452-461. uniquindio.edu.co

Balagopalan, A., Eyre, B., Robin, J., Rudzicz, F., & Novikova, J. (2021). Comparing pre-trained and feature-based models for prediction of Alzheimer's disease based on speech. *Frontiers in Aging Neuroscience*, 13, 635945. DOI: 10.3389/fnagi.2021.635945 PMID: 33986655

Ballard, C. (2021). Transmission's end? Cataclysm and chronology in Indigenous oral tradition. The Routledge companion to global indigenous history.

Bamodu, G. (2023). *Progressive harmonisation of international trade law in Africa: the role of UNCITRAL.* The Elgar Companion to UNCITRAL.

Bandi, A., Adapa, P. V. S. R., & Kuchi, Y. E. V. P. K. (2023). The power of generative ai: A review of requirements, models, input–output formats, evaluation metrics, and challenges. Future Internet.

Barreda-Ángeles, M., Aleix-Guillaume, S., & Pereda-Baños, A. (2021). Virtual reality storytelling as a double-edged sword: Immersive presentation of nonfiction 360-video is associated with impaired cognitive information processing. *Communication Monographs*, 88(2), 154–173. DOI: 10.1080/03637751.2020.1803496

Barthelmeß, U. & Furbach, U. (2023). A Different Look at Artificial Intelligence.

Belfiore, E. (2022). Is it really about the evidence? argument, persuasion, and the power of ideas in cultural policy. Cultural Trends.

Benvenuti, M., Cangelosi, A., Weinberger, A., Mazzoni, E., Benassi, M., Barbaresi, M., & Orsoni, M. (2023). Artificial intelligence and human behavioral development: A perspective on new skills and competences acquisition for the educational context. *Computers in Human Behavior*, 148, 107903. DOI: 10.1016/j.chb.2023.107903

Berov, L. (2023). From Narratology to Computational Story Composition and Back: An Exploratory Study in Generative Modeling.

Best, S. & Kellner, D. (2020). The postmodern adventure: Science technology and cultural studies at the third millennium.

Bishop, J. M. (2021). Artificial intelligence is stupid and causal reasoning will not fix it. Frontiers in Psychology. frontiersin.org

Brinkmann, L., Baumann, F., Bonnefon, J. F., Derex, M., Müller, T. F., Nussberger, A. M., Czaplicka, A., Acerbi, A., Griffiths, T. L., Henrich, J., Leibo, J. Z., McElreath, R., Oudeyer, P.-Y., Stray, J., & Rahwan, I. (2023). Machine culture. *Nature Human Behaviour*, 7(11), 1855–1868. DOI: 10.1038/s41562-023-01742-2 PMID: 37985914

Busse, R. (2021). *Folk tales and organizational change: an integrative model for Chinese management.* Inside the Changing Business of China.

Butler, P. (2023). *UNCITRAL and MSMEs: An enduring and successful marriage.* The Elgar Companion to UNCITRAL.

Çetin, E. (2021). Digital storytelling in teacher education and its effect on the digital literacy of pre-service teachers. *Thinking Skills and Creativity.*

Chakraborty, U., Roy, S., & Kumar, S. (2023). *Rise of Generative AI and ChatGPT: Understand how Generative AI and ChatGPT are transforming and reshaping the business world.* English Edition.

Chen, W., Li, J., Tang, C., & Sun, G. (2024, June). Developing an Intermediate Framework for Enhancing Comic Creation Through Generative AI. In International Conference on Human-Computer Interaction (pp. 292-306). Cham: Springer Nature Switzerland. DOI: 10.1007/978-3-031-60449-2_20

Chen, X., Xie, H., & Hwang, G. J. (2020). A multi-perspective study on artificial intelligence in education: Grants, conferences, journals, software tools, institutions, and researchers. Computers and Education: Artificial Intelligence.

Chen, Y., Ding, Z., Zheng, Q., Qin, Y., Huang, R., & Shah, N. (2020). A history and theory of textual event detection and recognition. *IEEE Access : Practical Innovations, Open Solutions*, 8, 201371–201392. DOI: 10.1109/ACCESS.2020.3034907

Chuang, Y. Y., Vollmer, M. L., Shafaei-Bajestan, E., Gahl, S., Hendrix, P., & Baayen, R. H. (2021). The processing of pseudoword form and meaning in production and comprehension: A computational modeling approach using linear discriminative learning. *Behavior Research Methods*, 53(3), 945–976. DOI: 10.3758/s13428-020-01356-w PMID: 32377973

Classen, C. (2023). Worlds of sense: Exploring the senses in history and across cultures.

Coeckelbergh, M. (2021). Time machines: Artificial intelligence, process, and narrative. Philosophy & Technology.

Cohen, S. (2024). I, Yantra: Exploring Self and Selflessness in Ancient Indian Robot Tales.

Cress, U., & Kimmerle, J. (2023). Co-constructing knowledge with generative AI tools: Reflections from a CSCL perspective. *International Journal of Computer-Supported Collaborative Learning*, 18(4), 607–614. DOI: 10.1007/s11412-023-09409-w

Davidson, I., Burke, H., Connelly, P., Porter, S., Sullivan, H., Sullivan, L., & Wallis, L. A. (2021). Oral tradition, history, and archaeohistory of Indigenous Australia. In *The Oxford Handbook of the Archaeology of Indigenous Australia and New Guinea* (pp. C5–S1). Oxford University Press.

de Guevara, M. R. L. (2022). Painting Algorithms.

Deakin, W. (2023). *Modern Language*. Philosophy and Criticism.

Djonov, E., Tseng, C. I., & Lim, F. V. (n.d.). Children's experiences with a transmedia narrative: Insights for promoting critical multimodal literacy in the digital age. Discourse.

Du, S., & Xie, C. (2021). Paradoxes of artificial intelligence in consumer markets: Ethical challenges and opportunities. *Journal of Business Research*, 129, 961–974. DOI: 10.1016/j.jbusres.2020.08.024

Dwivedi, D., & Mahanty, G. (2023). Human creativity vs. machine creativity: Innovations and challenges. In Multidisciplinary Approaches in AI, Creativity, Innovation, and Green Collaboration (pp. 19-28). IGI Global.

Dwivedi, Y. K., Kshetri, N., Hughes, L., Slade, E. L., Jeyaraj, A., Kar, A. K., Baabdullah, A. M., Koohang, A., Raghavan, V., Ahuja, M., Albanna, H., Albashrawi, M. A., Al-Busaidi, A. S., Balakrishnan, J., Barlette, Y., Basu, S., Bose, I., Brooks, L., Buhalis, D., & Wright, R. (2023). Opinion Paper: "So what if ChatGPT wrote it?" Multidisciplinary perspectives on opportunities, challenges and implications of generative conversational AI for research, practice and policy. *International Journal of Information Management*, 71, 102642. DOI: 10.1016/j.ijinfomgt.2023.102642

Feijóo, C., Kwon, Y., Bauer, J. M., Bohlin, E., Howell, B., Jain, R., Potgieter, P., Vu, K., Whalley, J., & Xia, J. (2020). Harnessing artificial intelligence (AI) to increase wellbeing for all: The case for a new technology diplomacy. *Telecommunications Policy*, 44(6), 101988. DOI: 10.1016/j.telpol.2020.101988 PMID: 32377031

Feuerriegel, S., Hartmann, J., Janiesch, C., & Zschech, P. (2024). Generative ai. *Business & Information Systems Engineering*, 66(1), 111–126. DOI: 10.1007/s12599-023-00834-7

Fischer, G., Lundin, J., & Lindberg, J. O. (2020). Rethinking and reinventing learning, education and collaboration in the digital age—From creating technologies to transforming cultures. *The International Journal of Information and Learning Technology*, 37(5), 241–252. DOI: 10.1108/IJILT-04-2020-0051

Forsler, I. (2024). *Marshall McLuhan (1967)*. The Medium Is the Massage. Classics in Media Theory.

Fui-Hoon Nah, F., Zheng, R., Cai, J., Siau, K., & Chen, L. (2023). Generative AI and ChatGPT: Applications, challenges, and AI-human collaboration. *Journal of Information Technology Case and Application Research*, 25(3), 277–304. DOI: 10.1080/15228053.2023.2233814

Gaiseanu, F. (2021). Information in the universal triangle of reality for non-living/living structures: From philosophy to neuro/life sciences. Philosophy Study.

Galaz, V., Centeno, M. A., Callahan, P. W., Causevic, A., Patterson, T., Brass, I., Baum, S., Farber, D., Fischer, J., Garcia, D., McPhearson, T., Jimenez, D., King, B., Larcey, P., & Levy, K. (2021). Artificial intelligence, systemic risks, and sustainability. *Technology in Society*, 67, 101741. DOI: 10.1016/j.techsoc.2021.101741

Galle, P. (2020). Christopher Alexander's Battle for Beauty in a World Turning Ugly: The Inception of a Science of Architecture? She Ji *The Journal of Design, Economics, and Innovation*, 6(3), 345–375. DOI: 10.1016/j.sheji.2020.03.002

Goldberg, A. E. & Ferreira, F. (2022). Good-enough language production. Trends in Cognitive Sciences.

Goltz, N., Zeleznikow, J., & Dowdeswell, T. (2020). From the tree of knowledge and the golem of Prague to kosher autonomous cars: The ethics of artificial intelligence through jewish eyes. Oxford Journal of Law and Religion, 9(1), 132-156. ecu.edu.au

Grba, D. (2022). Deep else: A critical framework for ai art. Digital.

Guan, J., Huang, F., Zhao, Z., Zhu, X., & Huang, M. (2020). A knowledge-enhanced pretraining model for commonsense story generation. *Transactions of the Association for Computational Linguistics*, 8, 93–108. DOI: 10.1162/tacl_a_00302

Gupta, P., Ding, B., Guan, C., & Ding, D. (2024). Generative AI: A systematic review using topic modelling techniques. Data and Information Management.

Guzman, A. L. & Lewis, S. C. (2020). Artificial intelligence and communication: A human–machine communication research agenda. New Media & Society.

Hagendorff, T., Bossert, L. N., Tse, Y. F., & Singer, P. (2023). Speciesist bias in AI: how AI applications perpetuate discrimination and unfair outcomes against animals. AI and Ethics.

Heitmeier, M., Chuang, Y. Y., & Baayen, R. H. (2021). Modeling morphology with linear discriminative learning: Considerations and design choices. Frontiers in Psychology.

Hermann, I. (2023). Artificial intelligence in fiction: between narratives and metaphors. AI & Society.

Herzig, M. (2021). On the Shoulders of Giants: Helene Wecker's Subversion of the Female Golem Myth. The Macksey Journal.

Hoffmann, C. H. (2022). Is AI intelligent? An assessment of artificial intelligence, 70 years after Turing. *Technology in Society*, 68, 101893. DOI: 10.1016/j.techsoc.2022.101893

Holloway-Attaway, L., & Vipsjö, L. (2020). *Using augmented reality, gaming technologies, and transmedial storytelling to develop and co-design local cultural heritage experiences*. Visual Computing for Cultural Heritage. DOI: 10.1007/978-3-030-37191-3_10

Holmström, J. & Carroll, N. (2024). How organizations can innovate with generative AI. Business Horizons.

Huang, Y. & Ferreira, F. (2021). What causes lingering misinterpretations of garden-path sentences: Incorrect syntactic representations or fallible memory processes?. Journal of Memory and Language.

Huettig, F., Audring, J., & Jackendoff, R. (2022). A parallel architecture perspective on pre-activation and prediction in language processing. Cognition.

Hughes, R. T., Zhu, L., & Bednarz, T. (2021). Generative adversarial networks–enabled human–artificial intelligence collaborative applications for creative and design industries: A systematic review of current .... Frontiers in artificial intelligence.

Illia, L., Colleoni, E., & Zyglidopoulos, S. (2023). Ethical implications of text generation in the age of artificial intelligence. *Business Ethics, the Environment & Responsibility*, 32(1), 201–210. DOI: 10.1111/beer.12479

Imdoukh, M., Ahmad, I., & Alfailakawi, M. G. (2020). Machine learning-based auto-scaling for containerized applications. *Neural Computing & Applications*, 32(13), 9745–9760. DOI: 10.1007/s00521-019-04507-z

Kantosalo, A., Falk, M., & Jordanous, A. (2021). Embodiment in 18th century depictions of human-machine co-creativity. Frontiers in Robotics and AI.

Kar, A. K., Varsha, P. S., & Rajan, S. (2023). Unravelling the impact of generative artificial intelligence (GAI) in industrial applications: A review of scientific and grey literature. *Global Journal of Flexible Systems Managment*, 24(4), 659–689. DOI: 10.1007/s40171-023-00356-x

Kedia, A. & Rasu, M. (2020). Hands-On Python Natural Language Processing: Explore tools and techniques to analyze and process text with a view to building real-world NLP applications.

Kidd, J. & Nieto Mcavoy, E. (2023). Deep Nostalgia: Remediated memory, algorithmic nostalgia and technological ambivalence. Convergence.

Kiss, D., Horváth, Z., Kassai, S., Gyarmathy, A. V., & Rácz, J. (2022). Folktales of recovery–from addiction to becoming a helper: deep structures of life stories applying Propp's theory: a narrative analysis. *Journal of Psychoactive Drugs*, 54(4), 328–339. DOI: 10.1080/02791072.2021.1990442 PMID: 34706624

Kitchener, P. D. & Hales, C. G. (2022). What neuroscientists think, and don't think, about consciousness. Frontiers in Human Neuroscience.

Köbis, N. & Mossink, L. D. (2021). Artificial intelligence versus Maya Angelou: Experimental evidence that people cannot differentiate AI-generated from human-written poetry. Computers in human behavior.

Korbak, T., Shi, K., Chen, A., Bhalerao, R. V., Buckley, C., Phang, J., & Perez, E. (2023, July). Pretraining language models with human preferences. In *International Conference on Machine Learning* (pp. 17506-17533). PMLR.

Kovacic, M. (2023). Between animated cells and animated cels: symbiotic turn and animation in multispecies life. Science as Culture.

Krishnan, R., & Butt, B. (2022). "The gasoline of the future:" points of continuity, energy materiality, and corporate marketing of electric vehicles among automakers and utilities. *Energy Research & Social Science*, 83, 102349. DOI: 10.1016/j.erss.2021.102349

Li, X. & Lin, B. (2021). The Development and Design of Artificial Intelligence in Cultural and Creative Products. Mathematical Problems in Engineering.

Liotsakis, V. (2024). Digressions as Meta-Literary Markers and Narrative Milestones in Arrian's Anabasis of Alexander. Trends in Classics–Supplementary Volumes.

Liu, Y., Yang, Z., Yu, Z., Liu, Z., Liu, D., Lin, H., Li, M., Ma, S., Avdeev, M., & Shi, S. (2023). Generative artificial intelligence and its applications in materials science: Current situation and future perspectives. *Journal of Materiomics*, 9(4), 798–816. DOI: 10.1016/j.jmat.2023.05.001

Lwakatare, L. E., Raj, A., Crnkovic, I., Bosch, J., & Olsson, H. H. (2020). Large-scale machine learning systems in real-world industrial settings: A review of challenges and solutions. *Information and Software Technology*, 127, 106368. DOI: 10.1016/j.infsof.2020.106368

Maestre, M. M., Vicente, M., Lloret, E., & Cueto, A. S. (2022). Extracting Narrative Patterns in Different Textual Genres: A Multilevel Feature Discourse Analysis. Information.

Maggs, D. & Robinson, J. (2020). Sustainability in an imaginary world: art and the question of agency.

Mars, M. (2022). From word embeddings to pre-trained language models: A state-of-the-art walkthrough. Applied Sciences.

McManus, M., & McManus, M. (2020). The Emergence of Post-modern Culture in Neoliberal Society. The Rise of Post-Modern Conservatism: Neoliberalism, Post-Modern Culture, and Reactionary Politics, 45-110.

Meskó, B. & Topol, E. J. (2023). The imperative for regulatory oversight of large language models (or generative AI) in healthcare. NPJ Digital Medicine.

Messer, U. (2024). Co-creating art with generative artificial intelligence: Implications for artworks and artists. Computers in Human Behavior: Artificial Humans.

Mikalef, P., Conboy, K., Lundström, J. E., & Popovič, A. (2022). Thinking responsibly about responsible AI and 'the dark side'of AI. *European Journal of Information Systems*, 31(3), 257–268. DOI: 10.1080/0960085X.2022.2026621

Molli, L. (2022). Just a pale shadow? The characterization of Briseis in Homer's Iliad. *Acta Antiqua Academiae Scientiarum Hungaricae*, 61(1), 1–9. DOI: 10.1556/068.2021.00001

Morgan, J., Halton, M., Qiao, Y., & Breslin, J. G. (2021). Industry 4.0 smart reconfigurable manufacturing machines. Journal of Manufacturing Systems.

Myers, D., Mohawesh, R., Chellaboina, V. I., Sathvik, A. L., Venkatesh, P., Ho, Y. H., Henshaw, H., Alhawawreh, M., Berdik, D., & Jararweh, Y. (2024). Foundation and large language models: Fundamentals, challenges, opportunities, and social impacts. *Cluster Computing*, 27(1), 1–26. DOI: 10.1007/s10586-023-04203-7

Ng, D. T. K., Luo, W., Chan, H. M. Y., & Chu, S. K. W. (2022). Using digital story writing as a pedagogy to develop AI literacy among primary students. *Computers and Education: Artificial Intelligence*, 3, 100054. DOI: 10.1016/j.caeai.2022.100054

Nielsen, W. C. (2022). Motherless creations: Fictions of artificial life, 1650-1890.

Nogueira, M. R., Menezes, P., & Maçãs de Carvalho, J. (2024). Exploring the impact of machine learning on dance performance: A systematic review. *International Journal of Performance Arts and Digital Media*, 20(1), 1–50. DOI: 10.1080/14794713.2024.2338927

Obiedat, A. Z. (2022). Modern Virtuous Ethics: Knowing the Good and Doing the Right in Scientific Humanism. In *Modernity and the Ideals of Arab-Islamic and Western-Scientific Philosophy: The Worldviews of Mario Bunge and Taha Abd al-Rahman* (pp. 241–283). Springer International Publishing. DOI: 10.1007/978-3-030-94265-6_8

Oksanen, A., Cvetkovic, A., Akin, N., Latikka, R., Bergdahl, J., Chen, Y., & Savela, N. (2023). Artificial intelligence in fine arts: A systematic review of empirical research. Computers in Human Behavior: Artificial Humans, 100004.

Paaß, G., & Giesselbach, S. (2023). Improving pre-trained language models. In Foundation Models for Natural Language Processing: Pre-trained Language Models Integrating Media (pp. 79-159). Cham: Springer International Publishing.

Pablos, A. B. (2024). Deleuze on Habit: Cognitive Science Beyond Prediction. *Journal of Archaeological Method and Theory.*

Papadakis, S. (2022). Apps to promote computational thinking and coding skills to young age children: A pedagogical challenge for the 21st century learners. Educational Process: International Journal (EDUPIJ).

Pataranutaporn, P., Danry, V., Leong, J., Punpongsanon, P., Novy, D., Maes, P., & Sra, M. (2021). AI-generated characters for supporting personalized learning and well-being. *Nature Machine Intelligence*, 3(12), 1013–1022. DOI: 10.1038/s42256-021-00417-9

Pescapè, A. (n.d.). Exploring the Current State and Future Potential of Generative Artificial Intelligence Using a Generative Artificial Intelligence. Mind.

Pinheiro, S., Mota, N. B., Sigman, M., Fernández-Slezak, D., Guerreiro, A., Tófoli, L. F., Cecchi, G., Copelli, M., & Ribeiro, S. (2020). The history of writing reflects the effects of education on discourse structure: Implications for literacy, orality, psychosis and the axial age. *Trends in Neuroscience and Education*, 21, 100142. DOI: 10.1016/j.tine.2020.100142 PMID: 33303107

Podlecki, A. J. (2021). *One Homer, or Two?* Some Suggested Stylistic Separators in the Homeric Poems. Mouseion.

Porteous, J., Ferreira, J. F., Lindsay, A., & Cavazza, M. (2021). Automated narrative planning model extension. *Autonomous Agents and Multi-Agent Systems*, 35(2), 19. DOI: 10.1007/s10458-021-09501-1

Pritoni, M., Paine, D., Fierro, G., Mosiman, C., Poplawski, M., Saha, A., Bender, J., & Granderson, J. (2021). Metadata schemas and ontologies for building energy applications: A critical review and use case analysis. *Energies*, 14(7), 2024. DOI: 10.3390/en14072024

Rajakannan, R. & Rukmini, S. (2021). Reading Paradigms of Digital Narratives: Reception of Hypertext Fictions and Its Implications. Journal of Narrative and Language Studies.

Rani, S., Jining, D., Shah, D., Xaba, S., & Shoukat, K. (2024). Examining the impacts of artificial intelligence technology and computing on digital art: A case study of Edmond de Belamy and its aesthetic values and techniques. *AI & Society*. Advance online publication. DOI: 10.1007/s00146-024-01996-y

Ray, P. P. (2023). ChatGPT: A comprehensive review on background, applications, key challenges, bias, ethics, limitations and future scope. Internet of Things and Cyber-Physical Systems.

Reddy, S. (2024). Generative AI in healthcare: an implementation science informed translational path on application, integration and governance. Implementation Science.

Romero, C., & Ventura, S. (2020). Educational data mining and learning analytics: An updated survey. *Wiley Interdisciplinary Reviews. Data Mining and Knowledge Discovery*, 10(3), e1355. DOI: 10.1002/widm.1355

Romero-Frías, E., & Barbecho, L. B. (2023). Digital Humanities Labs: Spaces for Innovation to Reconnect the Humanities With Society. In Digital Humanities and Laboratories (pp. 253-269). Routledge.

Roos, M. & Reccius, M. (2024). Narratives in economics. Journal of Economic Surveys.

Rosário, A. T. (2024). *Generative ai and generative pre-trained transformer applications: Challenges and opportunities*. Making Art With Generative AI Tools. DOI: 10.4018/979-8-3693-1950-5.ch003

Roth, R. E. (2021). Cartographic design as visual storytelling: synthesis and review of map-based narratives, genres, and tropes. The Cartographic Journal.

Roumeliotis, K. I. & Tselikas, N. D. (2023). Chatgpt and open-ai models: A preliminary review. Future Internet.

Rubinstein, Y. (2020). Uneasy listening: Towards a Hauntology of AI-generated music. Resonance: The Journal of Sound and Culture.

Safavi, G., & Ghazinoory, S. (2024). Creative bits: Challenges of applying industry 4.0 in digital creative industries. *Multimedia Tools and Applications*. Advance online publication. DOI: 10.1007/s11042-024-19701-y

Safely, A. C. (2023). Advanced Applications of Generative AI and Natural Language Processing Models. Advanced Applications of Generative AI and Natural Language Processing Models, 69.

Sartori, L. & Bocca, G. (2023). Minding the gap (s): public perceptions of AI and socio-technical imaginaries. AI & Society.

Sartori, L. & Theodorou, A. (2022). A sociotechnical perspective for the future of AI: narratives, inequalities, and human control. Ethics and Information Technology.

Shankar, P. (2024). Dwelling and landscape setting: Continuity of cultural ideas in the dwellings of Udaipur. Potency of the Vernacular Settlements.

Sharma, R. & Gupta, H. (2024). Leveraging cognitive digital twins in industry 5.0 for achieving sustainable development goal 9: An exploration of inclusive and sustainable industrialization strategies. Journal of Cleaner Production.

Sheikh, S. (2020). Understanding the role of artificial intelligence and its future social impact.

Sillett, M. (2020). Folklore and new Media Communications: An Exploration of Journey to the West, Its Modern Orality and Traditional Storytelling in Contemporary Online Spaces. canterbury.ac.uk

Škola, F., Rizvić, S., Cozza, M., Barbieri, L., Bruno, F., Skarlatos, D., & Liarokapis, F. (2020). Virtual reality with 360-video storytelling in cultural heritage: Study of presence, engagement, and immersion. *Sensors (Basel)*, 20(20), 5851. DOI: 10.3390/s20205851 PMID: 33081154

Smith, B. & Monforte, J. (2020). Stories, new materialism and pluralism: Understanding, practising and pushing the boundaries of narrative analysis. Methods in Psychology.

Spennemann, D. H. R. (2023). ChatGPT and the generation of digitally born "knowledge": How does a generative AI language model interpret cultural heritage values?. Knowledge.

Steffen, T. & Bjoraker, W. (2020). The return of oral hermeneutics: As good today as it was for the Hebrew Bible and first-century Christianity.

Sterledev, R., Sterledeva, T., & Abramenko, V. (2021, October). Artificial intelligence as the possible third front of humanity. In *International Perm Forum Science and Global Challenges of the 21st Century* (pp. 819-826). Cham: Springer International Publishing.

Sufi, F. (2024). Generative pre-trained transformer (GPT) in research: A systematic review on data augmentation. Information.

Sun, K., Luo, X., & Luo, M. Y. (2022, July). A survey of pretrained language models. In *International Conference on Knowledge Science, Engineering and Management* (pp. 442-456). Cham: Springer International Publishing.

Taeihagh, A. (2021). Governance of artificial intelligence. Policy and Society.

Tortorella, G. L., Fogliatto, F. S., Cauchick-Miguel, P. A., Kurnia, S., & Jurburg, D. (2021). Integration of industry 4.0 technologies into total productive maintenance practices. *International Journal of Production Economics*, 240, 108224. DOI: 10.1016/j.ijpe.2021.108224

Totschnig, W. (2020). Fully autonomous AI. Science and Engineering Ethics.

Trichopoulos, G., Alexandridis, G., & Caridakis, G. (2023). A survey on computational and emergent digital storytelling. Heritage.

Ugwuoke, E., & Onu, J. (2023). A Comparative Structuralist Analysis of Two Igbo folktales. Sprin Journal of Arts *Humanities and Social Sciences*, 2(05), 31–44.

von Davier, M. (2023). Training Optimus Prime, MD: A Case Study of Automated Item Generation Using Artificial Intelligence–From Fine-Tuned GPT2 to GPT3 and Beyond. In Advancing Natural Language Processing in Educational Assessment (pp. 90-106). Routledge.

Waardenburg, L. & Huysman, M. (2022). From coexistence to co-creation: Blurring boundaries in the age of AI. Information and Organization.

Waldron, A. (2022). Queer Screams: A History of LGBTQ+ Survival Through the Lens of American Horror Cinema.

Wasserman, R. (2021). Ancient and contemporary industries based on alkali and alkali-earth salts and hydroxides: the historical and technological. Ionic Liquids: Thermophysical Properties and Applications, 123.

Wienrich, C. & Latoschik, M. E. (2021). extended artificial intelligence: New prospects of human-ai interaction research. Frontiers in Virtual Reality.

Yeo, E., Pilson, A., Rutter, N., & Hasan, E. (2023). We Need to be as a Group: Using and Evaluating the Listening Guide in Feminist Collaborative Autoethnography With an Affective 'Fifth Listen'as a Tool to (re) construct Identities. *International Journal of Qualitative Methods*, 22. DOI: 10.1177/16094069231180166

Yigitcanlar, T., Desouza, K. C., Butler, L., & Roozkhosh, F. (2020). Contributions and risks of artificial intelligence (AI) in building smarter cities: Insights from a systematic review of the literature. Energies.

Young, M. (2022). "The Tablets I Spoke about Are Good to Preserve until Far-off Days": An Overview on the Creation and Evolution of Canons in Babylonia and Assyria from the .... Canonisation as Innovation.

Yuan, B., He, Y., Davis, J., Zhang, T., Dao, T., Chen, B., . . . Zhang, C. (2022). Decentralized training of foundation models in heterogeneous environments. Advances in Neural Information Processing Systems, 35, 25464-25477.

Zhang, B., Zhu, J., & Su, H. (2023). Toward the third generation artificial intelligence. *Science China. Information Sciences.*

Zhang, Y., & Chen, D. Z. (2023, October). GPT4MIA: Utilizing Generative Pretrained Transformer (GPT-3) as a Plug-and-Play Transductive Model for Medical Image Analysis. In International Conference on Medical Image Computing and Computer-Assisted Intervention (pp. 151-160). Cham: Springer Nature Switzerland. DOI: 10.1007/978-3-031-47401-9_15

Zwolińska-Ligaj, M. A. & Guzal-Dec, D. J. (2024). Rural Area Resilience during the COVID-19 Pandemic as Exemplified by Urban–Rural Communes in Poland. Sustainability.

Chapter 5
Exploring the Transformative Potential of Generative Artificial Intelligence

Mohsen Mahmoudi-Dehaki
https://orcid.org/0000-0002-4962-6827
Department of English, Islamic Azad University, Najafabad, Iran

Nasim Nasr-Esfahani
https://orcid.org/0000-0002-2388-6524
Department of English, Islamic Azad University, Isfahan, Iran

ABSTRACT

Generative AI represents a groundbreaking approach in artificial intelligence, focusing on creating new data instances that closely resemble existing datasets. Unlike traditional models that primarily classify or predict, generative models like generative adversarial networks (GANs) and variational autoencoders (VAEs) learn the underlying data distribution, enabling them to produce novel outputs. This chapter explores various generative models, their applications in industries such as entertainment, healthcare, and fashion, and their implications for creativity and originality. It highlights advancements in techniques like conditional generation and style transfer, emphasizing the potential of generative AI to redefine human creativity and foster collaboration between humans and machines in artistic endeavors.

DOI: 10.4018/979-8-3693-6255-6.ch005

1. INTRODUCTION

Generative AI represents a novel approach to artificial intelligence, creating new data instances resembling a given dataset. Unlike traditional AI models, which often rely on classification or regression to make predictions based on existing data, generative models are designed to learn the underlying data distribution, allowing them to generate new instances similar to the training data and exhibit a level of novelty (Feuerriegel et al., 2024).

One of the most striking applications of generative AI is in the realm of image generation. For instance, models like Generative Adversarial Networks (GANs) can produce hyper-realistic images of non-existent faces, as seen in projects like "This Person Does Not Exist" (Goodfellow et al., 2020). These systems leverage vast training data to understand the nuances of human features, lighting, and textures, ultimately synthesizing indistinguishable images from actual photographs.

Generative AI has broad implications across various industries. In entertainment, it can be used to create realistic animations and special effects. In healthcare, generative models can synthesize medical images for training purposes, helping to improve diagnostic algorithms without compromising patient privacy. In fashion, AI can generate new clothing designs based on current trends, allowing designers to explore creative avenues quickly.

The significance of generative AI extends beyond mere data generation. It challenges our understanding of creativity and originality, raising philosophical questions about authorship and the nature of art. As these models become more sophisticated, they may redefine the boundaries of human creativity, leading to new forms of collaboration between humans and machines.

2. OVERVIEW OF GENERATIVE MODELS

Generative models can be categorized into several types, each with unique characteristics and applications. Generative Adversarial Networks (GANs), Variational Autoencoders (VAEs), diffusion models, and normalizing flows are the most prominent (Bao & Davis, 2022). Understanding the differences between these models is crucial for selecting the right approach for specific tasks.

GANs operate on a two-network system: the generator and the discriminator (Saxena & Cao, 2021). The generator creates new data instances while the discriminator evaluates them against actual data. This adversarial setup leads to a dynamic where both networks improve over time. GANs have successfully generated high-quality images, enhanced video game graphics, and even produced art. However, they can be challenging to train due to issues like mode collapse, where the generator produces limited outputs.

VAEs are built on the principles of probabilistic graphical models (Klys et al., 2018). They consist of an encoder that maps input data to a latent space and a decoder that reconstructs the data from this latent representation. VAEs are particularly effective for tasks that require understanding the underlying data structure, such as anomaly detection and semi-supervised learning. They excel in generating new samples that maintain the diversity of the training data while allowing for smooth interpolation in the latent space.

Diffusion models have gained popularity for their ability to generate high-quality images through a unique process of adding and then removing noise from data. They work by gradually corrupting data with noise and then learning to reverse this process to generate new samples. Diffusion models have shown remarkable results in producing images that rival those generated by GANs, making them a powerful alternative in the generative modeling landscape (Chen et al., 2024)

Normalizing flows utilize a series of invertible transformations to model complex distributions. Normalizing flows can perform tasks such as density estimation and sample generation by transforming a simple base distribution (like a Gaussian) into a more complex one. They offer the advantage of exact likelihood computation, making them suitable for applications where understanding data distribution is critical.

Each model has strengths and weaknesses, making it suitable for different applications. The choice of a generative model often depends on the specific requirements of the task, such as the need for high-quality output, interpretability, or computational efficiency.

2.1. Generative Adversarial Networks (GANs)

Generative Adversarial Networks (GANs) revolutionized the field of generative modeling when they were introduced by Ian Goodfellow and his colleagues in 2014. The core idea behind GANs is the adversarial training process, which consists of two neural networks—the generator and the discriminator—engaged in a competitive game.

The generator creates new data instances while the discriminator evaluates these instances against actual data. The generator aims to produce data indistinguishable from the actual samples, while the discriminator strives to classify the data as real or fake accurately. This dynamic creates a feedback loop where both networks improve over time.

In regard to illustrating this concept, consider the analogy of a forger and an art critic. The forger (generator) attempts to create a painting that resembles a famous artwork, while the art critic (discriminator) evaluates the painting and provides feedback. If the critic identifies the painting as a forgery, the forger learns from this feedback and adjusts their techniques to produce a more convincing piece. Over time, the forger becomes better at mimicking the original artist's style, while the critic becomes more discerning in their evaluations.

One of the critical advantages of GANs is their ability to generate high-quality, high-resolution images. They have been successfully applied in various domains, including:

- Image Generation: GANs can create realistic images of faces, landscapes, and objects, often producing indistinguishable results from actual photographs.
- Text-to-Image Synthesis: GANs can generate images based on textual descriptions, creating visuals that match specific narratives.
- Video Generation: GANs have been adapted to generate video sequences, enabling the synthesis of realistic animations and dynamic content.

Despite their impressive capabilities, training GANs can be challenging. Issues such as mode collapse, where the generator produces a limited variety of outputs, and instability during training can hinder performance. Researchers have developed various techniques to address these challenges, including Wasserstein GANs (WGANs) and progressive growing GANs, which enhance stability and output quality (Gulrajani et al., 2017).

2.2. Variational Autoencoders (VAEs)

Variational Autoencoders (VAEs) represent a different approach to generative modeling, grounded in Bayesian inference and probabilistic graphical models. Introduced by Kingma and Welling (2013), VAEs are designed to learn a latent representation of the input data while enabling the generation of new samples.

The architecture of a VAE consists of two main components: the encoder and the decoder. The encoder maps input data to a latent space, producing a distribution over the latent variables. This distribution is typically modeled as a Gaussian, characterized by a mean and a variance. The decoder then samples from this latent distribution to reconstruct the original data.

A key feature of VAEs is their ability to learn meaningful latent representations (Kingma & Welling, 2013). By sampling from the latent space, VAEs can generate new data instances that share characteristics with the training data. For example, a VAE trained on handwritten digits can generate new digits that resemble those in the dataset, allowing for smooth interpolation between different digits. VAEs have several advantages, including:

- Continuous Latent Space: The latent space learned by VAEs is continuous, enabling smooth transitions between different data instances. This property is beneficial for tasks such as data interpolation and exploration.
- Generative Capability: VAEs can generate new samples by sampling from the learned latent distribution, making them suitable for data augmentation and synthesis applications.
- Regularization: The VAE framework incorporates a regularization term that encourages the learned latent distribution to be close to a prior distribution (usually a standard Gaussian). This helps prevent overfitting and improves generalization.

VAEs have been applied in various domains, including:

- Image Generation: VAEs can generate new images based on learned features, making them useful for tasks like generating new faces or objects.
- Anomaly Detection: By learning the normal distribution of data, VAEs can identify anomalies by measuring how well new instances fit within the learned distribution.
- Semi-Supervised Learning: VAEs can leverage labeled and unlabeled data, making them practical for tasks where labeled data is scarce.

While VAEs provide a robust framework for generative modeling, they may produce blurrier outputs compared to GANs due to their focus on reconstructing the data distribution rather than generating sharp samples. Nonetheless, their ability to learn meaningful latent representations and generate diverse outputs makes them a valuable tool in the generative AI toolkit.

3. GENERATIVE AI TECHNIQUES

3.1. Conditional Generation

Conditional Generative Adversarial Networks (cGANs) have revolutionized the field of image generation by allowing the creation of images based on specific conditions or attributes (Chrysos et al., 2021). Unlike traditional GANs, which generate images from random noise, cGANs take additional information as input, enabling them to produce outputs that meet specific criteria. This capability has profound implications in various applications, particularly in fashion, gaming, and personalized content creation.

One of the most compelling applications of conditional generation is in the fashion industry, where cGANs can generate images of clothing items tailored to individual preferences. For instance, a user could specify attributes such as color, style, and fabric type, and the cGAN would generate a corresponding outfit, enhancing the shopping experience and allowing designers to visualize new collections based on consumer trends and preferences.

Researchers (e.g., Yuan & Moghaddam, 2020) have employed cGANs to generate diverse hairstyles on faces in the hairstyle generation. Users can see how different hairstyles look in their images or models by conditioning the model based on hairstyle attributes, such as length, color, and texture. This application benefits hair salons and beauty apps, where customers can experiment with various looks before deciding.

Moreover, cGANs have been employed in art generation, where they can create artworks based on specific themes or styles. For example, a user could input a theme like "nature" or "urban life," and the cGAN would generate corresponding artworks that reflect those themes. This capability democratizes art creation and allows artists to explore and collaborate with AI.

The training process for cGANs involves a two-network architecture: the generator and the discriminator (Miyato & Koyama, 2018). The generator creates images based on the input conditions, while the discriminator evaluates the authenticity of the generated images against authentic images. This adversarial process continues until the generator produces images that the discriminator can no longer distinguish from real ones. Fine-tuning the conditioning information is crucial, as it directly influences the quality and relevance of the generated outputs.

Recent advancements in cGANs have focused on improving the quality and diversity of generated images (Rodriguez et al., 2019). Techniques such as attention mechanisms allow the model to focus on specific parts of the image, enhancing the details and realism of the generated outputs. Additionally, incorporating multimodal inputs—such as combining text descriptions with images—has further expanded the capabilities of cGANs, enabling them to generate images that are not only visually appealing but also contextually relevant.

Conditional generation through cGANs represents a significant leap forward in generative modeling. By allowing for the creation of tailored images based on specific attributes, these models have found applications across various industries, from fashion to art. As research advances, we can expect even more innovative applications that leverage the power of conditional generation to enhance creativity and personalization.

3.2. Style Transfer

Style transfer is a fascinating area of research that focuses on altering the visual appearance of an image while preserving its content. This technique has gained popularity due to its ability to transform photographs into the artistic styles of famous painters, such as Vincent van Gogh, Pablo Picasso, and Claude Monet. The underlying principle of style transfer lies in separating content and style, allowing for a unique blend of both in the final output.

At its core, style transfer typically employs convolutional neural networks (CNNs) to extract features from both the content and style images. The content representation captures the essential elements of the original image, such as shapes and objects, while the style representation encapsulates the textures, colors, and patterns characteristic of the artistic style. By combining these two representations, style transfer algorithms can generate a new image that reflects the original's content while adopting the chosen artwork's stylistic features.

One of the most notable advancements in style transfer is using neural style transfer (NST) techniques, which leverage deep learning to achieve high-quality results (Jing et al., 2019). The seminal work by Gatys et al. introduced a method that utilizes pre-trained CNNs to extract features at multiple layers, allowing for a more nuanced understanding of content and style. This approach has led to impressive results, enabling users to apply complex artistic styles to images with remarkable fidelity.

Real-time style transfer has also become a significant research focus, as it allows for the immediate application of artistic styles in interactive settings. Techniques such as adaptive instance normalization (AdaIN) have been developed to achieve this goal by normalizing feature maps based on the style image's statistics (Huang, 2022). This innovation enables the model to apply styles quickly, making it suitable for mobile and augmented reality applications.

In addition to artistic style transfer, researchers have explored various applications of this technology, including video style transfer, where the style is consistently applied across frames to create a cohesive artistic video. Furthermore, style transfer has found its way into the fashion industry, where it can generate clothing designs based on artistic influences, providing designers with new creative tools.

Despite its successes, style transfer also presents challenges. One significant issue is the potential loss of content fidelity, where the generated image may not accurately represent the original content. Researchers are actively working on improving the balance between content preservation and style application, ensuring that the final output maintains the integrity of both aspects.

Style transfer is a captivating technique that merges art and technology. Allowing users to transform images into renowned artists' styles has opened up new avenues for creativity and expression. As advancements continue in this field, we can anticipate even more sophisticated methods that enhance the quality and applicability of style transfer in various domains.

3.3. Unsupervised Learning

Unsupervised learning is a branch of machine learning that focuses on discovering data patterns and structures without needing labeled training samples (Colins, 2017). This approach is precious in generative modeling, which aims to create new data points that resemble a given dataset. Unsupervised generative models, such as clustering algorithms and generative models like VAEs and GANs, have gained prominence for their ability to learn from unstructured data.

Clustering algorithms are one of the most common techniques in unsupervised learning. They group similar data points into clusters based on their inherent characteristics, allowing for identifying patterns and relationships within the data. For example, in image datasets, clustering can reveal groups of images that share similar features, such as color palettes or object types. This capability benefits applications like image retrieval, where users can search for images based on visual similarity.

Generative models like VAEs and GANs take unsupervised learning a step further by identifying patterns and generating new data points that reflect those patterns. VAEs, for instance, learn a probabilistic representation of the input data, allowing them to sample from the learned distribution to generate new, similar data points. This approach has been successfully applied in various domains, including image synthesis, text generation, and music composition.

One of the critical advantages of unsupervised generative models is their ability to work with large amounts of unlabelled data, which is often more readily available than labeled datasets. This characteristic makes them particularly valuable in fields such as healthcare, where obtaining labeled data can be challenging and time-consuming. By leveraging unsupervised learning, researchers can uncover hidden patterns in medical imaging data, leading to improved diagnostic tools and treatment strategies.

Another exciting application of unsupervised generative models is in anomaly detection. By training on a dataset of typical instances, these models can learn to identify deviations from the norm, which can indicate potential issues. For example, in industrial settings, unsupervised models can monitor equipment performance and detect anomalies that may signal impending failures, enabling proactive maintenance and reducing downtime.

Despite the numerous advantages of unsupervised learning, it also presents challenges. One major hurdle is the difficulty in evaluating the quality of generated outputs, as traditional metrics used for supervised learning may not apply. Researchers are actively exploring new evaluation techniques that consider the diversity and realism of generated samples, ensuring that unsupervised models produce meaningful and high-quality outputs.

Unsupervised learning is a powerful approach in generative modeling that enables the discovery of patterns and the generating new data without needing labeled samples. Its applications span various domains, from clustering similar data points to generating realistic images and detecting anomalies. As the field continues to evolve, we can expect further advancements that enhance the capabilities and effectiveness of unsupervised generative models.

3.4. Reinforcement Learning in Generative Models

Reinforcement learning (RL) is a machine learning paradigm where an agent learns to make decisions by interacting with an environment. It is characterized by using rewards and penalties to guide the learning process, allowing the agent to optimize its actions over time (Ris-Ala, 2023). In the context of generative models, RL has emerged as a powerful tool for creating diverse and novel outputs, particularly in creative tasks such as game-level generation, music composition, and content creation.

One of the most compelling applications of RL in generative modeling is in game design. Traditional game-level design often relies on manual creation, which can be time-consuming and limited in scope. By applying RL, researchers can train generative models to create game levels that are playable, engaging, and varied. The RL agent learns to optimize the level design based on player feedback, adapting its strategies to create levels that maximize enjoyment and challenge.

For example, in a platformer game, the RL agent can generate levels by placing obstacles, enemies, and rewards in a way that balances difficulty and fun. The agent iteratively improves its designs by simulating player interactions and receiving feedback on the level's playability. This approach has the potential to revolutionize game development, enabling designers to explore a vast array of creative possibilities while minimizing manual effort.

In addition to game-level generation, RL has been applied to other creative tasks, such as music composition and storytelling. In music generation, RL can guide the creation of melodies and harmonies based on listener preferences, allowing for the production of unique and enjoyable compositions. Similarly, in storytelling, RL can help generate narratives that adapt to user choices, creating interactive and engaging experiences.

Integrating RL with generative models also facilitates the exploration of diverse outputs. By incorporating exploration strategies, RL agents can generate a wide range of variations, ensuring that the outputs are novel and relevant to the task at hand. This capability is precious in creative applications, where diversity and originality are paramount.

Despite its promise, applying RL in generative modeling also presents challenges. One significant issue is the need for a well-defined reward signal, which can be challenging to establish in creative tasks where subjective preferences vary widely. Researchers are exploring various approaches to define meaningful reward functions that capture the essence of creativity and user satisfaction.

Reinforcement learning is a powerful tool for enhancing generative models, particularly in creative domains such as game design and content generation. By leveraging the principles of RL, these models can learn to produce diverse and engaging outputs that adapt to user preferences. As research advances, we can expect even more innovative applications that harness the power of reinforcement learning in generative modeling.

3.5. Evolutionary Algorithms for Generation

Evolutionary algorithms (EAs) are optimization techniques inspired by natural selection and genetics principles (Yu & Gen, 2010). These algorithms simulate the process of evolution to improve solutions to complex problems iteratively. In generative modeling, EAs have shown great promise in optimizing generative models for specific tasks, such as evolving neural network architectures for image generation and enhancing the quality of generated outputs.

One of the key advantages of using evolutionary algorithms in generative modeling is their ability to explore a vast search space of potential solutions. Traditional optimization methods may struggle to navigate complex landscapes, particularly in high-dimensional spaces. EAs, on the other hand, utilize a population-based approach, where multiple candidate solutions are evaluated simultaneously. This allows for a more comprehensive exploration of the solution space, increasing the likelihood of discovering high-quality models.

In image generation, EAs can evolve neural network architectures tailored for specific tasks. For instance, researchers can define a population of neural networks with varying architectures, such as different numbers of layers, types of activation functions, and connectivity patterns. By evaluating the performance of these networks on a given dataset, EAs can select the best-performing architectures and apply genetic operators, such as crossover and mutation, to create new generations of networks. Over successive generations, the algorithm converges on architectures that yield superior performance in generating realistic images.

Moreover, EAs can be utilized to optimize hyperparameters of generative models, such as learning rates, batch sizes, and regularization techniques. By systematically exploring combinations of hyperparameters, EAs can identify configurations that lead to improved performance and stability during training. This capability is precious in complex models like GANs, where the choice of hyperparameters can significantly impact the quality of generated outputs.

In addition to optimizing neural networks, EAs have been applied in various creative domains, such as music composition and art generation. For example, in music generation, EAs can evolve musical sequences by evaluating their aesthetic qualities based on listener feedback. This approach allows for creating unique compositions that resonate with audiences while exploring diverse musical styles.

Despite the advantages of evolutionary algorithms, their application in generative modeling also presents challenges. One notable issue is the computational cost of evaluating multiple candidate solutions, which can be time-consuming, especially for complex models. Researchers actively explore parallelization techniques and more efficient evaluation methods to mitigate these challenges.

Evolutionary algorithms represent a powerful approach for optimizing generative models in various domains. By simulating the principles of natural selection, these algorithms can explore diverse architectures and configurations, leading to improved performance and creativity in generated outputs. As research continues to advance, we can anticipate further innovations that leverage the power of evolutionary algorithms in generative modeling, enhancing the capabilities of AI in creative tasks.

4. GENERATIVE AI TECHNIQUES

4.1. Bias and Fairness in Generative AI

Generative AI systems are increasingly integrated into various applications, from content creation to decision-making in sensitive areas like hiring and law enforcement. However, one of the most pressing concerns surrounding these technologies is the potential for bias and unfairness. Bias in AI can manifest in several ways, primarily stemming from the data used to train these models. If the training data is unrepresentative or contains historical biases, the AI system may learn and perpetuate these biases, leading to discriminatory outcomes. Sources of bias include:

- Data Bias: This occurs when the training dataset reflects societal biases. For instance, if a facial recognition system is trained predominantly on images of individuals from a specific demographic, it may struggle to accurately recognize faces from underrepresented groups. Studies have shown that commercial facial recognition systems have higher error rates for women and people of color, leading to significant implications for law enforcement and surveillance practices.

- Algorithmic Bias: Even with a balanced dataset, the algorithms can introduce bias through their design. Certain algorithms may prioritize specific features over others, inadvertently amplifying existing biases in the data. For example, an algorithm emphasizing speed over accuracy may produce biased outcomes if not carefully calibrated to account for fairness.
- User Bias: The biases of developers and users can also influence AI outcomes. If the individuals creating or using the AI systems harbor unconscious biases, these can seep into the design and implementation processes, further perpetuating unfairness.

In regard to address these biases, a multifaceted approach is necessary:

- Diverse Training Datasets: Ensuring that training datasets are representative of the population is crucial. This involves collecting data from various demographics and contexts to minimize the risk of bias. Techniques such as data augmentation can also help create a more balanced dataset.
- Algorithmic Fairness Techniques: Researchers are developing methods to assess and mitigate bias in AI algorithms. Techniques such as adversarial debiasing and fairness constraints can be integrated into the training process to promote fairness.
- Continuous Monitoring: Implementing a robust monitoring system post-deployment is essential. Regular audits of AI systems can help identify and rectify biases that may emerge over time, ensuring that the systems remain fair and equitable.
- Stakeholder Engagement: Engaging diverse stakeholders, including ethicists, community representatives, and affected individuals, can provide valuable insights into potential biases and their implications. This collaborative approach fosters a more inclusive development.

Addressing bias and fairness in generative AI is not merely a technical challenge but a societal imperative. By prioritizing fairness in AI development, we can create systems that enhance equity and justice rather than perpetuate existing inequalities.

4.2. Accountability and Transparency

The rapid advancement of generative AI technologies has raised significant concerns regarding accountability and transparency. Understanding how these systems operate becomes paramount as they increasingly influence critical decision-making processes. Transparency in AI algorithms is essential for fostering trust among users and stakeholders, ensuring these technologies are deployed responsibly. Transparency is essential due to:

- Understanding Decision-Making: Transparency allows users to comprehend how AI systems arrive at their conclusions. This understanding is vital in high-stakes applications, such as healthcare diagnosis or credit scoring, where decisions can profoundly impact individuals' lives. When users can trace the reasoning behind an AI's decision, it enhances their confidence in the system.
- Identifying Bias: Transparent AI models enable stakeholders to identify and address biases. By examining the input data and the decision-making process, developers can pinpoint areas where biases may exist and take corrective actions. This is particularly important in generative AI, where the potential for bias can have far-reaching consequences.
- Regulatory Compliance: As governments and organizations increasingly focus on ethical AI practices, transparency is becoming a regulatory requirement. Clear documentation of AI systems, including their design, training data, and decision-making processes, is essential for compliance with emerging regulations.

Also, accountability can be enhanced by:

- Model Interpretability: Techniques such as LIME (Local Interpretable Model-agnostic Explanations) and SHAP (SHapley Additive exPlanations) can help demystify AI models. These tools provide insights into how specific features contribute to the model's predictions, allowing stakeholders to understand the rationale behind decisions.
- Audit Trails: Implementing audit trails for AI systems can enhance accountability. Keeping detailed records of data sources, model training processes, and decision-making pathways allows for thorough investigations into disputes or errors.
- Stakeholder Involvement: Engaging diverse stakeholders in developing and evaluating AI systems can promote accountability. By incorporating feedback from various perspectives, developers can create more robust and transparent systems that better serve the needs of all users.
- Ethical Guidelines: Establishing clear ethical guidelines for AI development can help ensure accountability. Organizations should adopt frameworks prioritizing transparency, fairness, and ethical considerations throughout the AI lifecycle.

Accountability and transparency are critical components of responsible generative AI development. By fostering an environment of openness and engagement, we can build trust in these technologies and ensure they are used ethically and fairly.

4.3. Privacy Concerns

As generative AI technologies become more sophisticated, they raise significant privacy concerns that warrant careful examination (Santos & Radanliev, 2024). The ability of these systems to create realistic content, such as deepfakes, poses risks not only to individual privacy but also to societal trust and security. Risks associated with generative AI consist of:

- Deepfake Technology: Deepfakes utilize generative AI to create hyper-realistic images and videos that can manipulate reality. This technology has been used maliciously to create false representations of individuals, leading to potential reputational damage, harassment, and misinformation. The ease with which deepfakes can be produced raises alarms about their potential use in political manipulation, identity theft, and defamation.
- Misinformation: The proliferation of AI-generated content can contribute to the spread of misinformation. As generative AI becomes more accessible, it becomes easier for malicious actors to create deceptive content that can mislead the public. This poses a significant challenge to media literacy and trust in information sources.
- Identity Theft: Generative AI can be exploited to create convincing impersonations of individuals, leading to identity theft and fraud. For example, voice synthesis technology can replicate a person's voice, allowing scammers to impersonate them in phone calls and deceive their contacts.

In regard to addressing privacy concerns, it is essential to focus on:

- Regulatory Frameworks: Implementing robust regulations is essential for protecting individuals' privacy in the age of generative AI. Governments should establish clear guidelines regarding using AI technologies, particularly in sensitive areas such as identity verification and content creation.
- Data Protection Measures: Organizations developing generative AI systems must prioritize data protection. This includes implementing strong security measures to safeguard personal data and ensuring that data used for training is anonymized and ethically sourced.
- Public Awareness and Education: Raising public awareness about the potential risks associated with generative AI is crucial. Educational initiatives can

empower individuals to recognize deepfakes and other AI-generated content, fostering critical thinking and media literacy.

- Ethical AI Development: Developers should adhere to ethical principles, prioritizing user privacy. This includes conducting thorough impact assessments to understand how AI applications may affect individuals' privacy and implementing measures to mitigate risks.

Addressing privacy concerns related to generative AI is essential for maintaining public trust and ensuring the responsible use of these technologies. By implementing robust regulations and prioritizing ethical practices, we can harness the benefits of generative AI while safeguarding individuals' privacy.

4.4. Societal Impact of Generative AI

The societal implications of generative AI extend far beyond technical considerations, influencing public opinion, cultural norms, and social interactions. Understanding their potential impact is crucial for fostering a responsible and informed society as these technologies become more integrated into our daily lives. Influence on public opinion include:

- Content Creation and Manipulation: Generative AI enables the rapid creation of content, including articles, videos, and social media posts. This capability can be harnessed for positive purposes, such as enhancing creativity and accessibility. However, it also raises concerns about the manipulation of public opinion. AI-generated content can be used to spread propaganda, misinformation, or divisive narratives, potentially undermining democratic processes and societal cohesion.
- Erosion of Trust: The prevalence of AI-generated content, particularly deepfakes, can erode trust in media and information sources. As individuals become more skeptical of what they see and hear, it becomes increasingly challenging to discern fact from fiction. This erosion of trust can have far-reaching consequences for public discourse and civic engagement.

In addition, cultural norms and values include:

- Shaping Cultural Narratives: Generative AI can shape cultural narratives by influencing the stories we tell and the representations we see. AI-generated content can amplify certain voices while marginalizing others, impacting societal perceptions of identity, race, gender, and other critical issues. It is essential to ensure that generative AI systems are designed to promote diversity and inclusivity in the narratives they produce.

- Changing Creative Processes: Integrating generative AI into creative fields, such as art, music, and literature, transforms traditional creative processes. While AI can enhance creativity and provide new tools for artists, it also raises questions about authorship, originality, and the value of human creativity. As AI-generated content becomes more prevalent, society must grapple with what it means to be creative in an age of automation.

In the future, the concerned topics will be structured around:

- Public Dialogue and Engagement: Engaging the public in discussions about the implications of generative AI is crucial for fostering an informed society. Open dialogues can help individuals understand the benefits and risks of these technologies, empowering them to make informed decisions about their use.
- Ethical Frameworks: Establishing ethical frameworks for developing and deploying generative AI is essential for guiding its societal impact. These frameworks should prioritize human values, inclusivity, and accountability, ensuring AI technologies serve the public good.
- Interdisciplinary Collaboration: Addressing the societal implications of generative AI requires collaboration across disciplines, including technology, ethics, sociology, and law. By bringing together diverse perspectives, we can develop comprehensive solutions that consider the multifaceted nature of these technologies.

5. CREATIVE APPLICATIONS

5.1. Generative Art and Design

Generative art and design represent a revolutionary intersection of technology and creativity, where artists leverage artificial intelligence to produce innovative artworks. This field has gained momentum with the advent of sophisticated algorithms capable of learning from vast datasets of existing art. GANs, introduced by Ian Goodfellow in 2014, have become particularly influential. GANs consist of two neural networks: a generator that creates images and a discriminator that evaluates them. This adversarial process allows the generator to improve its output continuously, resulting in artworks that can be strikingly original and aesthetically pleasing.

One notable example of AI-generated art is the work of Refik Anadol, who utilizes machine learning algorithms to create immersive installations that blend data and art. His projects often involve training AI on large datasets, such as images from art history or architectural designs, to create dynamic visual experiences that challenge viewers' perceptions of space and creativity. Similarly, Obvious, a French art collective, gained international attention when their AI-generated portrait, "Edmond de Belamy," was auctioned at Christie's for $432,500. This event sparked discussions about the nature of authorship and the role of AI in the creative process.

The implications of generative art extend beyond mere aesthetics. Artists can use AI as a collaborator, enhancing their creative workflows and exploring new forms of expression. For instance, AI can suggest color palette compositions or generate entire pieces based on specific themes or emotions. This collaborative dynamic encourages artists to think outside traditional boundaries, leading to innovative works that might not have emerged through conventional methods.

Moreover, generative art raises philosophical questions about creativity and originality. If an AI creates a piece of art, who owns the rights to that work? Should the artist who trained the AI be credited, or does the credit lie with the machine? These questions are vital as the art world grapples with the implications of technology on creativity and intellectual property.

In addition to visual art, generative design makes waves in fields like architecture and product design. Designers can use AI algorithms to optimize structures and create functional yet aesthetically pleasing designs. For instance, Autodesk's Generative Design software allows architects to input design goals and constraints, and the AI generates multiple design alternatives, considering factors like materials, manufacturing methods, and environmental impact. This approach enhances creativity and promotes sustainability by optimizing resource use.

As generative art and design continue to evolve, they challenge our understanding of creativity, authorship, and the role of technology in artistic expression. The fusion of human creativity and AI capabilities opens up exciting possibilities for the future of art, making it an exhilarating area of exploration for artists, designers, and technologists alike.

5.2. Music Generation and Composition

Integrating AI into music generation and composition transforms how music is created, produced, and experienced. AI systems can analyze vast libraries of musical works, identifying patterns, structures, and stylistic elements that define various genres. This capability allows AI to compose original pieces that resonate with specific musical styles, offering musicians new tools for creativity.

One prominent example of AI in music is OpenAI's MuseNet, a deep learning model capable of generating compositions in various genres, from classical to jazz to pop. MuseNet can take user prompts, such as a specific genre or mood, and generate a complete musical piece that reflects those parameters. This technology not only aids composers in brainstorming ideas but also allows non-musicians to create music without extensive training.

AI-generated music is also making waves in the film and gaming industries, where soundtracks play a crucial role in enhancing the narrative experience. Companies like Aiva Technologies are developing AI systems that can compose original scores for films, advertisements, and video games. By analyzing existing soundtracks, these AI systems can create music that evokes specific emotions, ensuring that the audio complements the visual storytelling.

Moreover, AI can assist musicians in the creative process by providing real-time feedback and suggestions. Tools like Amper Music and Jukedeck allow users to create music by selecting parameters such as tempo, mood, and instrumentation. The AI then generates a unique composition that users can further modify, enabling a collaborative approach to music creation.

The implications of AI in music extend beyond composition. AI can also enhance music production through intelligent mixing and mastering tools. For example, LANDR uses AI algorithms to analyze audio tracks and provide automated mastering services, ensuring that the final product meets industry standards. This democratizes music production, allowing independent artists to achieve professional-quality sound without access to expensive studio equipment.

However, the rise of AI-generated music raises questions about authenticity and creativity. The line between human and machine-generated music blurs as AI systems become more sophisticated. This prompts discussions about the value of human creativity and the emotional depth that comes from personal experiences in music composition. While AI can mimic styles and structures, can it truly capture the nuances of human emotion and experience?

In conclusion, AI's role in music generation and composition is reshaping the landscape of the music industry. AI empowers musicians to explore uncharted territories in their craft by providing new tools for creativity and production. As technology advances, the collaboration between human artists and AI promises to yield innovative musical expressions that challenge traditional norms and redefine the future of music.

5.3. Text Generation and Storytelling

The advent of AI-driven text generation is revolutionizing the way stories are crafted and content is created. Natural language processing (NLP) models, particularly those based on deep learning, have demonstrated remarkable capabilities in generating coherent and contextually relevant text. These advancements open new avenues for writers, journalists, and content creators, allowing them to leverage AI as a powerful tool in their creative processes.

One of the most notable examples of AI in text generation is OpenAI's GPT-3, a language model that can produce human-like text based on user prompts. GPT-3 can generate everything from poetry to news articles to entire fiction chapters, showcasing its versatility. Writers can use this technology to brainstorm ideas, overcome writer's block, or even co-author narratives. Authors can receive suggestions that inspire new story directions by inputting specific themes or character traits.

In journalism, AI-generated content is becoming increasingly prevalent. News organizations are utilizing AI to automate the generation of routine news articles, such as sports scores, financial reports, and weather updates. For instance, The Associated Press employs AI to produce thousands of quarterly earnings reports, allowing journalists to focus on more in-depth reporting and analysis. This increases efficiency and ensures that timely information reaches audiences quickly.

AI's ability to analyze large datasets also enhances storytelling by providing insights that inform narrative development. For example, AI can analyze social media trends, audience preferences, and historical data to help writers craft stories that resonate with their target audience. This data-driven approach allows creators to make informed decisions about plotlines, character development, and thematic elements, ultimately enhancing the quality of their narratives.

Moreover, AI-generated text can serve as a foundation for interactive storytelling experiences. In gaming, AI can create dynamic narratives that adapt to player choices, providing a personalized experience. By generating dialogue and plot twists in real time, AI can enhance immersion and engagement, allowing players to feel more connected to the story.

However, the rise of AI in storytelling also raises ethical considerations. The potential for misinformation and spreading biased narratives is a significant concern, particularly in journalism. As AI systems learn from existing texts, they may inadvertently perpetuate biases in the data. Ensuring that AI-generated content adheres to ethical standards and promotes diversity and accuracy is crucial in maintaining the integrity of storytelling.

Additionally, the question of authorship arises in the context of AI-generated narratives. Who holds the rights to that content if an AI produces a story? Should the credit go to the programmer, the user who provided the prompt, or the AI?

These questions challenge traditional notions of creativity and ownership in the literary world.

AI-driven text generation transforms storytelling and content creation, offering new tools for writers and journalists. By leveraging AI's capabilities, creators can enhance their work, explore new narrative possibilities, and engage audiences innovatively. As technology continues to evolve, navigating the ethical implications and redefining our understanding of authorship and creativity in the digital age will be essential.

5.4. Fashion Design and Style Transfer

The intersection of AI and fashion design is an exciting frontier reshaping how clothing is conceptualized, created, and marketed. AI technologies enable designers to explore new aesthetics, optimize production processes, and personalize consumer fashion experiences. AI is revolutionizing the fashion industry in several ways by harnessing the power of machine learning and computer vision.

One of the most significant applications of AI in fashion is style transfer, a technique that allows designers to apply the visual characteristics of one garment or style to another. Using deep learning algorithms, AI can analyze the textures, colors, and patterns of existing clothing and then generate new designs that incorporate these elements. This process accelerates the design workflow and encourages experimentation, enabling designers to push the boundaries of traditional fashion aesthetics.

For instance, Google's DeepDream and similar neural networks have been used to create unique patterns and textures that can be applied to clothing designs. By inputting images of existing garments, designers can explore how different styles can be blended, resulting in innovative and unexpected pieces. This capability fosters creativity and allows designers to create collections that stand out in a competitive market.

AI is also playing a crucial role in trend forecasting. AI can identify emerging trends and consumer preferences by analyzing social media data, fashion blogs, and e-commerce platforms. This data-driven approach enables brands to stay ahead of the curve, ensuring their designs resonate with target audiences. Companies like Edited provide AI-powered analytics tools that help fashion retailers make informed decisions about inventory, pricing, and marketing strategies based on real-time data.

Moreover, AI is enhancing the personalization of fashion experiences for consumers. Virtual fitting rooms powered by AI allow shoppers to visualize how clothing will look on them before making a purchase. Augmented Reality (AR) and computer vision enable customers to try on clothes virtually, reducing the likelihood of returns and enhancing customer satisfaction. Brands like Zalando and ASOS have already implemented such features, creating a more engaging and tailored shopping experience.

In addition to design and retail, AI influences sustainable fashion practices. By optimizing supply chains and production processes, AI can help reduce waste and minimize the environmental impact of fashion manufacturing. For example, AI algorithms can predict demands more accurately, allowing brands to produce only what is needed, thereby reducing overproduction and excess inventory. This approach aligns with the growing consumer demand for sustainable and ethically produced fashion.

However, integrating AI into fashion design raises essential questions about creativity and originality. As AI systems generate designs based on existing styles, concerns about losing the human touch and fashion authenticity arise. Can AI truly replicate the emotional depth and cultural significance that human designers bring to their work? Furthermore, copyright and intellectual property issues come into play, as AI-generated designs may inadvertently infringe on existing trademarks or styles.

AI transforms the fashion industry by enhancing design processes, optimizing production, and personalizing consumer experiences. As designers and brands embrace these technologies, they can unlock new creative possibilities and respond to the evolving demands of the market. However, navigating the ethical implications and balancing technology and human creativity in the fashion landscape is essential.

5.5. Video and Image Synthesis

The applications of AI in video and image synthesis are rapidly evolving, offering innovative tools for content creation, editing, and manipulation. Generative AI technologies are transforming visual media, enabling creators to explore new artistic possibilities while raising critical ethical considerations.

One of the most prominent applications of AI in video synthesis is the creation of deepfake technology. Deepfakes use GANs to generate realistic videos where individuals appear to say or do things they never actually did. This technology has garnered significant attention for its potential in entertainment, allowing filmmakers to create realistic visual effects or resurrect deceased actors for new performances. However, deepfakes also pose severe ethical challenges, as they can be misused to spread misinformation or damage reputations. The ability to create hyper-realistic videos raises questions about trust and authenticity in visual media.

AI is also enhancing traditional video editing processes. Tools like Adobe Premiere Pro and Final Cut Pro incorporate AI features that automate scene detection, color correction, and audio enhancement tasks. These capabilities streamline the editing workflow, allowing creators to focus on storytelling rather than getting bogged down by technical details. For instance, AI can analyze footage and suggest the best shots for a scene, saving editors valuable time and effort.

In image synthesis, AI technologies create stunning visual effects and enhance image quality. Super-resolution algorithms, for example, can upscale low-resolution images, adding detail and clarity that was not present in the original. This technology is precious in the photography, gaming, and film industries, where high-quality visuals are essential for engaging audiences.

Another exciting application of AI in image synthesis is style transfer, where the visual characteristics of one image can be applied to another. This technique allows artists and designers to create unique visuals by blending different styles and aesthetics. For instance, an artist could take a photograph and apply the style of a famous painting, resulting in a visually striking piece that merges photography and traditional art.

AI-generated imagery is also making waves in the advertising and marketing sectors. Brands are using AI to create personalized advertisements that resonate with specific audiences. AI can generate tailored visuals and messages that enhance engagement and conversion rates by analyzing consumer data and preferences. This data-driven approach allows marketers to create more effective campaigns that speak directly to their target demographics.

However, the rise of AI in video and image synthesis raises ethical concerns regarding authenticity and copyright. As AI-generated content becomes more prevalent, distinguishing between human-created and machine-generated visuals may become increasingly challenging. This blurring of lines raises questions about the ownership of AI-generated content and the potential for misuse in creating misleading or harmful media.

Furthermore, the implications of AI-generated visuals extend to art and creativity. While AI can produce visually stunning images, can it replicate the emotional depth and cultural significance that human artists bring to their work? The debate over the role of AI in creative expression continues as artists and technologists explore the boundaries of machine-generated art.

AI is revolutionizing video and image synthesis, providing creators with powerful tools to enhance their work and explore new artistic avenues. As technology advances, it is essential to navigate the ethical implications and redefine our understanding of authenticity and creativity in the digital age. Visual media's future promises to be exciting and complex as AI plays an increasingly central role in shaping how we create and consume visual content.

6. PRACTICAL IMPLICATIONS

6.1. Natural Language Processing (NLP) Applications

Generative AI has significantly advanced the field of NLP, enabling various applications such as language translation, text summarization, and dialogue generation (Kumar, 2013). In language translation, generative models, particularly Large Language Models (LLMs), have enhanced machine translation capabilities, allowing for more accurate and context-aware translations. Techniques like neural machine translation leverage deep learning to maintain sentence structure and meaning across languages. For example, Google's Transformer model has achieved state-of-the-art performance on various translation tasks, outperforming previous statistical and rule-based approaches. These models can produce more fluent and natural translations by capturing long-range dependencies and understanding context.

Text summarization is another area where generative AI excels. AI models can automatically generate concise summaries of longer texts, making information more accessible. This involves understanding and rephrasing the main ideas effectively, which is crucial for applications in news aggregation and academic research. OpenAI's GPT-3 model has been used to generate high-quality summaries of articles, capturing the key points and insights while maintaining coherence. Researchers have also developed techniques like extractive summarization, where the most important sentences are identified and extracted from the original text, and abstractive summarization, where the summary is generated from scratch using natural language generation.

Dialogue generation is another critical application of generative AI in NLP. Chatbots and virtual assistants utilize generative AI to create human-like conversational responses. These systems are trained on vast datasets to understand context and user intent, improving customer service and engagement. For instance, Microsoft's XiaoIce chatbot has been designed to engage in long-term, empathetic conversations, building user relationships over time. By learning from human conversations and adapting its responses based on context, XiaoIce can maintain coherent and engaging dialogues.

Generative AI has also been applied to other NLP tasks, such as question answering, where models can answer questions accurately based on given information. This is particularly useful in educational settings and knowledge-sharing platforms. Researchers have also explored the use of generative AI for creative writing, where models can generate coherent and imaginative stories, poems, and scripts. While these applications are still in their early stages, they demonstrate the potential of generative AI to augment and enhance human creativity and productivity in NLP.

6.2. Computer Vision Applications

In computer vision, generative AI is applied to various tasks, including image generation, object detection, and image segmentation. Image generation is a fascinating application where models like GANs can create realistic images from scratch. This is useful in fields such as advertising and art, where AI-generated images can create unique and eye-catching visuals. For example, Nvidia's StyleGAN model can generate high-resolution, photorealistic images of human faces with impressive levels of detail and variation. These models learn to capture the underlying patterns and structures of images, allowing them to generate novel instances statistically similar to the training data.

Object detection is another area where generative AI enhances computer vision systems. By generating synthetic training data, models can improve their performance in identifying and classifying objects in images. This is particularly useful when real-world data is scarce or expensive to obtain. For instance, researchers have used GANs to generate realistic images of rare or dangerous objects, such as weapons or hazardous materials, to train object detection models without exposing them to actual examples. This approach helps avoid potential risks and ethical concerns while providing sufficient training data.

Image segmentation involves partitioning an image into multiple segments to simplify analysis. Generative models can assist in refining segmentation tasks, particularly in medical imaging, where precise delineation of structures is critical. For example, U-Net, a famous convolutional neural network architecture, has been used for medical image segmentation tasks such as identifying tumors or blood vessels in MRI scans. By leveraging generative models, researchers have improved the accuracy and robustness of these segmentation algorithms, leading to more reliable diagnoses and treatment planning.

Generative AI has also been applied to tasks like image inpainting, where missing or corrupted parts of an image are filled in based on the surrounding context. This can be useful for task removal, scratch removal, or restoration of damaged artwork. Models like Context Encoder and Partial Convolution have shown promising results in this area, demonstrating the ability to generate plausible and coherent image content to fill missing regions.

6.3. Healthcare Applications

Generative AI transforms healthcare through applications such as medical image analysis, disease diagnosis, and drug discovery. In medical image analysis, AI models can analyze medical images like X-rays, CT scans, and MRI scans to identify anomalies, aiding in early diagnosis. For instance, researchers have developed deep-learning models that can detect signs of breast cancer in mammograms with high accuracy, outperforming human radiologists in some cases. By leveraging generative models, these systems can enhance image quality or generate synthetic training data to improve model performance. This is particularly important in medical imaging, where data scarcity and high data collection costs can hinder the development of robust AI systems.

Disease diagnosis is another area where generative AI is making significant strides. By analyzing patient data, including medical histories, symptoms, and test results, AI models can assist in diagnosing diseases, predicting outcomes, and recommending treatment plans based on learned patterns from large datasets. For example, researchers have developed AI systems that can predict the onset of Alzheimer's disease several years before clinical symptoms appear by analyzing patterns in brain scans and cognitive test results. These models use generative techniques to learn the underlying representations of disease progression, allowing for earlier intervention and personalized treatment strategies.

Drug discovery is a complex and time-consuming process that involves screening millions of compounds to identify potential drug candidates. Generative AI is revolutionizing this field by accelerating the drug development pipeline. Researchers use generative models to predict molecular interactions and design new compounds with desired properties, such as high binding affinity to target proteins or low toxicity. For instance, Insilico Medicine has developed an AI platform called GENTRL that can design novel drug candidates for a specific target in a matter of days, compared to the traditional process that can take years. These AI systems are significantly speeding up the drug discovery process by leveraging generative models to explore vast chemical spaces and optimize drug-like properties.

Generative AI is also applied to personalized medicine, where treatment plans are tailored to individual patients based on their unique genetic profiles and medical histories. By generating synthetic patient data, AI models can learn to predict how different individuals will respond to various treatments, enabling more targeted and effective interventions. This approach can reduce adverse drug reactions, improve treatment outcomes, and ultimately lead to a more personalized and patient-centric healthcare system.

6.4. Finance and Business Applications

In finance, generative AI is utilized for fraud detection, risk assessment, and algorithmic trading tasks. Fraud detection is critical, as financial institutions face increasing threats from fraudulent activities like credit card fraud, money laundering, and identity theft. AI systems analyze transaction patterns to detect anomalies and potential fraud, improving security measures and reducing financial losses. Generative models play a crucial role in this process by learning the underlying patterns of legitimate transactions and generating synthetic data to train more robust fraud detection algorithms. For example, researchers have used GANs to generate realistic transaction data that captures real-world financial transactions' complex dependencies and temporal dynamics, enabling AI models to identify fraudulent activities better.

Risk assessment is another area where generative AI is making a significant impact in finance. By simulating various market conditions and predicting risks, AI models can help businesses make informed decisions regarding investments and resource allocation. For instance, researchers have developed generative models that can generate synthetic stock price data, capturing financial markets' complex dynamics and interdependencies. These models can stress-test investment portfolios, assess the potential impact of market shocks, and optimize risk-adjusted returns. Additionally, generative AI can be used to generate synthetic credit risk data, enabling financial institutions to assess the creditworthiness of borrowers better and make more informed lending decisions.

Algorithmic trading, where AI-driven algorithms analyze market data to execute trades at optimal times, is another application of generative AI in finance. By leveraging generative models to forecast market trends and identify profitable trading opportunities, these algorithms can generate higher returns than traditional trading strategies. For example, researchers have developed generative models to learn the complex patterns and dependencies in financial time series data, such as stock prices and macroeconomic indicators. These models can then be used to generate synthetic market data, which can be used to train and optimize trading algorithms, leading to more profitable and less risky trading decisions.

Generative AI is also applied to other business applications, such as demand forecasting, inventory optimization, and customer segmentation. By generating synthetic data that captures the complex relationships between various business variables, such as sales, customer behavior, and market trends, generative models can help businesses make more accurate predictions and optimize their operations. For instance, researchers have used GANs to generate synthetic customer data that captures the complex dependencies between customer attributes, purchase behavior, and demographic factors. This synthetic data can then train customer segmentation models, enabling businesses to understand their customer base better and tailor their marketing strategies accordingly.

6.5. Gaming and Virtual Reality (VR) Applications

Generative AI enhances gaming and VR through applications such as procedural content generation, character animation, and immersive VR environments. Procedural content generation is a technique where AI can automatically create game environments, levels, and assets, providing unique experiences for players and reducing development time. This approach is beneficial in open-world games, where the game world needs to be vast and diverse. For example, No Man's Sky, a space exploration game, uses procedural generation to create millions of unique planets, each with its terrain, flora, and fauna. By leveraging generative models, the game can generate these assets on the fly, reducing the need for manual creation and allowing for near-infinite replayability.

Character animation is another area where generative AI is making a significant impact in gaming and VR. AI can enhance immersion in gaming and virtual environments by generating realistic character movements and interactions. For instance, researchers have developed generative models that can learn from motion capture data to generate realistic human movements, such as walking, running, and jumping. These models can then be used to animate game characters, ensuring their movements are natural and responsive to player input. Additionally, generative AI can generate facial animations, allowing characters to express emotions and engage in believable conversations.

Immersive VR environments are another application of generative AI in gaming and VR. These environments become more dynamic and responsive to player actions by populating VR worlds with AI-generated content, improving user engagement and satisfaction. For example, researchers have developed generative models that can create realistic virtual environments, such as cities and landscapes, based on high-level parameters. These models can generate detailed buildings, streets, and vegetation, creating a sense of depth and realism in the virtual world. Additionally, generative AI can generate non-player characters (NPCs) that behave more realistically and engagingly, responding to player actions and engaging in meaningful conversations.

Generative AI also applies to gaming applications, such as game balancing and difficulty adjustment. By analyzing player behavior and performance data, AI models can generate optimal game settings and difficulty levels, ensuring the game remains challenging and engaging for players of all skill levels. For instance, researchers have developed generative models that can learn from player data to generate personalized game difficulty settings, adapting the game to each player's strengths and weaknesses. This approach helps to keep players engaged and motivated, reducing the likelihood of them abandoning the game due to frustration or boredom.

7. FUTURE DIRECTIONs

7.1. Challenges and Opportunities in Generative AI

Generative AI has made remarkable strides in recent years, yet it faces several challenges that must be addressed to unlock its full potential. One of the primary challenges is model robustness. Generative models, particularly those based on deep learning, can be sensitive to input variations, leading to unpredictable outputs. This unpredictability can be problematic, especially in critical applications such as healthcare, finance, and autonomous systems, where errors can have severe consequences. Researchers are actively exploring techniques to enhance robustness, such as adversarial training and ensemble methods, to ensure that generative models produce reliable outputs under various conditions.

Scalability is another significant challenge. As generative models grow in complexity and size, they require substantial computational resources for training and inference. This can limit accessibility, particularly for smaller organizations and researchers with limited resources. In regard to addressing this, there is a growing interest in developing more efficient architectures and training techniques, such as model pruning, quantization, and distillation, which can reduce the computational burden without sacrificing performance. Additionally, exploring distributed training methods and cloud-based solutions can democratize access to generative AI technologies, enabling broader participation in the field.

Ethical concerns also present a considerable challenge. Generative AI can be misused to create deepfakes, misinformation, and other harmful content, raising questions about accountability and regulation. The potential for bias in generated outputs is another critical issue, as models trained on biased datasets can perpetuate and amplify existing societal inequalities. Addressing these ethical challenges requires a multidisciplinary approach involving collaboration between technologists, ethicists, and policymakers to develop frameworks that promote responsible AI usage. This includes establishing transparency, fairness, and accountability guidelines in generative AI applications.

Despite these challenges, there are significant opportunities for growth and innovation in generative AI. The demand for personalized content is on the rise, and generative AI can play a pivotal role in meeting this need. Generative models can create tailored experiences in various domains by leveraging user data and preferences, from marketing to entertainment. Additionally, natural language processing and computer vision advancements pave the way for more sophisticated generative models that seamlessly integrate different modalities, enabling richer and more engaging user experiences.

Furthermore, the intersection of generative AI with other fields, such as neuroscience and cognitive science, holds promise for developing models that better mimic human creativity and cognition. This interdisciplinary approach can lead to breakthroughs in understanding how generative processes work in the human brain, informing the design of more effective AI systems. As researchers continue to explore these opportunities, the future of generative AI looks promising, with the potential to transform industries and enhance human creativity.

7.2. Emerging Trends and Research Directions

The landscape of generative AI is continuously evolving, with several emerging trends shaping the future of research in this field. One of the most exciting trends is multimodal generation, which involves the ability of generative models to create content across multiple modalities, such as text, images, audio, and video. This capability enables the development of more holistic AI systems that can understand and generate complex narratives that span different formats. For instance, a multimodal generative model could create a short film by generating a script, visual scenes, and accompanying music while maintaining coherence and thematic consistency.

Few-shot learning is another promising area of research in generative AI. Traditional machine learning models often require large amounts of labeled data to perform well, which can be a significant barrier in many applications. Few-shot learning aims to train models that can generalize from just a few examples, making them more adaptable and efficient. This approach is precious in domains where data is scarce or expensive to obtain, such as medical imaging or rare language translation. By developing generative models that excel in few-shot learning, researchers can create systems that are more efficient and capable of producing high-quality outputs with minimal input.

Meta-learning, or "learning to learn," is also gaining traction in generative AI research. Meta-learning algorithms enable models to adapt quickly to new tasks by leveraging prior knowledge from related tasks. This capability can significantly enhance the performance of generative models, allowing them to generate contextually relevant content based on limited input. For example, after being exposed to just a few examples, a meta-learning-based generative model could quickly adapt to generate text in a new writing style or produce artwork in a specific artistic genre. This adaptability is crucial for applications that require rapid iteration and personalization.

Another emerging trend is the focus on explainability and interpretability in generative AI. As generative models become more complex, understanding how they arrive at specific outputs becomes increasingly important. Researchers are exploring methods to make generative models more transparent, allowing users to comprehend the decision-making processes behind generated content. This focus on explainability is essential for building trust in AI systems, particularly in sensitive applications such as healthcare and legal domains.

In addition to these trends, a growing interest in sustainability within generative AI research exists. As the environmental impact of large-scale AI models becomes more apparent, researchers are seeking ways to reduce the carbon footprint associated with training and deploying generative models. This includes developing more energy-efficient architectures, optimizing training algorithms, and exploring alternative approaches such as federated learning, which allows models to be trained on decentralized data sources without compromising privacy.

Overall, the emerging trends in generative AI research present exciting opportunities for innovation and advancement. By exploring multimodal generation, few-shot learning, meta-learning, explainability, and sustainability, researchers can push the boundaries of what generative AI can achieve, leading to more powerful and versatile systems that can benefit various industries and applications.

7.3. Integration with Other AI Techniques

The integration of generative AI with other AI techniques presents a promising avenue for enhancing performance and expanding the capabilities of AI systems. One of the most notable integrations is with Reinforcement Learning (RL). In traditional generative models, the focus is often on producing high-quality outputs based on a given input. However, by incorporating reinforcement learning, generative models can be trained to optimize their outputs based on feedback from the environment or user interactions. This approach allows generative models to learn from their successes and failures, improving performance over time.

For instance, in the context of game design, a generative model could create levels or characters while receiving feedback on their playability and user engagement. By leveraging reinforcement learning, the model can iteratively refine its outputs to enhance user experience and satisfaction. This integration improves generated content quality and enables the model to adapt to user preferences and changing trends, making it a valuable tool for dynamic environments.

Transfer learning is another powerful technique that can be integrated with generative AI. Transfer learning allows models to leverage knowledge gained from one task and apply it to another, which is particularly beneficial in situations where labeled data is scarce. For generative models, this means that a model trained on a large dataset in one domain can be fine-tuned to generate content in a related domain with minimal additional training. This capability can significantly reduce the time and resources required to develop high-performing generative models across various applications.

For example, a generative model trained on a vast corpus of English literature could be adapted to create poetry in a less-represented language, drawing on its understanding of narrative structures and stylistic elements. This approach accelerates the development process and democratizes access to generative AI capabilities across different languages and cultures.

As previously mentioned, meta-learning also plays a crucial role in enhancing generative AI performance. By combining meta-learning with generative models, researchers can create systems that quickly adapt to new tasks and generate content that aligns with specific requirements. This integration is particularly valuable in creative industries, where the ability to produce contextually relevant and high-quality content on demand is essential. For instance, a meta-learning-enabled generative model could learn to create marketing materials tailored to different target audiences based on minimal input, streamlining the content creation process for businesses.

Moreover, integrating generative AI with unsupervised learning techniques can lead to more robust models capable of discovering patterns and structures within unlabelled data. This integration allows generative models to learn from vast amounts of data without extensive labeling, making them more efficient and scalable. By harnessing the power of unsupervised learning, generative models can generate content that reflects underlying trends and characteristics in the data, leading to more authentic and relevant outputs.

Integrating generative AI with other AI techniques also opens up new possibilities for interdisciplinary research. For example, combining generative AI with cognitive science and neuroscience techniques can lead to models that better mimic human creativity and cognition. By understanding how humans generate ideas and concepts, researchers can design generative models that emulate these processes, resulting in more sophisticated and nuanced outputs.

In summary, integrating generative AI with reinforcement learning, transfer learning, meta-learning, and unsupervised learning presents exciting opportunities for enhancing performance and expanding the capabilities of AI systems. By leveraging these techniques, researchers can develop generative models that are more efficient and adaptable and capable of producing high-quality content that meets the diverse needs of users across various domains.

7.4. Human-AI Collaboration and Co-Creation

The concept of human-AI collaboration and co-creation is transforming the creative landscape, offering new avenues for artistic expression and innovation. Generative AI is a powerful tool that can augment human creativity, enabling artists, musicians, writers, and other creators to explore new ideas and push the boundaries of their work. This collaboration is not about replacing human creativity but enhancing it, allowing for a synergistic relationship between humans and machines.

In the realm of visual arts, generative AI has already made significant strides. Artists can use AI algorithms to generate unique visual compositions, explore different styles, and experiment with color palettes. For instance, tools like DeepArt and Artbreeder allow users to blend their images with AI-generated art, resulting in novel creations that reflect human and machine input. This collaborative approach can inspire artists to think outside the box and explore new artistic directions they may not have considered otherwise.

Similarly, generative AI can assist musicians in creating melodies, harmonies, and arrangements in music composition. AI-driven platforms like Amper Music and OpenAI's MuseNet enable musicians to collaborate with AI to compose original pieces, offering suggestions and variations based on user input. This collaboration can lead to innovative musical styles and genres, as musicians can leverage AI's ability to analyze vast amounts of musical data and generate compositions that blend different influences.

In the realm of storytelling and writing, generative AI can serve as a brainstorming partner, helping authors generate plot ideas, character descriptions, and dialogue. Tools like GPT-3 and other language models can assist writers in overcoming creative blocks by providing prompts and suggestions that spark inspiration. This collaborative process allows writers to explore multiple narrative possibilities and refine their ideas, ultimately leading to more affluent and more engaging stories.

Moreover, human-AI collaboration extends beyond individual creative tasks to encompass collective creativity. In collaborative environments, teams can leverage generative AI to co-create content, whether it's designing marketing campaigns, developing video games, or producing films. By integrating AI into the creative workflow, teams can streamline the ideation process, generate diverse concepts, and enhance the overall quality of their projects.

The potential for human-AI collaboration also raises important questions about authorship and ownership. As AI-generated content becomes more prevalent, discussions around intellectual property rights and ethical considerations are becoming increasingly relevant. Who owns the rights to a piece of art created with AI? How do we attribute credit for collaborative works? Addressing these questions will be crucial for establishing clear guidelines and frameworks that govern the relationship between human creators and AI systems.

Furthermore, integrating generative AI into creative processes can foster inclusivity and diversity in artistic expression. By providing tools that enable individuals from various backgrounds and skill levels to engage in creative endeavors, generative AI can democratize access to artistic creation. This inclusivity can lead to a richer tapestry of voices and perspectives in the creative landscape, ultimately enriching the cultural fabric of society.

The potential for human-AI collaboration and co-creation is vast as we look to the future. By embracing generative AI as a partner in the creative process, individuals and teams can unlock new possibilities for innovation and expression. This collaborative approach enhances creativity and challenges traditional notions of authorship and creativity, paving the way for a more inclusive and dynamic creative ecosystem.

7.4. Speculations on the Future of Generative AI

The future of generative AI holds immense potential for transforming various aspects of society, creativity, and innovation. As research and development in this field continue to advance, we can speculate on several key trends and impacts that may shape the trajectory of generative AI in the coming years.

One of the most significant impacts of generative AI will likely be its influence on the creative industries. As generative models become more sophisticated, they will enable artists, writers, musicians, and designers to explore new forms of expression and storytelling. The ability to generate high-quality content quickly and efficiently will empower creators to experiment with diverse styles, genres, and formats, leading to a renaissance of artistic innovation. We may witness the emergence of entirely new art forms that blend human creativity with AI-generated elements, resulting in unique and immersive experiences for audiences.

Moreover, generative AI is expected to play a pivotal role in personalized content creation. As consumers increasingly seek tailored experiences, generative models can analyze user preferences and behaviors to generate content that resonates with individuals on a personal level. This personalization can extend to various domains, including marketing, entertainment, and education. For example, generative AI could create customized learning materials for students based on their learning styles and interests, enhancing engagement and retention.

In addition to its impact on creativity, generative AI may also revolutionize industries such as healthcare, finance, and design. In healthcare, generative models can assist in drug discovery by simulating molecular interactions and generating potential compounds for testing. This capability can accelerate the development of new treatments and therapies, ultimately improving patient outcomes. In finance, generative AI can analyze market trends and generate predictive models to inform investment strategies, enabling more informed decision-making.

As generative AI continues to evolve, ethical considerations will remain at the forefront of discussions surrounding its deployment. The potential for misuse, such as creating deepfakes and misinformation, poses significant challenges that society must address. Developing robust ethical frameworks and guidelines for responsible

AI usage will ensure that generative AI is harnessed for positive purposes. This includes fostering transparency, accountability, and fairness in developing and applying generative models.

Furthermore, the future of generative AI may see increased collaboration between humans and machines, leading to new paradigms of creativity and innovation. As AI systems become more capable of understanding human intent and context, they will serve as valuable partners in the creative process. This collaboration can enhance human creativity by providing new perspectives, insights, and inspiration, ultimately leading to groundbreaking ideas and solutions.

Speculating on the future of generative AI also raises questions about the nature of creativity itself. As AI-generated content becomes more prevalent, we may need to redefine our understanding of creativity and authorship. What does it mean to be creative in a world where machines can generate art, music, and literature? This philosophical inquiry will challenge traditional notions of artistic expression and prompt society to reevaluate the role of human creators in an increasingly automated landscape.

In conclusion, the future of generative AI is poised to bring about transformative changes across various sectors, enhancing creativity, personalization, and innovation. By embracing the potential of generative AI while addressing ethical considerations, society can harness its capabilities to create a more inclusive, dynamic, and creative future. As we navigate this evolving landscape, the collaboration between humans and AI will play a crucial role in shaping the next generation of artistic expression and technological advancement.

SUMMARY

Generative AI is a groundbreaking approach in artificial intelligence that focuses on creating new data instances that resemble a given dataset. Unlike traditional AI, which often relies on classification or regression, generative models learn the underlying data distribution to generate novel instances. A prominent application of generative AI is in image generation, exemplified by Generative Adversarial Networks (GANs), which can create hyper-realistic images of non-existent faces. Generative models can be categorized into several types, including GANs, Variational Autoencoders (VAEs), diffusion models, and normalizing flows. Each has unique characteristics and applications. GANs operate through a two-network system: a generator that creates data and a discriminator that evaluates it. This adversarial setup enhances the quality of the generated outputs.

VAEs, on the other hand, learn a latent representation of the input data, allowing for the generation of new samples that maintain the diversity of the training data. Diffusion models generate high-quality images by adding and then removing noise from data. Generative AI has vast implications across various industries, including entertainment, healthcare, and fashion. Entertainment can create realistic animations; in healthcare, it can synthesize medical images for training purposes; and in fashion, it can generate new clothing designs. Additionally, generative AI raises philosophical questions about creativity and originality, challenging traditional notions of authorship and art.

Moreover, techniques like conditional generation, style transfer, and reinforcement learning enhance generative modeling. Conditional Generative Adversarial Networks (cGANs) allow for image generation based on specific attributes, while style transfer can transform images into the artistic styles of famous painters. Reinforcement learning optimizes generative models by enabling them to create diverse and engaging outputs based on user feedback. Overall, generative AI represents a significant advancement in artificial intelligence, potentially redefining creativity and collaboration between humans and machines.

REFERENCES

Bao, J., Li, L., & Davis, A. (2022). Variational autoencoder or generative adversarial networks? a comparison of two deep learning methods for flow and transport data assimilation. *Mathematical Geosciences*, *54*(6), 1017–1042. DOI: 10.1007/s11004-022-10003-3

Chen, M., Mei, S., Fan, J., & Wang, M. (2024). An overview of diffusion models: Applications, guided generation, statistical rates and optimization. *arXiv*, *34*(2), 25-39.

Chrysos, G., Georgopoulos, M., & Panagakis, Y. (2021). Conditional generation using polynomial expansions. *Advances in Neural Information Processing Systems*, *34*(1), 28390–28404.

Colins, M. (2017). *Machine learning: an introduction to supervised and unsupervised learning algorithms*. CreateSpace.

Feuerriegel, S., Hartmann, J., Janiesch, C., & Zschech, P. (2024). Generative AI. *Business & Information Systems Engineering*, *66*(1), 111–126. DOI: 10.1007/s12599-023-00834-7

Goodfellow, I., Pouget-Abadie, J., Mirza, M., Xu, B., Warde-Farley, D., Ozair, S., & Bengio, Y. (2020). Generative adversarial networks. *Communications of the ACM*, *63*(11), 139–144. DOI: 10.1145/3422622

Gulrajani, I., Ahmed, F., Arjovsky, M., Dumoulin, V., & Courville, A. C. (2017). Improved training of Wasserstein gans. *Advances in Neural Information Processing Systems*, *30*(1), 56–68.

Huang, L. (2022). *Normalization techniques in deep learning*. Springer. DOI: 10.1007/978-3-031-14595-7

Jing, Y., Yang, Y., Feng, Z., Ye, J., Yu, Y., & Song, M. (2019). Neural style transfer: A review. *IEEE Transactions on Visualization and Computer Graphics*, *26*(11), 3365–3385. DOI: 10.1109/TVCG.2019.2921336 PMID: 31180860

Kingma, D. P., & Welling, M. (2013). Auto-encoding variational bayes. *arXiv*, *11*(4), 26-39.

Klys, J., Snell, J., & Zemel, R. (2018). Learning latent subspaces in variational autoencoders. *Advances in Neural Information Processing Systems*, *31*(3), 45–58.

Kumar, E. (2013). *Natural language processing*. IK International Pvt Ltd.

Miyato, T., & Koyama, M. (2018). cGANs with projection discriminator. *arXiv, 26*(3), 180-189.

Ris-Ala, R. (2023). *Fundamentals of reinforcement learning*. Springer. DOI: 10.1007/978-3-031-37345-9

Rodriguez, P., Velazquez, D., Cucurull, G., Gonfaus, J. M., Roca, F. X., & Gonzalez, J. (2019). Pay attention to the activations: A modular attention mechanism for fine-grained image recognition. *IEEE Transactions on Multimedia, 22*(2), 502–514. DOI: 10.1109/TMM.2019.2928494

Santos, O., & Radanliev, P. (2024). *Beyond the algorithm: AI, security, privacy, and ethics*. Addison-Wesley.

Saxena, D., & Cao, J. (2021). Generative adversarial networks (GANs) challenges, solutions, and future directions. *ACM Computing Surveys, 54*(3), 1–42. DOI: 10.1145/3446374

Walters, R., & Novak, M. (2021). *Cyber security, artificial intelligence, data protection & the law*. Springer. DOI: 10.1007/978-981-16-1665-5

Yu, X., & Gen, M. (2010). *Introduction to evolutionary algorithms*. Springer Science & Business Media. DOI: 10.1007/978-1-84996-129-5

Yuan, C., & Moghaddam, M. (2020). Attribute-aware generative design with generative adversarial networks. *IEEE Access : Practical Innovations, Open Solutions, 8*(1), 190710–190721. DOI: 10.1109/ACCESS.2020.3032280

ADDITIONAL READING

Banh, L., & Strobel, G. (2023). Generative artificial intelligence. *Electronic Markets, 33*(1), 63–75. DOI: 10.1007/s12525-023-00680-1

Cheng, K., & Wu, H. (2024). Policy framework for the utilization of generative AI. *Critical Care, 28*(1), 128–139. DOI: 10.1186/s13054-024-04917-z PMID: 38637898

Euchner, J. (2023). Generative AI. *Research Technology Management, 66*(3), 71–74. DOI: 10.1080/08956308.2023.2188861

Feuerriegel, S., Hartmann, J., Janiesch, C., & Zschech, P. (2024). Generative AI. *Business & Information Systems Engineering, 66*(1), 111–126. DOI: 10.1007/s12599-023-00834-7

Fui-Hoon Nah, F., Zheng, R., Cai, J., Siau, K., & Chen, L. (2023). Generative AI and ChatGPT: Applications, challenges, and AI-human collaboration. *Journal of Information Technology Case and Application Research*, *25*(3), 277–304. DOI: 10.1080/15228053.2023.2233814

Jo, A. (2023). The promise and peril of generative AI. *Nature*, *614*(1), 214–216.

KEY TERMS AND DEFINITIONS

Conditional Generative Adversarial Networks (cGANs): cGANs are an extension of GANs that generate data based on specific conditions or labels, allowing for targeted data generation, such as creating images of a particular category and enhancing control over the output.

Evolutionary Algorithms (EAs): An evolutionary algorithm is an optimization algorithm inspired by natural evolution. It is used to find approximate solutions to optimization problems, such as finding the minimum or maximum of a function.

Generative Adversarial Networks (GANs): GANs are a machine learning framework consisting of two networks: a generator that creates synthetic data and a discriminator that evaluates its authenticity. They are widely used for generating high-quality images and other data types.

Generative Artificial Intelligence (GEN AI): GEN AI refers to AI systems capable of creating new content—such as images, text, or music—by learning patterns from existing data. It encompasses various technologies, including GANs and VAEs, and is used in creative and data synthesis applications.

Variational Autoencoders (VAEs): VAEs are generative models that encode input data into a latent space and then decode it back to reconstruct the data. They allow for the generation of new, similar data instances and are helpful in image generation and anomaly detection.

Wasserstein GANs (WGANs): WGANs are a variant of GANs that use the Wasserstein distance as a loss function, improving training stability and convergence. They effectively generate high-quality images and address issues found in traditional GANs.

Chapter 6
A Review of Advances in Computer Vision, Multi/Hyperspectral Imaging, UAVs, and Agri-Bots

Muhammad Jawad Bashir
https://orcid.org/0000-0003-0942-7820
National University of Sciences and Technology, Pakistan

Rafia Mumtaz
National University of Sciences and Technology, Pakistan

ABSTRACT

Agriculture is vital to economic growth, contributing 4% to global GDP and over 25% in some developing countries. Most farming practices are outdated, necessitating modernization for improved efficiency. Advances in deep learning, multi- and hyperspectral imagery (MHSI), UAVs, and agri-bots have revolutionized precision agriculture (PA). Computer vision (CV) techniques, enhanced by MHSI, have automated tasks like crop classification, disease monitoring, and biomass estimation. UAVs assist in field scouting, disease detection, and precision spraying, while agri-bots with IoT sensors facilitate real-time data-driven actions such as fruit picking and weed control. This chapter reviews the latest developments in CV, MHSI, UAVs, and agri-bots, examining current methods, challenges, datasets, and future applications in precision agriculture.

DOI: 10.4018/979-8-3693-6255-6.ch006

INTRODUCTION

The necessity for increased food production, driven by an exponentially growing global population, has imposed unprecedented stress on the agricultural industry. This demand calls for innovative strategies to boost crop yields while minimizing input costs. Precision agriculture has emerged as a promising solution, leveraging sophisticated digital technologies and advanced analytics to optimize crop production processes and mitigate environmental impacts. Key technologies in this domain include computer vision, multispectral and hyperspectral imagery (MHSI), unmanned aerial vehicles (UAVs), and agri-bots equipped with IoT sensors. This chapter aims to elucidate contemporary technological advancements in precision agriculture and highlight critical research gaps requiring scholarly attention.

Recent breakthroughs in precision agriculture have opened up a new realm of possibilities for agricultural research. By leveraging modern technology in the form of sensors, drones, and other digital tools, precision agriculture has enabled us to better understand and manage the crop environment. By assessing environmental factors in real-time and responding to them with precision, we can drastically improve crop yields, reduce the amount of water and energy used, and even limit the need for chemical inputs.

Furthermore, the use of digital tools and platforms has allowed us to collect and analyze data more efficiently and accurately. This has led to improved efficiency, increased productivity, and more sustainable farming practices (Mohamed, et al., 2021). As such, the potential benefits of precision agriculture are manifold and have opened up a wealth of opportunities for further research. This paper will examine the current state of precision agriculture and explore avenues for further development.

Deep learning (DL) is crucial in precision agriculture, analyzing data from UAVs and IoT sensors to monitor crop health. DL algorithms identify patterns and predict trends, optimizing yields and reducing costs. Integrating computer vision with spectral features enhances plant health insights.

UAVs are vital for scalability and autonomy, capturing high-resolution images to identify crop health and soil composition. This data guides decisions on fertilizer application and irrigation, improving farming efficiency. UAVs also detect pests, diseases, and weeds for timely interventions to protect crops.

Multispectral and hyperspectral imaging (MHSI) are vital in precision agriculture, capturing data across the electromagnetic spectrum to reveal unique spectral signatures. MHSI aids climate change mitigation by monitoring carbon stocks and facilitates early disease detection by identifying plant diseases before visible symptoms. This preemptive approach reduces crop losses and optimizes yield and quality. Additionally, MHSI provides detailed nutrient monitoring, enabling precise fertilization strategies by detecting specific nutrient deficiencies, surpassing visible spectrum imaging.

The integration of IoT sensors is essential in precision agriculture, monitoring soil moisture, temperature, and nutrient levels to provide real-time data. This data helps farmers make informed decisions to optimize crop production and reduce costs. Additionally, agri-bots like FarmBot (Aronson, 2013) use data from UAVs, IoT sensors, and deep learning to monitor fields, detect pests, diseases, and weeds, and apply necessary treatments. Innovations in UAVs, IoT sensors, computer vision, and agri-bots are rapidly advancing precision agriculture, enhancing crop yields and reducing costs.

This chapter provides:

1. An overview of recent advancements in precision agriculture, encompassing computer vision, UAVs, hyperspectral imaging (HSI), and agri-bots within the IoT framework.
2. A curated selection of high-impact studies, ensuring the inclusion of influential research.
3. A comparative analysis of contemporary deep learning and spectral imaging techniques, evaluating their efficacy and limitations.
4. A summary of recent datasets and challenges in computer vision tasks for precision agriculture, highlighting current trends and research gaps.
5. A proposal for integrating spectral imaging and air quality monitoring with the existing FarmBot architecture to improve crop profiling and disease assessment.

This chapter reviews the methodology (PRISMA), developments in precision agriculture focusing on computer vision, multispectral and hyperspectral imaging (MHSI), UAVs, and agri-bots, future directions, and a comprehensive conclusion.

REVIEW METHODOLOGY

This chapter adheres to PRISMA (Preferred Reporting Items for Systematic Reviews and Meta-Analyses), selecting studies from Google Scholar, MDPI, and Elsevier, and assessing them for eligibility, novelty, and quality. Data extraction and analysis identified insights and trends, with results systematically organized for clarity.

Figure 1 presents a flowchart delineating the survey and selection methodology for the articles incorporated into this review. Figure 2 provides a visual representation, via a word cloud, of the keywords extracted from the reviewed articles. The temporal distribution and the journal origins of the reviewed articles are depicted in Figure 3 and Figure 4, respectively.

Figure 1. PRISMA flow diagram of review methodology

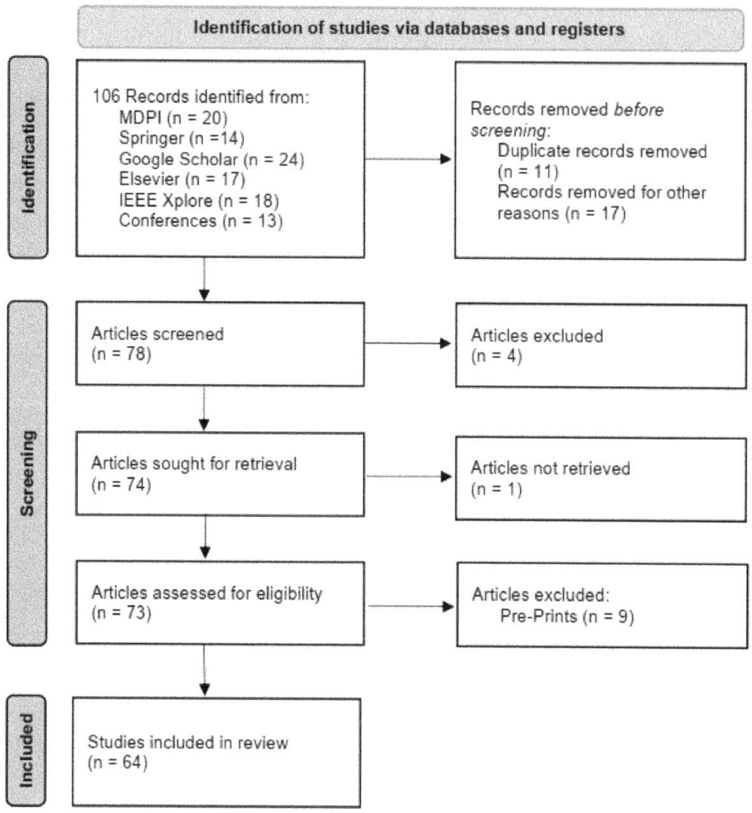

Figure 2. A visual illustration of keywords frequently used in reviewed articles

Figure 3. Distribution of reviewed articles

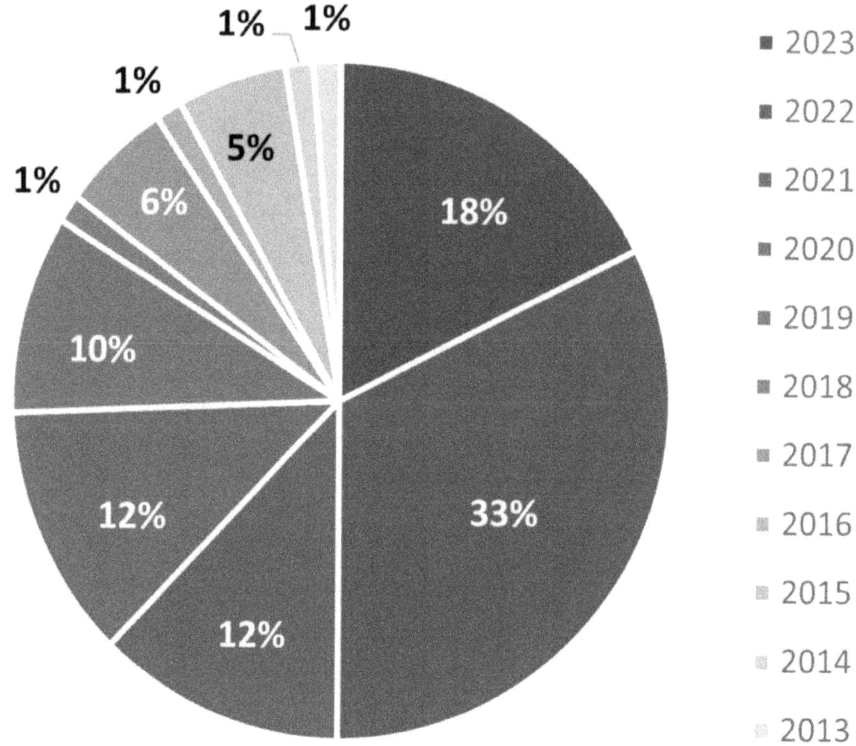

Figure 4. Reviewed articles, their respective journals, and impact factors

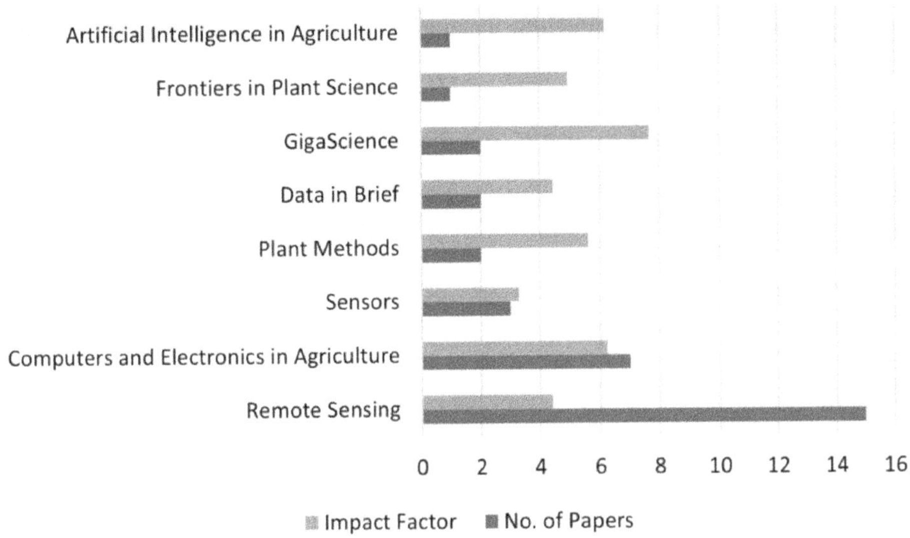

APPLICATIONS OF COMPUTER VISION IN PRECISION AGRICULTURE

Computer Vision (CV) has been increasingly used in precision agriculture to optimize crop performance and yield. By leveraging cameras, sensors and other machine learning algorithms that are easily deployed, farmers are able to leverage computer vision to detect pests and other diseases in the earliest stages, enabling early crop protection (Terentev, Dolzhenko, Fedotov, & Eremenko, 2022). Additionally, it enables low-cost monitoring and detection with higher accuracy than traditional methods, while reducing labor costs and crop loss. Following are the challenging avenues in Precision Agriculture that computer vision can offer solutions to:

1. **Automated Seed Detection:** To create an automated system for detecting seeds in soil. This can help farmers improve crop yield and crop quality.
2. **Disease Detection:** Crop diseases should be detected at their early stage in order to minimize the usage of pesticides.
3. **Weed Detection and Control:** To detect weeds and other forms of crop pests in order to reduce the number of herbicides and pesticides used.

4. **Soil Analysis:** To analyze soil properties such as pH, moisture, and nutrient levels in order to optimize crop growth.
5. **Irrigation System Automation:** To automate an irrigation system so that the crops are supplied with the right amount of water at the right time.
6. **Crop Yield Prediction:** To predict crop yield in order to maximize profits for the farmer. Multi- and hyperspectral imagery can be used to determine multiple vegetation indices to monitor multiple perspectives of crop health and to find their correlation with yield prediction (Candiago, Remondino, De Giglio, Dubbini, & Gattelli, 2015).
7. **Crop Phenotyping:** To analyze crop phenotypes in order to identify and select high-yielding plants for breeding.

The authors categorized numerous papers on computer vision applications in precision agriculture into four groups: Plant Disease Monitoring, Plant Seedling Monitoring, Crop & Weed Detection, and Plant Leaf Segmentation. They summarized the main information from each paper in Table 1, enumerated recent challenges in the field in Table 2, and provided a concise list of publicly available datasets along with their modality, crop type, and application type in Table 3.

Table 1. A survey of computer vision applications in precision agriculture

Paper	Method	Target	Result	Crop
(Reedha, Dericquebourg, Canals, & Hafiane, 2022)	ViT	Weed Crop Classification	F1Score: 99.4% (ViTB-16), 99.2% (ViT B-32)	Beet, Parsley and Spinach
(Li, Zhang, & Wang, 2022)	ViT (B16) + CNNs (ShuffleNet, EfficientNet-B0, MobileNet V3, RegNet)	Leaf Disease Classification	Accuracy: 99.23% (RegNet)	Apple
(Quan, et al., 2019)	Faster R-CNN (Customized)	Seedling Detection	Precision: 97.71% (F-RCNN)	Maize
(Peteinatos, Reichel, Karouta, Andújar, & Gerhards, 2020)	CNNs (VGG16, ResNet-50, Xception)	Weed and Plant Classification	Accuracy: 98% (Xception) 97% (ResNet50)	Maize, Sunflower and Potatoes
(Liu & Wang, 2020)	YOLO-v3	Pests Leaf Disease Detection	Accuracy: 92.39%	Tomato
(Jiang, Li, Paterson, & Robertson, 2019)	Faster-RCNN (feature extractor: Inception ResNet-v2)	Seedling Counting & Detection	F1 Score: 72.7% (IOU all), 96.9% (IOU 0.5)	Cotton

continued on following page

Table 1. Continued

Paper	Method	Target	Result	Crop
(Li, et al., 2022)	FCM + FHLSl (Framework of tray whole location and seedling identification)	Seedling Planting Control System	Accuracy: 92.35% Improvement in Planting: 15.5%	Tomato
(Yadav, et al., 2022)	YOLO-v5	Multi-stage Crop Identification	Accuracy: 98% (Max) 85% (Min)	Maize & Cotton
(Peng, et al., 2022)	DeNet	Plant Density Estimation	RMSE: 17.25% MAE: 12.63% (plants/ patch)	Wheat
(Yang, Yang, Hao, Xie, & Li, 2019)	CNN (10 layers)	Cold Damage Detection	Correlation Confidence: 82.19%	Maize
(Rasti, et al., 2021)	CNN (5 layers), VGG19 & SVM	Crop Growth Stage Determination	Accuracy: 94.2% (CNN) 99.7% (VGG19) 65.1% (SVM)	Wheat & Barley
(Ratnayake, Amarathunga, Zaman, Dyer, & Dorin, 2022)	CNN (5 layers), VGG19 & SVM	Insect Monitoring for Precision Pollination	Mean F1Score: 88%	Strawberry
(Yu, Xie, & Huang, 2023)	ViT (ICVT)	Plant Disease Identification	Accuracy: 99.94% (Village Plant) 99.22% (Ibean) 77.54% (PlantDoc)	Multi-crop (Apple, Pepper, Maize & Tomato)
(Salazar-Gomez, Darbyshire, Gao, Sklar, & Parsons, 2022)	YOLO-v5 & F-RCNN	Precision Spraying	WCR (Weed Coverage Rate): 96.96% (YOLO-v5) 95.03% (YOLO-v3) 92.8% (F-RCNN)	Sugar Beet
(Han, Hao, Sun, Xue, & Li, 2022)	YOLO-v5-AT2	Crop Maturity Detection	Accuracy: 81.25% (Green Tomato) 92.77% (Red Tomato)	Tomato
(Zhang, Huang, Zhou, Hu, & Li, 2023)	MAORANet	Leaf Disease Detection	Accuracy: 96.47%	Tomato

Table 2. Computer vision challenges in precision agriculture

Challenge Name	Crop	Target	Dataset(s)	Active Year(s)	Link
Global Wheat Challenge	Wheat	Wheat Head Counting, Crop Segmentation	GWHD20, GWHD21, 6000 Total Images (1024x1024), 300k+ instances	2020, 2021	C1
Sorghum Biomass Prediction	Sorghum	Biomass Prediction	277,327 images of 176 sorghum species	2021	C2
Arabidopsis Root Segmentation Challenge	Arabidopsis	Root Segmentation	Video Sequence Dataset	2021	C3
Leaf Segmentation Challenge	Tobacco, Arabidopsis	Leaf Instance Segmentation	284 Total Images (4 sets)	2014, 2017, 2021	C4
Leaf Counting Challenge	Tobacco, Arabidopsis	Leaf Counting, Key Point Detection	284 Total Images (4 sets)	2014, 2017, 2021	C5
FungiCLEF	Fungi	Species Identification	295,938 Training Images, 118676 Test Images	2022	C6
Herbarium Challenge	Vascular Plants	Species Identification	1.05M images	2022	C7
Sorghum Cultivars	Sorghum	Cultivar Prediction	Sorghum-100 Dataset (48106 images)	2022	C8
Cassava Leaf Disease Challenge	Cassava	Leaf Disease Identification	Cassava Leaf Dataset (Uganda) - 21367 images	2020	C9
Plant Pathology	Apple	Leaf Disease Identification	23000 RGB Images	2020, 2021	C10

Table 3. A survey of computer vision datasets in precision agriculture

Dataset	Modality	Application	Size	Crop(s)	Link
(Lac, Keresztes, Louargant, Donias, & Costa, 2022)	RGB Images (Annotated)	Crop Detection, Weed Detection	Total: 2801, Annotated: 2610	Maize, Leek, Bean	D1
(Nascimento, Ribeiro, Silva, Capobiango, & Silva, 2022)	RGB Images (Annotated)	Genotype Classification, Soil Condition Classification	Total: 1026 (30 Genotypes)	Soybean Seedlings	D2
(Bell & Dee, 2016)	RGB Images (Annotated)	Leaf Segmentation, Leaf Counting	Total Images: 56, Plant Instances: 916	Arabidopsis	D3
(Scharr, Minervini, Fischbach, & Tsaftaris, 2014)	RGB Images (Annotated)	Leaf Counting, Leaf Segmentation	Total: 284, Tobbaco: 83, Arabidopsis: 201	Tobbaco, Arabidopsis	D4

continued on following page

Table 3. Continued

Dataset	Modality	Application	Size	Crop(s)	Link
(Vélez, Ariza-Sentís, & Valente, 2023)	Spectral Images (Raw)	3D Reconstruction, Disease Detection, Crop Segmentation	Total: 16504	Grapevines	D5
(Veley, et al., 2017)	RGB Images (Annotated)	Nutrient Assessment, Stress Assessment, Crop Segmentation	Total: 96867 (30 Genotypes)	Sorghum	D6
(Lobet, et al., 2017)	RGB Images (Annotated)	Root Image Analysis	Total: 10000 (RSML Files)	Maize	D7
(Migicovsky, Li, Chitwood, & Myles, 2018)	RGB Images (Not Annotated)	Leaf Health Analysis, Leaf Segmentation	Total: 9000 (869 Accessions)	Apple	D8
(Seethepalli, et al., 2020)	RGB Images (Not Annotated)	Root Image Analysis	Total: 4400	Wheat, Soybean	D9
(Chitwood & Otoni, 2017)	RGB Images (Annotated)	Leaf Morphology Analysis, Leaf Shape Classification	Total: 3300	Passiflore	D10
(Atkinson, et al., 2017)	RGB Images (Annotated)	Root Health Analysis, Traits Identification	Total: 2614	Wheat	D11
(Murray, et al., 2019)	RGB & Spectral Images (Not Annotated)	Crop Health Analysis, Yield Prediction	Total: 1500	Maize	D12
(Pound, Atkinson, Wells, Pridmore, & French, 2017)	RGB Images (Annotated)	Spikes & Spikelet Counting, Spike Detection	Total: 500	Maize	D13
(Mattupalli, Seethepalli, York, & Young, 2019)	RGB Images (Annotated)	Root Disease Detection, Root Health Analysis	Total: 264	Alfalfa	D14

Plant Disease Monitoring

Numerous methods have been proposed for accurate identification and classification of plant leaves and their diseases based on leaf shape, color, and texture. Convolutional Neural Networks (CNNs) and other computer vision techniques like Vision Transformers (ViT), optical flow, background subtraction, and segmentation enhance accuracy and speed. Optical flow helps distinguish plant species by tracking leaf motion and subtle texture changes, while background subtraction isolates leaves, and segmentation identifies distinct image regions.

Vision Transformers (ViT) excel in plant leaf classification by learning long-term dependencies and complex visual relationships, outperforming traditional CNNs. (Li, Zhang, & Wang, 2022) developed a lightweight RegNet model, achieving 99.8% precision on the validation set and 99.23% on the test set using the Adam optimizer and an optimal learning rate of 0.0001.

(Liu & Wang, 2020) significantly improved the Yolo V3 algorithm for detecting tomato diseases and pests, achieving 92.39% accuracy with a detection time of 20.39ms. Their enhanced Yolo V3 outperformed SSD, Faster R-CNN, and the original Yolo V3 in accuracy and speed. (Yu, Xie, & Huang, 2023) introduced a novel transformer block for plant disease identification, combining transformer architecture, soft split token embedding, inception architecture, and cross-channel feature learning. This model achieved high accuracy on multiple datasets, demonstrating significant advancements in crop disease monitoring.

(Bibi, Moetesum, & Siddiqi, 2022) developed a YOLO-v5-based technique to address illumination variations, camouflage, and background clutter in automatic pest recognition, achieving 85.6% accuracy on the AgriPest dataset. (Zhang, Huang, Zhou, Hu, & Li, 2023) proposed a model for tomato leaf disease identification addressing inter-class similarity, intra-class variability, and noise interference, achieving 96.47% accuracy on a dataset of 7,943 images.

Most techniques rely on RGB image datasets, which may hinder timely disease detection. Utilizing multi and hyperspectral imagery-based datasets captures data beyond the visible spectrum, enabling early detection of plant diseases before visible symptoms appear.

Plant Seedlings Monitoring

Upon germination and emergence of the first leaves, a plant becomes a seedling, a critical phase for plant health and productivity. Computer Vision can automate seedling monitoring through image recognition and object detection, identifying diseases, pests, and monitoring growth to estimate yield. Initially, quantifying seedlings in the field is essential.

(Jiang, Li, Paterson, & Robertson, 2019) proposed a deep learning technique for counting seedlings in open fields, achieving an F1-score of 0.727 and 0.969 on the test set. Ablation experiments showed the importance of training data complexity on model generalizability, with an R^2 of 0.98 across 75 videos. The method proved accurate in instance counting, especially with generalized detection models.

(Li, et al., 2022) introduced a selective seedling planting control system to improve yield and transplant quality. The system, featuring a pneumatic pushrod, seed mechanisms, and sensors, used the FHLSI framework with the FCM segmentation algorithm. This vision-augmented process enhanced transplant quality by 15.4% and achieved 92.35% accuracy.

(Quan, et al., 2019) modified Faster R-CNN to identify maize seedlings in fields, achieving over 97.71% precision. The model trained on 20,000 images and was deployed on a field robot. However, performance dropped in low lighting, zero-degree shots, and six- to seven-leaf maize seedlings.

Automated crop monitoring must adapt to extreme weather due to climate change. High-throughput phenotyping, especially spectral image analysis, is crucial for assessing plant characteristics and cold stress resistance. (Yang, Yang, Hao, Xie, & Li, 2019) used a CNN to analyze spectral characteristics in corn seedlings, achieving an R^2 of 0.8219 in quantifying cold injury, showing the reliability of spectral evaluation using CNN modeling.

Crop and Weed Detection

Deep learning has advanced plant identification and disease recognition but requires large datasets and high computational costs. To address this, researchers are exploring vision transformers, which use self-attention mechanisms to process data more efficiently, reducing data size and computational needs. Vision transformers could revolutionize computer vision and enable faster, more efficient precision models.

Investigating the application of visual transformer (ViT) for recognizing weeds and crops in Unmanned Aerial Vehicles (UAVs) images, (Reedha, Dericquebourg, Canals, & Hafiane, 2022) discovered that the ViT model, even with minimal labeled training data, outperformed EfficientNet and ResNet. Despite the challenges posed by higher computation cost and the requirement of larger labeled datasets, the research outcomes point to the potential of ViT being used for a broad array of image analysis endeavors for high-throughput plant phenotyping.

(Peteinatos, Reichel, Karouta, Andújar, & Gerhards, 2020) investigated the capability of CNNs to differentiate thirteen categories of weeds and plants. In order to accurately determine the species, VGG16, ResNet-50, and Xception were used in combination with 93,000 images which contained only a single species. This technique enabled a Top-1 accuracy of 77-98% to determine plant species and distinguishing weed species. Tomatoes are a widely consumed vegetable, and their maturity detection is important for improving production.

(Han, Hao, Sun, Xue, & Li, 2022) proposes a YOLOv5 feature fusion network with an attention module that increases detection accuracy and reduces irrelevant features. An 1812- image, 4000-target tomato ripeness dataset was developed, achieving an mAP of 88.06%. The AP for green tomatoes was 86.12% and for red tomatoes, it was 90%. Red tomatoes were detected with an accuracy of 92.77%, and an accuracy of 81.25% was achieved on green tomatoes.

Shiitake mushroom cultivation is lucrative but inefficient with traditional methods. To address this, (Wang, et al., 2022) developed MushroomYOLO, an enhanced YOLOv5 algorithm, achieving a mean average precision (mAP) of 99.24%. The iMushroom prototype system was created for yield recognition, proving effective in real-world conditions and offering automated quality control in greenhouse farming.

(Cui, Lou, Ge, & Wang, 2023) proposed a low-resource pinecone identification method using a modified YOLOv4-Tiny algorithm. It achieved 95.33% precision, outperforming the original by 3.56%, while reducing parameters by 12.22% and detection time by 67.41%. It also surpassed YOLOv4, YOLOv5x, YOLOv5s, and YOLOX-Tiny in both precision and parameter reductions, identifying 135 images per second for efficient near-color hardware use.

Plant Leaf Segmentation

Computer vision techniques like semantic and instance segmentation reliably segment plants from their background, enabling accurate measurements of canopy size, leaf shape, and disease detection. This detailed analysis informs decisions on fertilization, irrigation, pest control, and crop selection. However, complex light conditions can impact leaf localization and segmentation.

In (Lin, et al., 2023)'s work, a novel self-supervised framework for leaf segmentation in image-based plant phenotyping was proposed. This framework contains a self-directed semantic segmentation approach combining CNNs and fully connected Conditional Random Fields (FCCRF) for feature extraction, a color-based leaf segmentation algorithm measuring "greenness" through a multivariate normal distribution in the HSV color space, and a self-supervised color correction algorithm adjusting distorted colors due to the usage of artificial grow lights. The evaluation of datasets of assorted plant specimens indicates the applicability and generality of the self-directed framework with an FBD (Foreground-Background Dice) of 94.8 and 94.5 on Cannabis and LSC datasets respectively (Scharr, Minervini, Fischbach, & Tsaftaris, 2014).

In another related work, (Islam, et al., 2022) developed a novel deep learning model, TheIR547v1, which is capable of robustly and autonomously segmenting images for plant phenotyping in varying backgrounds and illuminations. On backgrounds and leaves, a mean IoU of .87 and 0.94, and a mean BF (Boundary F1 score) of 0.86 and 0.93 was successfully achieved while evaluating on 37,328 augmented images. The designed framework has remarkable training precision and little training loss, enabling it to differentiate leaf/canopy pixels from background pixels quickly and with limited memory usage. However, its limitations include longer training time than DeepLab V3 variants and loss in segmentation accuracy of canopy boundaries due to a smaller dataset.

USAGE OF MULTISPECTRAL AND HYPERSPECTRAL IMAGERY IN PRECISION AGRICULTURE

Multispectral imagery(MSI) and hyperspectral imagery (HSI) are two forms of remote sensing that use the reflectance of objects to provide a detailed view of the Earth's surface. While MSI sensors measure the reflectance in a limited number of spectral bands, HSI provides data in a much wider range of spectral bands, offering higher resolution and more semantic information about the scene. This type of information can be utilized to surveil crop health, soil composition, biotic stress, biomass, carbon stock, and nutrient levels. It also offers rapid, accurate, and efficient analysis, meaning that farmers can quickly identify problems and make informed decisions about their crops (Omia, et al., 2023).

Multispectral imaging is relatively simple and cost-effective, making it a popular choice for farmers. It is able to detect a limited number of signals but can be used to provide information on vegetation indices and crop health. Hyperspectral imaging is more complex and expensive but provides more detailed information about the target, such as biochemical properties and mineral content. The spectral range can be divided into 6 groups i.e. Gamma Rays, X-Rays, UV, IR, Microwave, and Radiowaves. Figure 5 depicts different wavelength ranges and their respective usage in smart farming.

Figure 5. Band lengths, energy levels in electromagnetic spectrum and their respective agricultural usage. Source: (Omia, et al., 2023)

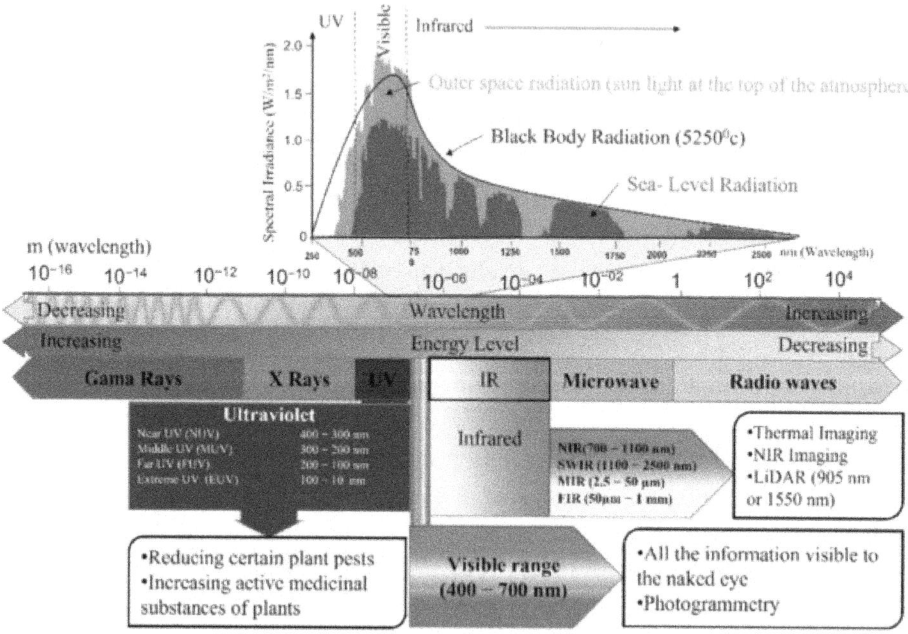

The use of MHSI in PA offers farmers a wide range of benefits (Table 4). This technology enables farmers to accurately assess crop stress, detect spectral variations in foliage, and monitor plant productivity while detecting plant disease in its early stages. It also allows growers to observe yield health and thereby reach their agronomic aims. Furthermore, this technology is low cost, consistent, simple to use, allows for rapid assessments, non-destructive, and highly accurate. Finally, this technology is a key component of Agriculture 4.0, which is an evolution of farming consisting of unmanned operations and autonomous decision-making.

Table 4. Multi and hyper-spectral imaging systems, their specifications, and usage in precision agriculture

HSI Camera	Spectral Type	Specification	Usage in PA
Specim IQ	Hyperspectral	400-1000nm band, 7nm resolution, 12bit output, CMOS sensors.	Measures NDVI, NDRE, biomass, nitrogen content, and water stress.
Sentera Double 4K	Multispectral	365-1000nm band, 5x e2v 5 MPIS CMOS sensors, >65dB dynamic range.	Analyzes plant health, leaf area index, and chlorophyll content.
Resonon Pika-IRL	Hyperspectral	925-1700nm band, 3.3nm bandwidth, 236 channels, airborne compatible.	Useful for NDVI, UV/vis, and NIR imagery to assess vegetative health.
Headwall Photonics SWIR-640	Hyperspectral	900-2500nm band, 267 spectral bands, 640 spatial bands, airborne and ground compatible.	Precisely identifies plant varieties, soil, and vegetation health.
Parrot Sequoia+	Multispectral	530-810nm band, 3.98mm focal length, airborne compatible.	Measures spectral reflectances like NDVI, NDRE, and chlorophyll ratio.
InnoSpec RedEye-1.7	Hyperspectral	950-1700nm band, 10nm resolution.	Hyperspectral imaging for nutrients, weeds, soil mapping, and water-stressed vegetation.
SOC710 - SWIR	Hyperspectral	900-1700nm band, 2.86/5.7nm resolution, 280/140 channels.	Measures and maps surfaces such as soils, crops, and vegetation.
imec SNAPSHOT SWIR-16	Hyperspectral	660-1650nm band, 30+ spectral bands, airborne and ground compatible.	Applications include canopy height, leaf area index, and soil moisture measurement.
ASD FieldSpec 4 Hi-Res NG	Hyperspectral	350-2500nm band, 2151 channels, 3nm resolution at 700nm, 6nm at 1400/2100nm.	Used for agricultural mappings like NDVI, growth rate, nitrogen, and biomass calculations.

In smart farming, hyperspectral imagery can be used to monitor crop health and detect disease, pests, and more importantly, nutrient deficiencies. The spectral signatures of different plant species and soil types can be detected, allowing for precise identification of crop types and assessment of soil fertility. It can also be used to detect water stress in plants, allowing farmers to optimize irrigation practices and reduce water usage. The reviewed articles were divided into 3 groups Pest & Disease Detection, Yield & Nutrient Assessment, and Crop Classification. Table 5 summarizes the survey details.

Table 5. A survey of Multispectral (MS) & Hyperspectral (HS) imagery usage in precision agriculture

Paper	Spectral Camera	Target	Method & Result	Crop
(Pinto, Powell, Peterson, Rosalen, & Fernandes, 2020)	Resonon PIKA-L (HS) (400-1000nm)	Defoliation Injury Detection	Random Forest Accuracy: 92%	Peanut
(Tanabe, Matsui, & Tanaka, 2023)	Parrot Sequoia (MS) (550-1000nm) Micasense Altum (MS) (560-1000nm)	Yield Prediction	CNN & MLR RMSE(test): 0.94, 0.99	Wheat
(Chancia, Bates, Heuvel, & van Aardt, 2021)	Headwall Nano (HS) (400-1000nm) Headwall Micro (MS) (900-2500nm) Micasense RedEdge-M (MS)	Nutrient Status Assessment	Ensemble & PLSR: Found wavelength 606nm, 641nm and 1168nm to be biochemically consistent for nitrogen content prediction	Grapevine
(Bu, et al., 2022)	Specim FX10 (HS) (400-1000nm) Specim FX17 (MS) (900-1700nm)	Starch Content Detection	GABPNN R-Square: 0.94 (Amylopectin), 0.97 (Amylose)	Sorghum
(Ramamoorthy, et al., 2022)	PSR +3500 (HS) (350-2500nm)	RKN Stress Detection	PCA & SLDA Overall Accuracy: 98%	Cotton
(Li, Chen, & Huang, 2018)	ImSpector N25E (HS) (1000-2500nm) ImSpector V10E (HS) (400-1000nm)	Bruise Detection	Watershed Segmentation Accuracy: 96.5%	Peaches
(Li, et al., 2022)	NEO - HySpex (HS) (409-989nm)	Yield Analysis and Biomass Estimation	AutoML Regression R-Square: 0.96 (wheat), 0.76 (oat and peas)	Wheat, Oat & Pea
(Wei, et al., 2021)	Headwall Nano (HS) (400-1000nm)	Crop Classification	DNN + CRF Overall Accuracy: 91.05% (images), 93.64% (Morphological Features)	Multi-Vegetable
(Sadeghi-Tehran, Virlet, & Hawkesford, 2021)	Headwall HyperSpec VNIR (HS) (400-1000nm)	Sunlit Shaded Plant Canopies Classification	CNN Accuracy: 98.6%	Wheat
(Candiani, et al., 2022)	HyPlant-DUAL (Siegmann et al., 2019) (HS) (370-2500nm)	Nitrogen & Chlorophyll Content Estimation	HYB & HAL R-Square: 0.82 (HYB), 0.95 (HAL)	Maize

Pest and Disease Detection

The finer resolution of MHSI images can be used to better detect and monitor pests that are often too small to be seen by the human eye, as well as to detect very low levels of pest and disease infestations that may be too small to be seen at all.

(Pinto, Powell, Peterson, Rosalen, & Fernandes, 2020) demonstrated hyperspectral proximal remote sensing as an effective tool for distinguishing between Stegasta bosqueella and Spodoptera cosmioides, two major peanut pests in South America. They found differences in leaf reflectance and various physiological parameters between the species, regardless of real or simulated defoliation. (Ramamoorthy, et al., 2022) studied the effect of root-knot nematode (RKN) and water shortage (DS) on two cotton genotypes, nematode-resistant (Rk-Rn-1) and nematode-susceptible (M8). Using high-resolution hyperspectral data, they detected early RKN stress with over 98% success. M8 showed a stronger response to all stressors compared to Rk-Rn-1. The study indicated that hyperspectral sensor data can distinguish between individual stress treatments, suggesting the potential for developing cotton varieties resistant to both nematodes and drought.

Yield Prediction and Nutrient Assessment

Using UAV-multispectral imagery, (Tanabe, Matsui, & Tanaka, 2023) assessed the performance of CNNs in predicting winter wheat grain yield. The CNN model achieved a lower RMSE of 0.94 t ha-1 compared to an EVI2-based linear regression model, suggesting enhanced prediction accuracy. The optimal data collection time was the heading stage; accuracy decreased as growth stages advanced, with the ripening stage being highly unreliable. Multi-temporal CNN models did not perform better when combining different growth stages. Further research is needed to evaluate the impact of image quality and temporal resolution on prediction accuracy.

(Chancia, Bates, Heuvel, & van Aardt, 2021) investigated the optimal spectral bands for monitoring grapevine nutrients using hyperspectral data from UAS. Machine learning feature selection methods, including PLSR and ensemble feature ranking, were used. Selected wavelengths (606, 614, and 1168 nm) effectively predicted nitrogen content, though larger datasets are needed for other nutrients. This study highlights the potential of different methods for nutrient-specific spectral response isolation.

(Bu, et al., 2022) utilized hyperspectral imaging fusion to quantify sorghum starch content. They applied watershed segmentation and methods like Pearson's correlation, PLSR, and PCA to create low- and mid-level fused data. GA-BPNN and PSO-SVR models were used for predictions, with mid-level fusion models outperforming NIR, single Vis, and low-level models. The GA-BPNN model, using

Pearson correlation-extracted data, predicted amylose content with an RMSEP of 0.0298 and R^2 of 0.9948. For amylopectin, PCA-extracted data achieved an RMSEP of 0.0213 and R^2 of 0.9985. This demonstrates the potential of hyperspectral imaging and data fusion for starch content identification in sorghum and other grains.

Crop Classification

Hyper- and multispectral imagery are effective and cost-efficient for crop classification, providing detailed spatial and spectral information. This technology enables the identification of crop species and varieties by analyzing spectral properties like reflectance and absorptance, as well as spatial characteristics such as size, shape, and distribution. This data helps classify crops into groups like cereals, vegetables, and fruits, enhancing agricultural monitoring and management.

Using airborne HSI, in (Wei, et al., 2021), a multi-feature fusion model combining a DNN (Deep Neural Network) and a CRF(conditional random field), was deployed for crops fine classification. The method extracted and fused three non-spectral features, such as texture, morphological profile, and endmember abundance, probability fusion, decision fusion, and stacking fusion. Evaluations on the Honshu and Xiong'an datasets demonstrated that the proposed method improved the accuracy of crop classification particularly relative to single feature classifications.

It was observed that the accuracy enhancement increased with an increase in the number of training samples and that incorporating neural networks and random fields further boosted accuracy.

(Sadeghi-Tehran, Virlet, & Hawkesford, 2021) used high-resolution hyperspectral imagery to analyze canopy biophysical and chemical traits and classify shaded and sunlit components. They developed two CNN-based models, CNN-RAW and CNN-LDA, achieving 98% and 97% accuracy respectively, surpassing conventional classifiers. Non-shadowed spikes and leaves had three times higher NIR reflectance than shaded ones, and vegetation indices (DVI, EVI, MSAVI, MTVI, TVI) showed distinct distributions between canopy components.

Figure 6 shows the qualitative results of their classification.

Figure 6. Classification of shadowed & non-shadowed regions.

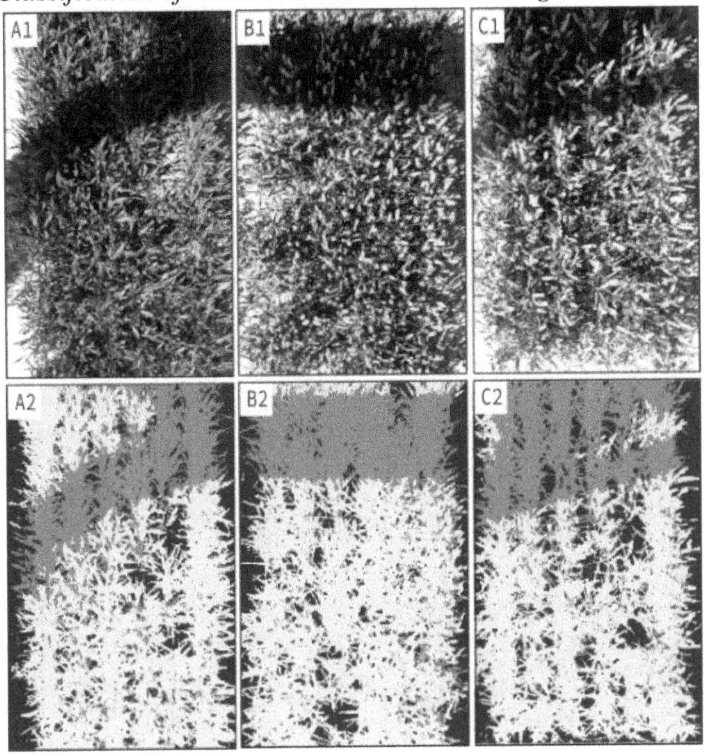

Source: (Sadeghi-Tehran, Virlet, & Hawkesford, 2021)

(Candiani, et al., 2022) evaluated a hybrid approach (HYB) and its variant with active learning heuristics (HAL) for estimating crop chlorophyll and nitrogen content using data from the ESA's Copernicus Hyperspectral Imaging Mission (CHIME). HYB reliably estimated canopy-level data, while HAL provided accurate predictions at both canopy and leaf levels. Further research is needed to optimize HYB's transferability to different contexts. The study supports the utility of spaceborne imaging spectroscopy for assessing crop traits.

(Farmonov, et al., 2023) applied Wavelet-Attention CNN (WA-CNN), Random Forest (RF), and Support Vector Machine (SVM) to hyperspectral images from the DESIS system in Hungary. WA-CNN achieved the highest accuracy with an OA of 97.89%, UA of 97-99%, and PA in the same range. Factor Analysis and wavelet transform improved WA-CNN's precision in crop-type mapping, outperforming RF and SVM. The findings highlight DESIS data's potential for detecting crop growth and predicting harvest volumes, benefiting farmers and decision-makers.

UAVS AND LOW-ALTITUDE REMOTE SENSING

Low-altitude sensing offers higher temporal and spatial resolution than satellite imagery, enabling more accurate crop health and soil condition monitoring (Zhang, Wang, Tian, & Yin, 2021). Data can be collected from aerial photographs, UAVs, and remote sensing systems like lidar and hyperspectral sensors (Cerro, Ulloa, Barrientos, & de León Rivas, 2021)UAVs equipped with sensors gather information on temperature, humidity, soil moisture, nutrient levels, and crop health. This data aids in analyzing crop health, soil conditions, mapping weeds, pests, diseases, and developing targeted treatments. It also helps optimize irrigation systems by providing soil fertility and drainage data, maximizing yields.

Figure 7 shows a DJI Phantom-4 UAV (SZ DJI Technology Co., Ltd, China) with a Sentera High Precision Multispectral Sensor (Sentera, USA) surveying the field.

Figure 7. UAV on survey in agricultural field

In addition to providing data, UAVs can also be used for applications such as crop spraying, seeding, and crop monitoring. UAVs can be programmed to fly over fields to identify areas for targeted applications, such as fertilizer or pest control. This can reduce costs associated with manual labor and improve crop yields. Furthermore, UAVs can provide farmers with detailed data on soil and crop health, enable them to identify and map pests and diseases and help them optimize their irrigation systems and crop management strategies. UAVs can also reduce costs and labor associated with crop spraying, seeding, and monitoring.

Paddy Yield Prediction

(Luo, et al., 2022) integrated UAV-based vegetation indices with tasselled cap transformation (TCT) parameters—brightness, greenness, and moisture—to enhance accuracy and avoid saturation in paddy yield predictions. The study, involving eight nitrogen gradients and UAV imaging during booting and heading phases, found that ground measurements at the booting stage provided the most accurate yield estimations. At the heading phase, combining vegetation indices with TCT metrics yielded reliable predictions, achieving an error rate below 7%.

Cotton Plant and LAI Estimation

(Wu, et al., 2022) evaluated UAV-derived RGB photos to predict cotton plant height and leaf area index (LAI) post-defoliant application. High correlation (R^2=0.962, RMSE=0.913) was observed three days post-spraying, which diminished over time (R^2=0.018, RMSE=0.027 at 10 days). Similar trends were noted in LAI estimation accuracy.

Wheat Plant Density Estimation

(Peng, et al., 2022) introduced DeNet, a deep learning model, for post-tillering wheat density estimation, outperforming SegNet and U-Net with an R^2 of 0.79. The study employed a key-point-based algorithm, exploring various heatmap-assembling techniques, sigma values, density levels, and zenith angles, indicating significant potential for precise fertilization and yield estimation.

Above-Ground Biomass Prediction

(Yue, et al., 2023) developed a UAV-based model to predict above-ground biomass (AGB) in vertically growing crops. The model, tested on winter wheat and summer maize across three stages, outperformed statistical regression models, achieving R^2 of 0.92-0.93 and RMSE of 68.82-75.15 g/m^2, demonstrating enhanced non-destructive AGB monitoring capabilities.

Impact of Soil Reflectance on Yield Estimates

(Almeida-Ñauñay, et al., 2023) highlighted the significance of soil background reflectance on UAV-based grain yield and quality estimates. Using a multispectral sensor, four vegetation indices were analyzed across 133 test plots with varying nitrogen doses. NDVI, MSAVI, and NDRE were effective in predicting wheat attributes, with the sequential cutting method improving yield and nitrogen output estimations.

Chickpea Yield Prediction

(Avneri, et al., 2023) explored the utility of Unmanned Aerial Systems (UAS) and RGB cameras to predict leaf area index (LAI), biomass, and yield for chickpeas during irrigation. Data from two field trials were analyzed using visual indices, morphological parameters, PLSR, SVM, and MLR models. The SVM model significantly improved biomass prediction accuracy, with R^2 rising from 0.62 to 0.96 for combined 2019-2020 data.

Sensor Placement Optimization for Agriculture

(Goodrich, Betancourt, Arias, & Zohdi, 2023) proposed an algorithm for optimizing sensor placement and multi-agent UAV flight paths using genetic algorithms. The study demonstrated that increasing drone swarm size reduced sensor examination time with minimal energy consumption impact, enhancing variable rate irrigation and precise biological control applications.

Nitrogen Estimation Using UAV Imagery

(Lee, Wang, & Leblon, 2020) investigated UAV multispectral imagery and Ratio Vegetation Index (RVI) for nitrogen canopy estimation in wheat and maize. The RVI-based models exhibited high reliability, with R^2 values of 0.93 and 0.83 for wheat and maize, respectively, indicating effective nitrogen requirement predictions.

Orchard Management with UAVs

(Tu, Johansen, Phinn, & Robson, 2019) showcased UAVs' potential in horticulture by measuring avocado tree attributes using aerial imagery. Accurate height models (R^2=0.65, RMSE=6%) and PPC determination (R^2=0.62) were achieved, with a random forest classifier providing 96% accuracy in tree condition classification.

UAV vs. Satellite Imagery for Crop Monitoring

(Li, Shamshiri, Weltzien, & Schirrmann, 2022) compared UAV and Sentinel-2 imagery for crop monitoring. UAV data correlated more strongly with agronomic parameters and identified management-driven features, proving more effective and cost-efficient than satellite imagery.

Genetic Dissection of NDVI in Maize

(Wang, et al., 2021) utilized UAV multispectral imagery for NDVI genetic dissection in maize. P-splines models and GWAS revealed significant gene-environment interactions affecting NDVI over the growth period, demonstrating UAV imagery's value in genetic studies.

AGRI-BOTS IN PRECISION FARMING

Agri-bots can be utilized for providing precise sensing and monitoring capabilities with regards to various aspects of precision agriculture, including temperature, humidity, soil moisture, light, and crop yield, and taking respective actions as well. The presence of agri-bots on large-scale farms enables the automated administration of fertilization and other inputs, as well as harvesting and weeding operations. This means that the need for manual labor is greatly reduced, saving on labor costs and increasing efficiency. Through IOT sensors, agri-bots can provide detailed and contextual data which can be used to monitor and analyze large-scale crop fields in real-time, enabling more precise management and improved decision-making, thus contributing to scalability. This section reviews a variety of agri-bots with distinct capabilities to fulfill unique functions in smart farming, along with Table 6.

Table 6. A survey of agri-bots in precision agriculture

Robot	Sensors	Application	Energy Source	Type
(Cubero, Marco-noales, Aleixos, Barbé, & Blasco, 2020)	RGB, thermal, multi- and hyperspectral cameras, GNSS, halogen lamps	Pest and Disease Detection	2000W Power Generator and Lithium Batteries	Rover
(Campbell, Dechemi, & Karydis, 2022)	Robotic Arm, Mountable	Leaf Detection and Retrieval	CNN & LiPo Battery	Depth Camera
(Quaglia, et al., 2020)	LiDAR, depth camera, soil sensors, IMU, GPS, barometer, accelerometer, gyroscope, compass, motor encoders	Multipurpose (Weed Identification, Crop Inspection, and Fertilization)	Solar Panels	Rover with Gripper
(Parsa, Debnath, Khan, & Amir Ghalamzan, 2023)	RGB Depth Sensor	Fruit Picking	Battery Powered	Rover with Gripper
(Aronson, 2013)	RGB Camera, Soil Sensor	Automated Gardening	Electricity	Fixed, Planter Bed

FarmBot Genesis v1.6

The FarmBot Genesis v1.6 (Aronson, 2013) is an advanced, open-source automated gardening system designed for residential food production. It integrates a robotic frame, web-based application, and sensors to simplify growing food (Figure 8). The robotic frame performs tasks like planting, watering, weeding, and harvesting. The web app allows users to customize their FarmBot experience with pre-configured plans and community support. Sensors monitor environmental conditions, enabling adaptive automation of gardening tasks. This versatile and user-friendly system is a significant innovation in automated agriculture, suitable for gardeners of all experience levels.

Figure 8. Farmbot (Aronson, 2013)

Robhortic

RobHortic (Cubero, Marco-noales, Aleixos, Barbé, & Blasco, 2020), a remotely-controlled robot designed for proximate sensing of pests and diseases in horticultural crops, was tested to detect 'Candidatus Liberibacter solanacearum' infections in carrots (Figure 9). This device was equipped with color, multispectral, and hyperspectral cameras, as well as a Global Navigation Satellite System, and three campaigns were conducted to assess its ability to detect infected plants.

Results from the Partial Least Squares-Discriminant Analysis showed the highest accuracy, which revealed a 66.4% detection rate for laboratory images and a 59.8% detection rate for field images.

Figure 9. RobHortic operating in field (Cubero et al., 2020)

Robotic Leaf Retrieval

Robotic automation in precision agriculture is growing, yet leaf sampling for stem water potential remains manual and labor-intensive. (Campbell, Dechemi, & Karydis, 2022) developed a system using a depth camera and a 6-DOF robotic arm, achieving a 95% success rate (Figure 10). Tests on avocado trees showed 80.0% leaf detection accuracy, 79.8% localization success, 69.2% viable leaf accuracy, and 77.8% precision cutting. Further research is needed to improve end-effector size, path planning, and system robustness.

Figure 10. Robotic leaf retrieval (Campbell et al., 2022)

Agri.q

Agri.q (Quaglia, et al., 2020) is a solar-powered, sustainable rover for precision agriculture, suitable for any terrain. It performs weed identification, crop inspection, and fertilization (Figure 11). Equipped with LiDAR, cameras, and various sensors, it monitors soil conditions and plant health. Data is transmitted to the cloud for analysis, enhancing agricultural output and reducing costs. The rover's accurate sensors, cost-effectiveness, ease of use, compatibility with farm management systems, and renewable energy usage make it a robust, eco-friendly solution.

Figure 11. The agri.q (Quaglia et al., 2020)

Strawberry Picking Robot

(Parsa, Debnath, Khan, & Amir Ghalamzan, 2023) developed an advanced robotic system for selectively harvesting strawberries in complex scenarios (Figure 12).

It features a modular platform, a patented 2.5-degree-of-freedom picking head, and a perceptual system. The picking head removes occlusions and harvests strawberries without contact to prevent damage. The perceptual system localizes strawberries, detects key points and ripeness.

Tested on two novel datasets in commercial and research farms with three strawberry varieties, the system showed promising results. Tests showed an 87% success rate for detected strawberries and 83% for pluckable fruits. The research highlights open questions and advances robotic strawberry harvesting, setting the stage for future improvements in the field.

Figure 12. Autonomous strawberry picking robot (Parsa et al., 2023)

DISCUSSION AND FUTURE DIRECTIONS

This chapter reviewed deep learning techniques in precision agriculture, identifying a generic pipeline involving image acquisition, pre-processing, and model development. A significant gap is the limited use of transfer learning due to the lack of suitable benchmark datasets. Developing these datasets is crucial for applying these techniques efficiently and reducing computational costs.

The study also noted that most methods for leaf segmentation and disease classification use simpler backgrounds than open-field environments, which are more complex due to occlusion, shadowing, and sunlight variability. Optimizing machine vision solutions for these conditions is essential. UAVs with multispectral and hyperspectral sensors could address the challenges of imaging large farms from low altitudes, potentially scaling deep learning models. However, further research is needed for real-time, scalable crop health monitoring solutions.

Climate change significantly threatens global crop yields, making precision agriculture vital for mitigating these risks. Current practices must be optimized to address climate change's diverse impacts on crop growth and yield. Agribots should be optimized with environmental parameters like air quality, climate trends, water stress, and temperature variability to improve farming practices and reduce climate change impacts. This involves developing predictive weather forecasting, deploying environmental sensors, and incorporating climate considerations into decision-making processes such as crop selection and fertilization. Sustainable Precision Agriculture (SPA) integrates Information and Communication Technologies (ICTs) to detect, analyze, and manage agricultural variability, promoting profitability and sustainability while protecting terrestrial resources. Despite extensive research, adoption remains limited among farming communities. The key challenges include:

1. The lack of benchmark agricultural RGB and MHSI-based imagery datasets and precision agriculture-based CV challenges.
2. Efficient use of farming inputs like water, seeds, and fertilizers.
3. Large-scale surveillance and mitigation of crop diseases, such as yellow rust in wheat, using UAVs.
4. Monitoring soil quality and carbon stocks with MHSI for informed crop rotation decisions.
5. Observing the environmental impact of irresponsible farming practices, such as excessive pesticide and fertilizer use.
6. Measuring the impact of air pollution on crop yields and identifying remedies.
7. Democratizing access to cost-effective agri-bots and fostering partnerships with local industries for their development.

One of our proposed studies is structured on the fundamentals of precision agriculture and Industry 4.0. The novelty of this work leverages spectral analysis techniques to examine crop & soil health. The system is supported by the Internet of Things (IoT) framework and AI, which will enable a qualitative data-driven study that aims to contribute by devising effective mechanisms to address the multiple problems mentioned above. The prospective system is illustrated in Figure 13 below.

Figure 13. Overview of proposed system for "multifaceted crop scouting using industry 4.0"

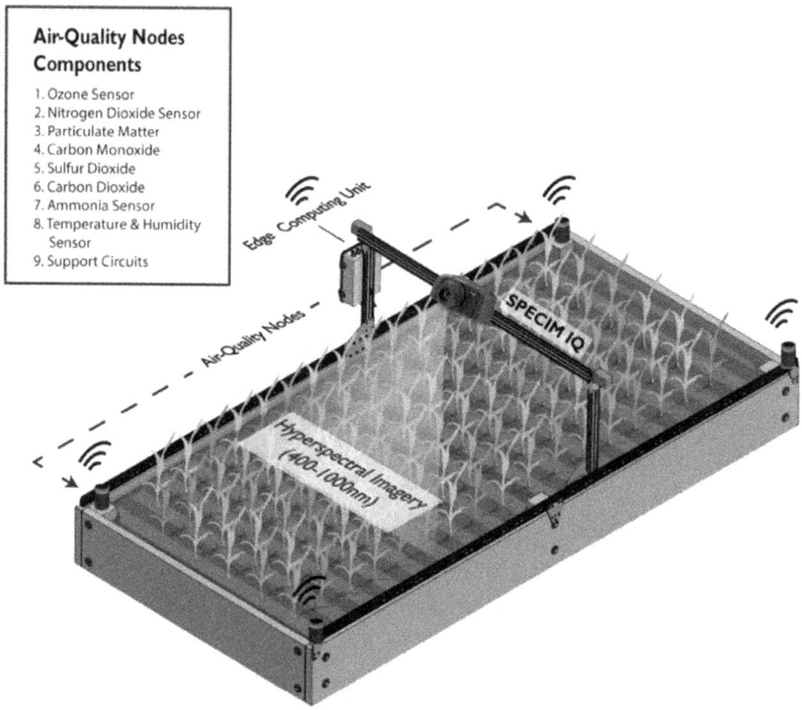

CONCLUSION

In conclusion, reviewed studies discussed various new and innovative technologies that have the potential to revolutionize the farming industry. UAVs, hyperspectral imagery, advancements in computer vision, and IoT sensor-equipped agri-bots are being used to increase the accuracy and effectiveness of the agricultural sector. By utilizing the power of these approaches, the farming industry can benefit from industry-wide efficiencies and cost savings while still producing high-quality and reliable, robust solutions. Research gaps in the field of precision agriculture include the need for the collection of MHSI-based benchmark datasets and the development of more efficient algorithms to process them, better ways to incorporate machine vision into farming systems to improve efficacy and scalability, and the need for data-driven and energy-efficient ways to manufacture more reliable and cost-effective IoT sensors & agri-bots. While the implementation of smart farming practices, has the potential to yield higher productivity and efficiency, these alone are not enough to adequately mitigate the risks associated with climate change, which vary in complexity and magnitude and require nuanced data collection and action optimization with environmental variables.

Additionally, the potential for deeper insight and forecasting of agricultural trends, allowing for improved management and decision-making processes, is made possible through the use of data-driven practices. It is important to note, however, that the successful implementation of such sophisticated automation on a large scale is reliant upon the continued development of suitable software and the acquisition of certain rich domain knowledge regarding the use and maintenance of such technology from all stakeholders involved in the agricultural industry. Thus, our proposed study took numerous research gaps into account and discussed them

ACKNOWLEDGMENT

Funding:

This research work is funded by Higher Education Commission (HEC), under Center of Excellence (COE) Grant, Grant.No COE-65.

Acknowledgments:

This research work is conducted at the NCIL lab at NUST-SEECS, Islamabad, Pakistan.

Declaration of Competing Interest / Conflict of Interest:

The authors declare no conflict of interest.

REFERENCES

Almeida-Ñauñay, A. F., Tarquis, A. M., López-Herrera, J., Pérez-Martín, E., Pancorbo, J. L., Raya-Sereno, M. D., & Quemada, M. (2023, February). Optimization of soil background removal to improve the prediction of wheat traits with UAV imagery. *Computers and Electronics in Agriculture*, 205, 107559. Advance online publication. DOI: 10.1016/j.compag.2022.107559

Aronson, R. L. (2013). FarmBot: Humanity's open-source automated precision farming machine. *Technology*, 19.

Atkinson, J. A., Lobet, G., Noll, M., Meyer, P. E., Griffiths, M., & Wells, D. M. (2017, August). Combining semi-automated image analysis techniques with machine learning algorithms to accelerate large-scale genetic studies. *GigaScience*, 6(10), gix084. Advance online publication. DOI: 10.1093/gigascience/gix084 PMID: 29020748

Avneri, A., Aharon, S., Brook, A., Atsmon, G., Smirnov, E., Sadeh, R., & Lati, R. N. (2023, February). UAS-based imaging for prediction of chickpea crop biophysical parameters and yield. *Computers and Electronics in Agriculture*, 205, 107581. Advance online publication. DOI: 10.1016/j.compag.2022.107581

Bell, J., & Dee, H. M. (2016, November). Aberystwyth Leaf Evaluation Dataset. *Aberystwyth Leaf Evaluation Dataset*. DOI: 10.5281/ZENODO.168158

Bibi, A., Moetesum, M., & Siddiqi, I. (2022). Deep Vision for Pest Detection in Corn Fields. *2022 19th International Bhurban Conference on Applied Sciences and Technology (IBCAST)* (pp. 343-348). DOI: 10.1109/IBCAST54850.2022.9990435

Bu, Y., Jiang, X., Tian, J., Hu, X., Fei, X., Huang, D., & Luo, H. (2022, October). Rapid and accurate detection of starch content in mixed sorghum by hyperspectral imaging combined with data fusion technology. *Journal of Food Process Engineering*, 45(10), e14129. Advance online publication. DOI: 10.1111/jfpe.14129

Campbell, M., Dechemi, A., & Karydis, K. (2022, October). An Integrated Actuation-Perception Framework for Robotic Leaf Retrieval: Detection, Localization, and Cutting. *An Integrated Actuation-Perception Framework for Robotic Leaf Retrieval: Detection, Localization, and Cutting*. IEEE. DOI: 10.1109/IROS47612.2022.9981118

Candiago, S., Remondino, F., De Giglio, M., Dubbini, M., & Gattelli, M. (2015). Evaluating multispectral images and vegetation indices for precision farming applications from UAV images. *Remote Sensing (Basel)*, 7(4), 4026–4047. DOI: 10.3390/rs70404026

Candiani, G., Tagliabue, G., Panigada, C., Verrelst, J., Picchi, V., Caicedo, J. P., & Boschetti, M. (2022, April). Evaluation of Hybrid Models to Estimate Chlorophyll and Nitrogen Content of Maize Crops in the Framework of the Future CHIME Mission. *Remote Sensing*, 14(8), 1792. Advance online publication. DOI: 10.3390/rs14081792 PMID: 36081596

Cerro, J. D., Ulloa, C. C., Barrientos, A., & de León Rivas, J. (2021, February). Unmanned aerial vehicles in agriculture: A survey. *Agronomy (Basel)*, 11(2), 203. Advance online publication. DOI: 10.3390/agronomy11020203

Chancia, R., Bates, T., Heuvel, J. V., & van Aardt, J. (2021, November). Assessing grapevine nutrient status from unmanned aerial system (UAS) hyperspectral imagery. *Remote Sensing (Basel)*, 13(21), 4489. Advance online publication. DOI: 10.3390/rs13214489

Chitwood, D. H., & Otoni, W. C. (2017, January). Morphometric analysis of Passiflora leaves: The relationship between landmarks of the vasculature and elliptical Fourier descriptors of the blade. *GigaScience*, 6(10). Advance online publication. DOI: 10.1093/gigascience/gix070 PMID: 28369351

Cubero, S., Marco-noales, E., Aleixos, N., Barbé, S., & Blasco, J. (2020). Robhortic: A field robot to detect pests and diseases in horticultural crops by proximal sensing. *Agriculture*, 10(7), 276. Advance online publication. DOI: 10.3390/agriculture10070276

Cui, M., Lou, Y., Ge, Y., & Wang, K. (2023, February). LES-YOLO: A lightweight pinecone detection algorithm based on improved YOLOv4-Tiny network. *Computers and Electronics in Agriculture*, 205, 107613. Advance online publication. DOI: 10.1016/j.compag.2023.107613

Dosovitskiy, A., Beyer, L., Kolesnikov, A., Weissenborn, D., Zhai, X., Unterthiner, T., . . . Houlsby, N. (2021). An Image is Worth 16x16 Words: Transformers for Image Recognition at Scale. *International Conference on Learning Representations.* Retrieved from https://openreview.net/forum?id=YicbFdNTTy

Farmonov, N., Amankulova, K., Szatmari, J., Sharifi, A., Abbasi-Moghadam, D., Nejad, S. M., & Mucsi, L. (2023). Crop Type Classification by DESIS Hyperspectral Imagery and Machine Learning Algorithms. *IEEE Journal of Selected Topics in Applied Earth Observations and Remote Sensing*, 16, 1–17. DOI: 10.1109/JSTARS.2023.3239756

Fukushima, K. (1980). Neocognitron: A self-organizing neural network model for a mechanism of pattern recognition unaffected by shift in position. *Biological Cybernetics*, 36(4), 193–202. DOI: 10.1007/BF00344251 PMID: 7370364

Goodrich, P., Betancourt, O., Arias, A. C., & Zohdi, T. (2023, February). Placement and drone flight path mapping of agricultural soil sensors using machine learning. *Computers and Electronics in Agriculture*, 205, 107591. Advance online publication. DOI: 10.1016/j.compag.2022.107591

Han, W., Hao, W., Sun, J., Xue, Y., & Li, W. (2022). Tomatoes Maturity Detection Approach Based on YOLOv5 and Attention Mechanisms. *2022 IEEE 4th International Conference on Civil Aviation Safety and Information Technology (ICCASIT)* (pp. 1363-1371). DOI: 10.1109/ICCASIT55263.2022.9986640

Hu, W., Yan, L., Liu, K., & Wang, H. (2015). PSO-SVR: A Hybrid Short-term Traffic Flow Forecasting Method. *2015 IEEE 21st International Conference on Parallel and Distributed Systems (ICPADS)* (pp. 553-561). DOI: 10.1109/ICPADS.2015.75

Islam, M. P., Hatou, K., Aihara, T., Kawahara, M., Okamoto, S., Senoo, S., & Sumire, K. (2022, November). ThelR547v1—An Asymmetric Dilated Convolutional Neural Network for Real-time Semantic Segmentation of Horticultural Crops. *Sensors (Basel)*, 22(22), 8807. DOI: 10.3390/s22228807 PMID: 36433404

Jafarbiglu, H., & Pourreza, A. (2022, June). A comprehensive review of remote sensing platforms, sensors, and applications in nut crops. *Computers and Electronics in Agriculture*, 197, 106844. Advance online publication. DOI: 10.1016/j.compag.2022.106844

Jiang, Y., Li, C., Paterson, A. H., & Robertson, J. S. (2019, November). DeepSeedling: Deep convolutional network and Kalman filter for plant seedling detection and counting in the field. *Plant Methods*, 15(1), 141. Advance online publication. DOI: 10.1186/s13007-019-0528-3 PMID: 31768186

Lac, L., Keresztes, B., Louargant, M., Donias, M., & Costa, J.-P. D. (2022). An annotated image dataset of vegetable crops at an early stage of growth for proximal sensing applications. *Data in Brief*, 42, 108035. DOI: 10.1016/j.dib.2022.108035 PMID: 35313502

LeCun, Y., Bengio, Y., & Hinton, G. (2015, May). Deep Learning. *Nature*, 521(7553), 436–444. DOI: 10.1038/nature14539 PMID: 26017442

Lee, H., Wang, J., & Leblon, B. (2020, July). Intra-Field Canopy Nitrogen Retrieval from Unmanned Aerial Vehicle Imagery for Wheat and Corn Fields. *Canadian Journal of Remote Sensing*, 46(4), 454–472. DOI: 10.1080/07038992.2020.1788384

Li, J., Chen, L., & Huang, W. (2018, January). Detection of early bruises on peaches (Amygdalus persica L.) using hyperspectral imaging coupled with improved watershed segmentation algorithm. *Postharvest Biology and Technology*, 135, 104–113. DOI: 10.1016/j.postharvbio.2017.09.007

Li, K. Y., de Lima, R. S., Burnside, N. G., Vahtmäe, E., Kutser, T., Sepp, K., & Sepp, K. (2022, March). Toward Automated Machine Learning-Based Hyperspectral Image Analysis in Crop Yield and Biomass Estimation. *Remote Sensing (Basel)*, 14(5), 1114. Advance online publication. DOI: 10.3390/rs14051114

Li, L., Zhang, S., & Wang, B. (2022, January). Apple leaf disease identification with a small and imbalanced dataset based on lightweight convolutional networks. *Sensors (Basel)*, 22(1), 173. Advance online publication. DOI: 10.3390/s22010173 PMID: 35009716

Li, M., Shamshiri, R. R., Weltzien, C., & Schirrmann, M. (2022, September). Crop Monitoring Using Sentinel-2 and UAV Multispectral Imagery: A Comparison Case Study in Northeastern Germany. *Remote Sensing (Basel)*, 14(17), 4426. DOI: 10.3390/rs14174426

Li, M., Xiao, L., Ma, X., Yang, F., Jin, X., & Ji, J. (2022, December). Vision-Based a Seedling Selective Planting Control System for Vegetable Transplanter. *Agriculture*, 12(12), 2064. Advance online publication. DOI: 10.3390/agriculture12122064

Lin, X., Li, C.-T., Adams, S., Kouzani, A. Z., Jiang, R., He, L., Hu, Y., Vernon, M., Doeven, E., Webb, L., Mcclellan, T., & Guskich, A. (2023). Self-Supervised Leaf Segmentation under Complex Lighting Conditions. *Pattern Recognition*, 135, 109021. DOI: 10.1016/j.patcog.2022.109021

Liu, J., & Wang, X. (2020, June). Tomato Diseases and Pests Detection Based on Improved Yolo V3 Convolutional Neural Network. *Frontiers in Plant Science*, 11, 898. Advance online publication. DOI: 10.3389/fpls.2020.00898 PMID: 32612632

Lobet, G., Koevoets, I. T., Noll, M., Meyer, P. E., Tocquin, P., Pagès, L., & Périlleux, C. (2017). Using a Structural Root System Model to Evaluate and Improve the Accuracy of Root Image Analysis Pipelines. *Frontiers in Plant Science*, 8. Advance online publication. DOI: 10.3389/fpls.2017.00447 PMID: 28421089

Luo, S., Jiang, X., Jiao, W., Yang, K., Li, Y., & Fang, S. (2022, September). Remotely Sensed Prediction of Rice Yield at Different Growth Durations Using UAV Multispectral Imagery. *Agriculture*, 12(9), 1447. DOI: 10.3390/agriculture12091447

Mattupalli, C., Seethepalli, A., York, L. M., & Young, C. A. (2019). Digital Imaging to Evaluate Root System Architectural Changes Associated with Soil Biotic Factors. *Phytobiomes Journal*, 3(2), 102–111. DOI: 10.1094/PBIOMES-12-18-0062-R

Migicovsky, Z., Li, M., Chitwood, D. H., & Myles, S. (2018). Morphometrics Reveals Complex and Heritable Apple Leaf Shapes. *Frontiers in Plant Science*, 8, 2185. Advance online publication. DOI: 10.3389/fpls.2017.02185 PMID: 29354142

Mohamed, E. S., Belal, A. A., Abd-Elmabod, S. K., El-Shirbeny, M. A., Gad, A., & Zahran, M. B. (2021). Smart farming for improving agricultural management. *The Egyptian Journal of Remote Sensing and Space Sciences*, 24(3), 971–981. DOI: 10.1016/j.ejrs.2021.08.007

Murray, S., Malambo, L., Popescu, S., Cope, D., Anderson, S., Chang, A., & Penna Cruzato, N. (2019, June). G2F Maize UAV Data, College Station, Texas 2017. *G2F Maize UAV Data, College Station, Texas 2017*. DOI: 10.25739/4ext-5e97

Nascimento, B., Ribeiro, M., Silva, L., Capobiango, N., & Silva, M. (2022). A soybean seedlings dataset for soil condition and genotype classification. *2022 35th SIBGRAPI Conference on Graphics, Patterns and Images (SIBGRAPI), 1*, 85-90. DOI: 10.1109/SIBGRAPI55357.2022.9991792

Omia, E., Bae, H., Park, E., Kim, M. S., Baek, I., Kabenge, I., & Cho, B. K. (2023, January). Remote Sensing in Field Crop Monitoring: A Comprehensive Review of Sensor Systems, Data Analyses and Recent Advances. *Remote Sensing (Basel)*, 15(2), 354. Advance online publication. DOI: 10.3390/rs15020354

Parsa, S., Debnath, B., Khan, M. A., & Amir Ghalamzan, E. (2023). Autonomous Strawberry Picking Robotic System (Robofruit). DOI: 10.48550/ARXIV.2301.03947

Peng, J., Rezaei, E. E., Zhu, W., Wang, D., Li, H., Yang, B., & Sun, Z. (2022, November). Plant Density Estimation Using UAV Imagery and Deep Learning. *Remote Sensing (Basel)*, 14(23), 5923. DOI: 10.3390/rs14235923

Peteinatos, G. G., Reichel, P., Karouta, J., Andújar, D., & Gerhards, R. (2020, December). Weed Identification in Maize, Sunflower, and Potatoes with the Aid of Convolutional Neural Networks. *Remote Sensing (Basel)*, 12(24), 1–22. DOI: 10.3390/rs12244185

Pinto, J., Powell, S., Peterson, R., Rosalen, D., & Fernandes, O. (2020, November). Detection of defoliation injury in peanut with hyperspectral proximal remote sensing. *Remote Sensing (Basel)*, 12(22), 1–16. DOI: 10.3390/rs12223828

Pound, M. P., Atkinson, J. A., Wells, D. M., Pridmore, T. P., & French, A. P. (2017). Deep Learning for Multi-task Plant Phenotyping. *2017 IEEE International Conference on Computer Vision Workshops (ICCVW)*, (pp. 2055-2063). DOI: 10.1109/ICCVW.2017.241

Quaglia, G., Visconte, C., Scimmi, L. S., Melchiorre, M., Cavallone, P., & Pastorelli, S. (2020, March). Design of a UGV powered by solar energy for precision agriculture. *Robotics (Basel, Switzerland)*, 9(1), 13. Advance online publication. DOI: 10.3390/robotics9010013

Quan, L., Feng, H., Lv, Y., Wang, Q., Zhang, C., Liu, J., & Yuan, Z. (2019, August). Maize seedling detection under different growth stages and complex field environments based on an improved Faster R–CNN. *Biosystems Engineering*, 184, 1–23. DOI: 10.1016/j.biosystemseng.2019.05.002

Ramamoorthy, P., Samiappan, S., Wubben, M. J., Brooks, J. P., Shrestha, A., Panda, R. M., Reddy, K. R., & Bheemanahalli, R. (2022, August). Hyperspectral Reflectance and Machine Learning Approaches for the Detection of Drought and Root–Knot Nematode Infestation in Cotton. *Remote Sensing (Basel)*, 14(16), 4021. Advance online publication. DOI: 10.3390/rs14164021

Rasti, S., Bleakley, C. J., Silvestre, G. C., Holden, N. M., Langton, D., & O'Hare, G. M. (2021, March). Crop growth stage estimation prior to canopy closure using deep learning algorithms. *Neural Computing & Applications*, 33(5), 1733–1743. DOI: 10.1007/s00521-020-05064-6

Ratnayake, M. N., Amarathunga, D. C., Zaman, A., Dyer, A. G., & Dorin, A. (2022, May). Spatial Monitoring and Insect Behavioural Analysis Using Computer Vision for Precision Pollination. *International Journal of Computer Vision*. Advance online publication. DOI: 10.1007/s11263-022-01715-4

Reedha, R., Dericquebourg, E., Canals, R., & Hafiane, A. (2022, February). Transformer Neural Network for Weed and Crop Classification of High Resolution UAV Images. *Remote Sensing (Basel)*, 14(3), 592. Advance online publication. DOI: 10.3390/rs14030592

Sadeghi-Tehran, P., Virlet, N., & Hawkesford, M. J. (2021, March). A neural network method for classification of sunlit and shaded components of wheat canopies in the field using high-resolution hyperspectral imagery. *Remote Sensing (Basel)*, 13(5), 1–17. DOI: 10.3390/rs13050898

Salazar-Gomez, A., Darbyshire, M., Gao, J., Sklar, E. I., & Parsons, S. (2022). Beyond mAP: Towards practical object detection for weed spraying in precision agriculture. *2022 IEEE/RSJ International Conference on Intelligent Robots and Systems (IROS)*, (pp. 9232-9238). DOI: 10.1109/IROS47612.2022.9982139

Scharr, H., Minervini, M., Fischbach, A., & Tsaftaris, S. (2014, July). Annotated Image Datasets of Rosette Plants. *Annotated Image Datasets of Rosette Plants.* Retrieved from https://juser.fz-juelich.de/record/154525/files/FZJ-2014-03837.pdf

Seethepalli, A., Guo, H., Liu, X., Griffiths, M., Almtarfi, H., Li, Z., Liu, S., Zare, A., Fritschi, F. B., Blancaflor, E. B., Ma, X.-F., & York, L. M. (2020). RhizoVision Crown: An Integrated Hardware and Software Platform for Root Crown Phenotyping. *Plant Phenomics (Washington, D.C.)*, 2020, 3074916. Advance online publication. DOI: 10.34133/2020/3074916 PMID: 33313547

Siegmann, B., Alonso, L., Celesti, M., Cogliati, S., Colombo, R., Damm, A., Douglas, S., Guanter, L., Hanuš, J., Kataja, K., Kraska, T., Matveeva, M., Moreno, J., Muller, O., Pikl, M., Pinto, F., Quirós Vargas, J., Rademske, P., Rodriguez-Morene, F., & Rascher, U. (2019, December). The high-performance airborne imaging spectrometer HyPlant-from raw images to top-of-canopy reflectance and fluorescence products: Introduction of an automatized processing chain. *Remote Sensing (Basel)*, 11(23), 2760. Advance online publication. DOI: 10.3390/rs11232760

Tanabe, R., Matsui, T., & Tanaka, T. S. (2023, February). Winter wheat yield prediction using convolutional neural networks and UAV-based multispectral imagery. *Field Crops Research*, 291, 108786. Advance online publication. DOI: 10.1016/j.fcr.2022.108786

Terentev, A., Dolzhenko, V., Fedotov, A., & Eremenko, D. (2022). Current state of hyperspectral remote sensing for early plant disease detection: A review. *Sensors (Basel)*, 22(3), 757. DOI: 10.3390/s22030757 PMID: 35161504

Tu, Y.-H., Johansen, K., Phinn, S., & Robson, A. (2019, January). Measuring Canopy Structure and Condition Using Multi-Spectral UAS Imagery in a Horticultural Environment. *Remote Sensing (Basel)*, 11(3), 269. DOI: 10.3390/rs11030269

Veley, K. M., Berry, J. C., Fentress, S. J., Schachtman, D. P., Baxter, I., & Bart, R. (2017). High-throughput profiling and analysis of plant responses over time to abiotic stress. *Plant Direct*, 1(4), e00023. DOI: 10.1002/pld3.23 PMID: 31245669

Vélez, S., Ariza-Sentís, M., & Valente, J. (2023). Dataset on unmanned aerial vehicle multispectral images acquired over a vineyard affected by Botrytis cinerea in northern Spain. *Data in Brief*, 46, 108876. DOI: 10.1016/j.dib.2022.108876 PMID: 36660442

Wang, J., Li, X., Guo, T., Dzievit, M. J., Yu, X., Liu, P., Price, K. P., & Yu, J. (2021, November). Genetic dissection of seasonal vegetation index dynamics in maize through aerial based high-throughput phenotyping. *The Plant Genome*, 14(3), e20155. Advance online publication. DOI: 10.1002/tpg2.20155 PMID: 34596348

Wang, L., Zeng, Y., & Chen, T. (2015, February). Back propagation neural network with adaptive differential evolution algorithm for time series forecasting. *Expert Systems with Applications*, 42(2), 855–863. DOI: 10.1016/j.eswa.2014.08.018

Wang, Y., Yang, L., Chen, H., Hussain, A., Ma, C., & Al-gabri, M. (2022). Mushroom-YOLO: A deep learning algorithm for mushroom growth recognition based on improved YOLOv5 in agriculture 4.0. *2022 IEEE 20th International Conference on Industrial Informatics (INDIN)* (pp. 239-244). DOI: 10.1109/INDIN51773.2022.9976155

Wei, L., Wang, K., Lu, Q., Liang, Y., Li, H., Wang, Z., Wang, R., & Cao, L. (2021, August). Crops fine classification in airborne hyperspectral imagery based on multi-feature fusion and deep learning. *Remote Sensing (Basel)*, 13(15), 2917. Advance online publication. DOI: 10.3390/rs13152917

Wu, J., Wen, S., Lan, Y., Yin, X., Zhang, J., & Ge, Y. (2022, December). Estimation of cotton canopy parameters based on unmanned aerial vehicle (UAV) oblique photography. *Plant Methods*, 18(1), 129. Advance online publication. DOI: 10.1186/s13007-022-00966-z PMID: 36482426

Yadav, P. K., Thomasson, J. A., Searcy, S. W., Hardin, R. G., Braga-Neto, U., Popescu, S. C., Martin, D. E., Rodriguez, R., Meza, K., Enciso, J., Diaz, J. S., & Wang, T. (2022). Assessing the performance of YOLOv5 algorithm for detecting volunteer cotton plants in corn fields at three different growth stages. *Artificial Intelligence in Agriculture*, 6, 292–303. DOI: 10.1016/j.aiia.2022.11.005

Yang, W., Yang, C., Hao, Z., Xie, C., & Li, M. (2019). Diagnosis of Plant Cold Damage Based on Hyperspectral Imaging and Convolutional Neural Network. *IEEE Access : Practical Innovations, Open Solutions*, 7, 118239–118248. DOI: 10.1109/ACCESS.2019.2936892

Yu, S., Xie, L., & Huang, Q. (2023, April). Inception convolutional vision transformers for plant disease identification. *Internet of Things : Engineering Cyber Physical Human Systems*, 21, 100650. DOI: 10.1016/j.iot.2022.100650

Yue, J., Yang, H., Yang, G., Fu, Y., Wang, H., & Zhou, C. (2023, February). Estimating vertically growing crop above-ground biomass based on UAV remote sensing. *Computers and Electronics in Agriculture*, 205, 107627. DOI: 10.1016/j.compag.2023.107627

Zhang, H., Wang, L., Tian, T., & Yin, J. (2021, March). A review of unmanned aerial vehicle low-altitude remote sensing (Uav-lars) use in agricultural monitoring in china. *Remote Sensing (Basel)*, 13(6), 1221. Advance online publication. DOI: 10.3390/rs13061221

Zhang, Y., Huang, S., Zhou, G., Hu, Y., & Li, L. (2023, February). Identification of tomato leaf diseases based on multi-channel automatic orientation recurrent attention network. *Computers and Electronics in Agriculture*, 205, 107605. DOI: 10.1016/j.compag.2022.107605

Zhong, Y., Hu, X., Luo, C., Wang, X., Zhao, J., & Zhang, L. (2020). WHU-Hi: UAV-borne hyperspectral with high spatial resolution (H2) benchmark datasets and classifier for precise crop identification based on deep convolutional neural network with CRF. *Remote Sensing of Environment*, 250, 112012. DOI: 10.1016/j.rse.2020.112012

Chapter 7
Natural Language Processing Applications

Piyal Roy
https://orcid.org/0009-0007-5378-2789
West Bengal State University, India

Rajat Pandit
West Bengal State University, India

ABSTRACT

Natural language processing (NLP) stands at the forefront of innovation, revolutionizing communication between humans and machines. The chapter discusses practical applications across diverse domains such as healthcare, finance, customer service, social media analysis, e-commerce, legal, education, and journalism, emphasizing NLP's pivotal role in enhancing efficiency and decision-making processes. However, challenges like bias, data quality, and ethical concerns necessitate interdisciplinary collaboration for mitigation. Recent advances in deep learning, pre-trained language models, transfer learning, multimodal NLP, and few-shot/zero-shot learning are highlighted for their transformative impact. Looking ahead, the chapter advocates for continued research to address model fairness, interpretability, and ethical considerations.

1. INTRODUCTION

A technical field called Natural Language Processing or NLP serves as the objective to let computers process human language while it also assists computers in creating meaning from language input. The natural evolution of NLP during recent years brought Gonzales important progress which transformed multiple industries.

DOI: 10.4018/979-8-3693-6255-6.ch007

The examination presents an extensive review of NLP starting with an introduction followed by field-based implementation perspectives and concluding research goals.

1.1. Overview of NLP

Artificial intelligence branch called NLP investigates human data transmission through commands and information along with possible automated computer simulation methods. A wide range of NLP tasks exists which includes speech recognition together with text mining and sentiment analysis and machine translation and question answering among others as per Sahoo et al., 2024. The fundamental principle of NLP exists in teaching machines to consume, understand and produce natural language data which ends the current information barrier between humans and machines (Roy et al., 2025a).

The Knowledge acquisition of written information happens through Machine Learning along with statisticians and linguists in Natural Language Processing (NLP). Natural language processing uses five major approaches with morphological linguistic approach being one of them. Syntactic linguistic approach along with the semantic linguistic approach and pragmatic linguistic approach and other approaches complete the set. The abilities of NLP systems rely on these methods to split input data into sentences, detect known entities and discover their relationships and understand textual surroundings.

The development of NLP technology relies on three main factors: utilizing extensive corpus and upgrading processing capabilities and implementing deep learning methodologies. Pre-trained generative models such as Generative Pre-trained Transformer (GPT) as well as Bidirectional Encoder Representations from Transformers (BERT) demonstrate exceptional performance in understanding human-like text and its generation hence contributing positively to natural language processing research and creating new applications.

1.2. Importance and Relevance of NLP in Various Fields

The multitude of fields where NLP creates business and societal effects makes this technological science extremely significant. Medical coding and electronic health record management and clinical documentation functions of NLP increase both patient satisfaction and reduce healthcare administration durations. The application in financial business supports trading functions and enables sentiment evaluation and fraud detection which allows organizations to control risks while making choices based on historical data (Cambria & White, 2014).

The critical role NLP plays in managing customer interaction stems from its foundational position in all chatbots and virtual assistants alongside public opinion examination systems. Such applications create better user experience while boosting operational speed and delivering customized experiences to multiple users. The NLP functionality of Twitter analysis consists of three elements: sentiment analysis, trends analysis and content moderation. omite the identification of new business matters along with ensuring brand image control and analyzing real-time public opinion trends through these tools.

NLP provides essential advantages to all e-commerce operations as well as legal entities and educational facilities and every sector you could imagine. NLP enables educational institutions to utilize its detection capabilities for plagiarism verification and to develop interactive teaching platforms while simultaneously enhancing educational outcomes across the education system. Journalism makes use of NLP to recommend news content and verify information sources and reduce lengthy stories into essential points. The news systems enable journalists to navigate through large amounts of data in order to deliver credible news items in a timely fashion.

1.3. Objectives

The paper discusses NLP applications across different industrial sectors throughout its fundamental sections. The study integrates real-life cases and literature to demonstrate how NLP handles diverse challenges and opportunities. The research explores established NLP practices while studying present trends which are now being utilized in this field and explains its base algorithms together with fundamental techniques. This article works to deepen understanding regarding NLP together with its application in academic and business operations and population settings.

2. FUNDAMENTALS OF NLP

NLP represents a branch of artificial intelligence and computational linguistics and other related domains with the mission of providing machines with natural language understanding abilities as well as analysis and generation capabilities. Here the explanation of NLP understanding and application commences while components receive a review along with an historical overview of NLP.

2.1. Definition and Scope of NLP

Natural language processing under AI refers to the computer interactions which duplicate human communication methods. The numerous tools managed by NLP include Speech recognition, text mining, Machine translation, question answering and sentiment analysis along with more tools. As Jurafsky & Martin (2009) explain NLP stands for "design and implementation of algorithms that allow computers to write and read with understanding". NLP finds practical applications throughout businesses within health, finance, customer support, social media monitoring, education, media and journalism and law departments. The system currently serves a large number of people who experience new growth in its coverage daily. Modern robots demonstrate the capability to learn contextual information as well as recognize specified entities within text while performing semantic analysis of the language and deriving relationships to generate text which displays human-level comprehension. Using the technology enhances interactions on business topics alongside social interactions which produces sound decision outcomes.

2.2. Key Components of NLP

Understandings of natural language require linguistic approaches such as pragmatics syntax and semantics while examining the NLP topic. Each linguistic component must be identified separately to achieve a complete understanding of language usage across various contexts according to Cooper (1982).

The study of word combination patterns which allows the creation of phrases and other words forms the basis of syntax. The simple sentence 'The cat sat on the mat' requires additional mention in my analysis for important reasons. The subject of this phrase is "cat" while the verb becomes "sat" and the preposition defines "on" and the object is "mat". This instance of syntactic dependency between phrase components appears in paragraph 2 to demonstrate this construction pattern. Nevertheless the grammatical structure of the phrase depends on parsing for understanding these dependencies between word elements. Part-of-speech tagging involves attributing speech parts to words for noun and verb and adjective and other categories identification. A machine's syntactic comprehension depends on syntactic analysis that decomposes sentences to extract phrases and clauses.

Semantics describes how words along with phrases together maintain meaning in real situations. Analyze the usage of "bank" within the range of subjects discussed earlier. A financial institution serves as the bank in this case but the bank term also illustrates the river shoreline ("I sat on the bank and watched the sun setting"). Word sense disambiguation serves as a method to identify which specific definition of a word should be applied when interpreting an instance of text. Semantic role labeling enables the identification of semantic roles from terms which determine their contributions to statement meaning through classifications such as agent and patient and place roles. Both machines and software benefit from semantic parsing because developers can normalize structured meaninfg in natural language text which enables machines to interpret word meanings in context.

In linguistics pragmatics provides explanations about additional meanings beyond words through evaluations of language usage in particular contexts. Conversation develops when Person A requests salt transfer from Person B who responds through an acceptance. In terms of direct response Person A is accurate when offering their seat to someone but examining this action requires analyzing social rules and conversational implications and social etiquette. The pragmatic analysis enables separation of speech actions for request and promise and speaker intentions derive from contextual information. Discourse analysis moves its attention to the structural aspects as well as coherence within extended language units including both texts and conversations since it analyzes the processes of meaning negotiation and interaction patterns. The predictive model provided by Conversational Inference enables the advancement of authentic robotic dialogue because it anticipates upcoming actions based on the recent conversation elements.

The NLP applications employ syntax semantics and pragmatics to process and generate textual language. The system enables various effective applications at high accuracy levels which include machine translation and sentiment analysis with question and answering functionalities.

2.3. Brief History and Evolution of NLP

The beginning of natural language processing history started with Alan Turing's paper in 1950 titled Turing (2009) together with Weaver's (1949) contribution. When Turing introduced the Turing Test as currency to check machine intelligence he began sparking growing interest in computational language models. Weaver reached the realization about machine language interpretation between languages which led him to invent the concept of machine translation.

Figure 1. Evolution of NLP

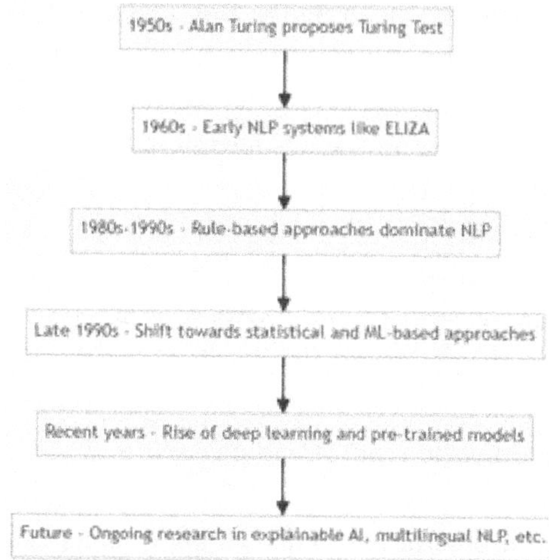

A basic text dialog system called ELIZA pioneered NLP technology when it became operational during the 1960s along with other early predecessors. During the first years the restricted capabilities to comprehend language and available computing power limited technological development.

Basic NLP practice with Symbolic methods became prevalent in the 1980s through 1990s and continues to be used in the present day. Knowledge-based and manually created language models enabled the creation of paradigms designed for information search and machine translation along with speech recognition systems. While these systems managed to be effective they proved inefficient for practical use since they never attained stable operation at scale. NLP experienced a transition between knowledge-based systems and machine learning together with statistical approaches during late 1990s and early 2000 (Manning & Schutze, 1999). Technical developments in large data availability along with processing power growth and data-learning algorithm development led to this evolution. The identification of named entities together with general language modeling benefits significantly from supervised and unsupervised learning approaches.

Pre-trained language models which became available together with deep learning structure advancements transformed NLP during the recent period. BERT along with GPT showcase powerful capabilities in retrieving and producing textual information like human beings for tasks like text generation and question answering and language translation.

NLP's future advancement path will emerge from current research domains about explainable AI, multilingual NLP, conversational AI and NLP for low-resource languages. These innovations will enable users to achieve outstanding outcomes when operating their computers and resolving practical problems across fields including finance and healthcare and learning.

3. NLP TECHNIQUES AND ALGORITHMS

NLP serves as a wide category that features numerous technological approaches and native systems that enable computers to interpret language besides generating textual output. The next part provides multiple explanations about NLP techniques alongside their practical applications across various fields.

3.1. Tokenization

Tokenization functions as a core NLP procedure with a critical purpose to turn text into tokens during this process. Tokens applied to this particular work in progress often consist of either sentences or phrases or individual letters. The practice of tokenization stands as a core element for numerous NLP applications throughout text analysis and information retrieval operations as well as machine learning algorithms development processes.

Machine learning algorithms together with efficient algorithm development become possible thanks to tokenization which establishes proper systematic organization for input text. NLP systems break text into tokens through tokenization which enables them to study individual meaningful units to perform detailed analytical work.

The process of lexical analysis reveals these specific words and phrases from the mentioned line: "the", "swift", "brown", "fox", "leaps", "over", "the", "slothful", "dog". NLP systems gain access to perform detailed text evaluation because each word is treated as an autonomous element during analysis.

NLP derives various additional tasks from tokenization such as named entity identification along with syntactic parsing and part of speech tagging. The tasks need to identify linguistic features and extract interesting patterns therefore text tokenization provides the necessary representation.

Humans achieve better language understanding from computers through tokenization which acts as an essential component during their language processing development. Text tokenization operates as a first step in advanced NLP since it breaks text content into distinct tokens that support complex language analysis.

3.2. Part-of-Speech Tagging

Within NLP processes POS tagging serves as an essential step to assign proper grammatical tags (parts of speech or POS) to each word in a text including noun, verb and adjective tags. Through this method NLP algorithms obtain important details about sentence structure while defining word meanings when placed in their context.

When reading "The cat sat on the mat" a person would encounter specific word marking that indicates parts of speech. Under a POS tagging process the statement would receive the following word designations:

The text contains six elements beginning with "the" (DT - determiner), "cat" (NN - noun), "sat" (VBD - verb, past tense), "on" (IN - preposition), moving to "the" (DT - determiner) before ending with "mat" (NN - noun).

The implementation of these tags enables NLP systems to detect both syntactic structures and recognize important texts because they specify how words function in sentences.

The NLP subdomains of syntax analysis and semantic analysis with information extraction develop their operations because of part of speech tagging technology. NLP systems analyze sentence words to derive syntax information because the systems automatically detect how each word functions within the sentence structure.

The syntactic analysis method named part-of-speech tagging requires sentence structure analysis to perform. Parse trees become possible with parsers who use this approach to show sentence hierarchical structure and discover working word syntactic relations.

Semantic parsing receives increased effectiveness through the implementation of part-of-speech tagging because tagging delivers precise details about word functions within sentences. The semantic parser acquires object-performance relations that let it understand sentence meaning.

The correct operation of computers when processing natural language content depends fundamentally on the implementation of part-of-speech tagging. Future tasks within NLP will benefit from POS tagging since this tagging method enables better language understanding through word classification according to POS categories.

3.3. Named Entity Recognition (NER)

When it comes to NLP one essential challenge lies in finding named entities through a process named named entity recognition. Named entities include specific objects which get distinguished through names that point to persons, locations, dates, firms and counted entities in expressions. The operation of NER serves to enable analysis of structured data derived from unstructured texts for downstream NLP operations.

The sentence "Apple is headquartered in Cupertino, California" presents NER with organizational data about "Apple" and locational data about "Cupertino, California". Named entities bring advantageous context through proper nouns that help understand text content while extracting useful info.

Named Entity Recognition appears multiple times in intelligent systems across entity linking and information retrieval systems as well as document summarization and question answering processes. The application of NER in information retrieval allows systems to recognize previously mentioned entities which speeds up the process of information delivery to users. The process of document summarization benefits from NER since it determines crucial entities that must appear in summaries as well as provides an overview of the text content. Entity and relation annotation enables systems to locate search terms in questions so they can generate correct answers from text corpora and knowledge bases in question answering systems. The NER systems employ machine learning approaches that include deep leaning models and conditional random fields (CRF) for training purposes based on annotated corpus. With previous processing experience the models establish patterns of named entities which they can use to apply to new text material.

NR proves essential for NLP systems to extract organized data from text inputs without structure. NER helps text understanding by identifying entities and categorization resulting in various practical applications through its entity tagging.

3.4. Sentiment Analysis

The NLP field requires opinion mining as an important task to analyze text documents so systems can determine their opinionated content (Liu, 2022). NLP systems employ this method to process consumer feedback and social media content and other materials that identify present trends while measuring both positive and negative sentiment reactions from customers. A restaurant review describing excellent service and delicious food appears in this format "The food was delicious and the service was excellent." The author expresses positive feelings in this review which positions it in the positive category showing the writer gave numerous good opinions about the restaurant. A review containing the complaint "The food was cold and service was slow" under the subject line would belong to the unsatisfactory group.

Sentiment analysis detects the overall sentiment of the text by allocating it into three possible groups that include positive, negative or neutral choices. Using sentiment analysis allows organizations to categorize feelings according to their sentiment level which determines the how strong or weak the expressed feeling is. Sentiment analysis serves organizations across different fields for market research purposes as well as analysis of customer feedback and brand monitoring and reputation management. Customer feedback enables firms to detect important changes that need attention while allowing them to evaluate customer satisfaction levels through sentiment analysis of these observations. Brand monitoring becomes possible with sentiment analysis because this technology enables businesses to track public perceptions of their brands together with potential PR failures or developing trends. Organisations conducting market research need this method to determine customer attitudes toward specific products and services.

The two main sentiment analysis methods include rule-based systems and supervised learning with recurrent neural networks (RNN) and support vector machines (SVM) as examples of training data sets. These models succeed at proper sentiment classification since their design includes the capabilities to understand the linguistic elements which express sentiment.

Sentiment analysis operates as an essential instrument which helps researchers understand public messages while examining how population sentiments appear within corresponding text documentation. Businesses alongside organizations gain easier access to strategic decision making through automated sentiment-based text determination which allows them to react efficiently to market sentiments and customer feedback.

3.5. Text Classification

The essential functionality of natural language processing constitutes text classification which assigns textual documents to pre-defined classification groups according to their written content. The classification method attains widespread use across multiple domains such as topics, emotions, spam, and documents (Sebastiani, 2002).

The process of sorting news articles between entertainment and sports and politics sections requires a specific sorting method. Each piece of article content will receive classification from text algorithms to determine the appropriate section for placement.

The classification algorithms employ machine learning functionality to find text material beyond user view since these systems examine labeled texts within training data. The text classification algorithms consist of either deep learning models using Convolutional neural networks and Recurrent neural networks together with traditional statistical models working with support vector machines and Naïve Bayes.

Text classification proves beneficial by developing an effective system to classify big document collections for knowledge management and information retrieval. Via text categorization we can detect spam in order to remove unwanted messages from non-desired emails along with real message content. Sentiment analysis classification requires assigning textual content to predefined response categories that include either positive or negative emotions or remaining neutral. The process generates beneficial insights that show what customers think about specific products and their services. The users gain clarity from extensive text data by applying topic modeling which sorts documents by their contained themes and subjects present in predefined document collections.

The initial training process utilizes labeled text documents to establish categories that will be used for classification purposes. During the learning phase these models extract patterns that enable them to connect text information with defined categories. New textual documents beyond their training set become their focus once they apply their learned patterns.

By summing up these points we can state that text classification constitutes a dynamic system that enhances computer handling of textual information with better organization and understanding. The classification of text based on algorithms enables numerous applications which generate user insights from substantial text collections because of predefined classification categories.

3.6. Machine Translation

Natural Language Processing (NLP) performs its major task in Machine Translation (MT) through text translation across different languages. The multilingual systems need support and information retrieval from different languages through this application. The system operates as a critical component in the development of multilingual communication procedures. The example shows a user translating an English paper for international readers with a target language of French. The analysis of English content through user-operated translation devices leads to automatic French translation output.

Machine translation systems implement several translation methods that generate accurate results with fluent wording. These methods consist of:

i. Machine translation through rules functions by applying dictionaries combined with linguistic rules which enable language migrations from one language to the other. The process of achieving decent machine translation output through these algorithms needs both deep language understanding and a series of manually built system rules.
ii. The analytical component of statistical machine translation systems uses extensive big bilingual corpora to discover typical translation patterns. Statistical machine translation systems perform two functions through their statistical models by determining probable translation options and linking pairs of linguistic elements between languages and their possible translation equivalents. SMT systems en-

hance translation quality standards through their current employment in almost all machine translation operations.

iii. NMT patterns derive from direct learning of data through transformers and recurrent neural networks along with other deep learning architectures. Machine translation systems maintain their position as top-rate because they optimize efficiency at levels higher than standard procedures did. When NMT models process translations the results become more natural and flowing than those generated by statistic MT models because the NMT algorithms understand complex syntactic structures and context dependencies.

Machine translation systems encounter two main challenges in addition to ambiguity and these are the occurrence of ambiguous content and industry-specific terminology along with colloquial language. Machine translation systems face specific translation problems while dealing with languages that have different word order and syntactical patterns.

Machine translation faces obstacles from minimal vocabulary along with scarce parallel data and confusing language structures yet the development of deep learning frameworks and big data resources and enhanced computational forces during the past years substantially advanced the speed of translation processing (Choudhury et al., 2024). Previous obstacles regarding language communication between users of different languages have transformed into crucial tools for intercultural communication through machine translation systems.

3.7. Question Answering

The core task of NLP known as Question Answering enables automated retrieval of appropriate natural language answers to human inquiries. Various operational systems including search engines and chatbots and information retrieval systems and virtual assistants already utilize this technological solution.

A situation where a person requests information by asking "What is the capital of France?" After processing the request the question-answering system retrieves suitable information from text or knowledge repositories before returning an answer like "Paris".

For question answering systems to produce responses they employ information retrieval methods together with natural language processing as well as knowledge representation techniques. Among these methods are:

i. Before answering user queries the systems engage in information retrieval to locate specific pertinent documents and structured databases which contain unstructured text documents among their content. The retrieval process within these sources generates specific documents or sections that relate to the request through information retrieval applications.

ii. Some systems using natural language understanding processes the provided query to comprehend its meaning as well as retrieve essential data from processed information. The natural language comprehension techniques along with syntactic and semantic analysis convert the query into an analyzable form which reveals important query elements and their relationships.
iii. Knowledge representation functions as an assistance tool for problem reasoning through systems which display acquired information combined with the query. The description methods used for information and knowledge include ontologies and semantic graphs which define entities together with their relational patterns.
iv. Question answering systems use acquired information from multiple sources to analyze user questions before generating precise answers for the queried information. The answer generation process can happen by two methods: synthesis from previous knowledge base data or retrieval of appropriate information from acquired papers.

The question answering system controls three types of questions: fact-based, definition-based and inference-based. The choice of solution depends on the particular task at hand as well as available data availability because it can be built with deep learning frameworks alongside statistical models and rule-based systems.

Question answering stands as a demanding yet crucial NLP operation that assists users to retrieve natural language-based answers to their inquiries.

3.8. Summarization

The process of document compression known as summarization functions as a core NLP technique which produces shorter materials from longer ones while keeping essential points intact. The readers can obtain essential concepts from long pieces through this method which produces short summaries of books or papers or news publications.

A long form news story from The Guardian about the recent incident serves as an excellent example I will share with you. The summarisation algorithm would examine the article's content before generating a brief that emphasizes significant arguments, opposes and highlights important article components. The summary provides essential content understanding for people who must read only a portion of the article (Nenkova & McKeown, 2011).

The summarizing algorithms mainly function in two different ways: extractive along with abstractive processing.

i. The algorithm extracts summaries from source material through manual selection of particular sentences or paragraphs. Most papers include their most important sentences directly in the selected summary. Several extractive summarization algorithms determine sentence scores from their document-based weightage calculations which include word frequencies and sentence position and relative importance to the whole document. Extracellular summarizing systems would arrange the summary of climate change papers to incorporate lines about causes and environmental effects before measures to counter the effects.
ii. The abstractive Summarization method creates new sentences through paraphrasing to convey the fundamental ideas present in original source materials. Model-based summarizing methods deviate from extractive models because they make unique phrases that differ from how content looks in the original material. Natural language generation together with semantic techniques enables the development of condensed reasonable summaries.

An algorithm performing abstractive summarization takes scientific content to create new text that presents the main research outcomes and study conclusions differently yet retains equivalent key points from the original piece.

Summarizing techniques function in four distinct ways which include literature review together with news clippings and documents and text summaries that appear in search engine results. Through automated summarization consumers can address extensive data volumes by basing their choices on the condensed interpretation of lengthy content.

The summarization process demonstrates excellent effectiveness for text processing through NLP methods which provides users rapid access to essential text information.

3.9. Language Generation

The primary activity of NLP involves generating language through automated systems that produces writing resembling human composition from given inputs. General content creation utilizes this technology alongside conversational platforms having both applications while it functions as a writing support system.

A bot system capable of interacting with clients through human language communication. User-friendly language generation by the chatbot produces sufficient responses for its environment so users experience interactions nearly equivalent to real person interactions. A user who asks about weather conditions The automated system will provide information about sunny and warm conditions that prevail in the present weather state.

Multiple language generation models employ recurrent neural networks (RNNs) that use extensive textual data for pattern identification before creating extensive textual data. The transformer designs of GPT alongside BERT make use of extensive textual data to learn these patterns for generating extensive textual data. The models require extensive exposure to text data which enables them to understand natural language syntax and meaning and pragmatic rules.

OpenAI showcases its most innovative language design approach within the GPT series of models. Transformer-based language models operate as part of this system after receiving Fine-tuning on multiple text datasets. The efficiency of these models proves reliable when producing contextually valid and grammatically correct responses for numerous tasks which include text generation and dialog generation and story writing.

Although factual or instructional content does not need language generative algorithms for its development. These models function creatively to create lyrics that serve both poems and songs as well as narratives. The training of language generation models on a body of poetry allows them to create fresh poetic lines which match the tone and style of the original writings.

Language Generation presents itself as a flexible method for computers to manufacture natural language materials which display near-human indistinguishable results for multiple utilization scenarios. The combination of self-organising language generation systems improves human-computer interaction in several fields through complex neural networks and big language models which decrease human content creation labor.

4. APPLICATIONS OF NLP IN VARIOUS DOMAINS

The widespread industrial application of NLP has made it a highly important technological field. NLP exerts substantial influence on information processing as well as communication promotion and commercial execution. The main areas that found substantial advancement in natural language processing are now open for our analysis.

4.1. Medical Care

The healthcare management relies heavily on NLP because it boosts both medical coding practices and EHR and clinical documentation operations. NLP systems demonstrate essential application in healthcare by assisting clinical choices of professionals while enhancing treatment quality and office workflow through examination of unstructured medical documentation and other study materials (Luo et al., 2019).

Patients benefit from NLP algorithms through automation of time-consuming summary procedures that present clinical information about patients. NLP has incorporated pharmacovigilance for two key purposes: patient safety improvement and adverse event identification and potential safety issue detection (Topaz & Lai, 2016).

4.2. Finance

The financial industry sees a meaningful advancement due to NLP implementations for fraud detection together with risk analysis and sentiment analysis of market news. The analysis performed by NLP systems on news stories and social media posts and financial reports reveals market mood and identifies new market trends while forecasting stock price movements (Pang & Lee, 2008).

NLP applications function as fundamental features within banking customer support through chatbots and virtual assistants which also enable banking staff to offer service guidance to clients and optimize bank account workflow. Finance organizations together with their customers receive better outcomes from their interaction with NLP because it handles mundane communication along with delivering better information.

4.3. Assistance to Customers

When NLP technology powers customer service applications it becomes essential to generate automatic feedback responses while reading through client feedback to enhance the entire service quality. The application of autonomous NLP in virtual assistants and chatbots allows them to deliver services to clients at any time (Oraby et al., 2019). These systems provide solutions to problems while answering questions through their interactions.

The use of sentiment analysis based on NLP technology enables organizations to monitor customer feedback across different platforms which include surveys and social media content and online review platforms. The acquisition of client sentiment patterns and behavioral shifts and business development needs through sentiment analysis enables companies to enhance their product and service personalization.

4.4. Social Media Analysis

The research of vast social media user-generated content depends heavily on NLP approaches. Three widely used NLP applications in social media analytics include sentiment analysis together with topic modeling and trend identification according to Wang et al. (2012).

An NLP system looks at social media conversations to detect customer emotions while it finds what people are discussing and tracks brand feedback levels. Social media monitoring systems apply NLP technology to track specific keywords and hashtags along with user interactions for marketing performance evaluation as a key system feature.

4.5. E-Commerce

Using NLP technology enables businesses to analyze customer reviews and generate product recommendations and sort merchandise by type. NLP algorithms perform three functions as Chen et al. (2019) report: they sort items and extract attributes from descriptions while offering personalized suggestions to each user based on their needs.

NLP-based sentiment analysis enables e-commerce systems to interpret user assessments and use the findings to identify product issues and gauge customer satisfaction for better inventory management decisions.

4.6. Legal

Legal entities employ NLP systems to analyze documents while researchers use it to perform legal research on cases and exam contracts. The NLP technology enables law professionals to search for legal documents and perform discovery operations and it helps to evaluate case law materials and extract significant legal text information (Ashley, 2017).

Legal practitioners utilize NLP to handle massive legal documents and find essential case references for legal assessments and identify necessary data to support case maintenance and litigation support. The evaluation of contracts by NLP-enabled contract analysis systems produces insights into potentially dangerous provisions and areas that require resolution.

4.7. Education

Through NLP education achieves the implementation of advanced tutoring systems along with automatic essay feedback and production of educational materials. The authors define NLP systems as systems which evaluate student-generated scripts and give feedback before measuring language proficiency according to Attali and Burstein.

ITISES uses NLP because the technology connects educational content to individual student requirements according to their learning achievements. Through NLP researchers can create instructional materials which directly fulfill curriculum demands and learning standards (Roy et al., 2025b).

4.8. Press and Publications

Natural language processing has introduced three main journalism applications which combine fact verification with news summaries that extract central data points. Natural language processing algorithms assist readers in obtaining simplified reports on essential events through processing news content and choosing relevant data along with summary generation (Giannakopoulos, 2009).

The ability of NLP to extract information proves beneficial for journalists in their mission to analyze verify facts sourced from multiple platforms. The fact-checking programs which implement NLP logic use its logic to evaluate information truthfulness while conducting fact-checks and cross-checks and performing claim analysis.

NLP methods have reached the threshold of becoming routine industrial practices while promoting economic sectors to automate their processes alongside fostering innovation and operational efficiency. Robots get their ability to interpret understand and create natural language text through the widely utilized technology known as NLP. The system improves user interfaces as well as supports business operations to deliver superior business decisions.

5. CHALLENGES AND LIMITATIONS OF NLP

The present NLP system experiences various limitations that restrict its widespread adoption to its maximum capacity. The next part of this article examines these problems with deeper analysis.

5.1. Natural Language Ambiguity

A word or phrase in natural language displays multiple possible contexts making the natural language inherently ambiguous. Natural language understanding becomes an elaborate task for NLP systems since Jurafsky and Martin note that people need to interpret various environmental contexts to distinguish multiple meanings. The term "bank" takes different meanings such as a financial institution handling money or the shoreline or an act of rotating toward one direction based on situational contexts.

Large text datasets receive training by NLP systems through contextual analytical methods and machine learning techniques to handle this issue. NLP ambiguity resolution research remains highly complex throughout the development process because no universal solution exists for managing this issue.

5.2. Domain Specific Considerations

The training of NLP models with general language data from large text collections produces problems when they operate in specific environments which display high formal language use along with professional terminology. Every industry sector including healthcare and banking together with legal practice features its unique terminology and phrases which exist throughout all human professions (Lever & Gimpel, 2021). The process of NLP technique application in specific domains demands both domain knowledge and training data to process textual semantics and identify textual relationships. The development of domain-specific NLP solutions requires direct involvement between NLP professionals and specialists from their target domains together with industrial partnership representatives.

5.3. Ethical Issues

Social impacts along with implications of NLP systems development and deployment do not allow us to disregard their ethical implications. The broader community along with researchers and policymakers demonstrate concerns about training biases and privacy intrusions which emerge from algorithm uses as well as data prejudices (Bolukbasi et al., 2016) (Keßler et al., 2020).

The multiplication of biased training data sources amplifies all forms of bias in NLP systems that eventually results in discriminatory treatment and sustains unfair societal standards. The total demands also involve implementing robust data protection regulations as well as open standards for personal information processing procedures.

Student teams should implement three preventive measures which include self-regulation procedures that enhance model transparency and fairness as well as impact analyses and standard ethical compliance requirements. Interdisciplinary teams with stakeholders need to resolve ethical issues which would rebuild trust among users regarding NLP technology.

5.4. Problems With Data Quality and Availability

Training data quality along with quantity represent vital elements that determine successful operation of NLP systems. Large diverse annotated datasets with a wide range of linguistic events and tasks must be obtained to train efficient NLP models (Gehrmann et al., 2019). Acquiring labeled data for NLP tasks can be difficult mainly in fields requiring specialized domains or for low resource languages.

Various hurdles emerge during the process of creating training datasets which are expected to be representative and high-quality. Research inadequacies caused by data bias or noise lead to faulty predictions that result in low accuracy rates while also reducing NLP's successful implementation. The NLP community requires proof of methods for data augmentation and high-quality datasets alongside best practice guidelines for collecting and annotating data to address data availability and quality challenges.

5.5. Explainability and Interpretability

Complex NLP models require functionality that allows users to understand the decision-making processes of the system. For critical applications that use models in healthcare, finance, and law the users and regulators want decision systems to deliver explanations about their predictions and logical reasoning (Ribeiro et al., 2016).

Most advanced NLP models that use deep neural networks operate as black boxes because their decision-making inner workings are difficult to understand and explain. To raise expert understanding of ways model modifications affect NLP system explainability and interpretability scientists need to advance their knowledge base because it directly enhances product confidence and protects against the algorithmic accountability issues.

The improvement of NLP methods requires both model-independent interpretability approaches and elegant architectural frameworks and built-in explainability protocols. The development of interpretable NLP solutions requires regular collaboration between NLP researchers and domain specialists with the ultimate decision-makers who use the solutions to achieve different requirements. The advancement of NLP as machine language analysis stands limited by challenges that need collaboration between academic researchers and corporate organizations and government officials and community members to solve. The scientific analysis of NLP-related challenges coupled with dedicated work allows us to access NLP technology's beneficial potential that leads to advantageous human advancements.

6. RECENT ADVANCES IN NLP

In the past few years, the development and creativity in the field of natural language processing (NLP) as a whole, along with new methodologies and techniques following advanced knowledge in machine learning, various forms of deep learning, and the rise of large language models, have been most spectacular. Well, we should dedicate some time seeing about the most important as well as ground breaking advancements in NLP within the last few years.

6.1. Deep Learning in NLP

Deep learning allows training and designing neural networks that learn very deep structure and develop rich patterns to represent large volumes of text data what have given enormous boost to natural language processing. Convolutional Neural Networks (CNNs), Recurrent Neural Networks (RNNs) and recently introduced transformers (Young et al., 2018) that are always known to deliver the best performance in NLP tasks can be worth using.

CNNs have one of the strengths, they possess the capability of learning local features of text i.e, word information content etc, which can be used in tasks such as sentiment analysis and text categorization. This is possible due to the dimensionality of processing that RNNs allow for, i.e. tasks such as machine translation and language modeling. One of the self attention techniques utilized by pretrained models like BERT are to point out the contextual features as well as dependencies of distant context in a text. It allows them to function very well and effectively on many natural language processing problems (Vaswani et al., 2017).

It is without a doubt that Deep learning models have made NLP stellar not just in the sense that they opened the opportunities for NLP to go full scale but also in the opportunities that they have brought about in applying NLP in the process of language creation, document summarization and conversational AI.

6.2. Pre-trained Language Models

Recent advances in particular that give relatively inexpensive, yet high efficiency ways to utilize large unlabeled corpora, have recast NLP with pre trained language models. These models were pre-trained from text corpora and fine tuned on such tasks as specified by BERT, GPT and so on; these models are very accurate when used in the standard NLP tests as mentioned by Devlin et al., 2018 and Radford et al., 2018.

In fact, the pre trained language models have the ability to understand complex syntactic and semantic patterns in the text as they have acquired extensive context representation of text and words to use while understanding it. By fine tuning on task specific data, practitioners can use these same models for many NLP tasks such as text categorization, named entity identification, question answering with minimal task specific data and computing resources. The emergence of pre trained language models has made NLP research and application development a lot more easier and the possibility that academics and practitioners to contribute in competitive fashion on variety of tasks and domains (Ghosh et al., 2025).

6.3. NLP Transfer Learning

Transfer learning had become quite popular in NLP as a powerful way to address problems with data scarcity and domain adaptation. With the prevailing need for NLP systems to generalize from few data, transfer learning aids systems to become more effective in generalizing to new tasks and domains using information from pre trained models on large scale data (Wijmans et al., 2019).

Optimizing pre trained language models or extracting features of an intermediate layer has shown to boost performance in the sequel task like text categorization, named entity identification, and sentiment analysis etc. Transfer learning techniques have succeeded in improving performance on subsequent tasks. Transfer learning has also made easy creation of domain specific langue models and customised embeddings for certain sectors or applications. Using the wealth of knowledge stored in pre trained models, transfer learning has become a leading strategy for getting better results and speeding up the development of NLP.

6.4. Multimodal NLP

Around standard NLP, we can incorporate data from several modalities such as text, graphics, audio to enrich the understanding and generate more complete content. The spread of multimedia content on the internet and social media platforms makes the task of picture captioning, video summarization and video retrieval cross modal, which makes multimodal NLP more significant (Wang et al., 2017).

For instance, to analyse text and visual data models like BERT and GPT expanded to multi modal inputs for image text matching and visual question answering among others. Multimodal NLP has many applications where one needs to understand and coalesce data from multiple modalities like recommendation systems, assistive technology, and autonomous cars.

6.5. Few-Shot and Zero-Shot Learning

To make NLP models generalize to new tasks and categories that were not seen during training, few shot and zero shot learning strategies attempt to train the models with a few annotated instances or without task specific training data at all. In particular, these methods are useful when it is expensive or infeasible to acquire the labeled data (Triantafillou et al., 2019).

Techniques such as generative modeling, prototype based learning and meta learning make few or zero shot learning possible in NLP. Using these methods, they attain the ability to quickly adjust to new assignments or untested classes with very little labeled data by employing meta knowledge acquired from a suite of jobs or even a set of families.

Few and zero shot learning techniques are widely used in cross lingual natural language processing and customized recommendation systems in low resource environments, where there is great need for flexibility in handling novel jobs and users with sparse data.

Recent development techniques in NLP, like deep learning, transfer learning, few-shot or zero-shot learning, pre-trained language models, and multimodal NLP have brought this field to unimaginable heights in the past decades, allowing language to be generated and comprehend with increasingly complexity in a plethora of domains and areas.

7. CONCLUSION AND FUTURE SCOPE

In this chapter, NLP is thoroughly researched from its core principles, practical implementations, recent advancement and current challenges. In this it is also stressed the importance of interdisciplinary collaboration between researchers, domain experts and stakeholders in order to advance the ethical integration of NLP technologies and design domain specific solutions. Such automation can help the industry improve its efficiency in the present scenario, warm up to AI and emerging technologies, and reshape the entire workflow from both customer as well as business prospects.

As such, future research in NLP should focus on reducing the biases in NLP models to foster regulatory compliance, instil more confidence in the users, and improve interpretability and explainability. Cross modal understanding research through multimodal NLP may help to carry a more prehensive and nuanced study of contents from multimedia mediums. Investigation of cross-lingual and low resource NLP approaches can enable inclusion and accessibility in NLP applications. Ethical, legal, and societal implications of NLP technologies should be a priority for industry stakeholders, policymakers and researchers to come to a term with.

REFERENCES

Ashley, K. D. (2017). *Artificial intelligence and legal analytics: new tools for law practice in the digital age*. Cambridge University Press. DOI: 10.1017/9781316761380

Attali, Y., & Burstein, J. (2006). Automated essay scoring with e-rater® V. 2. *The Journal of Technology, Learning, and Assessment*, 4(3).

Bolukbasi, T., Chang, K. W., Zou, J. Y., Saligrama, V., & Kalai, A. T. (2016). Man is to computer programmer as woman is to homemaker? debiasing word embeddings. *Advances in Neural Information Processing Systems*, 29.

Cambria, E., & White, B. (2014). Jumping NLP curves: A review of natural language processing research. *IEEE Computational Intelligence Magazine*, 9(2), 48–57. DOI: 10.1109/MCI.2014.2307227

Chen, F., Pan, S., Jiang, J., Huo, H., & Long, G. (2019, July). DAGCN: dual attention graph convolutional networks. In *2019 International Joint Conference on Neural Networks (IJCNN)* (pp. 1-8). IEEE.

Choudhury, R. R., Roy, P., Ghosh, S., & Ghosh, A. (2024). Machine Learning and Deep Learning Algorithms for Green Computing. In Kumar, K., Varadarajan, V., Nasser, N., & Poluru, R. (Eds.), *Computational Intelligence for Green Cloud Computing and Digital Waste Management* (pp. 1–23). IGI Global Scientific Publishing. DOI: 10.4018/979-8-3693-1552-1.ch001

Conroy, J. M., Schlesinger, J. D., & O'Leary, D. P. (2015). Automatic summarization of changes in documents. U.S. Patent No. 9,111,854. Washington, DC: U.S. Patent and Trademark Office.

Devlin, J., Chang, M. W., Lee, K., & Toutanova, K. (2018). Bert: Pre-training of deep bidirectional transformers for language understanding. arXiv preprint arXiv:1810.04805.

Gehrmann, S., Strobelt, H., & Rush, A. M. (2019). Gltr: Statistical detection and visualization of generated text. DOI: 10.18653/v1/P19-3019

Ghosh, S., Sarkar, S. K., Roy, P., Roy, B., & Podder, A. (2025). Role of Libraries in Promoting Digital Literacy and Information Fluency. In Sacco, K., Norton, A., & Arms, K. (Eds.), *Navigating AI in Academic Libraries: Implications for Academic Research* (pp. 77–108). IGI Global Scientific Publishing. DOI: 10.4018/979-8-3693-3053-1.ch005

Giannakopoulos, G. (2009). Automatic summarization from multiple documents. Department of Information and Communication Systems Engineering, University of the Aegean, 49-66.

Keßler, T., Rjasanow, S., & Weißer, S. (2020). Vlasov—Poisson System Tackled by Particle Simulation Utilizing Boundary Element Methods. *SIAM Journal on Scientific Computing*, 42(1), B299–B326. DOI: 10.1137/18M1225823

Liu, B. (2022). *Sentiment analysis and opinion mining*. Springer Nature.

Manning, C., & Schutze, H. (1999). *Foundations of statistical natural language processing*. MIT press.

Martin, J. H. (2009). *Speech and language processing: An introduction to natural language processing, computational linguistics, and speech recognition*. Pearson/ Prentice Hall.

Nenkova, A., & McKeown, K. (2011). Automatic summarization. Foundations and Trends® in Information Retrieval, 5(2–3), 103-233.

Oraby, S., Bhuiyan, M., Gundecha, P., Mahmud, J., & Akkiraju, R. (2019). Modeling and computational characterization of twitter customer service conversations. [TiiS]. *ACM Transactions on Interactive Intelligent Systems*, 9(2-3), 1–28. DOI: 10.1145/3213014

Pang, B., & Lee, L. (2008). Opinion mining and sentiment analysis. Foundations and Trends® in information retrieval, 2(1–2), 1-135.

Radford, A., Narasimhan, K., Salimans, T., & Sutskever, I. (2018). Improving language understanding by generative pre-training.

Ribeiro, M. T., Singh, S., & Guestrin, C. (2016, August). " Why should i trust you?" Explaining the predictions of any classifier. In *Proceedings of the 22nd ACM SIGKDD international conference on knowledge discovery and data mining* (pp. 1135-1144). DOI: 10.18653/v1/N16-3020

Roy, P., Ghosh, S., Podder, A., & Sarkar, S. K. (2025a). Opportunities and Challenges of Artificial Intelligence (AI) in the Banking and Finance Sector. Shaping Cutting-Edge Technologies and Applications for Digital Banking and Financial Services, 120.

Roy, P., Pandit, R., & Naskar, S. K. (2025b). Innovative Approaches to Problem-Solving Through Educational Technology Integration. In J. Zhang, W. Wan Yahaya, M. Sanmugam, & D. Lim (Eds.), Integrating Technology in Problem-Solving Educational Practices (pp. 375-402). IGI Global Scientific Publishing. DOI: 10.4018/979-8-3693-6745-2.ch016

Sahoo, T., Mondal, A., Roy, P., & Podder, A. (2024). Artificial Intelligence and Its Application in Engineering: A Comprehensive Review. In El Kacimi, Y., & Alaoui, K. (Eds.), *Emerging Engineering Technologies and Industrial Applications* (pp. 1–20). IGI Global Scientific Publishing. DOI: 10.4018/979-8-3693-1335-0.ch001

Sebastiani, F. (2002). Machine learning in automated text categorization. *ACM Computing Surveys*, 34(1), 1–47. DOI: 10.1145/505282.505283

Topaz, M., Lai, K., Dhopeshwarkar, N., Seger, D. L., Sa'adon, R., Goss, F., Rozenblum, R., & Zhou, L. (2016). Clinicians' reports in electronic health records versus patients' concerns in social media: A pilot study of adverse drug reactions of aspirin and atorvastatin. *Drug Safety*, 39(3), 241–250. DOI: 10.1007/s40264-015-0381-x PMID: 26715498

Triantafillou, E., Zhu, T., Dumoulin, V., Lamblin, P., Evci, U., Xu, K., . . . Larochelle, H. (2019). Meta-dataset: A dataset of datasets for learning to learn from few examples. arXiv preprint arXiv:1903.03096.

Turing, A. M. (2009). *Computing machinery and intelligence*. Springer Netherlands. DOI: 10.1007/978-1-4020-6710-5_3

Vaswani, A., Shazeer, N., Parmar, N., Uszkoreit, J., Jones, L., Gomez, A. N., & Polosukhin, I. (2017). Attention is all you need. *Advances in Neural Information Processing Systems*, 30.

Wang, H., Can, D., Kazemzadeh, A., Bar, F., & Narayanan, S. (2012, July). A system for real-time twitter sentiment analysis of 2012 us presidential election cycle. In *Proceedings of the ACL 2012 system demonstrations* (pp. 115-120).

Wang, X., Oxholm, G., Zhang, D., & Wang, Y. F. (2017). Multimodal transfer: A hierarchical deep convolutional neural network for fast artistic style transfer. In *Proceedings of the IEEE conference on computer vision and pattern recognition* (pp. 5239-5247). DOI: 10.1109/CVPR.2017.759

Weaver, W. (1949). In Locke, W. N., & Donald Booth, A. (Eds.), *Translation in Machine Translation of Languages: Fourteen Essays. Machine Translation of Languages: Fourteen Essays* (pp. 15–23). MIT Press.

Wijmans, E., Datta, S., Maksymets, O., Das, A., Gkioxari, G., Lee, S., & Batra, D. (2019). Embodied question answering in photorealistic environments with point cloud perception. In *Proceedings of the IEEE/CVF Conference on Computer Vision and Pattern Recognition* (pp. 6659-6668). DOI: 10.1109/CVPR.2019.00682

Young, T., Hazarika, D., Poria, S., & Cambria, E. (2018). Recent trends in deep learning based natural language processing. IEEE Computational Intelligence Magazine, 13(3), 55-75.

Chapter 8
Technology Adoption Alters the Insurance Industry's Competitive Landscape in India

S. Baby Latha
Bishop Heber College, India

S. Prettha
Bishop Heber College, India

ABSTRACT

Motor insurance is going through a radical change that will see usage-based pricing. This chapter addresses the development of a reasonable and reflecting pricing system, each driver's unique driving habits and risk factors is the main challenge. The solution involves developing a model that forecasts the likelihood of premium pricing based on insurance claims, the corresponding claim amounts, driving behaviour metrics, insured age, and other pertinent factors. Predictive modelling techniques, particularly a linear regression approach, are leveraged in this process. The model's coefficients, which are obtained using statistical techniques and domain expertise, are essential for allocating weights to different risk variables. This chapter should result in an understandable and transparent mechanism for calculating premiums, enabling insurance companies to dynamically modify rates according to individual driving habits and projected risk. Improving pricing accuracy, this model supports industry trends towards fairness, openness, and customer-oriented insurance processes.

DOI: 10.4018/979-8-3693-6255-6.ch008

1. INTRODUCTION

Being able to financially protect oneself against the hazards involved in owning and running a car makes motor insurance an essential part of the insurance sector. It assists people and companies in reducing the financial toll that accidents, theft, damage, or responsibility from occurrences involving vehicles might take. In many nations, it is legally required for drivers to carry motor insurance to guarantee that they have the resources to reimburse third parties for losses or injuries caused by their cars. In addition to meeting legal requirements, auto insurance gives car owners piece of mind by protecting their investment and helping in an emergency. To guarantee ethical behaviour, safeguarding consumers, and maintaining financial stability in the insurance sector, government agencies regulate motor insurance. Insurance businesses and agents are subject to licencing and conduct regulations, which also set minimum coverage requirements and criteria for policy terms and conditions. Maintaining lawful operations and the faith and confidence of policyholders and the public are contingent upon insurers adhering to regulatory regulations.

1.1 Early Motor Insurance Policies, Challenges, and Limitations

In the early 1900s, insurance firms started to offer specific policies to cover the risks associated with motor vehicles as the number of cars on the road rose. All the coverage was lacking, though, and these early policies were frequently simplistic. The protection against culpability for harm done to third parties was their primary concern. Limited data, absence of actuarial procedures, and uncertainty about the hazards connected with driving posed issues for insurers underwriting motor insurance. Throughout time, auto insurance plans have changed to include more extensive coverage choices, such as defence against fire, theft, and damage from collisions. The increase of automobile insurance coverage was further propelled by the implementation of mandatory insurance regulations in several countries. Car owners were required by these rules to maintain a certain amount of insurance to protect their liability for any harm or damages they may cause to third parties. Insurance companies changed their policies to cover new risks like cyberattacks and malfunctioning electrical systems as the automotive industry developed and cars got more technologically savvy. Automobile insurance has been greatly influenced by the advancement of actuarial science. Actuaries started estimating claims probability, determining suitable premium rates, and assessing risk using statistical techniques and mathematical models. An improved understanding of the variables impacting auto insurance risks, including driver demographics, car attributes, and geographic location, was made possible by actuarial techniques.

Henckaerts and Antonio 2022, the study focuses on how incorporating real-time driving behavior such as speed, acceleration, and braking can improve the accuracy of risk assessment and premium calculation. The authors use statistical models to demonstrate that continuously adjusting insurance prices based on telematics data leads to fairer pricing and better risk differentiation. Their findings suggest that dynamic pricing can enhance insurers' profitability while encouraging safer driving behavior among policyholders. When determining premium rates and assessing risk, traditional motor insurance pricing models frequently place a significant emphasis on demographic variables including age, gender, marital status, and region. Although these variables can offer valuable perspectives on specific risk concerns, they might not encompass all of the policyholders' unique driving habits and behaviours. Lack of personalisation is one of the main drawbacks of standard auto insurance pricing structures. Standard rating criteria are usually applied to entire demographic segments by these models, yielding generalised premium rates. Despite having quite different driving habits and risk profiles, policyholders with comparable demographic profiles could get the same premium quotes. Due to their reliance on demographic data and historical claims data, traditional pricing models frequently have few data inputs. Such as real-time driving behaviour data gathered by telematics devices, these models could miss important data sources. insurers may find it difficult to appropriately evaluate risk and establish premiums in the absence of access to large data sets. As road conditions, traffic patterns, and driver behaviour change, traditional motor insurance pricing models may find it difficult to adjust to these new risk factors. The premium estimates made by these algorithms may become inaccurate over time since they usually employ static rating variables that are updated seldom.

The conventional approaches to pricing vehicle insurance frequently depend on risk sharing and cross-funding to distribute the expenses of claims among participants. Even though this strategy lessens the financial impact of high-risk individuals, low-risk policyholders may end up paying more for their insurance than their high-risk counterparts due to discriminatory pricing. The flexibility of conventional auto insurance pricing models may be restricted by legal requirements and pricing restrictions. It can be more difficult for insurers to implement cutting-edge rating elements or modify premium prices in reaction to shifting market dynamics. Inadvertently suppressing competition and innovation in the insurance sector can be the result of consumer protection regulations. The absence of transparency in traditional automobile insurance pricing schemes can be a challenge for consumers seeking to comprehend the computation of their rates. A mistrust of the insurance sector may result from policyholders' frustration with what they see as an unfair or opaque premium pricing structure. Technological innovations in the auto insurance sector include telematics, artificial intelligence, and data analytics. Insurance companies can gather data on driving behaviour in real time using telematics devices fitted in cars, which enables customised risk assessment and pricing. Insurers may make more accurate underwriting and pricing decisions by using data analytics tools to assist them analyse massive volumes of data and find patterns, trends, and risk factors. Policies may be purchased, claims can be filed, and policy information can be accessed more easily with the help of digital platforms and mobile apps, which improves client convenience. Modern technology has completely changed the auto insurance market in the last several decades. The utilisation of telematics devices, GPS tracking systems, and data analytics tools has facilitated the collection of real-time driving behaviour data by insurers, hence enabling more customised risk assessment and pricing. Customers may now purchase policies, submit claims, and obtain policy information more easily thanks to the insurance industry's streamlining efforts brought about by digital platforms and mobile apps. With more innovation and upheaval on the horizon, the auto insurance sector is primed for growth. Artificial intelligence, usage-based insurance, and autonomous car technologies are predicted to change the distribution, pricing, and design of insurance products. In order to improve client experiences and risk management procedures, insurers will persist in utilising data analytics and predictive modelling tools. Moosavi and Ramnath 2023 their study focuses on how real-time driving behavior, combined with external contextual factors such as road conditions, weather, and traffic, can improve risk assessment for insurance and safety applications. By leveraging machine learning models, the authors demonstrate that integrating contextual data with telematics enhances the accuracy of predicting high-risk driving events. Their findings suggest that insurers and fleet managers can use this approach to refine premium pricing, optimize risk management, and promote safer driving practices.

2. INTRODUCTION TO TELEMATICS TECHNOLOGY AND ITS APPLICATION IN MOTOR INSURANCE

Data transmission across large distances is made possible by telematics technology, which combines informatics and telecommunication. When it comes to auto insurance, telematics devices are usually mounted in cars to gather and send data in real time about how people drive. The many parts that make up telematics devices are GPS receivers, gyroscopes, accelerometers, and onboard diagnostics (OBD) ports. Together, these parts enable the collection of data on variables like position, cornering, braking, acceleration, and speed of the vehicle. Telematics devices are designed to continuously gather data about driving behaviours, risky behaviours, and driving patterns while the car is being driven. Then, over wireless networks, this data is sent to insurance firms or other third-party providers for processing and analysis. A multitude of driving behaviour metrics can be gathered thanks to telematics technology, such as but not restricted to:

- Overcoming designated speed restrictions is known as speeding.
- Sharp Acceleration: A sudden increase in speed from a standing position.
- Applying the brakes suddenly and firmly is known as harsh braking.
- Turning abruptly or violently when driving is known as cornering.
- Distance and Time: The length of time and distance covered within predetermined window of time.

Because telematics technology makes it possible for insurers to more precisely assess risk and customise premiums based on the driving habits of specific policyholders, the motor insurance market has undergone massive transformation. Rather of depending just on historical claims data or demographic characteristics, insurers can now generate personalised premium rates based on driving performance thanks to telematics data. While those with higher-risk driving habits may pay higher premiums or surcharges, policyholders who exhibit safe driving habits and low-risk profiles may qualify for discounted premiums or other incentive programmes. For insurers and policyholders alike, telematics-based insurance provides several advantages, such as: Better Risk Assessment: More precise knowledge of each policyholder's risk profile is made possible by telematics data, which helps insurers manage and price risks more effectively. Increased Road Safety: Telematics-based insurance can lessen accident rates and improve road safety results by providing incentives for safe driving practices. Better Customer involvement: Based on their driving data, policyholders may receive tailored coaching and feedback that increases their involvement and knowledge of safe driving techniques. Possible Cost Savings: Insurers may experience a decrease in claims expenses and an improvement in profitability over time, while safe drivers may benefit from cheaper insurance rates.

2.1 Concept of Telematics Risk Pricing

To determine risk and set rates, traditional auto insurance pricing models often use historical claims data along with demographic variables (such as age, gender, and region). These models might not, however, adequately capture unique driving behaviours and behaviours. However, telematics risk pricing bases its risk assessment on real driving behaviour by using real-time data gathered from telematics devices fitted in vehicles. Insurance companies can more accurately adjust premiums using this method to the risk profile of each insured. Devices that track driving activity, such as speed, acceleration, braking, cornering, and time/distance travelled, are known as telematics devices. Insurers get this data and evaluate it to determine each policyholder's degree of risk. To evaluate telematics data and find behavioural patterns that are associated with either a higher or lower risk of accidents, insurers employ mathematical models and complex algorithms. When pricing telematics risk, many variables pertaining to driving behaviour are considered, such as Over speeding: This can lead to increased insurance costs and is a major cause of accidents. Sudden Braking and Acceleration: Sudden alterations in speed suggest aggressive driving, which raises the possibility of collisions. Cornering: Excessive or abrupt turns indicate a greater chance of losing control of the vehicle and getting into an accident. Time and Distance: An increased chance of accidents may arise when driving over long distances or at high-risk times, such as late at night. Insurers can create a thorough picture of each policyholder's risk profile and modify premiums in response by examining these variables. Providers can provide customised premium rates depending on individual driving habits thanks to telematics risk pricing. Premium discounts may be available to policyholders who exhibit low risk driving behaviours and safe driving practices. conversely, rates may increase for those who drive more recklessly.

This tailored strategy motivates policyholders to actively participate in lowering their risk of collisions and rewards safe driving behaviours. Telematics data gives insurers a more precise and detailed knowledge of the risk profile of each policyholder, which helps them manage risk and set prices more accurately. Policies for policyholders are more transparently priced since telematics risk pricing guarantees that premiums are determined by real driving behaviour rather than broad demographic characteristics. The implementation of telematics risk pricing incentivizes policyholders to adopt safer driving behaviours by connecting premiums to driving behaviour. This approach has been shown to reduce accident rates and enhance road safety outcomes. Berg Wahlstrom & Hagelberg 2023 this paper explores the benefits of usage-based insurance (UBI) models, which adjust premiums based on real-time driving data rather than traditional risk factors like age or demographics. The authors discuss data collection methods, privacy concerns, and the potential for more accurate and fair pricing in the insurance industry. Their findings suggest that telemetry-based pricing can reduce risk for insurers while incentivizing safer driving among policyholders.

2.2 Literature Reviews

Ahmad et al., 2024, this article clearly explain how the use of insurance technology in the insurance sector will raise the total insurance premium for the company. To examine the performance of the firm's premium based on technology investment, they employed a basic linear regression model using secondary data sources, which are investments in Insur-Tech and premium performance. The analysis of this data led to the conclusion that premium and technology investment have a substantial positive correlation. Their findings indicated that a higher investment correlated with a higher premium.

This study by Duval et al., 2024 they describe how actuarial neural networks and regression models were coupled in telematics to simulate cross-sectional and longitudinal claim count data using neural networks. To model the highest speed attained by insured drivers for the claim count, they employed longitudinal distributions such as the beta negative binominal distribution. The number of trips completed at maximum high speeds is positively connected with the frequency of claims.

Buthelezi et al.,2024 the author clearly explained how traditional methods like GLM, Autoregressive Integrated Moving Average, and Decision Trees are less accurate to model for pricing automobile insurance contracts. They also mentioned that these models only fit a limited collection of data. In the insurance industry, a lot of data sets are handled. Therefore, actuarial neural networks, generalised pareto distributions, and deep neural networks are alternate methods to predict the pricing of vehicle insurance. These models are perfect for making predictions with a lot of data. The insurer setting the prices for general insurance products can benefit most from these models.

Wilson et al. 2024," Their primary area of interest is the loss cost model for auto insurance pricing, which is accomplished by combining artificial neural networks and the generalised linear model in a hybrid model. The loss cost model, which is based on the combination of both claim severity and frequency, is a combination of the old way of projecting motor insurance premium. They are also contrasted with the artificial intelligence approach, which uses artificial neural networks and many criteria to calculate auto insurance pricing. In the end, they concluded that the hybrid model GLM & ANN provided a better estimate of how much auto insurance would cost with a low MSE.

Gao et al., 2022 this article used telemetry automobile driving data to model claim frequency giving a detailed explanation of the neural network's classical methodology and methods. The traditional method, which models the frequency of automobile insurance claims primarily using actuarial risk factors. Additionally, they evaluated a neural network model that modelled the frequency of claims using telematics data. Ultimately, they concluded that for both models to be the most accurate predictors of claim frequency, all components must be present.

Henckaerts & Antonio 2022 this study provided a clear explanation of how to price vehicle third-party liability insurance utilising both new technology telematics data and historical data in-house technical risk assessment expertise. Additionally, they examined this pricing model that was useful to marketers, actuaries, and managers.

Guillen et al.2021 in this paper, the method of pricing auto insurance utilising baseline insurance premiums plus data on dangerous driving is detailed in detail. This article is based on sample telematics data, which includes the base insurance premium plus additional costs related to drivers' activity. The pay as you drive programme was subject to certain limitations, and further references were contingent upon certain circumstances. Because of the difficulties in applying the PAYD with telemetry data, they mostly concentrated on traditional ratemaking principles based on the average claim cost model.

Meng Shengwang et al. 2022, this article's primary focus was on predicting motor insurance premiums using telematics vehicle driving data and data from auto insurance claims. For driving excursions in cars, they employ the supervised neural network model as an input risk score and an output. Additionally, they demonstrated a stronger improvement in the Poisson generalised linear model for telematics-based claim frequency prediction. They also demonstrated how insurers faced greater portfolio improvements and rewards for safer drivers when they used telematics.

Sun et al. 2020 study, "Assessing driving risk using internet of vehicles data: An analysis based on generalised linear models," The primary goal of this article is to examine the various risk factors that increase driving risk, such as accidents, faster speeds, higher RPMs, and more braking demands. Using binary logistics regressions and ordinary least squares, they utilised to model the driving risk. To model the driving risk, they combined accident and telemetry data analysis.

Eling & Kraft 2020, this article's primary goal, which used telematics data, had an impact on the actuarial, market, and sociological elements. Their conclusions about the actuarial features of the telematics data allowed for smaller risk pools, cost savings, lower claim expenses, and a decrease in fraud. According to the market perspective, a few criteria must result in premium reductions or discounts, and social considerations utilising telematics shown data security and standardisation.

Ekström & Chen 2020, article provided a good explanation of the typical approach of using a generalised linear model to model claim frequency. However, this model only considered significant factors that affect fixed auto insurance rates. They provided an additional alternative approach that uses telematics data and neural networks in conjunction with the gradient boosting model to model the frequency of policyholder claims. These two models have lower standard deviation and mean square error, making them superior predictors. Less telematics variables were employed to forecast improved performance.

Pesantez-Narvaez et al. 2019,this post provided a comprehensive explanation of how to use the XGBoost AI model and logistic regression to forecast accident claims using telematics data. These two models do a better job of forecasting accident claims. They concluded that larger data sets will increase the efficiency of their models despite the numerous constraints they experience in their research.

Huang et al., 2019 Auto insurance classification ratemaking based on telematics driving data. They concentrated on usage-based insurance, using telematics-derived data on motor insurance that showed a positive correlation with accidents. Consequently, the cost of cars was reduced. The claim amounts were modelled using the risk probability model by the authors, and the claim frequency model was modelled using Poisson regression. This study's primary goal was to use a data set to inform the ratemaking process for UBI vehicle insurance products.

Guillen et al.2019, they focused on insured automobiles that went greater distances in exchange for a higher premium and discounts for having no claims. Conventional auto insurance does not adjust for driving distance. Telematics data demonstrated that premiums would rise in proportion to the number of km drivers drive. Rather of using the traditional Poisson model, they employ the zero inflated Poisson model to fit the claim frequency. They demonstrated a positive correlation between the growth in claim numbers and the impact of the distance variable coefficients and traffic offences.

Ayuso et al. 2019, they employed traditional actuarial insurance pricing, but contemporary telematics-based pricing produced superior results. In conventional methods, many factors that have no bearing on insurance policy costs are seen as imposed penalties, such as the number of accidents. Long-distance driving was covered in this traditional method of determining insurance premiums, but it also discussed how a driver's habits and behaviours affected the various premium amounts.

Verbelen et al. (2018), this study's goal was to price auto insurance using telemetry data on insured drivers' driving habits. The conventional approach to pricing auto insurance relies on self-reported factors like age and postal code, which have little bearing on the likelihood of an accident. Claim frequency is modelled using a generalised additive model using telematics data. Their assessment of telematics data based on observation of drivers on highways or city streets in the evening or at night contributed to a riskier driving behaviour and usage-based pricing for auto insurance. Telematics data can be used to price auto insurance in a range between previous and posterior values.

Xie, 2024, this study's primary goal was to understand how general insurers make decisions and set rates for auto insurance. They were classified as risk factors based on their driving history, and the class employed two modelling techniques: GLM and minimum bias process. This article provided evidence of the value of utilising GLM to determine auto insurance rates. The best modelling technique for reviewing vehicle insurance rates is GLM.

Boucher et al. 2017 published a paper on exposure as duration and distance in telematics motor insurance using generalised additive models. The primary goal of this study is to better understand the new Pay As You Derive auto insurance plan, which bases premiums on data from GPS devices. Here, other risk factor data, such as travel distance and exposure duration, were also considered while estimating the insurance premium using the generalised additive model technique.

Baecke & Bocca 2017, they received a thorough explanation of the significance of telematics data, which is considered to enhance risk assessment when modelling usage-based insurance policies such as Pay As You Drive. These conventional variables were examined in this study together with variables from telematics data. The additional factors that go into determining the premium rate for auto insurance are the total number of miles driven within the specified time frame.

The 2016 book Innovation insurance schemes: pay as/how you drive, written by Tselentis et al. Pay as you drive and pay how you drive are the two categories of car insurance plans on which they mostly concentrated. These innovative plans use technology to forecast the risk premium to the insurance company. They concentrated on a linear combination of the telematics factors in addition to a premium charged on a fixed charge imposed on every motorist. Additionally, they employed the fuzzy linguistic approximation, which improved the prediction of huge number estimating estimation.

Husnjak et al. 2015, their primary concern was UBI legislation. The insurance firms must see tremendous possibilities in this kind of new business model. Users benefited from this usage-based insurance approach in addition to insurance providers and the social, economic, and environmental benefits. They described how the practical telematics system was put into practice.

Charity Mkajuma et al.2015 this paper about a company located in Kiambu. Their primary area of investigation was premium established by pay as you drive, which compensates for the miles driven by cars. The entire aggregate claim cost will be approximated by them using some significant data gathered from the device. They are modelling the overall claim cost, which is applicable to the zero inflated negative binomial distribution, using sophisticated statistical tools. Their findings show a strong correlation between mileage and the total cost of all claims combined.

3. METHODOLOGY

Irode 2017, this dissertation examines how telematics technology such as GPS tracking and onboard sensors can be used to assess driver behavior and adjust insurance premiums accordingly. The study discusses various data collection techniques, risk assessment models, and the benefits of a usage-based insurance (UBI) approach. He argues that telematics-based pricing can lead to fairer premiums, reduce fraud, and promote safer driving habits. The research also highlights potential challenges, including data privacy concerns and implementation costs for insurers. Before explaining the modelling of this research work, we start some of the initial work will be taken to the telematics data which normally called graduation of data and clearly gave the information about which are the factors to be consider in this paper. The target variables for risk pricing, the dataset used in this paper includes a variety of factors pertaining to driving behaviour and motor insurance. An extensive summary of the dataset may be found here:

- The length of time, expressed in days, that the policyholder is covered.
- Insured Driver Age: The insured driver's age expressed in whole years.
- Insured Sex: The insured driver's gender.
- Age of Car: How old the car is.
- Marital status: The insured driver's marital status.
- Car Use: The reason the vehicle is used (such as commuting or personal use).
  Credit Score: The policyholder's credit score.
- Region: The area in which the insured car is situated.
- Annual Miles Driven: The total distance travelled each year.
- Years Without Claims: This refers to the amount of time without an insurance claim.
- Territory: The car's geographic location code.
- Annual Percentage Driven: The proportion of days the policyholder drives the car each year.
- Percentage of Driving Behaviour: Compositional variables that show how driving behaviour is distributed across the week's several days.
- Brake and Acceleration Intensity: This section includes metrics for brake and acceleration intensity.
- Left and Right Turn Intensity: This section contains metrics pertaining to the degree of left and right turns.
- Administrative expenses: Expenses related to the insurance policy's administration.
- Profit Margin: An insurance company's profit margin.
- Number of Claims (NB_Claim): The total number of insurance claims that the policyholder has submitted.
- Claim Amount (AMT_Claim): The total of all insurance claims.

3.1 Statistical Summary of Numerical Columns

Table 1. Dimensions of the dataset (rows, columns): 100000, 49

Variables	Duration	Insured age	Car age	Credit score	Annual miles drive	Years no claim	Territory
Mean	314.2041	51.37895	5.63972	800.8889	9124.123	28.83996	56.53139
S.Deviation	79.74622	15.46707	4.062135	83.38232	3826.145	16.12372	24.03652
Minimum	27	16	-2	422	0	0	11
Maximum	366	103	20	900	56731.17	79	91
25%	200	39	2	766	6213.71	15	35
50%	365	51	5	825	7456.452	29	62
75%	366	63	8	856	12427.42	41	78

Table 2.

Variables	Annual pct driven	Total miles driven	Pct drive mon	Pct drive tue	Pct drive wed	Pct drive thu	Pct drive fri
Mean	0.502294	4833.575	0.139365	0.151262	0.148288	0.153009	0.157641
S. Deviation	0.299189	4545.943	0.042807	0.047612	0.044609	0.044418	0.043716
Minimum	0.00274	0.095298	0	0	0	0	0
Maximum	1	47282.6	0.998172	1	1	0.9979	0.998617
25%	0.249315	1529.897	0.120894	0.130084	0.129348	0.133619	0.138615
50%	0.490411	3468.288	0.137909	0.1479	0.147083	0.151377	0.155996
75%	0.753425	6779.877	0.155203	0.168479	0.165925	0.170582	0.174473

Table 3.

Variables	Pct drive sat	Pct drive sun	Pct drive 2hrs	Pct drive 3hrs	Pct drive 4hrs	Pct drive wkdys	Pct drive wked
Mean	0.137912	0.112524	0.003931	0.000868	0.000242	0.74955	0.25045
S.Deviation	0.053069	0.049864	0.008122	0.004005	0.002592	0.083039	0.083039
Minimum	0	-1.9E-09	0	0	0	0	0
Maximum	0.946596	0.976063	0.455742	0.323831	0.265887	1	1
25%	0.109415	0.085258	0	0	0	0.710336	0.204727
50%	0.134668	0.110706	0.001308	0	0	0.752464	0.247536
75%	0.161304	0.134756	0.004791	0.000584	0	0.795273	0.289664

Table 4.

Variables	Pct drive rush am	Pct drive rush pm	Avgdays week	Accel.06 miles	Accel.08 miles	Accel.09 miles	Accel.11 miles
Mean	0.097823	0.137598	5.533067	43.09712	4.53249	1.75355	0.92915
S.Deviation	0.078752	0.069939	1.248339	62.10494	19.53138	14.56016	11.93603
Minimum	0	0	0.200902	0	0	0	0
Maximum	0.988042	0.993178	7	621	621	621	621
25%	0.037389	0.090424	4.911596	9	0	0	0
50%	0.078013	0.129842	5.890227	24	1	0	0
75%	0.140843	0.174353	6.487471	52	3	1	0

Table 5.

Variables	Accel.12 miles	Accel.14 miles	Brake.06 miles	Brake.08 miles	Brake.09 miles	Brake.11 miles	Brake.12 miles
Mean	0.52509	0.35703	83.65254	9.59409	3.10253	1.34924	0.5899
S.Deviation	9.699139	8.433604	80.22937	18.13882	12.70102	10.59141	9.124862
Minimum	0	0	0	0	0	0	0
Maximum	621	621	621	621	621	621	621
25%	0	0	33	3	1	0	0
50%	0	0	60	6	2	1	0
75%	0	0	107	11	3	1	0

Table 6.

Variables	Brake. 14miles	Left turn intensity 08	Left turn Intensity 09	Left turn Intensity 10	Left turn Intensity 11	Left turn Intensity 12	Right turn Intensity 08
Mean	0.35499	915.6763	718.0536	551.574	487.3407	447.7584	843.4618
S.Deviation	8.234056	16330.9	15666.07	14687.93	14198.33	13719.79	11630.19
Minimum	0	0	0	0	0	0	0
Maximum	621	794740	794676	794380	793926	793170	841210
25%	0	7	2	0	0	0	11
50%	0	66	22	3	1	0	122
75%	0	361	146	30	9	2	680

Table 7.

Variables	Right turn intensity09	Right turn intensity10	Right turn intensity11	Right turn intensity12	NB Claim	AMT Claim
Mean	565.0561	326.6548	246.7131	198.7537	0.04494	137.6023
S.Deviation	10657.4	9460.244	8977.57	8585.177	0.21813	1264.32
Minimum	0	0	0	0	0	0
Maximum	841207	841200	841176	841144	3	104074.9
25%	3	0	0	0	0	0
50%	43	7	2	0	0	0
75%	321	81	27	9	0	0

From table no. 1-7, we are using some statistical properties like mean, variance, minimum, maximum and finally estimated the quartiles ranges all the targeted variables. Pre-processing the dataset, handling missing values, encoding categorical variables, and carrying out any required transformations are crucial steps to take before moving further with analysis and modelling to guarantee data quality and suitability for modelling. During the data pre-processing stage, carry out multiple procedures to guarantee that the data is uncontaminated, coherent, and prepared for examination. Below is a thorough breakdown of every steps.

3.2 Handling Missing Values

Common in datasets, missing values must be fixed before further analysis can be done. There are various approaches we can take to address missing values. Imputation: Using a suitable alternative (such as the mean, median, or mode) to fill in the gaps in data.

- ✓ Removal: Eliminating any rows or columns that have values missing.
- ✓ One method of predicting missing values based on other features is to use machine learning techniques.
- ✓ Prediction: Using other features as a basis for machine learning algorithms to forecast missing data.
- ✓ The type of data and degree of missingness determine which approach is best.

3.3 Encoding Categorical Variables

Utilise strategies like label encoding to convert categorical variables like "Insured sex," "Marital," "Car use," and "Region" into numerical format.

Figure 1. Converting categorical variables into numerical format

```
# Initialize LabelEncoder
label_encoder = LabelEncoder()

# Encode 'Car.use' and 'Region' columns
data['Car.use_encoded'] = label_encoder.fit_transform(data['Car.use'])
data['Region_encoded'] = label_encoder.fit_transform(data['Region'])
data['Insured.sex_encoded'] = label_encoder.fit_transform(data['Insured.sex'])
data['Marital_encoded'] = label_encoder.fit_transform(data['Marital'])
```

Car.use	Car.use_encoded	Region	Region_encoded	Marital	Marital_encoded	Insured.sex	Insured.sex_encoded
Private	3	Urban	1	Single	1	Male	1
Commute	1	Urban	1	Married	0	Male	1
Commute	1	Rural	0	Single	1	Male	1
Private	3	Rural	0	Married	0	Male	1
Commercial	0	Rural	0	Single	1	Female	0

3.4 Deleting Unwanted Columns

Once one-hot encoding (or any alternative encoding) is completed, the original categorical column should be removed from the dataset. This is because the newly formed binary columns fully capture the information that was previously redundant in the original column. It's possible that some of the dataset's columns don't support our modelling or analytic attempts. These columns can be safely eliminated if they are deemed redundant or superfluous. We have identified number in this document that might not be pertinent to risk pricing analysis. These columns can be removed to simplify the dataset and cut down on complexity without losing any crucial information.

Figure 2. Data set column

```
data.drop(['Insured.sex', 'Car.use', 'Region', 'Marital','s.no'], axis=1, inplace=True)
```

3.5 Random Forest Regressor

Generate a strong prediction model, several decision trees are combined using the Random Forest Regressor, an ensemble learning technique. A strong predictive model is produced by combining several decision trees using the Random Forest Regressor, an ensemble learning technique. Regression tasks, such estimating insurance rates using driving behaviour data, are a good fit for its capabilities. A random subset of the training data and features is used to train each of the numerous decision trees that Random Forest creates during training. The model produces more accurate predictions by combining the predictions from several trees, which lessens overfitting. Each feature's significance in forecasting the target variable that is insurance premiums is determined via Random Forest. By doing this, we may determine which measures related to driving behaviour have the biggest influence on insurance rates.

3.6 Linear Regression

The link between a dependent variable (insurance premiums) and one or more independent variables (driving behaviour metrics) can be modelled using the traditional statistical technique of linear regression. Between the independent variables and the target variable, it is assumed that there is a linear relationship.

$$P = \alpha + \beta B + error$$

Where P is the dependent variable the variable, we are trying to predict that is insurance premium (P)

B is the independent variable the variable used to make predictions that is driving behaviors (B)

α is the P-intercept the value of Q when P is 0

β is the slope of the line the change in P for a one-unit change in B

The error term the difference between the observed and predicted values of P

In the case of multiple independent variables, the formula can be extended to

$$P = \beta_0 + \beta_1 B_1 + \beta_2 B_2 + \ldots\ldots\ldots + \beta_n B_n + error$$

$B_1, B_2.....B_n$ are the independent variables that is driving behavioral factors

$\beta_0, \beta_1, \beta_2 \ldots\ldots \beta_n$ are the coefficients or weights associated with each independent variable.

To determine the feature significance scores and weights for every feature in the dataset, this bit of Python code uses the Random Forest Regressor model from the scikit-learn module.

Figure 3. Python code with the random forest regressor model

```
from sklearn.ensemble import RandomForestRegressor
import pandas as pd


# Drop target variable and any unnecessary columns
X = data.drop(["AMT_Claim", "NB_Claim"], axis=1)
y = data["AMT_Claim"]  # or "NB_Claim" depending on your target variable

# Initialize Random Forest model
rf_model = RandomForestRegressor()

# Train the model
rf_model.fit(X, y)

# Get feature importance scores
feature_importance = rf_model.feature_importances_

# Normalize importance scores
normalized_importance = feature_importance / sum(feature_importance)

# Assign weights to features
weights = normalized_importance

# Print feature importance scores and weights
for i, feature in enumerate(X.columns):
    print(f"Feature: {feature}, Importance Score: {feature_importance[i]}, Weight: {weights[i]}")
```

The Random Forest Regressor model from the scikit-learn module is used in this snippet of Python code to determine the weights and feature significance scores for each feature in the dataset. Import Random Forest Regressor from sk learn.ensemble: Utilises the scikit-learn ensemble module to import the Random Forest Regressor class. To manipulate data, import the pandas library as pd.

3.6.1 Prepare Data

B = data.drop([“AMT_Claim”, “NB_Claim”], axis=1): Assigns the independent variables (features) to B by dropping the target variables (“AMT_Claim” and “NB_Claim”) and any unnecessary columns from the dataset.

P = data[“AMT_Claim”]: Assigns the target variable “AMT_Claim” to P.

3.6.2 Initialize Random Forest Model

rf_model = RandomForestRegressor(): Initializes a RandomForestRegressor model without specifying any hyperparameters.

3.6.3 Train the Model

rf_model.fit (B, P): Trains the RandomForestRegressor model using the independent variables (B) and the target variable (P).

3.6.4 Calculate Feature Importance Scores

feature_importance = rf_model.feature_importances_: Retrieves the feature importance scores calculated by the RandomForestRegressor model.

3.6.5 Normalize Importance Scores

normalized_importance = feature_importance / sum(feature_importance): Normalizes the feature importance scores by dividing each score by the sum of all scores, ensuring they sum up to 1.

3.6.6 Assign Weights to Features

weights = normalized_importance: Assigns the normalized importance scores (weights) to the variable "weights".

3.6.7 Print Feature Importance Scores and Weights

Iterates through each feature in X. columns and prints its name, original importance score, and corresponding weight.

The loop prints the feature name, importance score, and weight for each feature in the dataset.

This code helps in understanding the importance of each feature in predicting the target variable "AMT_Claim" using the Random Forest Regressor model. The importance scores and weights provide insights into which features have the most significant impact on the target variable, aiding in feature selection and model interpretation. This output displays the feature importance scores and weights calculated by the Random Forest Regressor model for each feature in the dataset.

Feature: The name of the feature.
Importance Score: The original importance score assigned to the feature by the Random Forest Regressor model.
Weight: The normalized importance score or weight of the feature, calculated by dividing the importance score by the sum of all importance scores.

For example,

The feature "Duration" has an importance score of approximately 0.0066, and its weight is also approximately 0.0066.

The feature "Insured.age" has an importance score of approximately 0.0278, and its weight is also approximately 0.0278.

The feature "Car.age" has an importance score of approximately 0.0352, and its weight is also approximately 0.0352.

These weights represent the relative importance of each feature in predicting the target variable. Features with higher weights are considered more important in the prediction process. This information can be used for feature selection, model interpretation, and understanding the driving factors behind the target variable.

Figure 4. Data frame feature_importance_df

```
import pandas as pd

# Feature names
features = X.columns.tolist()

# Create DataFrame
feature_importance_df = pd.DataFrame({
    'Feature': features,
    'Importance_Score': feature_importance,
    'Weight': weights
})

# Display the DataFrame
df2 = pd.DataFrame(feature_importance_df)
```

This code creates a DataFrame named feature_importance_df containing three columns: 'Feature', 'Importance_Score', and 'Weight'.

Import pandas: Imports the pandas library, which is commonly used for data manipulation and analysis.

Feature names: Extracts the names of the features from the columns of the DataFrame B (assuming B our feature matrix).

Create DataFrame: Constructs a DataFrame named feature_importance_df with three columns:

'Feature': Contains the names of the features.

'Importance_Score': Contains the importance scores calculated by the RandomForestRegressor model.

'Weight': Contains the normalized importance scores or weights calculated by dividing the importance scores by the sum of all importance scores.

Display the DataFrame: Creates a new DataFrame named df2 to store the feature_importance_df, and then displays the DataFrame.

After executing this code, df2 will contain the feature names along with their importance scores and weights, allowing you to analyze and visualize the importance of each feature in predicting the target variable.

Figure 5. Feature names and their importance scores and weights

	Feature	Importance_Score	Weight
0	Duration	0.006603	0.006603
1	Insured.age	0.027841	0.027841
2	Car.age	0.035237	0.035237
3	Credit.score	0.054765	0.054765
4	Annual.miles.drive	0.014531	0.014531
5	Years.noclaims	0.023212	0.023212
6	Territory	0.020405	0.020405
7	Annual.pct.driven	0.025802	0.025802
8	Total.miles.driven	0.082904	0.082904
9	Pct.drive.mon	0.027056	0.027056
10	Pct.drive.tue	0.024940	0.024940
11	Pct.drive.wed	0.019649	0.019649
12	Pct.drive.thr	0.019008	0.019008
13	Pct.drive.fri	0.036637	0.036637
14	Pct.drive.sat	0.020839	0.020839
15	Pct.drive.sun	0.019663	0.019663
16	Pct.drive.2hrs	0.028251	0.028251
17	Pct.drive.3hrs	0.030154	0.030154
18	Pct.drive.4hrs	0.017336	0.017336
19	Pct.drive.wkday	0.013213	0.013213
20	Pct.drive.wkend	0.011336	0.011336
21	Pct.drive.rush am	0.048040	0.048040
22	Pct.drive.rush pm	0.025282	0.025282
23	Avgdays.week	0.036626	0.036626
24	Accel.06miles	0.036108	0.036108
25	Accel.08miles	0.016314	0.016314
26	Accel.09miles	0.006253	0.006253
27	Accel.11miles	0.004958	0.004958
28	Accel.12miles	0.005349	0.005349
29	Accel.14miles	0.003101	0.003101
30	Brake.06miles	0.025220	0.025220
31	Brake.08miles	0.050847	0.050847
32	Brake.09miles	0.026773	0.026773
33	Brake.11miles	0.014363	0.014363
34	Brake.12miles	0.004910	0.004910
35	Brake.14miles	0.003950	0.003950
36	Left.turn.intensity08	0.013268	0.013268
37	Left.turn.intensity09	0.010480	0.010480
38	Left.turn.intensity10	0.008759	0.008759
39	Left.turn.intensity11	0.007740	0.007740
40	Left.turn.intensity12	0.011251	0.011251
41	Right.turn.intensity08	0.013953	0.013953
42	Right.turn.intensity09	0.012599	0.012599
43	Right.turn.intensity10	0.014228	0.014228
44	Right.turn.intensity11	0.012069	0.012069
45	Right.turn.intensity12	0.014953	0.014953
46	Car.use_encoded	0.004142	0.004142
47	Region_encoded	0.004024	0.004024
48	Insured.sex_encoded	0.002809	0.002809
49	Marital_encoded	0.002248	0.002248

3.6.8 Summary Statistics of the Data

Table 8. Summary statistics of the data

Statistics	Weights
count	50.0000
Mean	0.0200
S. Deviation	0.0157
Minimum	0.0225
25%	0.0092
50%	0.0156
75%	0.0265
Maximum	0.0829

This summary provides statistical information about the “Importance_Score” and “Weight” columns using table no.8

- count: Indicates the number of observations in each column, which is 50 in this case.
- mean: Represents the average value of the importance scores and weights across all features. The mean importance score and weight are both approximately 0.02.
- std: Denotes the standard deviation, which measures the dispersion or spread of the importance scores and weights around the mean. It shows how much variation or dispersion exists from the average. The standard deviation for both columns is approximately 0.0157.
- min: Shows the minimum value observed in each column. The smallest importance score and weight are both approximately 0.0022.
- 25%: Represents the first quartile, also known as the lower quartile or 25th percentile. It indicates that 25% of the observations fall below this value. For importance scores and weights, this value is approximately 0.0092.
- 50%: Corresponds to the median, which is the middle value of the dataset when it is ordered from smallest to largest. Approximately 50% of the observations have importance scores and weights below this value, which is approximately 0.0156.
- 75%: Represents the third quartile, also known as the upper quartile or 75th percentile. It indicates that 75% of the observations fall below this value. For importance scores and weights, this value is approximately 0.0265.

- max: Shows the maximum value observed in each column. The largest importance score and weight are both approximately 0.0829.

These statistics provide insights into the distribution and variability of the importance scores and weights across the features in the dataset.

3.6.9 Most Important Feature

Figure 6. Data frame feature_importance_df

```
# Sort the DataFrame by the "Weight" column in descending order
sorted_feature_importance_df = feature_importance_df.sort_values(by='Weight', ascending=False)

# Display the sorted DataFrame
df3 = pd.DataFrame(sorted_feature_importance_df)
df3
```

This code sorts the Data Frame feature_importance_df by the "Weight" column in descending order and stores the sorted Data Frame in sorted_feature_importance_df. Then, it creates a new Data Frame df3 to display the sorted Data Frame. Here's what each part of the code does:

- Sort the Data Frame: Uses the sort_values() method to sort the Data Frame feature_importance_df based on the values in the "Weight" column. The parameter ascending=False specifies that the sorting should be done in descending order.
- Create a new Data Frame: Constructs a new Data Frame named df3 to store the sorted DataFrame sorted_feature_importance_df.
- Display the sorted Data Frame: Displays the sorted Data Frame sorted_feature_importance_df using the pd.Data Frame() function.

After executing this code, df3 will contain the feature names along with their importance scores and weights, sorted by the weight in descending order, which can help in identifying the most important features for predicting the target variable.

Figure 7. Feature names with their importance scores and weights

	Feature	Importance_Score	Weight	626
8	Total.miles.driven	0.082904	0.082904	108
3	Credit.score	0.054765	0.054765	314
31	Brake.08miles	0.050847	0.050847	253
21	Pct.drive.rush am	0.048040	0.048040	958
13	Pct.drive.fri	0.036637	0.036637	349
23	Avgdays.week	0.036626	0.036626	101
24	Accel.06miles	0.036108	0.036108	220
2	Car.age	0.035237	0.035237	847
17	Pct.drive.3hrs	0.030154	0.030154	773
16	Pct.drive.2hrs	0.028251	0.028251	363
1	Insured.age	0.027841	0.027841	910
9	Pct.drive.mon	0.027056	0.027056	950
32	Brake.09miles	0.026773	0.026773	268
7	Annual.pct.driven	0.025802	0.025802	480
22	Pct.drive.rush pm	0.025282	0.025282	759
30	Brake.06miles	0.025220	0.025220	740
10	Pct.drive.tue	0.024940	0.024940	251
5	Years.noclaims	0.023212	0.023212	953
14	Pct.drive.sat	0.020839	0.020839	599
6	Territory	0.020405	0.020405	228
15	Pct.drive.sun	0.019663	0.019663	069
11	Pct.drive.wed	0.019649	0.019649	953
12	Pct.drive.thr	0.019008	0.019008	142
18	Pct.drive.4hrs	0.017336	0.017336	024
25	Accel.08miles	0.016314	0.016314	
45	Right.turn.intensity12	0.014953	0.014953	
4	Annual.miles.drive	0.014531	0.014531	
33	Brake.11miles	0.014363	0.014363	
43	Right.turn.intensity10	0.014228	0.014228	
41	Right.turn.intensity08	0.013953	0.013953	
36	Left.turn.intensity08	0.013268	0.013268	
19	Pct.drive.wkday	0.013213	0.013213	
42	Right.turn.intensity09	0.012599	0.012599	
44	Right.turn.intensity11	0.012069	0.012069	
20	Pct.drive.wkend	0.011336	0.011336	
40	Left.turn.intensity12	0.011251	0.011251	
37	Left.turn.intensity09	0.010480	0.010480	
38	Left.turn.intensity10	0.008759	0.008759	
39	Left.turn.intensity11	0.007740	0.007740	
0	Duration	0.006603	0.006603	
26	Accel.09miles	0.006253	0.006253	
28	Accel.12miles	0.005349	0.005349	
27	Accel.11miles	0.004958	0.004958	
34	Brake.12miles	0.004910	0.004910	
46	Car.use_encoded	0.004142	0.004142	
47	Region_encoded	0.004024	0.004024	
35	Brake.14miles	0.003950	0.003950	
29	Accel.14miles	0.003101	0.003101	
48	Insured.sex_encoded	0.002809	0.002809	
49	Marital_encoded	0.002248	0.002248	

Figure 8. Code snippet calculating predicted premium values

```
# Initialize an empty list to store the predicted values
predicted_values = []

# Iterate over each row in the standardized dataframe
for index, row in data.iterrows():
    # Initialize the predicted value for the current row
    pred_value = 0
    # Multiply each standardized independent variable by its corresponding coefficient
    for feature, weight in zip(feature_importance_df['Feature'], feature_importance_df['Weight']):
        pred_value += row[feature] * weight
    # Append the predicted value to the list
    predicted_values.append(pred_value)

# Convert the list of predicted values to a pandas Series
premium = pd.Series(predicted_values)
```

This code snippet calculates the predicted premium values using the feature importance weights obtained from the Random Forest Regressor model.

- Initialize an empty list to store the predicted values: This list, named predicted_values, will hold the predicted premium values for each row in the dataset.
- Iterate over each row in the dataset: This loop iterates over each row in the dataset using the iterrows() method.
- Initialize the predicted value for the current row: Inside the loop, pred_value is initialized to 0 for each row. This variable will hold the predicted premium value for the current row.
- Multiply each standardized independent variable by its corresponding coefficient: Within the nested loop, the code iterates through each feature and its corresponding weight (importance score) calculated from the Random Forest Regressor model. It multiplies each standardized independent variable in the row by its corresponding weight and adds it to pred_value.
- Append the predicted value to the list: After calculating the predicted premium value for the current row, it appends this value to the predicted_values list.
- Convert the list of predicted values to a pandas Series: Finally, the list of predicted premium values is converted into a pandas Series named premi-

um, which can be easily integrated into the Data Frame or used for further analysis.

This process effectively calculates the predicted premium values for each row in the dataset based on the feature importance weights obtained from the Random Forest Regressor model.

Table 9. Data set

S. No.	Premium in terms of rupees
0	868.77
1	929.39
2	507.41
3	165.59
4	518.05
5	678.63
6	455.25
7	440.00
8	997.16

3.6.10 Summary Statistics of Premium

The summary statistics provided for the predicted premium values (Premium) indicate the following using table no.9

- Count: There are 100,000 predicted premium values in total.
- Mean: The mean predicted premium value is approximately Rs.650.12.
- Standard Deviation: The standard deviation of the predicted premium values is approximately Rs.1081.40, indicating the dispersion of values around the mean.
- Minimum: The minimum predicted premium value is approximately Rs.59.49.
- 25th Percentile (Q1): 25% of the predicted premium values are below approximately Rs.322.44.
- Median (50th Percentile, Q2): The median predicted premium value is approximately Rs.495.61, which indicates that 50% of the predicted premiums are below this value.

- 75th Percentile (Q3): 75% of the predicted premium values are below approximately Rs.785.65.
- Maximum: The maximum predicted premium value is approximately Rs.57,260.51, which represents the highest predicted premium in the dataset.

These summary statistics provide insights into the distribution and central tendency of the predicted premium values, helping to understand the variability and range of premiums across the dataset.

3.6.11 Who Will Pay Premium More?

Figure 9. Code sorts data frame by the "premium" column

```
df5 = df4.sort_values(by='Premium', ascending=False)

# Display the sorted DataFrame
df5
```

This code sorts the Data Frame by the "Premium" column in descending order and stores the sorted Data Frame in df5.

- Sort the Data Frame: Uses the sort_values() method to sort the Data Frame based on the values in the "Premium" column. The parameter ascending=-False specifies that the sorting should be done in descending order.
- Create a new Data Frame: Constructs a new Data Frame named df5 to store the sorted Data Frame.
- Display the sorted Data Frame: Displays the sorted Data Frame using the pd.Data Frame() function.

After executing this code, df5 will contain the premiums, sorted by the premium in descending order, to know who pays premium the most

Table 10. Data set

S. No	Premium in terms of rupees
99250	57260.51
99924	52670.51
88658	50876.05

continued on following page

Table 10. Continued

S. No	Premium in terms of rupees
27531	50727.67
61535	49636.57
79174	44792.78
33090	44767.70
62203	44365.68
66779	41402.72

4. CONCLUSION

This study's primary goal is to estimate the risk premium for auto insurance by using drivers' driving habits. Using telematics data as support, the analysis and investigation predicted that, for all 1,00,000 usage-based insurance telematics data, the lowest estimated risk premium would be Rs. 59.49 and the highest risk premium would be Rs. 57,260.51(table no. 10). The range of premiums computed is from Rs. 59.49 to Rs. 57260.51. This is not a vehicle's engine size or type-specific premium rather, it is the cost of comprehensive coverage, which includes protection against theft, fire, and natural catastrophes. Rather, the driver's estimation of the likelihood of an accident and driving behaviour measurements are the only factors that decide it. Regardless of their driving habits, all customers paid the average premium in the early phases. Some customers paid a high premium for low-risk drivers, while others paid a low premium for high-risk drivers. Typically, several variables, including age, gender, driving record, kind of vehicle, location, and occasionally credit score, are considered when determining car insurance rates. Following their classification into risk pools based on these characteristics, premiums are determined.

Customary approaches to premium calculation rely on actuarial tables and statistical data to forecast risk using broad driver profiles. In the event where safe drivers are categorised as greater risk due to other considerations, their rates may still be higher. For example, premiums are set for a year and are subject to small adjustments depending on yearly updates or shifts in risk variables. Traditional insurers may offer competitive prices to drivers with average or safer profiles, but the savings are unrelated to individual driving behaviour. Insurance firms do not usually monitor driving behaviour in real time, but they do use personal data. Rate adjustments for PAYD insurance are made in accordance with the vehicle's actual usage. It keeps track of how much, how well, and when a car is driven using technologies like GPS and telematics. These variables have a direct impact on the premium, which is designed to incentivize safer and less frequent drivers with reduced rates. Drivers that exhibit safe driving habits, such as staying under speed limits, avoiding abrupt stops or accelerations, and travelling during more secure hours of the day, are rewarded. This promotes more cautious driving practices.

Based on driving habits, premiums may change more frequently possibly even monthly. This makes it possible to more quickly modify premiums to reflect the true risk that the motorist poses. When compared to conventional insurance costs, drivers who drive carefully or infrequently use their cars can save a lot of money. As a result, insurance may become more inexpensive for infrequent drivers or those with safe driving habits. Tracking devices or smartphone apps that measure driving behaviour are required under PAYD. Because precise driving data is collected and transmitted, privacy and data security concerns may surface. To put it simply, PAYD insurance offers a more dynamic and individualised strategy based on actual driving behaviour, whereas older systems base rates on statistical averages and broad risk categories. For those who drive safely and less frequently, this may result in more equitable pricing, which could result in financial savings for those who are eligible for lower-risk premiums. Research effort limitation, data is gathered from secondary sources. It varies from nation to nation and area to area. Due to the secondary source of data, the anticipated risk premium for auto insurance has changed slightly. For their future research, the authors want to use the same nation data that provides the most accurate estimate of auto insurance premiums.

REFERENCES

Ahmad, S., Saxena, C., Islam, S., & Karim, R. (2024). Impact of Insur-Tech on the Premium Performance of Insurance Business. *SN Computer Science*, *5*(1), 138. DOI: 10.1007/s42979-023-02462-0

Ayuso, M., Guillen, M., & Nielsen, J. P. (2019). Improving automobile insurance ratemaking using telematics: Incorporating mileage and driver behaviour data. *Transportation*, *46*(3), 735–752. DOI: 10.1007/s11116-018-9890-7

Baecke, P., & Bocca, L. (2017). The value of vehicle telematics data in insurance risk selection processes. *Decision Support Systems*, *98*, 69–79. DOI: 10.1016/j.dss.2017.04.009

Berg Wahlström, M., & Hagelberg, A. (2023). Analysis and Use of Telemetry Data for Car Insurance Premiums.

Boucher, J. P., Côté, S., & Guillen, M. (2017). Exposure as duration and distance in telematics motor insurance using generalized additive models. *Risks*, *5*(4), 54. DOI: 10.3390/risks5040054

Buthelezi, S. J., Hungwe, T., Seeletse, S. M., & Mbirimi-Hungwe, V. (2024). Non-life insurance: The state of the art of determining the superior method for pricing automobile insurance premiums using archival technique. *International Journal of Research in Business and Social Science, 13*(2), 180-188.

Duval, F., Boucher, J. P., & Pigeon, M. (2024). Telematics combined actuarial neural networks for cross-sectional and longitudinal claim count data. *ASTIN Bulletin: The Journal of the IAA*, 1-24.

Ekström, F., & Chen, A. (2020). Machine Learning and Telematics for Risk Assessment in Auto Insurance.

Eling, M., & Kraft, M. (2020). The impact of telematics on the insurability of risks. *The Journal of Risk Finance*, *21*(2), 77–109. DOI: 10.1108/JRF-07-2019-0129

Gao, G., Wang, H., & Wüthrich, M. V. (2022). Boosting Poisson regression models with telematics car driving data. *Machine Learning*, *111*(1), 243–272. DOI: 10.1007/s10994-021-05957-0

Guillen, M., Nielsen, J. P., Ayuso, M., & Pérez-Marín, A. M. (2019). The use of telematics devices to improve automobile insurance rates. *Risk Analysis*, *39*(3), 662–672. DOI: 10.1111/risa.13172 PMID: 30566751

Guillen, M., Nielsen, J. P., & Pérez-Marín, A. M. (2021). Near-miss telematics in motor insurance. *The Journal of Risk and Insurance*, *88*(3), 569–589. DOI: 10.1111/jori.12340

Henckaerts, R., & Antonio, K. (2022). The added value of dynamically updating motor insurance prices with telematics collected driving behavior data. *Insurance, Mathematics & Economics*, *105*, 79–95. DOI: 10.1016/j.insmatheco.2022.03.011

Huang, Y., & Meng, S. (2019). Automobile insurance classification ratemaking based on telematics driving data. *Decision Support Systems*, *127*, 113156. DOI: 10.1016/j.dss.2019.113156

Husnjak, S., Peraković, D., Forenbacher, I., & Mumdziev, M. (2015). Telematics system in usage-based motor insurance. *Procedia Engineering*, *100*, 816–825. DOI: 10.1016/j.proeng.2015.01.436

Irode, P. L. (2017). *An Auto Telematics System for Insurance Premium Rating & Pricing* (Doctoral dissertation, University of Nairobi).

Meng, S., Wang, H., Shi, Y., & Gao, G. (2022). Improving automobile insurance claims frequency prediction with telematics car driving data. *ASTIN Bulletin*, *52*(2), 363–391. DOI: 10.1017/asb.2021.35

Moosavi, S., & Ramnath, R. (2023). Context-aware driver risk prediction with telematics data. *Accident; Analysis and Prevention*, *192*, 107269. DOI: 10.1016/j.aap.2023.107269 PMID: 37696064

Pesantez-Narvaez, J., Guillen, M., & Alcañiz, M. (2019). Predicting motor insurance claims using telematics data—XGBoost versus logistic regression. *Risks*, *7*(2), 70. DOI: 10.3390/risks7020070

Sun, S., Bi, J., Guillen, M., & Pérez-Marín, A. M. (2020). Assessing driving risk using internet of vehicles data: An analysis based on generalized linear models. *Sensors (Basel)*, *20*(9), 2712. DOI: 10.3390/s20092712 PMID: 32397508

Verbelen, R., Antonio, K., & Claeskens, G. (2018). Unravelling the predictive power of telematics data in car insurance pricing. *Applied Statistics*, *67*(5), 1275–1304. DOI: 10.1111/rssc.12283

Wamwea, C. M., Muema, B. K., & Mung'atu, J. K. (2015). Modelling a pay-as-you-drive insurance pricing structure using a generalized linear model: Case study of a company in Kiambu. *American Journal of Theoretical and Applied Statistics*, *4*(6), 527–533. DOI: 10.11648/j.ajtas.20150406.23

Wilson, A. A., Nehme, A., Dhyani, A., & Mahbub, K. (2024). A Comparison of Generalised Linear Modelling with Machine Learning Approaches for Predicting Loss Cost in Motor Insurance. *Risks*, *12*(4), 62. DOI: 10.3390/risks12040062

Xie, S. (2024). Estimating Risk Relativity of Driving Records using Generalized Additive Models: A Statistical Approach for Auto Insurance Rate Regulation. *Asia-Pacific Journal of Risk and Insurance*, *18*(1), 55–86. DOI: 10.1515/apjri-2023-0032

Chapter 9

Exploring Attitudes of First-Year Medical and Dental Students Toward Acquiring Communication Skills:

Student Perspectives on Communication Skills

Sadaf Mumtaz
https://orcid.org/0000-0003-2945-1393
Rawalpindi Medical University, Pakistan

Rabia Latif
Imam Abdul Rahman Bin Faisal University, Saudi Arabia

Tayyaba Faisal
https://orcid.org/0009-0002-8461-9734
College of Physicians and Surgeons, Pakistan

Sadia Ashraf
University of Malaya, Malaysia

Shakeel Ahmed
Allama Iqbal Open University, Islamabad, Pakistan

DOI: 10.4018/979-8-3693-6255-6.ch009

ABSTRACT

The study has investigated attitudes of medical and dental students toward acquiring communication skills using 'Communication Skills Attitude Scale' where 95% of students considered learning communication a lifelong skill. Students from British curriculum had significantly stronger positive attitudes compared to Pakistani curriculum. Themes identified using focal group discussions include allocating more time, training, resources, and standardized assessments for learning communication skills.

INTRODUCTION

In medical education, communication skill is an essential competency, as recognized by WHO (World Health Organization, 1995), CanMeds competency framework 2015 (CanMEDS, 2015), Tomorrow's Doctors document, 2015 (General Medical Council [GMC], 2015), The Scottish Doctor (Simpson et al., 2002), College of Physicians and Surgeons, Pakistan, 2017 (College of Physicians and Surgeons Pakistan, 2017) and many other similar international organizations. Strong communication skills are crucial, since successful doctor/patient communication has been associated with an enhancement in patient gratification (Williams, Weinman, & Dale, 1998), compliance with treatment regimens (DiMatteo, 2004) and patient health outcomes/follow-up (Stewart, 1995). The standard procedure to assess communication skills, adopted by many medical schools is to measure attitude predicting intention and behavior toward learning communication skills, as evidenced by the reasoned action approach (RAA) (McEachan et al., 2016).

Despite rigorous efforts at the national level, Pakistan still lacks a well-structured undergraduate or postgraduate communication skills training program. Grievances and lawsuits brought against doctors point to the poor experiences of patients and the community at large and raises serious concerns and questions on the communication skills training of undergraduate and postgraduate doctors, as well as practicing physicians in various hospitals (Tamblyn et al., 2007).

Including both medical and dental colleges, the HITEC institute of medical sciences is a budding private institution in Pakistan. A vertically integrated curriculum is followed in the medical college, whereas the dental college follows a traditional curriculum. In both colleges, communication skills are not explicitly incorporated into the curriculum in the first year. A handful of studies have focused on determining the awareness of learning this important skill especially in first year medical and dental students (Simpson et al., 2002) (Amanat, Yasmin, Sohail, & Amanat, 2016) (Lichtenstein et al., 2018) (Timilsina, Karki, & Singh, 2019) (Badaam, Shaikh, & Badaam, 2022). Moreover, the perceptions of dental students have been reported recently in a single study conducted in Germany (Lichtenstein et al., 2018), even though it would be important for their future practice in terms of patient treatment and outcome.

The present study, therefore, investigated the attitudes toward communication skill acquisition in the early years of medical and dental school. Our objectives were to a) explore the attitudes toward communication skill acquisition in the early years of medical and dental school, b) compare the attitude between groups of students based on their gender, program discipline, and educational background, c) find the association of positive and negative attitudes towards communication skills with age, gender, discipline, and educational background, and d) find a way to improve attitude toward communication skills.

Highlights of the Study

1. Doctor-patient communication is a rigorous task, poorly addressed in curriculum and requires standardization for assessment.
2. Negative attitudes toward learning communication skills should be scrutinized and addressed.
3. We propose a 'conceptual map' for preclinical and clinical years by assigning more time, training and resources by implementing Kolb's experiential learning cycle.

METHODOLOGY

Ethical approval was sought and granted by our Institutional Review Board, HITEC-Institute of Medical Sciences (IMS); ERC/21/02 for this cross-sectional descriptive study. The sample was obtained by using a non-probability convenience method.

The HITEC-IMS offers five and four-year, graduate entry medical (MBBS, Bachelor of Medicine and Surgery) and dental (BDS, Bachelor of Dental Surgery) programs, respectively. First and second-year students enrolled in the medical program study Physiology, Anatomy, and Biochemistry as major subjects, with integrated lectures of medicine and surgery along with a flavor of history taking and clinical examination spread over a period of two years. Contrastingly, first-year dental students must complete their Physiology, Biochemistry, Anatomy, and Oral Biology through a discipline-based curriculum in one year and are assessed in the same year. Dental students are exposed mainly to clinical examinations with real subjects during their first year, especially in Physiology.

Our subjects were first-year undergraduate medical and dental students enrolled in our institute; 2021-2022 entry (100 in medical and 48 in dental). The students practice communication skills through class presentations, role play, counseling sessions, and clinical examination during their practical sessions. The students who gave consent completed the questionnaire. A modified version of the 'Communication Skills Attitude Scale' (CSAS) Questionnaire by Amanat et al, 2016 (Amanat, Yasmin, Sohail, & Amanat, 2016) was used which was originally designed by Rees et al (Rees, Sheard, & Davies, 2002). These modifications have been made after assessing the reliability and validity of CSAS in our population (Amanat, Yasmin, Sohail, & Amanat, 2016). Rees et al, 2002 (Rees, Sheard, & Davies, 2002) have also done several refinements in CSAS. To further address the ambiguity of items, Marambe et al, 2012 (Marambe, Edussuriya, & Dayaratne, 2012) further improved item number 8 of the CSAS questionnaire. The questionnaire consists of 21 items (1, 2, 3, 5, 6, 7, 8, 9, 10, 11, 13, 14, 17, 18, 19, 20, 21, 22, 23, 24, and 25) with two subscales; positive attitude scale (PAS) and negative attitude scale (NAS). Ten items represent positive attitudes and the remaining eleven items represent negative attitudes toward communication skills education. Items were accompanied by a 5-point Likert scale ranging from strongly disagree (1) to strongly agree (5). By adding scores of items 1, 5, 7, 9, 10, 14, 17, 21, 23, and 25, the positive attitude scale was obtained. NAS, on the contrary, was measured by adding the scales of items 2, 3, 6, 8, 11, 13, 18, 19, 20, 22, and 24. The range of both scales was from 13 to 65, and higher scores represented stronger positive or negative attitudes. The versatility of synonymous responses was grouped as 1 = disagree & strongly disagree, 2 = neutral, and 3 = agree & strongly agree, for ease of presentation (Mumtaz & Zahra, 2016) at a few places.

To check the questionnaire's reliability and validity, we adopted a test-retest technique supervised by one of the authors. The same questionnaire was given to twenty students again 2 weeks later, to check if they responded in a similar way. A measured value of Cronbach's α [0.71] was considered reliable for test items. All responses were anonymous, and only to be used to improve the quality of prospective training and for publication in our professional community.

To enhance a positive attitude towards learning communication skills, focal group discussions with groups of at least twenty students from first-year MBBS and BDS was carried out after obtaining their consent. The session was moderated by one of the authors trained in medical education having a minimum degree of Masters in medical education. The session started with an introduction followed by questions and discussions. Questions were asked to improve ways of effective communication skills. Themes were identified from students' responses. The discussion was recorded for documentation.

STATISTICAL ANALYSIS

SPSS version 27 (IBM Statistics) was used for data analysis. For between-the-groups comparison, an independent sample t-test was used. For the association of the dependent variables (PAS and NAS scores) with the independent variables (age, gender, educational background, program discipline), Pearson correlation was used for numerical data (Age & PAS, NAS Scores) and chi-square association for categorical variables (gender, educational background, discipline). To run the chi-square test, continuous scales of PAS and NAS were converted to categorical scales through "Median Split" technique. Briefly, median values were identified for both PAS & NAS Scales (PAS Median: 39; NAS Median 28.5). The participants with scores ≥ median values were labeled as having a strong attitude, and those with < mean scores were labeled as having a weak attitude. Significance was assumed to be $P < 0.05$ in all tests.

Results

Out of 148 potential study participants, 114 (77%) students responded to our questionnaire. The mean age of our study participants was 19.42±0.871 years. Most of the students were females (75%), Punjabis (73%), belonged to MBBS discipline (58%), and followed the Pakistani curriculum (83%) at their high schools. Mean PAS and NAS scores were 39.01±4.387 and 29.31±5.527 respectively (table 1).

Table 1. Characteristics of study participants (N=114)

Variables	Mean±SD or N (%)
Age (years)	19.42±0.871
Gender	
Male	29 (25%)
Female	85 (75%)
Ethnic Group	
Punjabi	83 (73%)
Pashtun	17 (15%)
Kashmiri	8 (7%)
Saraiki	3 (2.5%)
Baloch	2 (1.7%)
Hindku	1 (0.8%)
Discipline	

continued on following page

Table 1. Continued

Variables	Mean±SD or N (%)
MBBS	66 (58%)
BDS	48 (42%)
Educational Background	
Pakistani curriculum	95 (83%)
British curriculum	19 (17%)
CSAS Scale	
PAS	39.01±4.387
NAS	29.31±5.527

CSAS: Communication Skills Attitude Scale; PAS: Positive Attitude Scale; NAS: Negative Attitude Scale

Table 2. Descriptive analysis of items on positive attitude scale

Statements	Options	Responses N (%)
In order to be a good doctor, I must have good communication skills	A	110(96)
	N	1 (1)
	D	3 (3)
Learning communication skills will help me to respect patients	A	108(95)
	N	5(4)
	D	1(1)
Learning communication skills is interesting	A	99(87)
	N	11(10)
	D	4(3)
Learning communication skills will help to facilitate my team-working skills	A	110(96)
	N	3(3)
	D	1(1)
Learning communication skills will improve my ability to communicate with patients	A	109(96)
	N	5(4)
	D	0(0)

continued on following page

Table 2. Continued

Statements	Options	Responses N (%)
Learning communication skills will help me to respect my colleagues	A	99(87)
	N	11(10)
	D	4(3)
Communication skills teaching would have a better image if it sounded more like a science subject	A	54(47)
	N	35(32)
	D	25(21)
I think it's really useful learning communication skills on the medical or dental degree	A	100(87)
	N	11(10)
	D	3(3)
Learning communication skills is applicable to learning medicine	A	87(76)
	N	19(17)
	D	8(7)
Learning communication skills is important because my ability to communicate is a lifelong skill	A	107(94)
	N	6(5)
	D	1(1)

Note: For ease 5-point Likert scale was converted to 3-point for this table (Strongly agree/Agree=3, Neutral=2, Strongly disagree/Disagree=1) N=114

In PAS, ≥ 95% of study participants realized the importance of having good communication skills and agreed that learning such skills will facilitate their teamwork and help them in dealing with patients (table 2). In NAS, ≥ 30% of study participants thought that learning communication skills is easy and nobody is going to fail them if they do not have good communication skills (table 3).

Table 3. Descriptive analysis of items on negative attitude scale

Statements	Options	Responses N (%)
I can't see the point in learning communication skills	A	6(5)
	N	52 (46)
	D	56 (49)
Nobody is going to fail their medical degree for having poor communication skills	A	38(33)
	N	11(10)
	D	65(57)

continued on following page

Table 3. Continued

Statements	Options	Responses N (%)
I haven't got time to learn communication skills	A	20(17)
	N	18(16)
	D	76 (67)
It will be too much trouble to attend sessions on communication skills	A	20(18)
	N	21(17)
	D	73(65)
Communication skills teaching states the obvious and then complicates it	A	21(18)
	N	6(5)
	D	87(77)
Learning communication skills is too easy	A	43(38)
	N	5(4)
	D	66(58)
When applying for medicine or dentistry, I thought it was a really good idea to learn communications kills	A	61(53)
	N	2(2)
	D	51(45)
I don't need good communication skills to be a doctor	A	10(9)
	N	47(41)
	D	57(50)
I find it hard to admit having some problems with my communication skills	A	33(29)
	N	15(13)
	D	66(58)
My ability to pass exams will get me through medical school rather than my ability to communicate	A	35(31)
	N	9(8)
	D	70(61)
I find it difficult to take communication skills learning seriously	A	21(18)
	N	21(18)
	D	72(64)

Note: For ease 5-point Likert scale was converted to 3-point for this table (Strongly agree/Agree=3, Neutral=2, Strongly disagree/Disagree=1) N=114

No statistically significant differences were found either in PAS or NAS mean scores when groups were compared in terms of gender, and program (MBBS vs BDS). However, students from British Curriculum had significantly higher PAS mean scores in comparison to Pakistani curriculum (table 4).

Table 4. Comparisons of positive and negative attitudes scores between groups of the students

Variables	Positive Attitude Scale		Negative Attitude Scale	
	Mean±SD	p-value	Mean±SD	p-value
Gender Male Female	 37.45±4.95 38.54±4.07	0.05	 30.17±5.61 29.01±5.50	0.33
Discipline MBBS BDS	 38.82±3.65 39.27±5.27	0.61	 28.83±5.46 29.96±5.61	0.29
Educational Background Pakistani curriculum British curriculum	 37.26±3.51 39.36±4.48	0.03	 29.42±5.57 28.74±5.44	0.62

None of the variables (age, gender, educational background, program discipline) was found to be associated with any of the attitude scales (PAS or NAS) (table 5).

Table 5. Association of positive and negative attitudes scales with demographic variables

Positive Attitude Scale		
Variables	X^2 (df) or Pearson Correlation	p-value
Gender Male Female	2.022 (1)	0.155
Program Discipline Medicine Dentistry	0.162 (1)	0.687
Educational Background Pakistani curriculum British curriculum	0.3448 (1)	0.063
Age	0.085	0.370
Negative Attitude Scale		
Variables	**X^2 (df) or Pearson Correlation coefficient**	**p-value**
Gender Male Female	1.156 (1)	0.282
Discipline Medicine Dentistry	0.935 (1)	0.671

continued on following page

Table 5. Continued

	Positive Attitude Scale	
Educational Background Pakistani curriculum British curriculum	0.063 (1)	0.802
Age	-0.137	0.145

X^2 (df)=Chi-square & degree of freedom

Focus Group Discussion

Themes identified on focus group discussion were, 1) More time allocation to communication skills training 2) Training 3) Resources 4) Standardized assessment for improving the communication skills of medical students.

Few responses were;

"Allocating sufficient time for practicing communication skills with real patients"

"More time to practice communication skills"

"Standardized training techniques should be incorporated in the curriculum of medical students"

"SPIKES, role playing and simulation techniques to be used"

"Resources be made available such as internet connectivity for online courses, webinars or training sessions"

"Measuring assessment that aligns with specific needs and goals"

"A systematic approach implemented for measuring communication skill"

DISCUSSION

Our results show that students in their preclinical years carry both positive and negative attitudes toward learning communication skills. Comparatively, positive attitude is stronger than negative attitude as PAS mean scores are higher than NAS mean scores. A similar, predominant positive attitude was observed in a previous study conducted in Pakistan (Amanat, Yasmin, Sohail, & Amanat, 2016) and Indonesia (Widyahening, 2011). Our study results are similar to a Srilankan study in which approximately a quarter of first-year students indicated that their ability to pass exams, rather than to communicate, will get them through medical school. They also reported that they found it difficult to take communication skills learning seriously (Marambe, Edussuriya, & Dayaratne, 2012). In our study, nearly 30-38% of the students considered that nobody could fail them for having poor communication skills, it's too easy, difficult for them to admit having problems with communication skills and their ability to pass exams would get them through medical or dental school rather than communication skills. To our surprise, when applying for medicine or dentistry, 45% (n=51) of students did not think it was a good idea to learn communication skills.

Our results do not show a significant male–female difference in positive or negative attitudes with regard to learning communication skills. Previous studies show similar results in the context of gender and attitude (Amanat, Yasmin, Sohail, & Amanat, 2016) (Marambe, Edussuriya, & Dayaratne, 2012) (Shankar et al., 2006). This is possibly the result of globalization, development in rural areas, awareness through media campaigns, and a rise in literacy rates.

Regarding educational background, the students from the British curriculum had a significantly stronger positive attitude as compared to the students trained by the local curriculum (Cambridge system of examination i.e A-level students). This suggests a lack of students' communication skills training, trained staff, and resources -particularly in the context of the traditional Pakistani curriculum. Similar results were revealed in a German study which showed that traditional teaching schools did not focus on educating pupils with such skills when compared to other schools. However, students from the German problem-based school system were more inclined toward acquiring communication skills (Sellenthin, 2012).

We found no association between most of the demographic and education-related characteristics and NAS or PAS scores. This could be due to rapid developments in cultural practices and globalization. Similar results have been obtained in a recent study conducted on first- and second-year medical undergraduates in Malaysia (Foong, Sow, Ramasamy, & Yap, 2019).

Based on focus group discussions with the students, we propose a 'conceptual map' for communication skills training and assessment in early preclinical and clinical years as shown in Figure 1. In this revised map, we have assigned more time, training, and resources by implementing Kolb's experiential learning cycle. Strategies that will be implemented in first-year medical and dental curricula include role play, debate, problem-based learning, journal clubs, presentations, exposure to standardized or real patients along with generative artificial intelligence techniques such as augmented reality integration using virtual patient dialogues, empathy training and real time feedbacks. Learning will occur through practicing, planning strategies for learning, thinking critically, and monitoring the process. As a result, learners' motivation will be enhanced. During clinical years there will be an addition of teaching tools, including clinical-pathological conferences, case-based discussions, community visits, and seminars incorporating theories such as communities of practice, social constructivism, self-regulated learning, and Schon's Reflection in/on the action. Quantitative standardized assessment tools will be developed and increased weighting has been assigned to communication skills in the blueprint for final assessment during preclinical and clinical years i.e. 30% and 40% respectively. Finally, this reform in the curriculum will be evaluated by using KirkPatrick's Model (Fig 1).

Figure 1. Communication skills training and assessment "conceptual map" for medical and dental students of preclinical and clinical curricula.

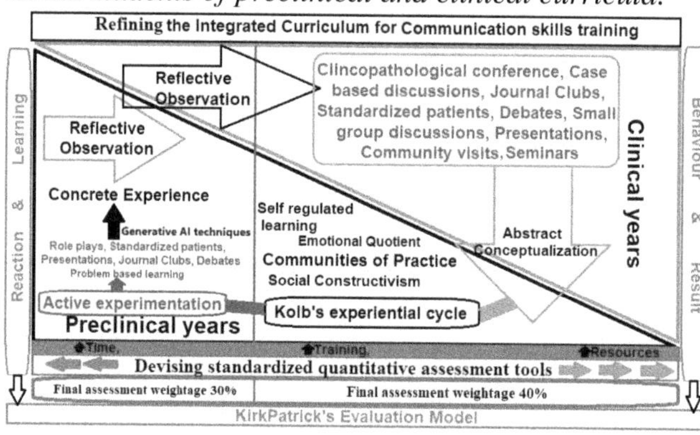

The solid red bar at the bottom indicates more time, training and resources assigned by implementing Kolb's experiential learning cycle i.e. active experimentation, concrete experiences, reflective observations and finally abstract conceptualization.

Limitations: Although the responses were sought through a validated structured questionnaire, there are several limitations to our study. Firstly, we have included participants from only one institution. This, and the fact that most participants were of Punjabi ethnic origin, can affect the generalizability of the results. That there is a higher percentage of female than male respondents may have biased the scores, especially while making gender-based comparisons. The findings of this study highlight that the decline in knowledge of communication skills concepts can be largely attributed to the lack of a longitudinal emphasis, which is compounded by limited exposure to real-world patient scenarios and a dearth of role models.

CONCLUSION

Our students exhibited a relatively stronger positive attitude toward learning communication skills, especially the students trained in British curriculum were significantly more positive compared to those trained in a traditional Pakistani curriculum. There was no association between most of the demographic and education-related characteristics and NAS or PAS scores. Efforts should be made to allocate adequate time, training, and resources to prioritize the learning of communication skills. Using cutting edge technology through generative artificial intelligence techniques can be utilized to practice communicating in virtual clinical environment. This would help to address the identified issue of the deterioration in understanding of CS concepts and enhance the overall quality of CS education. Our findings stipulate that substantial effort may be required to institute a reform in students' attitudes in relation to communication skills learning. Based on our findings, we further suggest revisiting the curriculum of health professionals for incorporation of training programs using artificial intelligence tools and standardized assessment modalities for communication skills explicitly.

ACKNOWLEDGMENT

Statement of Ethics:

Ethical approval was sought and granted by the Institutional Review Board and subjects have given their written informed consent before the start of the study.

Conflict of Interest:

The authors have no conflicts of interest to declare.

Funding Sources:

Funding was not received for this study.

Author Contributions:

Author 1 and author 2 have made a substantial contribution to the concept or design of the article; or the acquisition, analysis, or interpretation of data for the article; AND 2. Drafted the article or revised it critically for important intellectual content; AND 3. Approved the version to be published; AND 4. Agreed to be accountable for all aspects of the work in ensuring that questions related to the accuracy or integrity of any part of the work are appropriately investigated and resolved.

Data Availability Statement:

The data that support the findings of this study are available on request from Author 1 who is also the corresponding author.

REFERENCES

Amanat, R., Yasmin, M., Sohail, A., & Amanat, M. (2016). Pakistani Medical Students' Attitudes towards Communication Skills Learning: A Correlation of Demographic and Education-Related Characteristics. *Open Journal of Social Sciences*, 4(1), 67–73. DOI: 10.4236/jss.2016.41009

Badaam, K. M., Shaikh, S. M., & Badaam, A. M. (2022, May). Assessment of Attitude of First Year Medical Undergraduate Students Towards Communication Skills Training: A Cross-sectional Study. *Journal of Clinical and Diagnostic Research : JCDR*, 16(5), JC05–JC08. DOI: 10.7860/JCDR/2022/53468.16313

CanMEDS. (2015). Framework. http://canmeds.royalcollege.ca/en/framework

DiMatteo, M. (2004). The role of effective communication with children and their families in fostering adherence to pediatric regimens. *Patient Education and Counseling*, 55(3), 339–344. DOI: 10.1016/j.pec.2003.04.003 PMID: 15582339

Foong AL, Sow CF, Ramasamy S, & Yap PS. (2019). Pre-tertiary education, ethnicity, and attitudes of Asian medical undergraduates towards communication skills. Int J Med Educ., 10, 1-8. DOI: 10.5116/ijme.5c30.988d

Lichtenstein NV, Haak R, Ensmann I, Hallal H, Huttenlau J, Krämer K, Krause F, Matthes J, & Stosch C (2018) Does teaching social and communicative competences influence dental students' attitudes towards learning communication skills? A comparison between two dental schools in Germany. GMS J Med Educ., 35(2).

Marambe, K. N., Edussuriya, D. H., & Dayaratne, K. (2012). Attitudes of Sri Lankan Medical Students toward Learning Communication Skills. *Education for Health*, 25(3), 165–171. DOI: 10.4103/1357-6283.109796 PMID: 23823636

McEachan, R., Taylor, N., Harrison, R., Lawton, R., Gardner, P., & Conner, M. (2016). Meta-analysis of the Reasoned Action Approach (RAA) to understanding health behaviours. *Annals of Behavioral Medicine*, 50(4), 592–612. DOI: 10.1007/s12160-016-9798-4 PMID: 27169555

Mumtaz, S., & Zahra, T. (2016). Role-play as a learning modality in Pakistan. *The Clinical Teacher*, 13(2), 124–129. DOI: 10.1111/tct.12406 PMID: 26084372

Outcomes for graduates. Tomorrow's Doctor's. (2015). GMC. https://www.gmc-uk.org/static/documents/content/Outcomes_for_graduates_Dec_16.pdf

Rees, C., Sheard, C., & Davies, S. (2002). The development of a scale to measure medical students' attitudes towards communication skills learning: The Communication Skills Attitude Scale (CSAS). *Medical Education*, 36(2), 141–147. DOI: 10.1046/j.1365-2923.2002.01072.x PMID: 11869441

Sellenthin, A. L. (2012). Students' attitudes towards learning communication skills: Correlating attitudes, demographic and metacognitive variables. *International Journal of Medical Education*, 3, 201–208. DOI: 10.5116/ijme.5066.cef9

Shankar, R. P., Dubey, A. K., Mishra, P., Deshpande, V. Y., Chandrasekhar, T. S., & Shivananda, P. G. (2006). Student attitudes towards communication skills training in a medical college in Western Nepal. *Education for Health (Abingdon)*, 19(1), 71–84. DOI: 10.1080/13576280500534693 PMID: 16531304

Simpson, J., Furnace, J., Crosby, J., Cumming, A., Evans, P., Friedman, M., David, B., Harden, R., Lloyd, D., & McKenzie, H. (2002). The Scottish Doctor –learning outcomes for the medical undergraduate in Scotland: A foundation for competent and reflective practice. *Medical Teacher*, 24(2), 136–143. DOI: 10.1080/01421590220120713 PMID: 12098432

Stewart, M. (1995). Effective physician-patient communication and health outcomes: A review. *Canadian Medical Association Journal*, 152, 1423–1433. PMID: 7728691

Tamblyn, R., Abrahamowicz, M., Dauphinee, D., Wenghofer, E., Jacques, A., Klass, D., Smee, S., Blackmore, D., Winslade, N., Girard, N., Du Berger, R., Bartman, I., Buckeridge, D. L., & Hanley, J. A. (2007). Physician scores on a national clinical skills examination as predictors of complaints to medical regulatory authorities. *Journal of the American Medical Association*, 298(9), 993–1001. DOI: 10.1001/jama.298.9.993 PMID: 17785644

Timilsina S, Karki S, & Singh JP. (2019). Attitudes Of Recently Admitted Undergraduate Medical Students Towards Learning Communication-Skills: A Cross-Sectional Study From Chitwan Medical College. Adv Med Educ Pract., 10, 963-969. DOI: 10.2147/AMEP.S229951

Widyahening, I. S. (2011) Negative attitudes of fi rst year medical students of University of Indonesia towards communication skills learning. *Proceedings of the 8th Asia Pacifi c Medical Education Conference.*

Williams, S., Weinman, J., & Dale, J. (1998). Doctor-patient communication and patient satisfaction: A review. *Family Practice*, 15(5), 480–492. DOI: 10.1093/fampra/15.5.480 PMID: 9848436

World Health Organization. (1995). The five-star doctor: An asset to health care reform? https://www.who.int/hrh/en/HRDJ_1_1_02.pdf

Chapter 10
Prompt Engineering in Generative AI Systems

Qazi Mudassar Ilyas
https://orcid.org/0000-0003-4238-8093
Department of Information Systems, King Faisal University, Saudi Arabia

ABSTRACT

Generative AI has become the disruptive technology of this decade, which has profoundly impacted our lives. Prompt engineering is at the heart of interactions with these models. The skill of designing effective prompts is quickly becoming an essential tool for the entire white-collar workforce. This chapter explores fundamental concepts, challenges, strategies, advanced techniques, and future directions of prompt engineering, providing a comprehensive understanding of how this skill set enables the user to benefit from generative AI systems. Furthermore, the chapter highlights several strategies for troubleshooting prompts that fail to produce the desired results. The chapter concludes with future directions and trends in prompt engineering, such as auto-prompting and dynamic prompt adoption, where AI models are becoming increasingly adept at optimizing prompts autonomously. Ultimately, this chapter provides a detailed view of current practices in prompt engineering and the future potential for effective and responsible human-AI collaboration.

1. INTRODUCTION

Generative artificial intelligence (AI) has become one of the most disruptive, helpful, and impactful technologies in a few years. It is quickly changing the way we carry out our daily tasks. It profoundly impacts individuals, businesses, societies, and governments in ways no one had imagined in the recent past. Generative AI has not only been able to pass the Turing test proposed by Allan Turing in 1950 (Turing,

DOI: 10.4018/979-8-3693-6255-6.ch010

1950), but these systems are challenging human intelligence, even though they are still in their infancy. Today, generative AI can outsmart the most brilliant human in the board games (Silver et al., 2017), medicine (Jumper et al., 2021), scientific research (Zhavoronkov et al., 2019), law (Katz et al., 2017), and creative arts (Elhoseiny & Mazzone, n.d.). These systems are capable of a variety of "intelligent" tasks, including but not limited to brainstorming, holding conversations, solving complex problems, giving logical explanations, writing code, and even producing stunning art. A key concept called prompt engineering is central to these capabilities – the art and science of designing effective prompts that guide these systems to produce the desired output.

The rise of generative AI technologies has not only opened new dimensions of what AI can achieve but has also shifted how we interact with these technologies. All users, from ordinary individuals to researchers, consumers to businesses, learners to scientists, and novices to experts, engage in conversations with these systems to produce desired outputs for their unique tasks. This interaction is made possible through prompts, commands, instructions, or questions framing their intentions and requirements. In many cases, the quality of prompts posed to these systems directly impacts the output quality, relevance, and utility. This makes prompt engineering essential for individuals who want to augment their tasks with generative AI.

This chapter explores the foundations, strategies, and applications of prompt engineering. We discuss its importance, unique challenges, and the future directions of this evolving field. By the end of this chapter, readers will have a clear understanding of the essential skill required for every individual, its impact on their tasks, and the different techniques used to make their prompts as effective as possible to get high-quality outputs from the generative AI systems.

1.1. The Significance of Prompts in Generative AI

Prompts are a gateway to a generative AI system through which users interact with the generative AI models. A prompt is a set of instructions conveying the user intent and requirements for generating responses in the form of text, images, computer code, music, or other creative outputs. As generative AI systems rely on prompts to understand user intent and context, the quality and structure of prompts are crucial in generating high-quality responses.

While traditional computer programs are deterministic, generative AI systems are probabilistic. These systems respond to the user prompts probabilistically, producing an output from multiple plausible outcomes. Due to the probabilistic nature of these systems, it is extremely crucial to provide clear instructions and exact requirements in the prompt passed to the model. A slight change in the choice of terms, phrases, or input structure might lead to a drastically different response from the model.

For example, a poorly structured prompt in text generation may "confuse" the model, misunderstand the user intent, and produce poor-quality content that lacks relevance and focus. The same question posed to the model's carefully crafted choice of words, phrases, and clear instructions might produce a focused, high-quality, and relevant response, resulting in higher user satisfaction. The essence of prompt engineering is the ability to craft such prompts with clear instructions, intention, constraints, and the specification of the desired output. Effective utilization of the powerful capabilities of generative models relies heavily on the ability of users to "ask them the right questions" in the form of carefully crafted prompts.

Although the main objective of prompts is to give instructions to the models to generate the required responses, effective, prompt engineering also allows users to mitigate some well-known limitations of such systems. For example, a carefully crafted prompt might avoid known biases in the model or direct the system to consider specific ethical considerations. Thus, prompting is as much about controlling and refining the systems' behavior to suit specific needs or ethical behavior as it is about generating the desired content. Thus, designing prompts becomes a key competency for maximizing the model's capabilities while minimizing their drawbacks and limitations.

1.2. Evolution of Prompt Engineering

Prompt engineering has evolved significantly since its inception with the advent of generative models. This evolution has followed the evolution in capabilities and performance of the generative models. As early models were relatively simpler, naïve prompts, such as "translate this text," "generate a story," or "summarize the text," would suffice for user interaction with these models. However, as the models grew more sophisticated, the users needed to give more elaborate and sophisticated prompts to get the best results from these models.

The concept of zero-shot learning – where the model performs new tasks on which it has been explicitly trained before – profoundly impacted the evolution of prompt engineering. Instead of training a model for a new task with new data, the model could exploit its existing general understanding of knowledge and context to perform new tasks effectively using transfer learning.

Today, prompt engineering has moved from simple instructions for generative models to enhancing their understanding and guiding them through complex tasks. This evolution has resulted in many innovations in prompt engineering, such as thread of thought, chain of note, chain of verification, emotional prompt, expert prompting, and agenting workflows, to name a few. The subsequent sections of this chapter explore several advanced techniques of prompt engineering that can synergize the existing generative models without requiring retraining or fine-tuning them for improved performance.

1.3. Prompt Engineering in Different Domains

As generative models are not generally domain-specific, users across several domains interact with them with prompts to carry out tasks in their domains. Due to vast differences between the domain characteristics and user requirements, background knowledge, and nature of tasks, there is no one-size-fits-all set of guidelines for prompt engineering. Instead, every domain has its requirements and criteria for prompt design. In the following, we discuss a few use cases for generative models to highlight their differences in prompt design.

1.3.1. Content Creation

Prompt engineering plays a vital role in brainstorming new ideas, generating creative content, refining it, and making it coherent and consistent in creative content creations such as journalism, marketing, social media content generation, and storytelling. The prompts in these domains must clearly describe the target audience, desired format, content focus, and constraints such as minimum or maximum text length.

1.3.2. Healthcare and Diagnostics

Generative models are already playing a key role in various aspects of healthcare, such as clinical note summarization, medical diagnostics, and treatment recommendations. The content requirements in healthcare differ dramatically from those in the creative content domain because of their sensitivity. Accordingly, the prompt design in this domain must focus on high accuracy and reliability instead of creativity. Careful consideration must be given to prevent the model from hallucinations or providing harmful recommendations.

1.3.3. Visual Arts

In creative fields, such as visual arts, prompt engineering inspires creativity by guiding the model to the desired theme or style. Artists and designers use visual prompts to precisely capture their creative thoughts by describing objects, colors, styles, and other visual elements and effects. These precise instructions help the model generate creative artists' desired output.

1.3.4. Scientific Research and Synthetic Data Generation

Scientific research is another domain that is being revolutionized due to generative models. Researchers use these models to generate synthetic data, analyze their data, generate insights, identify patterns, or suggest potential research narratives. High accuracy and specificity in this domain required precisely designed prompts, especially when dealing with highly technical or domain-specific language.

We have discussed a diverse range of domains and highlighted how the requirements of prompts change based on the task, context, and user background. It is crucial for prompt designers to understand the unique requirements of the target domain and the capabilities and limitations of the generative model to craft the most suitable prompts to serve the task at hand.

2. FUNDAMENTALS OF PROMPT ENGINEERING

At the core of generative AI systems is their ability to receive user inputs, interpret these inputs, understand their context and user intention, and generate the desired output (Figure 1). The user input, called prompt, must be designed in such a way that it captures input context and user intention. It might look like a conventional user interaction with the software, but due to the subjective nature of generative systems, generating effective prompts involves a deeper understanding of the internal design and working of generative models and how the structure, length, and syntax of a prompt influences the model output.

Figure 1. Basic process of prompt engineering

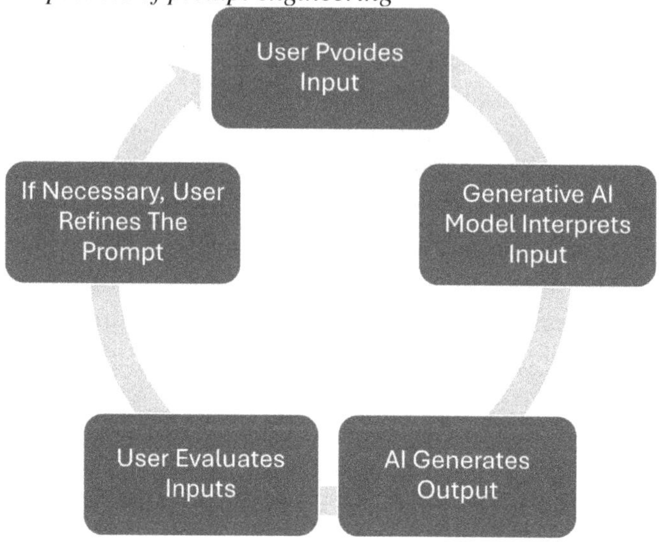

In traditional software development, user requirements are calculated and clearly articulated by the system designer to identify the problems and desired outputs of the system. All system responses are deterministic, resulting in the same result for the same input every single time. Any improvements in the system are made through mini-development cycles in which new user requirements are gathered and analyzed, logical and physical designs of the proposed solution are produced, followed by construction and testing phases before the upgraded system can be delivered to the users. The system implements a well-defined set of user-defined requirements and behaves deterministically. On the other hand, generative systems are designed to learn to carry out new tasks and solve problems they have not been explicitly designed to solve. This non-deterministic behavior is made possible by vast training data and several learning iterations. This intricate process enables these systems to effectively reason and solve unseen problems and generate new and creative artifacts to which they have never been exposed. As user requirements are not fixed in a way similar to traditional software systems, prompt engineering plays a vital role in guiding the system responses. A carefully crafted response designed by an expert engineer who understands the workings of generative systems has a higher potential to generate the desired results with high accuracy, precision, and consistency. Hence, prompt engineering is crucial to getting the best results from these systems.

This section delves into the fundamentals of prompt engineering, beginning with its definition and significance, highlighting key factors affecting prompt quality, and contrasting prompt engineering with traditional software development approaches.

2.1. Definition and Significance of Prompt Engineering

In the simplest terms, a prompt is an input given by a user to a generative model to produce their desired output. A prompt can be as simple as a few keywords or as complex as the detailed instructions about use case scenario, context, output format, length, structure, and style to carry out a complex multi-step task. The term prompt engineering refers to the art and science of designing these prompts that lead to more effective, accurate, contextually appropriate outputs without having any potential to cause harm to the end users.

Prompts are crucial because generative systems are not designed to produce a fixed set of deterministic outputs. However, their behavior and the final probabilistic results are greatly influenced by the input given by the users in the form of these prompts. A well-designed prompt can lead to system responses that are coherent, relevant, and valuable to the users. Conversely, a poorly designed prompt can produce vague, irrelevant, and even harmful output for end users. This makes prompt engineering a crucial skill to learn for maximizing the utility of generative AI systems.

The skill of prompt engineering is paramount in complex and multi-step tasks in which the model needs specific instructions to understand the task, user intention, and exact output requirements. For example, if the system is required to generate a technical report for a highly skillful and experienced audience, a simple set of keywords about the subject matter will not suffice. In addition to the clear information about the subject matter, the user needs to give clear instructions about the target audience, intended purpose of the report, structure, tone, length, and any other aspects of the report to generate one that suits the intended audience and purpose of the report. The most recent phenomenon in prompt engineering - agentic workflows – might also be considered by an experienced prompt engineer to instruct the model to research the topic, extract the required information from these sources, synthesize the knowledge, generate the first draft, test for consistency, accuracy, and coherence, reproduce the second draft and present in the required length and format most suitable for the consumption of this information. These detailed instructions guide the model in understanding the user requirements, breaking this complex task into manageable sub-tasks, executing these tasks independently, and merging the final output into a beneficial output for the target audience.

The significance of prompt engineering can be broken down into the following key areas:

- **Precision**: By following the best practices in prompt engineering, the users can design effective prompts to generate precise information, minimizing irrelevant or inaccurate results.

- **Creativity**: Carefully crafted prompts guide the generative models to produce novel and creative content. This is useful not only in creative fields like art, literature, and music generation but also in scientific, engineering, and applied domains, which can also benefit from it in code generation, data generation and analysis, and problem-solving.
- **Efficiency**: The more well-designed the prompt, the more efficiently the resources are utilized, and the desired output is generated in fewer iterations, making the overall process more resource-efficient.
- **Control**: Following prompt engineering guidelines and best practices provide more control to the user and ensures any harmful outputs are filtered and the final response is safe and appropriate for consumption.

2.2. Factors Affecting Prompt Quality

The art and science of prompt engineering rely on understanding and optimizing several factors that contribute to the quality of prompts. These factors can be categorized into two broad categories: semantic and syntactic (Figure 2). The factors related to the semantics of the prompts include clarity, specificity, and contextual richness. The syntactic or structural factors include prompt syntax, structure, and tokenization considerations. These factors are discussed briefly in the following.

Figure 2. Factors affecting prompt quality

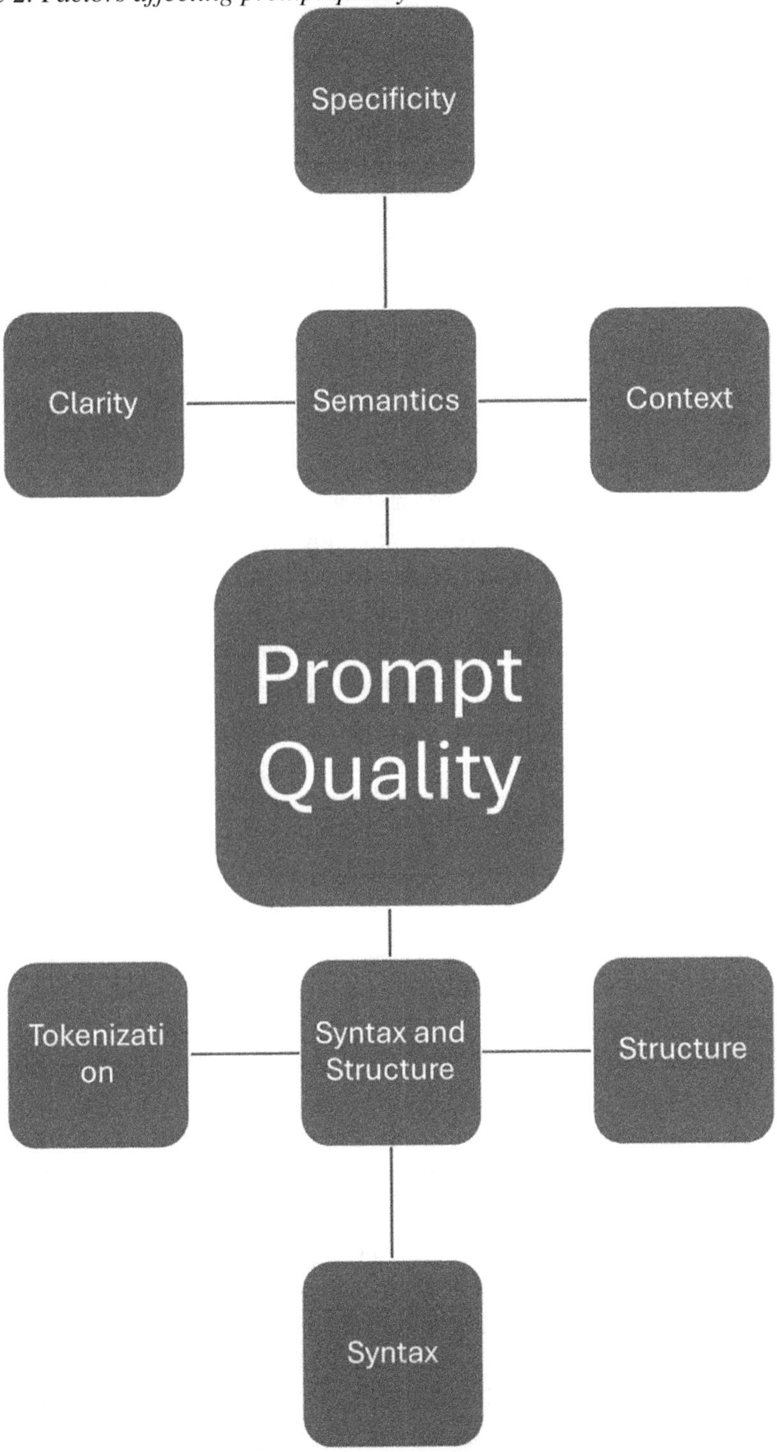

2.2.1. Semantic Considerations

- **Clarity**: An unambiguous prompt can convey the intent and requirements of the user precisely, thus resulting in a clear and coherent response from the model. An ambiguous or vague prompt does not provide precise context to the generative AI system to produce the desired output.
- **Specificity**: As generative AI systems possess broad information about almost every topic in our lives, general instructions lead to very generic and broad responses. However, the users are often interested in more specific information. The user must provide prompts with the level of granularity they are expected from the system. For example, a prompt like "write a 300-word summary on the effects of climate change on coastal regions" gives the system clear instructions about the subject matter, desired length, and geographic focus to generate the desired response.
- **Context**: As in our communication and interaction in our daily lives, it is crucial to put things in perspective by providing enough contextual background to avoid any misunderstanding. Generative systems rely heavily on context to generate the output. Without this contextual information, the AI system may struggle to generate responses perfectly aligned with the user expectations. For example, suppose a prompt is designed to generate a marketing campaign for a particular product. In that case, the necessary contextual information must be provided regarding the target audience, product specifications, and marketing goals for the generative model to generate an appropriate response.

2.2.2. Syntactic and Structural Considerations

- **Syntax**: Although semantic aspects of the query stated above are crucial for effective prompt engineering, the importance of syntactic components should not be ignored either. The prompt syntax, including the language and grammar used in the prompt, can also influence the response generated by the AI. Although the models perform pretty well on slang, informal language, and poor sentence structure, it is pertinent to mention that these models are trained on high-quality data from various sources, and they excel at understanding the user input when proper language and grammar are used in prompts. Poorly structured syntax and grammar can hamper the ability of generative systems to produce coherent and sensible responses.
- **Structure**: The general "divide and conquer" guideline also applies to generative systems. Several studies have shown that well-structured prompts significantly improve the model responses (Wei et al., 2022). A well-structured prompt that breaks down a complex task into simpler sub-tasks guides the AI

model in solving the puzzle pieces and combining them as a coherent whole. This logical progression results in a more organized output, impossible if the model is asked to solve the complete puzzle through a complex prompt. Agentic flows take it to the next level by guiding the systems to decide various paths based on intermediate outputs and user requirements and consult different sources for solving a complex problem (Park et al., 2023).

- **Tokenization**: Tokenization refers to how the AI model breaks down and processes the text. Every word and phrase in the prompt is split into smaller units called tokens, which the model uses to generate its sequence of tokens. Very long or convoluted prompts may result in poor tokenization, making it harder for the model to process them and produce the desired results. Hence, keeping the prompt concise and well-formed is essential to ensure efficient tokenization and better model performance.

2.3. Prompt Engineering vs Traditional Programming

Generative AI systems are probabilistic in contrast to the deterministic design of traditional software programs. In traditional programming, every program function is deterministically designed through conditions, loops, and functions. This results in code performing specific tasks with predictable outcomes.

In contrast, prompt engineering with models that are not explicitly programmed to produce deterministic outputs. This means the same prompt can produce different outputs each time it is run. This introduces an element of unpredictability and requires a different mindset of problem-solving and task execution from that of traditional software programs.

In addition to the differences in fundamental interactions and expectations of the systems, there is a significant shift in handling the situation where the system does not produce the required output. In traditional programming, the software designer elaborates step-by-step instructions to solve problems. The programmers then convert these algorithms and logic into code using programming languages. In case of gaps between the desired and actual outputs, software designers and developers trace the errors in the program or the algorithm to produce the desired output for the user.

In contrast, there is no bug to fix when the output aligns with user expectations. Instead, the prompt engineer must try different prompts, prompt structures, or other approaches to guide the systems' behavior. This involves more trial and error and creativity than traditional debugging, as the objective is to guide the system to produce the desired output instead of changing the internal logic or structure of code.

3. STRATEGIES FOR EFFECTIVE PROMPT DESIGN

As mentioned above, the prompts given to the generative AI systems significantly impact the output produced by these systems. Effective prompt design requires understanding how these models work and strategies to maximize their potential. This section explores several strategies for effective prompt design, focusing on the text's importance, prompt types, optimization techniques, and advanced prompt engineering.

3.1. The Role of Context in Prompting

As in interpersonal communication, context is crucial in generative AI systems. A clear description of the task at hand is crucial for these models to generate accurate, relevant, and coherent responses. The more effectively a user can express the task with an appropriate contextual background, the generative models produce the better results.

Context in a prompt to generative AI models refers to the additional information provided by the user to help the system understand the current task more effectively. This might include precise information about the desired output's subject matter, target audience, constraints, format, or structure. When the model lacks sufficient contextual information, it might produce incomplete, inaccurate, off-topic, or even non-sensical responses.

Some ways to provide context in a prompt are as follows:

3.1.1. Directly Include Background Information

This simple and popular strategy is used to provide context to the model. For example, if you ask the model to summarize a research article, you may include salient details, such as field of study, target audience, and main findings. An example prompt might look like as follows:

"Summarize key findings of the study on the effectiveness of planting more trees, focusing on scientific insights relevant to environmental policymakers."

3.1.2. Incorporate Constraints

Constraints help the generative model produce more focused output within boundaries defined by the prompt and its context. For instance, if you ask the model to generate a marketing campaign email, specifying constraints like length, tone, product specifications, and target audience characteristics will lead to a more customized response.

3.1.3. Use Multi-Part Instructions

It is often helpful to break complex tasks into multiple parts or sub-tasks, describe each sub-task, and how they relate to each other. This detailed step-by-step approach helps the model understand the big picture and the specific details to perform the task more effectively.

Although the techniques mentioned above can be used to provide background information and task descriptions usually produce improved results, it is pertinent to mention that context is not merely about adding background information. It must also ensure that the prompt aligns with the larger goals and that the model understands the application environment or user characteristics who will use the final output. For instance, when asking the model to write a report on renewable energy, an effective prompt would clearly state whether readers will use the report in technical, financial, or environmental domains. This contextual information enables the model to focus on the relevant aspects and produce the desired report.

3.2. Types of Prompts and Their Usage

As generative AI systems are not designed for particular functional requirements and use cases, different prompts may be required for different use case scenarios. There are several types of prompts depending on the characteristics of the task at hand. Knowledge of these types is essential to effectively guide the generative model in generating the desired responses. This section explored open-ended vs. closed prompts and instruction-based vs. creative prompts, highlighting their unique nature and advantages.

3.2.1. Open-Ended vs. Closed Prompts

A prompt given to a generative AI system might require it to be as creative as possible and generate freeform text without any specific constraints on the generated output's style, structure, or format. Such prompts are called open-ended prompts, and they are helpful in tasks involving high creativity, exploration, or generative diversity. For example, asking the generative model to "Write a story about an astronaut stranded on Mars" gives the model complete freedom to create the story's setting, plot, characters, narrative style, and ending. These prompts allow the AI to explore several possibilities and generate a truly creative story without constraints or limitations. Open-ended prompts are well-suited to tasks that are more creative or have no fixed structure or constraints. Some such tasks include storytelling, brainstorming, and exploratory research. However, since the generated content is highly unpredictable, open-ended prompts are unsuitable for tasks requiring high precision or consistency.

On the other hand, closed prompts contain certain constraints on the output generated by the model. They are used when users need factual, accurate, or well-structured information. These constraints are used to limit the responses from the model. Closed prompts are helpful for summarization, data analysis, or data retrieval tasks. They may also be used to generate more focused responses. Table 1 shows a comparison between open-ended and closed-ended prompts.

Table 1. Open-ended vs. closed ended prompts

	Open-Ended Prompts	**Closed-Ended Prompts**
Example	Write a story about a space adventure.	List three causes of deforestation
Outcome	Creative, unpredictable	Factual, precise
Use Case	Creative writing, brainstorming	Data retrieval, summarization

3.2.2. Instruction-Based vs. Creative Prompts

Instruction-based prompts provide specific step-by-step instructions to the model. They are more useful for tasks requiring clear directions or adherence to a structured process. These prompts may require the model to generate a step-by-step procedure for a particular task. For example, "Explain the step-by-step procedure for setting up a cloud server for a small business." Instruction-based prompts are handy in educational settings, where learners may need step-by-step guides to carry out tasks.

Creative prompts encourage the model to "think" more freely and generate imaginative, novel, or artistic outputs. These prompts are more useful in creative fields such as art, storytelling, brainstorming, or marketing.

3.2.3. Single-Turn vs. Multi-Turn Prompts

Single-turn prompts result in a single response from the model. The interaction is complete when the model generates the desired output—for example, a prompt requiring the model to translate a text into another language.

Multi-turn prompts are conversational in nature. The model response to the user's first prompt results in a follow-up question from the user. Thus, the user and AI engage in a back-and-forth interaction that involves several prompts and user responses. Each response builds on all the previous prompts and responses to generate the most suitable response. Multi-turn prompts are helpful for tasks like dialogue generation, problem-solving, or interviews.

3.3. Optimizing Prompts for Different AI Systems

As there are different generative models, each one responds differently to the prompts depending on their capabilities and internal working. There is a massive difference in the internal working of text and image generation models, which is why they interpret the same prompts differently. The user must understand how to optimize prompts for these models to optimize their potential across different tasks and modalities. In the following, we discuss popular models and prompt engineering guidelines for the following types of generative models:

- Text generation and natural language processing
- Image generation
- Code generation
- Text-to-speech (TTS)
- Speech-to-text (speech recognition)
- Music generation
- Text-to-3D

3.3.1. Text Generation and Natural Language Processing

Generative Pre-trained Transformers (GPTs) are the predominant class of models designed primarily for natural language processing and text generation. For these text generation models, the prompt quality is determined by clarity, specificity, and context. To design effective prompts for text generation, the user must clearly describe the purpose, tone, required out format, and any limitations on output length or other aspects. For complex tasks, output examples guide the model in generating practical outputs. A balanced prompt length is also crucial. Too short prompts may result in vague responses, and overly long prompts may confuse the model. An iterative strategy usually results in better final outputs. Table 2 below lists popular text generation and natural language processing models with their salient properties to help users better understand these models and design effective prompts.

Table 2. Popular text generation and natural language processing models

Model Name	Developer	Architecture	Release Year	Supported Languages	Key Features
GPT-4	OpenAI	Transformer-based	2023	Multilingual (many languages)	Large-scale text generation, multimodal support; excels in complex reasoning and text generation.
GPT-3.5	OpenAI	Transformer-based	2022	Multilingual (many languages)	Powers many AI-based applications like ChatGPT; high-quality contextual understanding.
BLOOM	BigScience (Hugging Face)	Transformer-based	2022	46 languages, 13 programming languages	Open-source; multilingual text generation, capable of code generation as well.
OPT	Meta AI	Transformer-based	2022	Multilingual	Open-source; optimized for efficient scaling.
PaLM 2	Google Research	Transformer-based	2023	Multilingual	Specialized in reasoning and knowledge-intensive tasks, text generation in complex domains.
LLaMA 2	Meta AI	Transformer-based	2023	Multilingual	Lightweight, open-source model; designed for low-resource applications with high performance.
GLaM	Google Research	Mixture of Experts	2022	Multilingual	Large, sparse model optimized for fewer active parameters, efficient in resource use.
Claude 2	Anthropic	Transformer-based	2023	English	Focuses on ethical text generation with safety and alignment in mind; chat-like and instructional outputs.
Jurassic-2	AI21 Labs	Transformer-based	2022	English, Hebrew, Spanish	Excels in long-form content generation; offers customization for domain-specific text.
T5 (Text-to-Text Transfer Transformer)	Google Research	Transformer-based	2019	Multilingual	Unified model for a wide range of text-based tasks (e.g., translation, summarization, and Q&A).
GPT-NeoX	EleutherAI	Transformer-based	2021	English	Open-source; large model with strong general-purpose text generation capabilities.

continued on following page

Table 2. Continued

Model Name	Developer	Architecture	Release Year	Supported Languages	Key Features
T5-XXL	Google Research	Transformer-based	2021	Multilingual	Large-scale model optimized for natural language understanding, summarization, and translation.
Megatron-Turing NLG	NVIDIA + Microsoft	Transformer-based	2021	English	Largest language model (530B parameters); designed for enterprise-scale text generation tasks.
ChatGLM	Tsinghua University	Transformer-based	2022	Chinese, English	Bilingual (Chinese-English) model optimized for chat and dialogue generation.
Flan-T5	Google Research	Transformer-based	2022	Multilingual	Fine-tuned for instruction following, high performance across a wide range of natural language tasks.
Ultrachat	Ultraleap	Transformer-based	2022	Multilingual	Focuses on conversational AI with optimized chatbot performance and contextual awareness.
Cohere Command R	Cohere	Transformer-based	2023	English, Multilingual	Optimized for retrieval-augmented generation (RAG) tasks; excels at generating and retrieving text.

3.3.2. Image generation

Specificity is crucial for prompts in image generation models. Prompts containing detailed descriptions of colors, style, context, and other visual elements yield better results. Using adjectives to describe visual mood, composition, or artistic style adds value to the prompts. Other essential aspects are location or action-based clues to guide the model in generating the required images. The prompt may be broken down into parts specific to the background, foreground, objects, their relationship, and placement for complex scenes. Starting with a relatively broad prompt and progressively adding more details to images may result in finer outputs. Table 3 lists popular image generation models with salient capabilities to help the users write effective prompts and generate the required images.

Table 3. Popular image generation models

Model Name	Developer	Architecture	Release Year	Image Types	Key Features
DALL·E	OpenAI	Transformer	2021	Surreal, creative, high-resolution	Generates realistic and creative images from text prompts; handles complex scenes; good at abstraction.
DALL·E 2	OpenAI	Diffusion + Transformer	2022	Realistic, high-detail	Uses diffusion-based models for higher image fidelity; excels at photorealism and fine details.
Stable Diffusion	Stability AI	Latent Diffusion Model	2022	High-resolution, artistic	Open-source; can run on consumer hardware (GPUs); produces high-quality artistic and photorealistic images.
MidJourney	MidJourney Inc.	Proprietary (Transformer)	2022	Abstract, stylized, high-quality	Known for stunning, artistic, and stylized images; excels at creative interpretations and surreal landscapes.
Imagen	Google DeepMind	Diffusion	2022	High-quality, photorealistic	Focuses on generating high-quality photorealistic images with text-to-image generation.
Latent Diffusion	CompVis (LMU Munich)	Latent Diffusion Model	2021	General-purpose, diverse styles	Efficient, open-source model; generates diverse styles of images, good at photorealism and creative tasks.
Make-a-Scene	Meta AI	Autoregressive Transformer	2022	Multi-object scenes, complex layouts	Allows users to provide scene layouts; models handle complex multi-object interactions with fidelity.
Parti	Google DeepMind	Autoregressive Transformer	2022	Realistic, creative, high-resolution	Autoregressive model; focuses on large-scale, high-quality image generation from detailed text prompts.
Muse	Google Research	Masked Generative Model	2023	High-resolution, photorealistic	Masked generative transformer that uses a non-autoregressive process; focuses on fast image generation.

continued on following page

Table 3. Continued

Model Name	Developer	Architecture	Release Year	Image Types	Key Features
BigGAN	DeepMind	GAN (Generative Adversarial Network)	2018	Realistic, diverse styles	Known for generating high-quality, large-scale images with great diversity in objects and backgrounds.
eDiff-I	NVIDIA	Diffusion	2022	High-quality, photorealistic	High-quality image generation from diffusion models; excellent for detailed, real-world object representation.
Artbreeder	Collaborative project	GAN	2019	Stylized, portraits, landscapes	Focused on breeding and morphing images; allows users to combine multiple images to create unique artworks.
DreamBooth	Google Research	Diffusion	2022	Personalizable, realistic, creative	Fine-tunes pre-trained diffusion models to generate personalized images based on user-specific data.
DeepDream	Google	Convolutional Neural Network (CNN)	2015	Psychedelic, abstract	Alters images to enhance patterns; known for surreal, dream-like, and psychedelic visuals.

3.3.3. Code Generation

A clear problem definition is crucial in code generation models. Providing input-output examples, edge cases, constraints, or expected time/space complexities significantly enhances the quality of code produced by these models. The models are smart enough to interpret any comments in the prompt to guide them in the code-generation process. Breaking down the code requirements into smaller modular components also facilitates the code generation process for the code generation models. Table 4 lists some popular code generation models along with their key characteristics to help the user write effective prompts for these models.

Table 4. Popular code generation models

Model Name	Developer	Architecture	Release Year	Supported Languages	Key Features
Codex	OpenAI	GPT (Transformer)	2021	Python, JavaScript, SQL, etc.	Powers GitHub Copilot; translates natural language to code; multi-language support.
AlphaCode	DeepMind	Transformer-based	2022	Python, C++, etc.	Focuses on competitive programming; capable of solving complex algorithmic tasks.
CodeT5	Salesforce	T5-based Transformer	2021	Python, Java, C++, etc.	Supports multiple programming languages and tasks like code summarization.
Polycoder	OpenAI	GPT-2 based	2021	C, Python, Java, JavaScript, etc.	Open-source; focuses on generating syntactically correct and functional code.
InCoder	Meta AI	Autoregressive Transformer	2022	Python, C++, Java, etc.	Combines code generation and infilling; can generate complete functions or fill in code.
Cogram	Cogram AI	GPT-based	2021	Python, SQL	Focuses on assisting with data science tasks like writing SQL queries and Python code.
Tabnine	Tabnine (private)	Transformer-based	2020	Multiple languages (20+)	AI code completion for many languages; focuses on integration with developer tools.
CodeBERT	Microsoft	BERT (Bidirectional Encoder)	2020	Python, Java, JavaScript, etc.	Pre-trained on both source code and natural language, excels in code understanding and generation.
CodeParrot	Hugging Face	GPT-2 based	2021	Python	Open-source; trained on large Python datasets from GitHub.

3.3.4. Text-to-Speech (TTS)

Prompt engineering for text-to-speech models focuses on clarity and natural expression. Correct use of grammar, textual cues for intonation in the form of pauses, punctuation, and the desired style (formal vs. conversational) significantly enhance the generated speech. For multilingual tasks, mentioning the language and even accents can guide the model in generating the desired speech. Table 5 lists some popular text-to-speech models along with their key characteristics to help the user write effective prompts for these models.

Table 5. Popular text-to-speech models

Model Name	Developer	Architecture	Release Year	Languages Supported	Key Features
Tacotron 2	Google	Sequence-to-Sequence (RNN)	2018	Multilingual	Generates high-quality speech; paired with WaveNet for audio synthesis.
WaveNet	DeepMind	Convolutional Neural Network	2016	Multilingual	Autoregressive model that generates high-fidelity, human-like speech.
FastSpeech 2	Microsoft	Transformer-based	2021	Multilingual	Non-autoregressive TTS model; generates high-quality, fast, and stable speech.
VITS	NVIDIA	Variational Autoencoder (VAE) + GAN	2021	Multilingual	Combines VAEs and GANs for expressive, high-quality text-to-speech synthesis.
HiFi-GAN	Kakao Enterprise	GAN-based	2020	Multilingual	Efficient and fast neural vocoder; generates high-fidelity speech from mel-spectrograms.
SpeechT5	Microsoft	Transformer-based	2021	English	Unified model for speech-to-text, text-to-speech, and speech translation.

3.3.5. Speech-to-Text (Speech Recognition)

Prompt engineering for speech-to-text models requires attention to environment and speaker characteristics. A prompt specifying language, accent, background noise, or domain-specific terms can produce better text. These models are commonly used for transcription, for which clearly describing the format (e.g., verbatim or clean transcription) helps refine the output. Table 6 lists some popular speech-to-text models along with their key characteristics to help the user write effective prompts for these models.

Table 6. Popular speech-to-text models

Model Name	Developer	Architecture	Release Year	Languages Supported	Key Features
Whisper	OpenAI	Transformer-based	2022	Multilingual (50+ languages)	High accuracy for noisy and multi-language environments; supports multiple speech tasks like translation.
DeepSpeech	Mozilla	RNN-based (Recurrent Neural Network)	2017	English, Mandarin	Efficient, open-source STT model; designed for real-time speech recognition; uses Connectionist Temporal Classification (CTC).
Wav2Vec 2.0	Meta AI	Transformer-based	2020	Multilingual	Self-supervised learning from raw audio data; high accuracy with low-labeled data.
Conformer	Google Research	Hybrid (CNN + Transformer)	2020	English, Multilingual	Combines convolutional and transformer layers; excels at long-range dependencies and local feature extraction.
Jasper	NVIDIA	RNN-based (Deep CNN)	2019	English	Highly parallelized model, optimized for GPUs; designed for fast and efficient ASR tasks.
QuartzNet	NVIDIA	Convolutional Neural Networks (CNN)	2019	English	Lightweight model; lower computational cost compared to Jasper, with high performance in STT tasks.
Kaldi	Johns Hopkins Univ.	HMM + DNN hybrid	2011	Multilingual	Modular and open-source; supports traditional ASR pipelines; widely used in academic research and industry.
Google Speech-to-Text	Google Cloud	Transformer-based	2018	Multilingual	Industry-grade ASR; real-time transcription with high accuracy and scalability in cloud environments.
Azure Speech-to-Text	Microsoft Azure	Transformer-based	2018	Multilingual	Offers customizable models; strong integration with Microsoft services for enterprise applications.
ASR by AssemblyAI	AssemblyAI	Transformer-based	2021	Multilingual	API-first ASR solution; specializes in real-time speech recognition and speaker diarization.

continued on following page

Table 6. Continued

Model Name	Developer	Architecture	Release Year	Languages Supported	Key Features
SpeechBrain	Open-source community	Transformer-based	2021	Multilingual	Open-source; supports speech recognition, translation, and speaker identification.
Rev AI	Rev.com	Transformer-based	2018	English	Human-assisted transcription; combines AI with human verification for highly accurate results.
Vosk	Alpha Cephei	DNN-based (Deep Neural Network)	2020	Multilingual (20+ languages)	Offline, lightweight STT model; optimized for real-time, on-device ASR.
Silero Models	Silero	Deep Neural Network (DNN)	2020	English, Russian, German, etc.	Real-time, lightweight models designed for edge devices; supports multiple languages.

3.3.6. Music Generation

For music generation models, clear instructions about instruments, genre, mood, and tempo are crucial details to be included in the prompts. Additional details in the form of keys, time signatures, instrument combinations, and musical structure (e.g., verse-chorus structure) can also help guide the model in producing the desired music. Table 7 lists some popular music generation models along with their key characteristics to help the user write effective prompts for these models.

Table 7. Popular music generation models

Model Name	Developer	Architecture	Release Year	Music Types	Key Features
Jukedeck	Jukedeck (acquired by ByteDance)	Deep Learning	2019	Various (background, cinematic)	AI-generated music based on user preferences; focuses on creating background scores.
OpenAI Jukebox	OpenAI	VQ-VAE (Variational Autoencoder)	2020	Pop, classical, jazz	Generates raw audio in different styles; can replicate artist styles and lyrics.
MuseNet	OpenAI	Transformer-based	2019	Classical, jazz, pop, rock	Can generate multi-instrument compositions; supports various styles and time durations.

continued on following page

Table 7. Continued

Model Name	Developer	Architecture	Release Year	Music Types	Key Features
AIVA	AIVA Technologies	Deep Neural Networks	2016	Orchestral, classical, cinematic	Specialized in creating symphonic music and cinematic soundtracks.
Riffusion	Independent (HarmonAI)	Stable Diffusion-based	2022	Synth, electronic	Generates music by using spectrograms, leveraging diffusion models for creating sounds.
MusicLM	Google Research	Transformer-based	2023	Diverse genres, complex structures	Generates long and coherent pieces from text descriptions; fine-tuned for genre and mood.

3.3.7. Text-to-3D

The high-quality prompts for text-to-3D models include details about the scene's physical characteristics, e.g., object shapes, materials, and structures. Furthermore, geometric properties of the objects, dimensions, positions, environment, and interaction with light are crucial to generating high-quality 3D models. The usual divide-and-conquer strategy for text-to-3D models comprises prompts to contain parts related to foreground, background, and layer specifications. Table 8 lists some popular text-to-3D models along with their key characteristics to help the user write effective prompts for these models.

Table 8. Popular text-to-3D models

Model Name	Developer	Architecture	Release Year	3D Outputs	Key Features
DreamFusion	Google Research	NeRF (Neural Radiance Fields)	2022	3D scenes, objects	Leverages text prompts to generate detailed 3D models; uses diffusion for texture generation.
Point-E	OpenAI	Transformer-based	2022	3D point clouds	Generates 3D point clouds from text; focuses on lightweight and efficient model creation.
GET3D	NVIDIA	GAN-based	2022	3D meshes, textured models	Generates textured 3D models from random noise; creates high-fidelity 3D objects.
SJC	DeepMind	Diffusion + Transformer	2023	3D models, detailed objects	Generates 3D objects and textures from text-based descriptions; efficient generation.

4. ADVANCED PROMPT ENGINEERING TECHNIQUES

Although basic prompt engineering techniques and best practices detailed above suffice in several simple applications and use cases, advanced prompt engineering techniques are necessary for unlocking the full potential of the generative models. The capabilities of generative AI systems have improved dramatically recently. These models' applications, use cases, and user expectations have also followed this development. Hence, simple prompts fail to meet user expectations, especially in complex tasks involving reasoning, problem-solving, or domain-specific applications. Several advanced techniques for prompt engineering have emerged in recent years that have the potential to handle complicated tasks and use case scenarios (Figure 3). Advanced techniques such as chain of thought, ReACT, and expert prompting allow for more structured and task-oriented interaction, guiding generative models through the reasoning process and facilitating real-time interactions. In the following, we explore recent research trends and discuss advanced prompt engineering techniques for optimizing the responses from generative models.

Figure 3. Advanced prompt engineering techniques

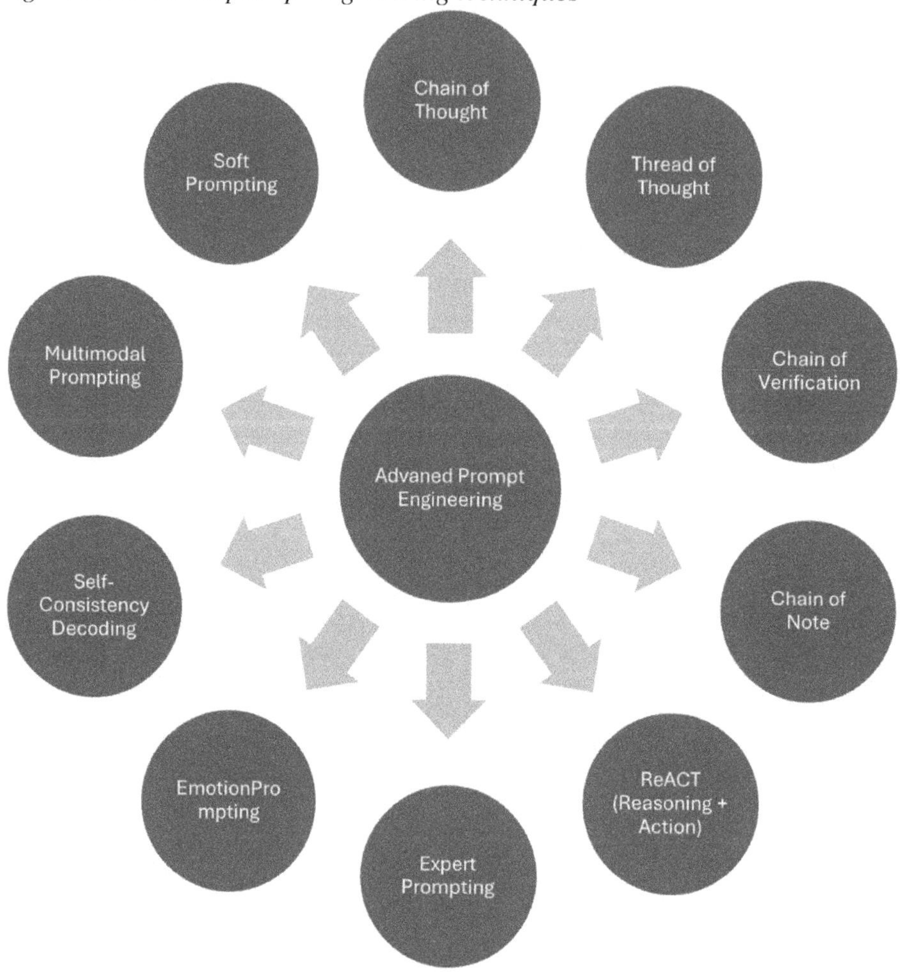

4.1. Chain of Thought Prompting

Chain of thought prompting is one of the earliest advanced prompt engineering techniques mimicking the human reasoning process for solving complex problems (Wei et al., 2023). Instead of overwhelming the generative model with a long prompt, the task is broken down into logical sub-tasks comprising a series of intermediate reasoning steps, and the model is asked to work through this process, providing a detailed explanation of each process used for arriving at the conclusion. This technique is particularly useful for tasks that require multi-step reasoning, such as arithmetic problems, logic puzzles, or intricate tasks involving several sub-tasks.

4.2. Thread of Thought

Thread of thought is an extension of the chain of thought prompt engineering used to maintain coherence and continuity during reasoning (Zhou et al., 2023). While a chain of thought encourages step-by-step execution and explanation, the thread of thought ensures a continuous logical thread connects each part of the reasoning process, preventing the model from losing focus or veering off track. This technique is recommended for handling complex, multi-turn dialogues, legal case reviews, or long-form storytelling.

4.3. Chain of Verification

Chain of verification is a prompt engineering technique that builds upon chain of thought reasoning but performs extra caution to reduce model hallucinations (Dhuliawala et al., 2023). Instead of guiding the model to follow a step-by-step process, the chain of verification also requires the model to verify the result of each intermediate step for accuracy, correctness, and completeness before moving to the next step. The model reviews and verifies intermediate results, fixes any hallucinations, and moves to the next step only after a certain level of confidence is achieved for the current step. This technique is particularly useful in scenarios where precision or accuracy are critical, such as legal reasoning, scientific problem-solving, or complex calculations.

4.4. Chain of Note

This technique uses a chain of notes to guide the model to the desired output. For example, before asking the model to summarize a paper, the prompt might remind the model with a series of notes: "Remember that this is a biography paper on robotics. The key focus is on using large language models and the impact of hallucinations that may adversely affect the performance of robots." These notes ensure that the model builds context before performing the task, leading to a more accurate and contextually relevant response. This promoting technique is proper when detailed background knowledge is necessary before performing the task.

4.5. ReACT (Reasoning + Action)

Generally, the generative models are frozen in time, and their world knowledge is limited to the data on which they were trained. Hence, the classical use case of generative models is to take input from the user, apply a reasoning process using their existing knowledge, and present a solution to a user. However, agentic frameworks expose these models to the outside world and use information from the World Wide Web, databases, or even other programs to assist in their reasoning and content generation process. ReACT prompt engineering is one such technique that combines the reasoning process with any external actions that might be required to augment the model problem-solving process and arrive at the final result (Yao et al., 2023). For example, using a ReACT prompt in a coding task can require the model to understand the problem, generate some code, and then "act" by testing it and refining the results if necessary. This prompting technique is useful for complex multi-step tasks requiring external knowledge, validation, or verification.

4.6. Expert Prompting

The expert prompting technique involves crafting prompts in which the model is asked to emulate a domain expert and use domain knowledge and understanding to solve the problem (Xu et al., 2023). This technique guides the generative model by embedding the domain knowledge in domain-specific jargon, technical details, and expert-level instruction to guide the generation process. For example, instead of a general question like "What is the process of filing a US patent?" the expert prompting technique would provide, "As a patent attorney, explain the specific procedural steps and legal requirements for filing a utility patent under US law, including the required forms and submission guidelines." This technique is more useful in professional domains, such as medicine, law, and engineering, where specificity and accuracy are critical.

4.7. EmotionPrompting

Scientists have long explored the impact of emotional intelligence on human behavior. Several theories and models prove emotional stimuli's strong connection to our actions and decisions. Although it is still debatable whether AI possesses consciousness and emotions, Li et al. found a significant impact of emotional stimuli on the performance of generative AI (Li et al., 2023). EmotionPrompting, proposed by the authors, includes appending an emotional phrase in a prompt to evoke emotional reactions or motivations in the model. Instead of giving a simple prompt, appending it with "This is extremely important to my career" or "Believe in your abilities and strive for excellence" improved the generated responses significantly. This technique is more suitable for big-bench tasks – tasks that challenge the capabilities of generative models – and truthfulQA.

4.8. Self-Consistency Decoding

The generative model usually gets stuck in its first wrong solution. Self-consistency decoding attempts to resolve such situations by requiring the model to generate multiple reasoning paths for the given problem, compare and evaluate them, and select the best one (Wang et al., 2023). This technique is advantageous in complex reasoning tasks where the model gets stuck in an incorrect path.

4.9. Multimodal Prompting

Several complex use cases involve multiple input modalities and processing these inputs as a group to produce the desired output. Multimodal prompting involves diverse input modalities, such as text, images, audio, and video (Radford et al., 2021). For instance, a physician might upload a patient's laboratory results and ask the model to summarize the report, highlighting any anomalies. Multimodal prompting is usually appropriate for text-to-image, text-to-video, and multimedia analysis applications.

4.10. Soft Prompting

Soft prompting is an advanced technique in which prompts are represented as trainable vectors instead of plain text. This enables the model to learn more subtle features from the vectors instead of relying on natural language understanding (Lester et al., 2021). For instance, instead of specifying the exact wording of a prompt in natural language, a soft prompt might be embedded in the latent space of the model as a vector, which the model can interpret in a more abstract form. This approach is beneficial for fine-tuning models in a parameter-efficient way. Soft prompting often adapts a pre-trained model to new tasks with minimal changes.

5. CHALLENGES IN PROMPT ENGINEERING

Although prompt engineering has emerged as an essential skill to extract helpful information from generative AI systems, it presents some serious challenges. The root causes of these issues include inherent complexities in human languages, limitations of AI models, and difficulties in managing unpredictable or biased results. In this section, we briefly explore these areas so that prompt engineers know the pitfalls and may take necessary actions to mitigate them.

5.1. Ambiguity and Bias in Prompts

As no fixed structure is required for prompts to generative models, the users are free to give these models very general or precise prompts. A prompt is ambiguous when the language used in the prompt is too broad and lacks clarity or specificity, leading the model to generate unpredictable or off-topic results. Throughout this chapter, we have emphasized the importance of clear and specific instructions for a model in the prompt. Clear and specific prompts have a higher chance of generating the desired content for the users.

Bias is another important issue in prompt engineering. Poorly designed prompts may reflect cultural, social, or racial biases that the generative models amplify. The biases in the model output ethical concerns, especially in applications where AI output influences decision-making, public opinion, or business operations. Hence, prompt engineers must be aware of implicit biases in prompts and the potential for generative models to exacerbate harmful stereotypes.

5.2. Limitations of Current Generative Models

Although generative models have made significant progress quickly, they have certain limitations that demand caution when using their outputs, especially in sensitive applications. Even with well-designed prompts, the generative models have the potential to hallucinate, where models believe it is producing the correct output. At the same time, the response is fabricated, inaccurate, or incorrect. This is because the generative models are usually frozen in time and do not have real-time access to the current information and fact-checking and verification mechanisms to validate the generated responses.

Misinterpretation is another limitation of generative models. AI models sometimes misunderstand the nuances of a prompt and generate irrelevant or illogical responses. Prompt engineers must be mindful of these limitations and use the generated outputs responsibly and cautiously.

5.3. Troubleshooting Prompts

Whenever a prompt does not produce the desired output, the prompt engineer may employ several troubleshooting strategies to refine the prompt and produce the desired output. Some strategies include:

- **Iterative prompt refinement:** This is one of the most commonly used and most effective strategies for troubleshooting prompts. When a prompt does not produce the desired results, the user can rephrase the prompt to provide more explicit instruction or additional context. In most cases, the revised prompt would produce the desired results.

- **Experimenting with prompt length and structure:** Sometimes, short prompts fail to provide enough contextual background or task details to the model. Similarly, overly long prompts may prevent the model from identifying the content's actual focus to be generated. Trying prompts with varying lengths and structures may guide the model in generating the desired response.
- **Using examples in few-shot prompting:** If the first prompt does not yield the desired results, users may try giving a few examples to specify their expectations from the model regarding the generated content. The model may readjust the content generation process to produce output better aligned with the examples provided by the user.
- **Employing post-processing techniques:** In some cases, if everything fails, the users may employ post-processing techniques to edit and filter AI's output, ensuring that the final result aligns with the intended goal.

6. FUTURE DIRECTIONS AND TRENDS IN PROMPT ENGINEERING

The recent advancements show that the science and art of prompt engineering are poised for significant evolution as the generative models continue to improve. Generative models are increasingly becoming more sophisticated at interpreting natural language. This somewhat shifts the burden of crafting careful prompts from prompt engineers. The models are expected to become more adept at understanding context and intent, making these models more accessible and intuitive.

Emerging technologies like auto-prompting (Zhang et al., 2022) and dynamic prompting (Fan et al., 2023) also change prompt engineering dynamics. Such techniques help AI systems self-optimize by adjusting real-time prompts based on user input and feedback.

Looking ahead, ethical and social considerations will play a crucial role in defining the future of prompt engineering. As AI systems become more autonomous, the responsibility of the service providers to ensure fairness, reduce bias, and ensure the safety of these systems will grow. This evolving relationship between humans and AI will ultimately drive more meaningful collaboration as prompt engineers help bridge the gap between human intent and machine-generated outputs.

7. CONCLUSION

With the increasing proliferation of generative AI in our everyday tasks, the skill of prompt engineering is quickly becoming an essential tool to perform our tasks more effectively and efficiently. These models are still in the early stages. With further developments in these models, the ability to craft precise, context-aware prompts is expected to become essential for optimizing AI responses. This chapter explores the fundamentals of prompt engineering, several strategies for making these prompts as effective as possible, various challenges, and evolving trends in prompt engineering.

The art and science of prompt engineering relied on understanding human language's nuances, generative models' capabilities, and the application environment. With the development of more advanced models, the domain of prompt engineering is also expected to change. Future interactions between humans and AI models are expected to be fluid and more intuitive. At the same time, with more infiltration of these systems in our daily lives, the ethical responsibilities of prompt engineers would also increase, requiring greater consideration for safety, transparency, and fairness.

In the future, prompt engineers will have a crucial impact on how users benefit from AI and how humans and machines collaborate. The role of prompt engineers will shift from simple command developers to enablers of more interactive and adaptive forms of communication with AI. This will result in more responsive, intelligent, and socially conscious AI systems. This transformation holds immense potential for improving how we work, create, and innovate with AI.

FUNDING

This work was supported by the Deanship of Scientific Research, Vice Presidency for Graduate Studies and Scientific Research, King Faisal University, Saudi Arabia [Grant No. KFU250566]

REFERENCES

Dhuliawala, S., Komeili, M., Xu, J., Raileanu, R., Li, X., Celikyilmaz, A., & Weston, J. (2023). *Chain-of-Verification Reduces Hallucination in Large Language Models* (No. arXiv:2309.11495). arXiv. http://arxiv.org/abs/2309.11495

Elhoseiny, A. E. B. L. M., & Mazzone, M. (n.d.). *CAN: Creative Adversarial Networks Generating "Art" by Learning About Styles and Deviating from Style Norms.*

Fan, L., Wang, H. J., Zhang, K., Pei, Z., & Li, A. (2023). Towards an Automatic Prompt Optimization Framework for AI Image Generation. In Stephanidis, C., Antona, M., Ntoa, S., & Salvendy, G. (Eds.), *HCI International 2023 Posters* (Vol. 1836, pp. 405–410). Springer Nature Switzerland. DOI: 10.1007/978-3-031-36004-6_55

Jumper, J., Evans, R., Pritzel, A., Green, T., Figurnov, M., Ronneberger, O., Tunyasuvunakool, K., Bates, R., Žídek, A., Potapenko, A., Bridgland, A., Meyer, C., Kohl, S. A. A., Ballard, A. J., Cowie, A., Romera-Paredes, B., Nikolov, S., Jain, R., Adler, J., & Hassabis, D. (2021). Highly accurate protein structure prediction with AlphaFold. *Nature*, *596*(7873), 583–589. DOI: 10.1038/s41586-021-03819-2 PMID: 34265844

Katz, D. M., Bommarito, M. J., & Blackman, J. (2017). A general approach for predicting the behavior of the Supreme Court of the United States. *PLoS One*, *12*(4), e0174698. DOI: 10.1371/journal.pone.0174698 PMID: 28403140

Lester, B., Al-Rfou, R., & Constant, N. (2021). *The Power of Scale for Parameter-Efficient Prompt Tuning* (No. arXiv:2104.08691). DOI: 10.18653/v1/2021.emnlp-main.243

Li, C., Wang, J., Zhang, Y., Zhu, K., Hou, W., Lian, J., Luo, F., Yang, Q., & Xie, X. (2023). *Large Language Models Understand and Can be Enhanced by Emotional Stimuli* (No. arXiv:2307.11760). arXiv. http://arxiv.org/abs/2307.11760

Park, J. S., O'Brien, J. C., Cai, C. J., Morris, M. R., Liang, P., & Bernstein, M. S. (2023). *Generative Agents: Interactive Simulacra of Human Behavior* (Version 2). arXiv. DOI: 10.1145/3586183.3606763

Radford, A., Kim, J. W., Hallacy, C., Ramesh, A., Goh, G., Agarwal, S., Sastry, G., Askell, A., Mishkin, P., Clark, J., Krueger, G., & Sutskever, I. (2021). *Learning Transferable Visual Models From Natural Language Supervision* (No. arXiv:2103.00020). arXiv. http://arxiv.org/abs/2103.00020

Silver, D., Schrittwieser, J., Simonyan, K., Antonoglou, I., Huang, A., Guez, A., Hubert, T., Baker, L., Lai, M., Bolton, A., Chen, Y., Lillicrap, T., Hui, F., Sifre, L., Van Den Driessche, G., Graepel, T., & Hassabis, D. (2017). Mastering the game of Go without human knowledge. *Nature, 550*(7676), 354–359. DOI: 10.1038/nature24270 PMID: 29052630

Turing, A. M. (1950). Computing Machinery and Intelligence. *Mind, LIX*(236), 433–460. DOI: 10.1093/mind/LIX.236.433

Wang, X., Wei, J., Schuurmans, D., Le, Q., Chi, E., Narang, S., Chowdhery, A., & Zhou, D. (2023). *Self-Consistency Improves Chain of Thought Reasoning in Language Models* (No. arXiv:2203.11171). arXiv. http://arxiv.org/abs/2203.11171

Wei, J., Wang, X., Schuurmans, D., Bosma, M., Ichter, B., Xia, F., Chi, E., Le, Q., & Zhou, D. (2022). *Chain-of-Thought Prompting Elicits Reasoning in Large Language Models* (Version 6). arXiv. DOI: 10.48550/ARXIV.2201.11903

Wei, J., Wang, X., Schuurmans, D., Bosma, M., Ichter, B., Xia, F., Chi, E., Le, Q., & Zhou, D. (2023). *Chain-of-Thought Prompting Elicits Reasoning in Large Language Models* (No. arXiv:2201.11903). arXiv. http://arxiv.org/abs/2201.11903

Xu, B., Yang, A., Lin, J., Wang, Q., Zhou, C., Zhang, Y., & Mao, Z. (2023). *ExpertPrompting: Instructing Large Language Models to be Distinguished Experts* (No. arXiv:2305.14688). arXiv. http://arxiv.org/abs/2305.14688

Yao, S., Zhao, J., Yu, D., Du, N., Shafran, I., Narasimhan, K., & Cao, Y. (2023). *ReAct: Synergizing Reasoning and Acting in Language Models* (No. arXiv:2210.03629). arXiv. http://arxiv.org/abs/2210.03629

Zhang, Y., Fei, H., Li, D., & Li, P. (2022). PromptGen: Automatically Generate Prompts using Generative Models. *Findings of the Association for Computational Linguistics: NAACL, 2022*, 30–37. DOI: 10.18653/v1/2022.findings-naacl.3

Zhavoronkov, A., Ivanenkov, Y. A., Aliper, A., Veselov, M. S., Aladinskiy, V. A., Aladinskaya, A. V., Terentiev, V. A., Polykovskiy, D. A., Kuznetsov, M. D., Asadulaev, A., Volkov, Y., Zholus, A., Shayakhmetov, R. R., Zhebrak, A., Minaeva, L. I., Zagribelnyy, B. A., Lee, L. H., Soll, R., Madge, D., & Aspuru-Guzik, A. (2019). Deep learning enables rapid identification of potent DDR1 kinase inhibitors. *Nature Biotechnology*, *37*(9), 1038–1040. DOI: 10.1038/s41587-019-0224-x PMID: 31477924

Zhou, Y., Geng, X., Shen, T., Tao, C., Long, G., Lou, J.-G., & Shen, J. (2023). *Thread of Thought Unraveling Chaotic Contexts* (No. arXiv:2311.08734). arXiv. http://arxiv.org/abs/2311.08734

Chapter 11
Unsupervised Learning

Akshay Bhuvaneswari Ramakrishnan
https://orcid.org/0009-0000-1578-0984
Johns Hopkins University, USA

S. Srijanani
https://orcid.org/0009-0008-4233-2958
Velammal Engineering College, India

ABSTRACT

Unsupervised learning, an essential component of machine learning, has a substantial impact on the advancement and implementation of generative AI. Incorporating unsupervised learning into generative AI models has the potential to transform businesses by automating and improving creative processes. This chapter explores the fundamental principles, techniques, and progress in unsupervised learning. The authors delve into a range of methods and approaches, including clustering, dimensionality reduction, data mining, feature extraction, neural networks, and anomaly detection, emphasizing their use in generative models. This chapter provides a detailed explanation and use cases to demonstrate how unsupervised learning allows generative AI to produce new and high-quality outputs without the need for labeled data.

1. INTRODUCTION

Unsupervised learning, an essential division of machine learning, concentrates on revealing concealed patterns in data without the requirement for labeled instances (Vincent, Sakthivel, Kumari, Nisha, & Rohini, 2024). Unsupervised learning algorithms operate independently to discover the inherent patterns in data, without relying on input-output pairs for training. This means that the algorithm primarily

DOI: 10.4018/979-8-3693-6255-6.ch011

learns from the structure of the input data itself, rather than applying predefined knowledge to solve a specific task.Unsupervised learning techniques have demonstrated growing progress in recent research on Generative AI.The reasons for this phenomenon are diverse, including factors such as the availability of unmarked data and advancements in modeling techniques.Unsupervised learning is especially beneficial when there is a limited availability or high cost associated with obtaining labeled data (Muneer, Farooq, Athar, Ahsan Raza, Ghazal, & Sakib, 2024).

Unsupervised learning is essential in the field of generative AI since it allows machines to produce new data of superior quality.Generative artificial intelligence (AI) has gained considerable interest, although there is a lack of research on its economic effects.Generative AI models are quickly changing the way we interact, create, and work (Wilmers, 2024). These models utilize unsupervised learning to analyze patterns and relationships in a dataset, allowing them to understand the probability distribution of the data and greatly profit from it. These models have the potential to generate new outputs that are both logical and relevant to the situation.

This chapter seeks to offer a thorough comprehension of the use of unsupervised learning methods in generative AI through in-depth explanations and practical illustrations. We will examine how these methods contribute to the generation of artificial data in different forms, such as photos, text, and audio. We also go into the fundamental principles of unsupervised learning, examining the diverse algorithms and techniques that constitute the core of this field. We will analyze clustering techniques, including K-Means and hierarchical clustering, which group similar data points together. Additionally, we will explore dimensionality reduction methods such as Principal Component Analysis (PCA) and t-Distributed Stochastic Neighbor Embedding (t-SNE), which simplify data complexity while retaining its fundamental characteristics. In addition, we will explore anomaly detection techniques that may effectively find outliers and detect strange patterns in datasets.

2. RELATED WORKS

Unsupervised learning has a long and significant history, with many studies and advances that have contributed to its progress. This section provides an overview of important contributions and related research that have influenced the current state of unsupervised learning and its applications in generative artificial intelligence. According to Watson et al. (Watson, 2023), unsupervised learning is considered the most fundamental branch of artificial intelligence, making it a subject of great importance in philosophical investigation. Nevertheless, the author emphasizes that unsupervised learning is generally ineffective without certain restrictions being imposed. This underscores the importance of carefully considering the underlying assumptions and frameworks that guide unsupervised learning methodologies. (Sharma et al., 2021) examine different emerging techniques that are more worrisome in the realm of unsupervised learning for artificial intelligence, particularly in the field of generation (Sharma, Saxena, & Rana, 2021). These findings indicate that unsupervised learning is becoming more significant in the advancement of generative AI capabilities. (Viswanath et al., 2024) investigate the potential of unsupervised learning in enabling generative AI models to adhere to privacy regulations like the General Data Protection Regulation (GDPR) (Viswanath, Jamthe, Lokiah, & Bianchini, 2024). Unsupervised learning, through the analysis of unlabelled data, enables "machine unlearning" and the protection of privacy in generative AI. This is an important factor to consider when ethically deploying these models.Patel et al. (Patel, 2019) offer a practical manual for constructing practical machine learning solutions using Python, specifically focusing on unlabelled data. The book provides an explanation of commonly used supervised and unsupervised learning methods. It suggests that unsupervised learning could be the key to reaching general artificial intelligence by making use of the large amount of unlabelled data that is available. The authors (Usama et al., 2019) (Usama, Qadir, Raza, Arif, Yau, Elkhatib, ... & Al-Fuqaha, 2019) examine the versatile, comprehensive, and automated techniques of unsupervised machine learning and their utilization in the fields of artificial intelligence (AI) and machine learning (ML). The authors emphasize the significance of unsupervised learning in networking and other fields, showcasing its wide applicability and potential influence on the advancement of generative AI.Generative Adversarial Network (GAN) is being discussed in the paper (Lim et al.,) is used for generating images which makes the images look realistic and Recurrent Neural Network (RNN) (Yu & Guo, 2023) which is used in NLP for generating new textual data. Also, the recent invention ChatGPT (2022) which is the best example for Generative AI which increases the potential impact on education.It has been found through earlier research on GAN interpretation that GANs encode semantics in feature maps in a form that is linearly separable. In (Xu, Zhang, & Hu, 2023) (Jianjin et al.,) novel clustering algorithm KLiSH imparts on extracting the delicate syntactic of GANs trained on objects like non-living and living things. Using KLiSH, the sample images can be collected along with segmentation masks and synthesize paired image-segmentation datasets.Research (Bandi, Adapa, & Kuchi, 2023) commences by explaining the implementation phases of generative AI models, such as variational autoencoders (VAEs) which clarifies what generative AI structures require in order to devise, design, and perform at their fine. A taxonomy of models facilitates the choice of appropriate solutions and promotes innovation. Classifying input-output codecs makes it viable to use quite a few formats for bespoke systems, and assessment metrics provide standardized ways to rate the performance and high-quality of performance. In order to explain and are expecting visible items that aren't presently in the library,

(Kara et al.,) (Combs, Bihl, & Ganapathy, 2024) proposes the Image Recognition Using the Analogical Reasoning Algorithm (IRTARA) and its "generative AI" version, known as "GIRTARA," IRTARA makes use of a list of phrases called the "time period frequency list" to describe the out-of-library object. To determine the nature of the out-of-library item, GIRTARA uses the term frequency listing. We evaluate the exceptional IRTARA effects using both quantitative and qualitative methods, and compare the automated strategies and human-generated outcomes against a baseline. We use the cosine similarity analysis to determine the accuracy of GIRTARA's predictions.

3. FOUNDATIONAL CONCEPT

Comprehending the fundamental principles of unsupervised learning is crucial for understanding and valuing its uses in generative artificial intelligence. This section provides an overview of the fundamental principles, distinguishing characteristics from supervised learning, and the typical tasks that unsupervised learning algorithms are designed to handle.

i) Definition and Key Principles

Unsupervised refers to the machine or computer learning patterns from data without relying on any predetermined response.The objective of the learner is to identify the innate patterns in the data that may be utilized to ascertain the accurate output value for new data instances. Unsupervised learning techniques are highly advantageous in diverse applications due to the following reasons:

- The process of gathering labeled data requires a significant amount of resources and time.
- Achieving precise labeling is a challenging task.

ii) Comparison with Supervised Learning

In supervised learning, the practitioner provides labeled data to the system, such as images of various flowers with corresponding tags indicating their species, such as iris, rose, etc. This allows the system to learn through examples. In the context of unsupervised learning, a data scientist only supplies photographs, and it is the responsibility of the system to analyze the data (Park, Ko, Park, Yim, & Kim, 2024) and ascertain whether they represent images of flowers or not. For instance, if you train a model using unlabeled data and then input an image of a tree, the system will be capable of accurately identifying it as not being a flower. This example is Illustrated in Figure 1. Unsupervised learning refers to the process by which humans acquire the ability to recognize and categorize items that they contemplate.

Figure 1. Simple unsupervised learning model

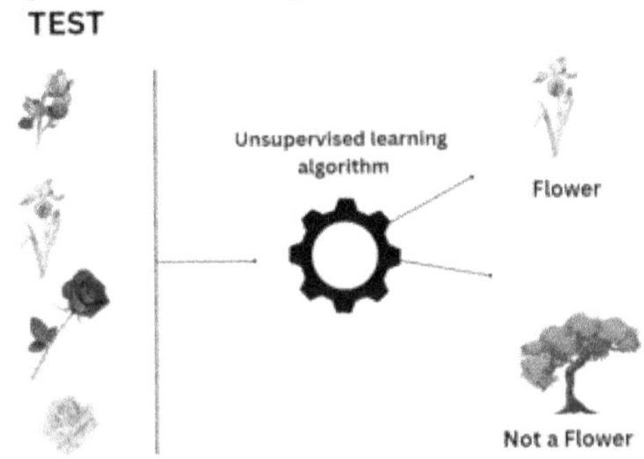

iii) Types of Unsupervised Learning Tasks

a) Clustering

Clustering, often known as cluster analysis, is a type of unsupervised learning. It is commonly used in jobs involving pattern recognition and detecting activities (Nurmamatovich & Azizjon o'g, 2024).Clustering can be categorized into several forms, such as partitioning, hierarchical, overlapping, and probabilistic. The data is divided into partitions, ensuring that each piece of information is exclusively assigned to a single cluster. An instance of a clustering algorithm is the K-means clustering algorithm.The process employs a straightforward and uncomplicated approach to categorize a given dataset into a specific number of clusters (Huang, Zheng, Li, & Che, 2024). The primary concept is to establish k centers, with each center representing a distinct cluster represented in Figure 2.

Figure 2. K- means algorithm implementation

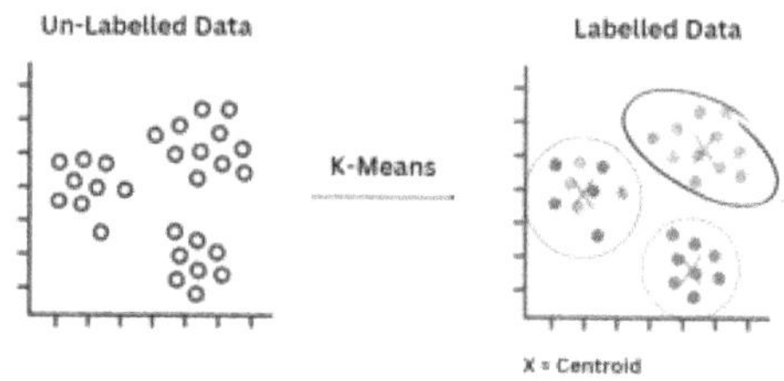

b) Dimensionality Reduction

Dimensionality reduction is a crucial component of unsupervised learning that aims to simplify datasets by decreasing the number of features or variables while retaining as much significant information as feasible (Dessureault & Massicotte, 2024).Several algorithms have been created to achieve dimensionality reduction, one of which is Principal Component Analysis (PCA). PCA is a traditional technique that generates a series of optimal linear approximations for a given set of high-dimensional observations (Bashir, Mzoughi, Shahid, Alturki, & Saidani, 2024). It is a widely used method for reducing the number of dimensions in data.

Below is a detailed breakdown of the process of Principal Component Analysis:

- Data Standardization: Normalize the data by calculating the difference between each feature's value and the average, and then dividing it by the standard deviation. This guarantees that all features are measured using the same scale.
- Covariance Matrix Calculation: Compute the covariance matrix using the standardized data. The covariance matrix quantifies the variability and interdependence among each pair of attributes.
- Perform eigenvalue and eigenvector calculation to determine the eigenvalues and eigenvectors of the covariance matrix. Eigenvectors correspond to the orientations of the new axes, whereas eigenvalues indicate the amount of variability accounted for by each primary component.
- Component Selection: Choose the k eigenvectors that correspond to the k largest eigenvalues. These components are the primary factors that account for the most amount of variability in the data.

- Transformation: Project the original data onto the new coordinate system specified by the selected major components. This process decreases the number of dimensions in the data while still preserving the majority of the information.

c) Anomaly Detection

Anomaly detection refers to any process that identifies outliers in a given data set. These anomalies may indicate atypical network activity, a malfunctioning sensor, or data that need preprocessing prior to analysis (Jaiswal, Bhavsagar, Chavan, Tikekar, & Chaurasia, 2024).Irrelevant traits can obscure the existence of anomalies. An anomaly occurs when data models deviate or diverge from the typical models. Anomalies are detected or anticipated by identifying or predicting data points that deviate from the standard model.One-class Support Vector Machines are widely used for unsupervised anomaly detection. Typically, their objective is to represent the fundamental pattern of normal data while being unaffected by any irrelevant or abnormal data in the training records (Ghiasi, Khan, Sorrentino, Diaine, & Malekjafarian, 2024). A kernel function effectively transforms the input space into a higher-dimensional feature space, facilitating a more distinct differentiation between normal and anomalous data.

d) Association

Association rule mining, a crucial duty in data mining, encounters difficulties in managing extensive, multi-dimensional datasets, extracting significant and understandable rules, dealing with computational intricacy, and guaranteeing scalability and effectiveness. The Apriori algorithm is a well-known algorithm (Mudumba & Kabir, 2024) utilized in data mining to extract frequent itemsets and significant connection rules (Chen, Yang, & Tang, 2024). The algorithm functions on a database of transactions, where each transaction consists of a collection of items, with the objective of identifying itemsets that occur frequently in conjunction. Subsequently, these recurring groupings of things are utilized to generate association rules, which can unveil intriguing connections between the objects.

4. APPLICATIONS IN GENERATIVE AI

Unsupervised learning approaches, including clustering, dimensionality reduction, and association rule mining, are important for developing and improving generative AI models.Generative models seek to generate novel data instances that exhibit similarities to the data used for training. Unsupervised learning is essential for this process as it aids in comprehending the inherent structure and distribution of the data without the need for labeled examples. Through the acquisition of these patterns, generative models have the ability to generate outputs that are both realistic and innovative.

i) Image Generation

Generative AI is well recognized as a leading and thrilling field for creating fresh images that are frequently indistinguishable from genuine ones. Unsupervised learning is essential in this field as it allows models to acquire knowledge about the underlying patterns in picture datasets without the need for labeled input. Generative AI is widely acknowledged as a prominent and exhilarating domain for producing novel visuals that often cannot be distinguished from authentic ones. Unsupervised learning is crucial in this domain as it enables models to gain understanding of the underlying patterns in image datasets without the requirement of labeled input. It is important to mention the concept of utilizing a GAN to implicitly acquire knowledge about the geographical distribution of. The capabilities for generating synthetic images can also be expanded to include more elements.Various types of applications Generative AI is widely acknowledged as a prominent and exhilarating discipline for producing novel visuals that are often indiscernible from authentic ones. Unsupervised learning is crucial in this domain as it enables models to get insights into the underlying patterns in image collections without requiring labeled input.

ii) Text Generation

Text creation is a prominent use of generative AI, in which models produce coherent and contextually appropriate text. Unsupervised learning approaches play a crucial role in this field, allowing models to comprehend and imitate the intricate patterns of human language without the need for large amounts of labeled data. Recurrent Neural Networks (RNNs) are a specific sort of neural network that are specifically built to process sequential data. They accomplish this by keeping a hidden state that stores information about previous items in the sequence. This renders them appropriate for text generating jobs.Due to its repetitive nature, Recurrent Neural Network (RNN) is well-suited for processing sequential input. There are no limitations on the length of the sequence when using this model, and the hidden unit is updated at each time-step.

iii) Music and Audio Synthesis

Generative AI is an exhilarating field that applies music and audio synthesis. In this application, models are capable of producing fresh musical compositions, generating lifelike audio samples, and improving pre-existing audio content. WaveNet, created by DeepMind, is a sophisticated generative model designed specifically for unprocessed audio waveforms. The system utilizes expanded causal convolutions to produce audio samples sequentially, capturing intricate details and subtleties.

5. CONCLUSION AND FUTURE DIRECTIONS

Although generative AI has made notable advancements in recent years, there are still some obstacles that need to be overcome in order to fully unlock its potential.Generative artificial intelligence (AI) is a permanent fixture in our society. The progress in generative AI is rapidly increasing, and its impact on businesses and industries will become more pronounced. Generative AI is significantly influencing our work and lifestyles to the extent where engaging and cooperating with generative AI will soon become a standard practice, if it hasn't already.In this regard, we pinpoint some fundamental obstacles in the existing generative modeling frameworks in terms of their flexibility across various domains, efficient usage of resources, and dependable and secure deployment. There are multiple obstacles that prevent the broad use and practical implementation of generative AI. These tasks involve guaranteeing the excellence and uniformity of produced results across different areas, dealing with the reliance on data and computational resources, managing ethical issues related to bias, privacy, and misuse, enhancing the clarity and openness of model behavior, reducing the susceptibility to adversarial attacks, enhancing the ability to apply knowledge to new situations, creating user-friendly interfaces, and promoting cooperation between humans and AI. We are of the opinion that addressing or reducing these difficulties to a significant degree, along with recent progress in scaling, can unleash the full potential of generative models, which has significant technological and societal consequences.In the last ten years, the potential range of automation has increased significantly, allowing for the automation of several virtual social interactions. This also applies to creative efforts that focus on merging existing concepts. Furthermore, progress in computer vision has facilitated the automation of a wider range of perception activities.

REFERENCES

Bandi, A., Adapa, P. V. S. R., & Kuchi, Y. E. V. P. K. (2023). The power of generative ai: A review of requirements, models, input–output formats, evaluation metrics, and challenges. *Future Internet*, 15(8), 260. DOI: 10.3390/fi15080260

Bashir, R. N., Mzoughi, O., Shahid, M. A., Alturki, N., & Saidani, O. (2024). Principal Component Analysis (PCA) and feature importance-based dimension reduction for Reference Evapotranspiration (ET0) predictions of Taif, Saudi Arabia. *Computers and Electronics in Agriculture*, 222, 109036. DOI: 10.1016/j.compag.2024.109036

Chen, H., Yang, M., & Tang, X. (2024). Association Rule Mining of Aircraft Incident Causes based on Apriori Algorithm.

Combs, K., Bihl, T. J., & Ganapathy, S. (2024). Utilization of generative AI for the characterization and identification of visual unknowns. *Natural Language Processing Journal*, 7, 100064. DOI: 10.1016/j.nlp.2024.100064

Dessureault, J. S., & Massicotte, D. (2024). DPDR: A novel machine learning method for the Decision Process for Dimensionality Reduction. *SN Computer Science*, 5(1), 1–15.

Ghiasi, R., Khan, M. A., Sorrentino, D., Diaine, C., & Malekjafarian, A. (2024). An unsupervised anomaly detection framework for onboard monitoring of railway track geometrical defects using one-class support vector machine. *Engineering Applications of Artificial Intelligence*, 133, 108167. DOI: 10.1016/j.engappai.2024.108167

Huang, Z., Zheng, H., Li, C., & Che, C. (2024). Application of Machine Learning-Based K-Means Clustering for Financial Fraud Detection. *Academic Journal of Science and Technology*, 10(1), 33–39. DOI: 10.54097/74414c90

Jaiswal, A. S., Bhavsagar, D. V., Chavan, S. R., Tikekar, P. C., & Chaurasia, S. (2024). Exploring the Role of Generative Adversarial Networks in Cybersecurity: Techniques, Applications, and Advancements. In Enhancing Security in Public Spaces Through Generative Adversarial Networks (GANs) (pp. 246-258). IGI Global.

Mudumba, B., & Kabir, M. F. (2024). Mine-first association rule mining: An integration of independent frequent patterns in distributed environments. Decision Analytics Journal, 100434.

Muneer, S., Farooq, U., Athar, A., Ahsan Raza, M., Ghazal, T. M., & Sakib, S. (2024). A Critical Review of Artificial Intelligence Based Approaches in Intrusion Detection: A Comprehensive Analysis. *Journal of Engineering*, 2024(1), 3909173. DOI: 10.1155/2024/3909173

Nurmamatovich, T. I., & Azizjon o'g, N. A. Z. (2024). Neural network clustering methods. *American Journal of Open University Education*, 1(1), 16–18.

Park, J., Ko, E. Y., Park, Y. S., Yim, J., & Kim, J. (2024, March). DynamicLabels: Supporting Informed Construction of Machine Learning Label Sets with Crowd Feedback. In *Proceedings of the 29th International Conference on Intelligent User Interfaces* (pp. 209-228). DOI: 10.1145/3640543.3645157

Patel, A. A. (2019). *Hands-on unsupervised learning using Python: how to build applied machine learning solutions from unlabeled data*. O'Reilly Media.

Sharma, R., Saxena, K., & Rana, A. (2021). Unsupervised learning in accordance with new aspects of artificial intelligence. Machine learning approach for cloud data analytics in IoT, 429-459.

Usama, M., Qadir, J., Raza, A., Arif, H., Yau, K. L. A., Elkhatib, Y., Hussain, A., & Al-Fuqaha, A. (2019). Unsupervised machine learning for networking: Techniques, applications and research challenges. *IEEE Access : Practical Innovations, Open Solutions*, 7, 65579–65615. DOI: 10.1109/ACCESS.2019.2916648

Vincent, R. R., Sakthivel, E., Kumari, M., Nisha, F., & Rohini, A. (2024). Machine Learning for Geospatial Analysis: Enhancing Spatial Understanding and Decision-Making. In Ethics, Machine Learning, and Python in Geospatial Analysis (pp. 168-195). IGI Global.

Viswanath, Y., Jamthe, S., Lokiah, S., & Bianchini, E. (2024). Machine unlearning for generative AI. Journal of AI. *Robotics & Workplace Automation*, 3(1), 37–46. DOI: 10.69554/KZRS2422

Watson, D. S. (2023). On the philosophy of unsupervised learning. *Philosophy & Technology*, 36(2), 28. DOI: 10.1007/s13347-023-00635-6

Wilmers, N. (2024). Generative AI and the Future of Inequality.

Xu, J., Zhang, Z., & Hu, X. (2023). Extracting semantic knowledge from gans with unsupervised learning. *IEEE Transactions on Pattern Analysis and Machine Intelligence*, 45(8), 9654–9668. DOI: 10.1109/TPAMI.2023.3262140 PMID: 37030793

Yu, H., & Guo, Y. (2023, June). Generative artificial intelligence empowers educational reform: Current status, issues, and prospects. *Frontiers in Education*, 8, 1183162. DOI: 10.3389/feduc.2023.1183162

Compilation of References

Aguiar, M., & Araújo, S. (2024). Final Thoughts: Digital Humanities Looking at Generative AI. In Digital Humanities Looking at the World: Exploring Innovative Approaches and Contributions to Society (pp. 367-380). Cham: Springer Nature Switzerland.

Ahmad, S., Saxena, C., Islam, S., & Karim, R. (2024). Impact of Insur-Tech on the Premium Performance of Insurance Business. *SN Computer Science*, *5*(1), 138. DOI: 10.1007/s42979-023-02462-0

Aizenberg, E. & Van Den Hoven, J. (2020). Designing for human rights in AI. Big Data & Society.

Al Naqbi, H., Bahroun, Z., & Ahmed, V. (2024). Enhancing work productivity through generative artificial intelligence: A comprehensive literature review. Sustainability.

Alharbi, R., Almajnooni, N., Albishry, M., Alotaibi, A., Alsaadi, F., Alsulami, G., Alharbi, A., Alotaibi, R., Alharbi, R., Alharbi, A., Alkhodidi, T., Alafif, T., Al-bassam, A., & Sabban, S. (2020). GEAD: Generating and Evaluating Handwritten Eastern Arabic Digits Using Generative Adversarial Networks. DOI: 10.13140/RG.2.2.24679.06561

Almeida-Ñauñay, A. F., Tarquis, A. M., López-Herrera, J., Pérez-Martín, E., Pancorbo, J. L., Raya-Sereno, M. D., & Quemada, M. (2023, February). Optimization of soil background removal to improve the prediction of wheat traits with UAV imagery. *Computers and Electronics in Agriculture*, *205*, 107559. Advance online publication. DOI: 10.1016/j.compag.2022.107559

Alto, V. (2023). Modern Generative AI with ChatGPT and OpenAI Models: Leverage the capabilities of OpenAI's LLM for productivity and innovation with GPT3 and GPT4.

Amanat, R., Yasmin, M., Sohail, A., & Amanat, M. (2016). Pakistani Medical Students' Attitudes towards Communication Skills Learning: A Correlation of Demographic and Education-Related Characteristics. *Open Journal of Social Sciences, 4*(1), 67–73. DOI: 10.4236/jss.2016.41009

Amankwah-Amoah, J., Abdalla, S., Mogaji, E., Elbanna, A., & Dwivedi, Y. K. (2024). The impending disruption of creative industries by generative AI: Opportunities, challenges, and research agenda. *International Journal of Information Management, 79*, 102759. DOI: 10.1016/j.ijinfomgt.2024.102759

Anantrasirichai, N. & Bull, D. (2022). Artificial intelligence in the creative industries: a review. Artificial intelligence review.

Andoni, A., & Indyk, P. (2008). Near-optimal hashing algorithms for approximate nearest neighbor in high dimensions. *Communications of the ACM, 51*(1), 117–122. DOI: 10.1145/1327452.1327494

Ansag, R. A., & Gonzalez, A. J. (2023). State-of-the-art in automated story generation systems research. *Journal of Experimental & Theoretical Artificial Intelligence, 35*(6), 877–931. DOI: 10.1080/0952813X.2021.1971777

Aronson, R. L. (2013). FarmBot: Humanity's open-source automated precision farming machine. *Technology*, 19.

Ashley, K. D. (2017). *Artificial intelligence and legal analytics: new tools for law practice in the digital age*. Cambridge University Press. DOI: 10.1017/9781316761380

Atkinson, J. A., Lobet, G., Noll, M., Meyer, P. E., Griffiths, M., & Wells, D. M. (2017, August). Combining semi-automated image analysis techniques with machine learning algorithms to accelerate large-scale genetic studies. *GigaScience, 6*(10), gix084. Advance online publication. DOI: 10.1093/gigascience/gix084 PMID: 29020748

Attali, Y., & Burstein, J. (2006). Automated essay scoring with e-rater® V. 2. *The Journal of Technology, Learning, and Assessment, 4*(3).

Avneri, A., Aharon, S., Brook, A., Atsmon, G., Smirnov, E., Sadeh, R., & Lati, R. N. (2023, February). UAS-based imaging for prediction of chickpea crop biophysical parameters and yield. *Computers and Electronics in Agriculture, 205*, 107581. Advance online publication. DOI: 10.1016/j.compag.2022.107581

Ayuso, M., Guillen, M., & Nielsen, J. P. (2019). Improving automobile insurance ratemaking using telematics: Incorporating mileage and driver behaviour data. *Transportation, 46*(3), 735–752. DOI: 10.1007/s11116-018-9890-7

Bacchi, A. (2020). *Uncovering Jewish Creativity in Book III of the Sibylline Oracles: Gender*. Intertextuality, and Politics. DOI: 10.1163/9789004426078

Badaam, K. M., Shaikh, S. M., & Badaam, A. M. (2022, May). Assessment of Attitude of First Year Medical Undergraduate Students Towards Communication Skills Training: A Cross-sectional Study. *Journal of Clinical and Diagnostic Research : JCDR, 16*(5), JC05–JC08. DOI: 10.7860/JCDR/2022/53468.16313

Baecke, P., & Bocca, L. (2017). The value of vehicle telematics data in insurance risk selection processes. *Decision Support Systems, 98*, 69–79. DOI: 10.1016/j.dss.2017.04.009

Bagherian, S., & Yaghoobi-Derabi, J. (2022). Langue at work: a review and comparison of the narrative theories in literature. Revista de Investigaciones Universidad del Quindío, 34(S2), 452-461. uniquindio.edu.co

Balagopalan, A., Eyre, B., Robin, J., Rudzicz, F., & Novikova, J. (2021). Comparing pre-trained and feature-based models for prediction of Alzheimer's disease based on speech. *Frontiers in Aging Neuroscience, 13*, 635945. DOI: 10.3389/fnagi.2021.635945 PMID: 33986655

Ballard, C. (2021). Transmission's end? Cataclysm and chronology in Indigenous oral tradition. The Routledge companion to global indigenous history.

Bamodu, G. (2023). *Progressive harmonisation of international trade law in Africa: the role of UNCITRAL*. The Elgar Companion to UNCITRAL.

Bandi, A., Adapa, P. V. S. R., & Kuchi, Y. E. V. P. K. (2023). The power of generative ai: A review of requirements, models, input–output formats, evaluation metrics, and challenges. Future Internet.

Bandi, A., Adapa, P. V. S. R., & Kuchi, Y. E. V. P. K. (2023). The power of generative ai: A review of requirements, models, input–output formats, evaluation metrics, and challenges. *Future Internet, 15*(8), 260. DOI: 10.3390/fi15080260

Bao, J., Li, L., & Davis, A. (2022). Variational autoencoder or generative adversarial networks? a comparison of two deep learning methods for flow and transport data assimilation. *Mathematical Geosciences, 54*(6), 1017–1042. DOI: 10.1007/s11004-022-10003-3

Barreda-Ángeles, M., Aleix-Guillaume, S., & Pereda-Baños, A. (2021). Virtual reality storytelling as a double-edged sword: Immersive presentation of nonfiction 360-video is associated with impaired cognitive information processing. *Communication Monographs, 88*(2), 154–173. DOI: 10.1080/03637751.2020.1803496

Barthelmeß, U. & Furbach, U. (2023). A Different Look at Artificial Intelligence.

Bashir, R. N., Mzoughi, O., Shahid, M. A., Alturki, N., & Saidani, O. (2024). Principal Component Analysis (PCA) and feature importance-based dimension reduction for Reference Evapotranspiration (ET0) predictions of Taif, Saudi Arabia. *Computers and Electronics in Agriculture, 222*, 109036. DOI: 10.1016/j.compag.2024.109036

Belfiore, E. (2022). Is it really about the evidence? argument, persuasion, and the power of ideas in cultural policy. Cultural Trends.

Bell, J., & Dee, H. M. (2016, November). Aberystwyth Leaf Evaluation Dataset. *Aberystwyth Leaf Evaluation Dataset.* DOI: 10.5281/ZENODO.168158

Benvenuti, M., Cangelosi, A., Weinberger, A., Mazzoni, E., Benassi, M., Barbaresi, M., & Orsoni, M. (2023). Artificial intelligence and human behavioral development: A perspective on new skills and competences acquisition for the educational context. *Computers in Human Behavior, 148*, 107903. DOI: 10.1016/j.chb.2023.107903

Berg Wahlström, M., & Hagelberg, A. (2023). Analysis and Use of Telemetry Data for Car Insurance Premiums.

Berov, L. (2023). From Narratology to Computational Story Composition and Back: An Exploratory Study in Generative Modeling.

Best, S. & Kellner, D. (2020). The postmodern adventure: Science technology and cultural studies at the third millennium.

Bibi, A., Moetesum, M., & Siddiqi, I. (2022). Deep Vision for Pest Detection in Corn Fields. *2022 19th International Bhurban Conference on Applied Sciences and Technology (IBCAST)* (pp. 343-348). DOI: 10.1109/IBCAST54850.2022.9990435

Bingham, E., & Mannila, H. (2001). Random projection in dimensionality reduction: Applications to image and text data. *Proceedings of the Seventh ACM SIGKDD International Conference on Knowledge Discovery and Data Mining*, 245–250. DOI: 10.1145/502512.502546

Bishop, J. M. (2021). Artificial intelligence is stupid and causal reasoning will not fix it. Frontiers in Psychology. frontiersin.org

Bolukbasi, T., Chang, K. W., Zou, J. Y., Saligrama, V., & Kalai, A. T. (2016). Man is to computer programmer as woman is to homemaker? debiasing word embeddings. *Advances in Neural Information Processing Systems*, 29.

Bondarenko, A., Braslavski, P., Völske, M., Aly, R., Fröbe, M., Panchenko, A., Biemann, C., Stein, B., & Hagen, M. (2020). Comparative Web Search Questions. *Proceedings of the 13th International Conference on Web Search and Data Mining*, 52–60. DOI: 10.1145/3336191.3371848

Boucher, J. P., Côté, S., & Guillen, M. (2017). Exposure as duration and distance in telematics motor insurance using generalized additive models. *Risks*, *5*(4), 54. DOI: 10.3390/risks5040054

Brinkmann, L., Baumann, F., Bonnefon, J. F., Derex, M., Müller, T. F., Nussberger, A. M., Czaplicka, A., Acerbi, A., Griffiths, T. L., Henrich, J., Leibo, J. Z., McElreath, R., Oudeyer, P.-Y., Stray, J., & Rahwan, I. (2023). Machine culture. *Nature Human Behaviour*, *7*(11), 1855–1868. DOI: 10.1038/s41562-023-01742-2 PMID: 37985914

Busse, R. (2021). *Folk tales and organizational change: an integrative model for Chinese management*. Inside the Changing Business of China.

Buthelezi, S. J., Hungwe, T., Seeletse, S. M., & Mbirimi-Hungwe, V. (2024). Non-life insurance: The state of the art of determining the superior method for pricing automobile insurance premiums using archival technique. *International Journal of Research in Business and Social Science, 13*(2), 180-188.

Butler, P. (2023). *UNCITRAL and MSMEs: An enduring and successful marriage*. The Elgar Companion to UNCITRAL.

Bu, Y., Jiang, X., Tian, J., Hu, X., Fei, X., Huang, D., & Luo, H. (2022, October). Rapid and accurate detection of starch content in mixed sorghum by hyperspectral imaging combined with data fusion technology. *Journal of Food Process Engineering*, *45*(10), e14129. Advance online publication. DOI: 10.1111/jfpe.14129

Cambria, E., & White, B. (2014). Jumping NLP curves: A review of natural language processing research. *IEEE Computational Intelligence Magazine*, *9*(2), 48–57. DOI: 10.1109/MCI.2014.2307227

Campbell, M., Dechemi, A., & Karydis, K. (2022, October). An Integrated Actuation-Perception Framework for Robotic Leaf Retrieval: Detection, Localization, and Cutting. *An Integrated Actuation-Perception Framework for Robotic Leaf Retrieval: Detection, Localization, and Cutting*. IEEE. DOI: 10.1109/IROS47612.2022.9981118

Candiago, S., Remondino, F., De Giglio, M., Dubbini, M., & Gattelli, M. (2015). Evaluating multispectral images and vegetation indices for precision farming applications from UAV images. *Remote Sensing (Basel)*, *7*(4), 4026–4047. DOI: 10.3390/rs70404026

Candiani, G., Tagliabue, G., Panigada, C., Verrelst, J., Picchi, V., Caicedo, J. P., & Boschetti, M. (2022, April). Evaluation of Hybrid Models to Estimate Chlorophyll and Nitrogen Content of Maize Crops in the Framework of the Future CHIME Mission. *Remote Sensing*, *14*(8), 1792. Advance online publication. DOI: 10.3390/rs14081792 PMID: 36081596

CanMEDS. (2015). Framework. http://canmeds.royalcollege.ca/en/framework

Cecotti, H. (2016). Active graph based semi-supervised learning using image matching: Application to handwritten digit recognition. *Pattern Recognition Letters*, *73*, 76–82. DOI: 10.1016/j.patrec.2016.01.016

Cerro, J. D., Ulloa, C. C., Barrientos, A., & de León Rivas, J. (2021, February). Unmanned aerial vehicles in agriculture: A survey. *Agronomy (Basel)*, *11*(2), 203. Advance online publication. DOI: 10.3390/agronomy11020203

Çetin, E. (2021). Digital storytelling in teacher education and its effect on the digital literacy of pre-service teachers. *Thinking Skills and Creativity*.

Chakraborty, U., Roy, S., & Kumar, S. (2023). *Rise of Generative AI and ChatGPT: Understand how Generative AI and ChatGPT are transforming and reshaping the business world*. English Edition.

Chancia, R., Bates, T., Heuvel, J. V., & van Aardt, J. (2021, November). Assessing grapevine nutrient status from unmanned aerial system (UAS) hyperspectral imagery. *Remote Sensing (Basel)*, *13*(21), 4489. Advance online publication. DOI: 10.3390/rs13214489

Chen, H., Yang, M., & Tang, X. (2024). Association Rule Mining of Aircraft Incident Causes based on Apriori Algorithm.

Chen, M., Mei, S., Fan, J., & Wang, M. (2024). An overview of diffusion models: Applications, guided generation, statistical rates and optimization. *arXiv, 34*(2), 25-39.

Chen, W., Li, J., Tang, C., & Sun, G. (2024, June). Developing an Intermediate Framework for Enhancing Comic Creation Through Generative AI. In International Conference on Human-Computer Interaction (pp. 292-306). Cham: Springer Nature Switzerland. DOI: 10.1007/978-3-031-60449-2_20

Chen, X., Xie, H., & Hwang, G. J. (2020). A multi-perspective study on artificial intelligence in education: Grants, conferences, journals, software tools, institutions, and researchers. Computers and Education: Artificial Intelligence.

Chen, C., Zhou, S., Liao, L., Wu, H., Sun, W., Yan, Q., & Lin, W. (2024). Iterative Token Evaluation and Refinement for Real-World Super-resolution. *Proceedings of the AAAI Conference on Artificial Intelligence*, *38*(2), 1010–1018. DOI: 10.1609/aaai.v38i2.27861

Chen, F., Pan, S., Jiang, J., Huo, H., & Long, G. (2019, July). DAGCN: dual attention graph convolutional networks. In *2019 International Joint Conference on Neural Networks (IJCNN)* (pp. 1-8). IEEE.

Chen, Y., Ding, Z., Zheng, Q., Qin, Y., Huang, R., & Shah, N. (2020). A history and theory of textual event detection and recognition. *IEEE Access : Practical Innovations, Open Solutions*, *8*, 201371–201392. DOI: 10.1109/ACCESS.2020.3034907

Chitwood, D. H., & Otoni, W. C. (2017, January). Morphometric analysis of Passiflora leaves: The relationship between landmarks of the vasculature and elliptical Fourier descriptors of the blade. *GigaScience*, *6*(10). Advance online publication. DOI: 10.1093/gigascience/gix070 PMID: 28369351

Choudhury, R. R., Roy, P., Ghosh, S., & Ghosh, A. (2024). Machine Learning and Deep Learning Algorithms for Green Computing. In Kumar, K., Varadarajan, V., Nasser, N., & Poluru, R. (Eds.), *Computational Intelligence for Green Cloud Computing and Digital Waste Management* (pp. 1–23). IGI Global Scientific Publishing. DOI: 10.4018/979-8-3693-1552-1.ch001

Chrysos, G., Georgopoulos, M., & Panagakis, Y. (2021). Conditional generation using polynomial expansions. *Advances in Neural Information Processing Systems*, *34*(1), 28390–28404.

Chuang, Y. Y., Vollmer, M. L., Shafaei-Bajestan, E., Gahl, S., Hendrix, P., & Baayen, R. H. (2021). The processing of pseudoword form and meaning in production and comprehension: A computational modeling approach using linear discriminative learning. *Behavior Research Methods*, *53*(3), 945–976. DOI: 10.3758/s13428-020-01356-w PMID: 32377973

Classen, C. (2023). Worlds of sense: Exploring the senses in history and across cultures.

Coeckelbergh, M. (2021). Time machines: Artificial intelligence, process, and narrative. Philosophy & Technology.

Cohen, S. (2024). I, Yantra: Exploring Self and Selflessness in Ancient Indian Robot Tales.

Colins, M. (2017). *Machine learning: an introduction to supervised and unsupervised learning algorithms*. CreateSpace.

Combs, K., Bihl, T. J., & Ganapathy, S. (2024). Utilization of generative AI for the characterization and identification of visual unknowns. *Natural Language Processing Journal, 7*, 100064. DOI: 10.1016/j.nlp.2024.100064

Conroy, J. M., Schlesinger, J. D., & O'Leary, D. P. (2015). Automatic summarization of changes in documents. U.S. Patent No. 9,111,854. Washington, DC: U.S. Patent and Trademark Office.

Cress, U., & Kimmerle, J. (2023). Co-constructing knowledge with generative AI tools: Reflections from a CSCL perspective. *International Journal of Computer-Supported Collaborative Learning*, *18*(4), 607–614. DOI: 10.1007/s11412-023-09409-w

Cubero, S., Marco-noales, E., Aleixos, N., Barbé, S., & Blasco, J. (2020). Robhortic: A field robot to detect pests and diseases in horticultural crops by proximal sensing. *Agriculture*, *10*(7), 276. Advance online publication. DOI: 10.3390/agriculture10070276

Cui, M., Lou, Y., Ge, Y., & Wang, K. (2023, February). LES-YOLO: A lightweight pinecone detection algorithm based on improved YOLOv4-Tiny network. *Computers and Electronics in Agriculture*, *205*, 107613. Advance online publication. DOI: 10.1016/j.compag.2023.107613

Davidson, I., Burke, H., Connelly, P., Porter, S., Sullivan, H., Sullivan, L., & Wallis, L. A. (2021). Oral tradition, history, and archaeohistory of Indigenous Australia. In *The Oxford Handbook of the Archaeology of Indigenous Australia and New Guinea* (pp. C5–S1). Oxford University Press.

de Guevara, M. R. L. (2022). Painting Algorithms.

Deakin, W. (2023). *Modern Language*. Philosophy and Criticism.

Dessureault, J. S., & Massicotte, D. (2024). DPDR: A novel machine learning method for the Decision Process for Dimensionality Reduction. *SN Computer Science*, *5*(1), 1–15.

Devlin, J., Chang, M. W., Lee, K., & Toutanova, K. (2018). Bert: Pre-training of deep bidirectional transformers for language understanding. arXiv preprint arXiv:1810.04805.

Dhuliawala, S., Komeili, M., Xu, J., Raileanu, R., Li, X., Celikyilmaz, A., & Weston, J. (2023). *Chain-of-Verification Reduces Hallucination in Large Language Models* (No. arXiv:2309.11495). arXiv. http://arxiv.org/abs/2309.11495

DiMatteo, M. (2004). The role of effective communication with children and their families in fostering adherence to pediatric regimens. *Patient Education and Counseling, 55*(3), 339–344. DOI: 10.1016/j.pec.2003.04.003 PMID: 15582339

Djonov, E., Tseng, C. I., & Lim, F. V. (n.d.). Children's experiences with a transmedia narrative: Insights for promoting critical multimodal literacy in the digital age. Discourse.

Dosovitskiy, A., Beyer, L., Kolesnikov, A., Weissenborn, D., Zhai, X., Unterthiner, T., . . . Houlsby, N. (2021). An Image is Worth 16x16 Words: Transformers for Image Recognition at Scale. *International Conference on Learning Representations.* Retrieved from https://openreview.net/forum?id=YicbFdNTTy

Dowson, D., & Landau, B. (1982). The Fréchet distance between multivariate normal distributions. *Journal of Multivariate Analysis, 12*(3), 450–455. DOI: 10.1016/0047-259X(82)90077-X

Du, S., & Xie, C. (2021). Paradoxes of artificial intelligence in consumer markets: Ethical challenges and opportunities. *Journal of Business Research, 129*, 961–974. DOI: 10.1016/j.jbusres.2020.08.024

Duval, F., Boucher, J. P., & Pigeon, M. (2024). Telematics combined actuarial neural networks for cross-sectional and longitudinal claim count data. *ASTIN Bulletin: The Journal of the IAA*, 1-24.

Dwivedi, D., & Mahanty, G. (2023). Human creativity vs. machine creativity: Innovations and challenges. In Multidisciplinary Approaches in AI, Creativity, Innovation, and Green Collaboration (pp. 19-28). IGI Global.

Dwivedi, Y. K., Kshetri, N., Hughes, L., Slade, E. L., Jeyaraj, A., Kar, A. K., Baabdullah, A. M., Koohang, A., Raghavan, V., Ahuja, M., Albanna, H., Albashrawi, M. A., Al-Busaidi, A. S., Balakrishnan, J., Barlette, Y., Basu, S., Bose, I., Brooks, L., Buhalis, D., & Wright, R. (2023). Opinion Paper: "So what if ChatGPT wrote it?" Multidisciplinary perspectives on opportunities, challenges and implications of generative conversational AI for research, practice and policy. *International Journal of Information Management, 71*, 102642. DOI: 10.1016/j.ijinfomgt.2023.102642

Ekström, F., & Chen, A. (2020). Machine Learning and Telematics for Risk Assessment in Auto Insurance.

Elazar, Y., Kassner, N., Ravfogel, S., Ravichander, A., Hovy, E., Schütze, H., & Goldberg, Y. (2021). Measuring and Improving Consistency in Pretrained Language Models. *Transactions of the Association for Computational Linguistics, 9*, 1012–1031. DOI: 10.1162/tacl_a_00410

Elhoseiny, A. E. B. L. M., & Mazzone, M. (n.d.). *CAN: Creative Adversarial Networks Generating "Art" by Learning About Styles and Deviating from Style Norms*.

Eling, M., & Kraft, M. (2020). The impact of telematics on the insurability of risks. *The Journal of Risk Finance*, *21*(2), 77–109. DOI: 10.1108/JRF-07-2019-0129

Elleuch, M., Maalej, R., & Kherallah, M. (2016). A New Design Based-SVM of the CNN Classifier Architecture with Dropout for Offline Arabic Handwritten Recognition. *Procedia Computer Science*, *80*, 1712–1723. DOI: 10.1016/j.procs.2016.05.512

Fan, L., Wang, H. J., Zhang, K., Pei, Z., & Li, A. (2023). Towards an Automatic Prompt Optimization Framework for AI Image Generation. In Stephanidis, C., Antona, M., Ntoa, S., & Salvendy, G. (Eds.), *HCI International 2023 Posters* (Vol. 1836, pp. 405–410). Springer Nature Switzerland. DOI: 10.1007/978-3-031-36004-6_55

Farmonov, N., Amankulova, K., Szatmari, J., Sharifi, A., Abbasi-Moghadam, D., Nejad, S. M., & Mucsi, L. (2023). Crop Type Classification by DESIS Hyperspectral Imagery and Machine Learning Algorithms. *IEEE Journal of Selected Topics in Applied Earth Observations and Remote Sensing*, *16*, 1–17. DOI: 10.1109/JSTARS.2023.3239756

Feijóo, C., Kwon, Y., Bauer, J. M., Bohlin, E., Howell, B., Jain, R., Potgieter, P., Vu, K., Whalley, J., & Xia, J. (2020). Harnessing artificial intelligence (AI) to increase wellbeing for all: The case for a new technology diplomacy. *Telecommunications Policy*, *44*(6), 101988. DOI: 10.1016/j.telpol.2020.101988 PMID: 32377031

Feuerriegel, S., Hartmann, J., Janiesch, C., & Zschech, P. (2024). Generative ai. *Business & Information Systems Engineering*, *66*(1), 111–126. DOI: 10.1007/s12599-023-00834-7

Fischer, G., Lundin, J., & Lindberg, J. O. (2020). Rethinking and reinventing learning, education and collaboration in the digital age—From creating technologies to transforming cultures. *The International Journal of Information and Learning Technology*, *37*(5), 241–252. DOI: 10.1108/IJILT-04-2020-0051

Foong AL, Sow CF, Ramasamy S, & Yap PS. (2019). Pre-tertiary education, ethnicity, and attitudes of Asian medical undergraduates towards communication skills. Int J Med Educ., 10, 1-8. DOI: 10.5116/ijme.5c30.988d

Forsler, I. (2024). *Marshall McLuhan (1967)*. The Medium Is the Massage. Classics in Media Theory.

Fui-Hoon Nah, F., Zheng, R., Cai, J., Siau, K., & Chen, L. (2023). Generative AI and ChatGPT: Applications, challenges, and AI-human collaboration. *Journal of Information Technology Case and Application Research, 25*(3), 277–304. DOI: 10.1080/15228053.2023.2233814

Fukushima, K. (1980). Neocognitron: A self-organizing neural network model for a mechanism of pattern recognition unaffected by shift in position. *Biological Cybernetics, 36*(4), 193–202. DOI: 10.1007/BF00344251 PMID: 7370364

Gaiseanu, F. (2021). Information in the universal triangle of reality for non-living/living structures: From philosophy to neuro/life sciences. Philosophy Study.

Galaz, V., Centeno, M. A., Callahan, P. W., Causevic, A., Patterson, T., Brass, I., Baum, S., Farber, D., Fischer, J., Garcia, D., McPhearson, T., Jimenez, D., King, B., Larcey, P., & Levy, K. (2021). Artificial intelligence, systemic risks, and sustainability. *Technology in Society, 67*, 101741. DOI: 10.1016/j.techsoc.2021.101741

Galle, P. (2020). Christopher Alexander's Battle for Beauty in a World Turning Ugly: The Inception of a Science of Architecture? She Ji *The Journal of Design, Economics, and Innovation, 6*(3), 345–375. DOI: 10.1016/j.sheji.2020.03.002

Gao, G., Wang, H., & Wüthrich, M. V. (2022). Boosting Poisson regression models with telematics car driving data. *Machine Learning, 111*(1), 243–272. DOI: 10.1007/s10994-021-05957-0

Garg, S., Pundir, P., Jindal, H., Saini, H., & Garg, S. (2021, July). Towards a multimodal system for precision agriculture using IoT and machine learning. In 2021 12th international conference on computing communication and networking technologies (ICCCNT) (pp. 1-7). IEEE. DOI: 10.1109/ICCCNT51525.2021.9579646

Geetha, R., Jebamalar, G. B., Shiney, S. A., Dao, N. N., Moon, H., & Cho, S. (2024). Enhancing Upscaled Image Resolution Using Hybrid Generative Adversarial Network-Enabled Frameworks. *IEEE Access : Practical Innovations, Open Solutions, 12*, 27784–27793. DOI: 10.1109/ACCESS.2024.3367763

Gehrmann, S., Strobelt, H., & Rush, A. M. (2019). Gltr: Statistical detection and visualization of generated text. DOI: 10.18653/v1/P19-3019

Ghiasi, R., Khan, M. A., Sorrentino, D., Diaine, C., & Malekjafarian, A. (2024). An unsupervised anomaly detection framework for onboard monitoring of railway track geometrical defects using one-class support vector machine. *Engineering Applications of Artificial Intelligence, 133*, 108167. DOI: 10.1016/j.engappai.2024.108167

Ghosh, S., Sarkar, S. K., Roy, P., Roy, B., & Podder, A. (2025). Role of Libraries in Promoting Digital Literacy and Information Fluency. In Sacco, K., Norton, A., & Arms, K. (Eds.), *Navigating AI in Academic Libraries: Implications for Academic Research* (pp. 77–108). IGI Global Scientific Publishing. DOI: 10.4018/979-8-3693-3053-1.ch005

Giannakopoulos, G. (2009). Automatic summarization from multiple documents. Department of Information and Communication Systems Engineering, University of the Aegean, 49-66.

Goldberg, A. E. & Ferreira, F. (2022). Good-enough language production. Trends in Cognitive Sciences.

Goltz, N., Zeleznikow, J., & Dowdeswell, T. (2020). From the tree of knowledge and the golem of Prague to kosher autonomous cars: The ethics of artificial intelligence through jewish eyes. Oxford Journal of Law and Religion, 9(1), 132-156. ecu.edu.au

Goodfellow, I., Pouget-Abadie, J., Mirza, M., Xu, B., Warde-Farley, D., Ozair, S., & Bengio, Y. (2020). Generative adversarial networks. *Communications of the ACM*, *63*(11), 139–144. DOI: 10.1145/3422622

Goodrich, P., Betancourt, O., Arias, A. C., & Zohdi, T. (2023, February). Placement and drone flight path mapping of agricultural soil sensors using machine learning. *Computers and Electronics in Agriculture*, *205*, 107591. Advance online publication. DOI: 10.1016/j.compag.2022.107591

Grba, D. (2022). Deep else: A critical framework for ai art. Digital.

Guan, J., Huang, F., Zhao, Z., Zhu, X., & Huang, M. (2020). A knowledge-enhanced pretraining model for commonsense story generation. *Transactions of the Association for Computational Linguistics*, *8*, 93–108. DOI: 10.1162/tacl_a_00302

Guillen, M., Nielsen, J. P., Ayuso, M., & Pérez-Marín, A. M. (2019). The use of telematics devices to improve automobile insurance rates. *Risk Analysis*, *39*(3), 662–672. DOI: 10.1111/risa.13172 PMID: 30566751

Guillen, M., Nielsen, J. P., & Pérez-Marín, A. M. (2021). Near-miss telematics in motor insurance. *The Journal of Risk and Insurance*, *88*(3), 569–589. DOI: 10.1111/jori.12340

Gulrajani, I., Ahmed, F., Arjovsky, M., Dumoulin, V., & Courville, A. C. (2017). Improved training of Wasserstein gans. *Advances in Neural Information Processing Systems*, *30*(1), 56–68.

Gupta, P., Ding, B., Guan, C., & Ding, D. (2024). Generative AI: A systematic review using topic modelling techniques. Data and Information Management.

Gupta, S., Ranjan, R., & Singh, S. N. (2024). *A Comprehensive Survey of Retrieval-Augmented Generation (RAG): Evolution, Current Landscape and Future Directions* (Version 1). arXiv. DOI: 10.48550/ARXIV.2410.12837

Guzman, A. L. & Lewis, S. C. (2020). Artificial intelligence and communication: A human–machine communication research agenda. New Media & Society.

Hagendorff, T., Bossert, L. N., Tse, Y. F., & Singer, P. (2023). Speciesist bias in AI: how AI applications perpetuate discrimination and unfair outcomes against animals. AI and Ethics.

Han, W., Hao, W., Sun, J., Xue, Y., & Li, W. (2022). Tomatoes Maturity Detection Approach Based on YOLOv5 and Attention Mechanisms. *2022 IEEE 4th International Conference on Civil Aviation Safety and Information Technology (ICCASIT)* (pp. 1363-1371). DOI: 10.1109/ICCASIT55263.2022.9986640

Haque, Shahinoor, Rabby, Abujar, & Hossain. (2019). OnkoGan: Bangla Handwritten Digit Generation with Deep Convolutional Generative Adversarial Networks. DOI: 10.1007/978-981-13-9187-310

He, Zhang, Ren, & Sun. (2015). Deep Residual Learning for Image Recognition.

Heitmeier, M., Chuang, Y. Y., & Baayen, R. H. (2021). Modeling morphology with linear discriminative learning: Considerations and design choices. Frontiers in Psychology.

Henckaerts, R., & Antonio, K. (2022). The added value of dynamically updating motor insurance prices with telematics collected driving behavior data. *Insurance, Mathematics & Economics*, *105*, 79–95. DOI: 10.1016/j.insmatheco.2022.03.011

Hermann, I. (2023). Artificial intelligence in fiction: between narratives and metaphors. AI & Society.

Herzig, M. (2021). On the Shoulders of Giants: Helene Wecker's Subversion of the Female Golem Myth. The Macksey Journal.

Heusel, M., Ramsauer, H., Unterthiner, T., Nessler, B., & Hochreiter, S. (2017). GANs trained by a two time-scale update rule converge to a local nash equilibrium. In *Advances in Neural Information Processing Systems 30*. Morgan Kaufmann Publishers Inc.

Hoffmann, C. H. (2022). Is AI intelligent? An assessment of artificial intelligence, 70 years after Turing. *Technology in Society*, *68*, 101893. DOI: 10.1016/j.techsoc.2022.101893

Holloway-Attaway, L., & Vipsjö, L. (2020). *Using augmented reality, gaming technologies, and transmedial storytelling to develop and co-design local cultural heritage experiences*. Visual Computing for Cultural Heritage. DOI: 10.1007/978-3-030-37191-3_10

Holmström, J. & Carroll, N. (2024). How organizations can innovate with generative AI. Business Horizons.

Hu, W., Yan, L., Liu, K., & Wang, H. (2015). PSO-SVR: A Hybrid Short-term Traffic Flow Forecasting Method. *2015 IEEE 21st International Conference on Parallel and Distributed Systems (ICPADS)* (pp. 553-561). DOI: 10.1109/ICPADS.2015.75

Huang, Liu, van der Maaten, & Weinberger. (2017). Densely Connected Convolutional Networks. .DOI: 10.1109/CVPR.2017.243

Huang, Y. & Ferreira, F. (2021). What causes lingering misinterpretations of garden-path sentences: Incorrect syntactic representations or fallible memory processes?. Journal of Memory and Language.

Huang, Y., & Huang, J. (2024). *A Survey on Retrieval-Augmented Text Generation for Large Language Models* (Version 2). arXiv. DOI: 10.48550/ARXIV.2404.10981

Huang, L. (2022). *Normalization techniques in deep learning*. Springer. DOI: 10.1007/978-3-031-14595-7

Huang, Y., & Meng, S. (2019). Automobile insurance classification ratemaking based on telematics driving data. *Decision Support Systems*, *127*, 113156. DOI: 10.1016/j.dss.2019.113156

Huang, Z., Zheng, H., Li, C., & Che, C. (2024). Application of Machine Learning-Based K-Means Clustering for Financial Fraud Detection. *Academic Journal of Science and Technology*, *10*(1), 33–39. DOI: 10.54097/74414c90

Huettig, F., Audring, J., & Jackendoff, R. (2022). A parallel architecture perspective on pre-activation and prediction in language processing. Cognition.

Hughes, R. T., Zhu, L., & Bednarz, T. (2021). Generative adversarial networks–enabled human–artificial intelligence collaborative applications for creative and design industries: A systematic review of current…. Frontiers in artificial intelligence.

Husnain, M., Missen, M. M. S., Mumtaz, S., Jhanidr, M. Z., Coustaty, M., Muzzamil Luqman, M., Ogier, J. M., & Choi, G. S. (2019). Recognition of Urdu Handwritten Characters Using Convolutional Neural Network. *Applied Sciences (Basel, Switzerland)*, *9*(13), 2758. Advance online publication. DOI: 10.3390/app9132758

Husnjak, S., Peraković, D., Forenbacher, I., & Mumdziev, M. (2015). Telematics system in usage-based motor insurance. *Procedia Engineering*, *100*, 816–825. DOI: 10.1016/j.proeng.2015.01.436

Illia, L., Colleoni, E., & Zyglidopoulos, S. (2023). Ethical implications of text generation in the age of artificial intelligence. *Business Ethics, the Environment & Responsibility*, *32*(1), 201–210. DOI: 10.1111/beer.12479

Imdoukh, M., Ahmad, I., & Alfailakawi, M. G. (2020). Machine learning-based auto-scaling for containerized applications. *Neural Computing & Applications*, *32*(13), 9745–9760. DOI: 10.1007/s00521-019-04507-z

Irode, P. L. (2017). *An Auto Telematics System for Insurance Premium Rating & Pricing* (Doctoral dissertation, University of Nairobi).

Islam, M. P., Hatou, K., Aihara, T., Kawahara, M., Okamoto, S., Senoo, S., & Sumire, K. (2022, November). ThelR547v1—An Asymmetric Dilated Convolutional Neural Network for Real-time Semantic Segmentation of Horticultural Crops. *Sensors (Basel)*, *22*(22), 8807. DOI: 10.3390/s22228807 PMID: 36433404

Izacard, G., & Grave, E. (2021). *Leveraging Passage Retrieval with Generative Models for Open Domain Question Answering* (No. arXiv:2007.01282). DOI: 10.18653/v1/2021.eacl-main.74

Jafarbiglu, H., & Pourreza, A. (2022, June). A comprehensive review of remote sensing platforms, sensors, and applications in nut crops. *Computers and Electronics in Agriculture*, *197*, 106844. Advance online publication. DOI: 10.1016/j.compag.2022.106844

Jaiswal, A. S., Bhavsagar, D. V., Chavan, S. R., Tikekar, P. C., & Chaurasia, S. (2024). Exploring the Role of Generative Adversarial Networks in Cybersecurity: Techniques, Applications, and Advancements. In Enhancing Security in Public Spaces Through Generative Adversarial Networks (GANs) (pp. 246-258). IGI Global.

Jégou, H., Douze, M., & Schmid, C. (2011). Product Quantization for Nearest Neighbor Search. *IEEE Transactions on Pattern Analysis and Machine Intelligence*, *33*(1), 117–128. DOI: 10.1109/TPAMI.2010.57 PMID: 21088323

Jha, G., & Cecotti, H. (2020). Data augmentation for handwritten digit recognition using generative adversarial networks. *Multimedia Tools and Applications*, *79*(47-48), 35055–35068. Advance online publication. DOI: 10.1007/s11042-020-08883-w

Jiang, Y., Li, C., Paterson, A. H., & Robertson, J. S. (2019, November). DeepSeedling: Deep convolutional network and Kalman filter for plant seedling detection and counting in the field. *Plant Methods*, *15*(1), 141. Advance online publication. DOI: 10.1186/s13007-019-0528-3 PMID: 31768186

Jing, Y., Yang, Y., Feng, Z., Ye, J., Yu, Y., & Song, M. (2019). Neural style transfer: A review. *IEEE Transactions on Visualization and Computer Graphics*, *26*(11), 3365–3385. DOI: 10.1109/TVCG.2019.2921336 PMID: 31180860

Jumper, J., Evans, R., Pritzel, A., Green, T., Figurnov, M., Ronneberger, O., Tunyasuvunakool, K., Bates, R., Žídek, A., Potapenko, A., Bridgland, A., Meyer, C., Kohl, S. A. A., Ballard, A. J., Cowie, A., Romera-Paredes, B., Nikolov, S., Jain, R., Adler, J., & Hassabis, D. (2021). Highly accurate protein structure prediction with AlphaFold. *Nature*, *596*(7873), 583–589. DOI: 10.1038/s41586-021-03819-2 PMID: 34265844

Kantosalo, A., Falk, M., & Jordanous, A. (2021). Embodiment in 18th century depictions of human-machine co-creativity. Frontiers in Robotics and AI.

Kar, S., Mohammad, R., Zaman, M. T., Reza, S. M., Talukder, O., & Hasan, M. (2023, December). Farmbot: an IoT-Based Wireless Agricultural Robot for Smart Cultivation. In 2023 26th International Conference on Computer and Information Technology (ICCIT) (pp. 1-6). IEEE. DOI: 10.1109/ICCIT60459.2023.10441291

Kar, A. K., Varsha, P. S., & Rajan, S. (2023). Unravelling the impact of generative artificial intelligence (GAI) in industrial applications: A review of scientific and grey literature. *Global Journal of Flexible Systems Managment*, *24*(4), 659–689. DOI: 10.1007/s40171-023-00356-x

Katz, D. M., Bommarito, M. J., & Blackman, J. (2017). A general approach for predicting the behavior of the Supreme Court of the United States. *PLoS One*, *12*(4), e0174698. DOI: 10.1371/journal.pone.0174698 PMID: 28403140

Kedia, A. & Rasu, M. (2020). Hands-On Python Natural Language Processing: Explore tools and techniques to analyze and process text with a view to building real-world NLP applications.

Keßler, T., Rjasanow, S., & Weißer, S. (2020). Vlasov—Poisson System Tackled by Particle Simulation Utilizing Boundary Element Methods. *SIAM Journal on Scientific Computing*, *42*(1), B299–B326. DOI: 10.1137/18M1225823

Kidd, J. & Nieto Mcavoy, E. (2023). Deep Nostalgia: Remediated memory, algorithmic nostalgia and technological ambivalence. Convergence.

Kingma, D. P., & Welling, M. (2013). Auto-encoding variational bayes. *arXiv, 11*(4), 26-39.

Kiss, D., Horváth, Z., Kassai, S., Gyarmathy, A. V., & Rácz, J. (2022). Folktales of recovery–from addiction to becoming a helper: deep structures of life stories applying Propp's theory: a narrative analysis. *Journal of Psychoactive Drugs, 54*(4), 328–339. DOI: 10.1080/02791072.2021.1990442 PMID: 34706624

Kitchener, P. D. & Hales, C. G. (2022). What neuroscientists think, and don't think, about consciousness. Frontiers in Human Neuroscience.

Klys, J., Snell, J., & Zemel, R. (2018). Learning latent subspaces in variational autoencoders. *Advances in Neural Information Processing Systems, 31*(3), 45–58.

Köbis, N. & Mossink, L. D. (2021). Artificial intelligence versus Maya Angelou: Experimental evidence that people cannot differentiate AI-generated from human-written poetry. Computers in human behavior.

Kong, Q., Tong, B., Klinkigt, M., Watanabe, Y., Akira, N., & Murakami, T. (2019). Active Generative Adversarial Network for Image Classification. *Proceedings of the AAAI Conference on Artificial Intelligence, 33*(1), 4090–4097. DOI: 10.1609/aaai.v33i01.33014090

Kora, S., & Ravula, S. (2020). Evaluation of Deep Convolutional Generative Adversarial Networks for Data Augmentation of Chest X-ray Images. *Future Internet, 13*(1), 8. DOI: 10.3390/fi13010008

Korbak, T., Shi, K., Chen, A., Bhalerao, R. V., Buckley, C., Phang, J., & Perez, E. (2023, July). Pretraining language models with human preferences. In *International Conference on Machine Learning* (pp. 17506-17533). PMLR.

Kovacic, M. (2023). Between animated cells and animated cels: symbiotic turn and animation in multispecies life. Science as Culture.

Krishnan, R., & Butt, B. (2022). "The gasoline of the future:" points of continuity, energy materiality, and corporate marketing of electric vehicles among automakers and utilities. *Energy Research & Social Science, 83*, 102349. DOI: 10.1016/j.erss.2021.102349

Kumar, E. (2013). *Natural language processing*. IK International Pvt Ltd.

Lac, L., Keresztes, B., Louargant, M., Donias, M., & Costa, J.-P. D. (2022). An annotated image dataset of vegetable crops at an early stage of growth for proximal sensing applications. *Data in Brief, 42*, 108035. DOI: 10.1016/j.dib.2022.108035 PMID: 35313502

Lahat, D., Adali, T., & Jutten, C. (2015). Multimodal data fusion: An overview of methods, challenges, and prospects. *Proceedings of the IEEE, 103*(9), 1449–1477. DOI: 10.1109/JPROC.2015.2460697

LeCun, Y., Bengio, Y., & Hinton, G. (2015, May). Deep Learning. *Nature, 521*(7553), 436–444. DOI: 10.1038/nature14539 PMID: 26017442

Lee, H., Wang, J., & Leblon, B. (2020, July). Intra-Field Canopy Nitrogen Retrieval from Unmanned Aerial Vehicle Imagery for Wheat and Corn Fields. *Canadian Journal of Remote Sensing, 46*(4), 454–472. DOI: 10.1080/07038992.2020.1788384

Lester, B., Al-Rfou, R., & Constant, N. (2021). *The Power of Scale for Parameter-Efficient Prompt Tuning* (No. arXiv:2104.08691). DOI: 10.18653/v1/2021.emnlp-main.243

Lewis, P., Perez, E., Piktus, A., Petroni, F., Karpukhin, V., Goyal, N., Küttler, H., Lewis, M., Yih, W., Rocktäschel, T., Riedel, S., & Kiela, D. (2020). *Retrieval-Augmented Generation for Knowledge-Intensive NLP Tasks* (Version 4). arXiv. DOI: 10.48550/ARXIV.2005.11401

Lewis, P., Perez, E., Piktus, A., Petroni, F., Karpukhin, V., Goyal, N., Küttler, H., Lewis, M., Yih, W., Rocktäschel, T., Riedel, S., & Kiela, D. (2021). *Retrieval-Augmented Generation for Knowledge-Intensive NLP Tasks* (No. arXiv:2005.11401). arXiv. http://arxiv.org/abs/2005.11401

Li, C., Wang, J., Zhang, Y., Zhu, K., Hou, W., Lian, J., Luo, F., Yang, Q., & Xie, X. (2023). *Large Language Models Understand and Can be Enhanced by Emotional Stimuli* (No. arXiv:2307.11760). arXiv. http://arxiv.org/abs/2307.11760

Li, X. & Lin, B. (2021). The Development and Design of Artificial Intelligence in Cultural and Creative Products. Mathematical Problems in Engineering.

Lichtenstein NV, Haak R, Ensmann I, Hallal H, Huttenlau J, Krämer K, Krause F, Matthes J, & Stosch C (2018) Does teaching social and communicative competences influence dental students' attitudes towards learning communication skills? A comparison between two dental schools in Germany. GMS J Med Educ., 35(2).

Li, H., Ai, Q., Zhan, J., Mao, J., Liu, Y., Liu, Z., & Cao, Z. (2023). Constructing Tree-based Index for Efficient and Effective Dense Retrieval. *Proceedings of the 46th International ACM SIGIR Conference on Research and Development in Information Retrieval*, 131–140. DOI: 10.1145/3539618.3591651

Li, J., Chen, L., & Huang, W. (2018, January). Detection of early bruises on peaches (Amygdalus persica L.) using hyperspectral imaging coupled with improved watershed segmentation algorithm. *Postharvest Biology and Technology, 135*, 104–113. DOI: 10.1016/j.postharvbio.2017.09.007

Li, K. Y., de Lima, R. S., Burnside, N. G., Vahtmäe, E., Kutser, T., Sepp, K., & Sepp, K. (2022, March). Toward Automated Machine Learning-Based Hyperspectral Image Analysis in Crop Yield and Biomass Estimation. *Remote Sensing (Basel), 14*(5), 1114. Advance online publication. DOI: 10.3390/rs14051114

Li, L., Zhang, S., & Wang, B. (2022, January). Apple leaf disease identification with a small and imbalanced dataset based on lightweight convolutional networks. *Sensors (Basel), 22*(1), 173. Advance online publication. DOI: 10.3390/s22010173 PMID: 35009716

Li, M., Shamshiri, R. R., Weltzien, C., & Schirrmann, M. (2022, September). Crop Monitoring Using Sentinel-2 and UAV Multispectral Imagery: A Comparison Case Study in Northeastern Germany. *Remote Sensing (Basel), 14*(17), 4426. DOI: 10.3390/rs14174426

Li, M., Xiao, L., Ma, X., Yang, F., Jin, X., & Ji, J. (2022, December). Vision-Based a Seedling Selective Planting Control System for Vegetable Transplanter. *Agriculture, 12*(12), 2064. Advance online publication. DOI: 10.3390/agriculture12122064

Lin, X., Li, C.-T., Adams, S., Kouzani, A. Z., Jiang, R., He, L., Hu, Y., Vernon, M., Doeven, E., Webb, L., Mcclellan, T., & Guskich, A. (2023). Self-Supervised Leaf Segmentation under Complex Lighting Conditions. *Pattern Recognition, 135*, 109021. DOI: 10.1016/j.patcog.2022.109021

Liotsakis, V. (2024). Digressions as Meta-Literary Markers and Narrative Milestones in Arrian's Anabasis of Alexander. Trends in Classics–Supplementary Volumes.

Liu, F., Jung, J., & Feinstein, W. (2024). *Aggregated Knowledge Model: Enhancing Domain-Specific QA with Fine-Tuned and Retrieval-Augmented Generation Models* (Version 1). DOI: 10.48550/ARXIV.2410.18344

Liu, B. (2022). *Sentiment analysis and opinion mining*. Springer Nature.

Liu, J., & Wang, X. (2020, June). Tomato Diseases and Pests Detection Based on Improved Yolo V3 Convolutional Neural Network. *Frontiers in Plant Science*, *11*, 898. Advance online publication. DOI: 10.3389/fpls.2020.00898 PMID: 32612632

Liu, Y., Yang, Z., Yu, Z., Liu, Z., Liu, D., Lin, H., Li, M., Ma, S., Avdeev, M., & Shi, S. (2023). Generative artificial intelligence and its applications in materials science: Current situation and future perspectives. *Journal of Materiomics*, *9*(4), 798–816. DOI: 10.1016/j.jmat.2023.05.001

Lobet, G., Koevoets, I. T., Noll, M., Meyer, P. E., Tocquin, P., Pagès, L., & Périlleux, C. (2017). Using a Structural Root System Model to Evaluate and Improve the Accuracy of Root Image Analysis Pipelines. *Frontiers in Plant Science*, *8*. Advance online publication. DOI: 10.3389/fpls.2017.00447 PMID: 28421089

Luo, S., Jiang, X., Jiao, W., Yang, K., Li, Y., & Fang, S. (2022, September). Remotely Sensed Prediction of Rice Yield at Different Growth Durations Using UAV Multispectral Imagery. *Agriculture*, *12*(9), 1447. DOI: 10.3390/agriculture12091447

Lwakatare, L. E., Raj, A., Crnkovic, I., Bosch, J., & Olsson, H. H. (2020). Large-scale machine learning systems in real-world industrial settings: A review of challenges and solutions. *Information and Software Technology*, *127*, 106368. DOI: 10.1016/j.infsof.2020.106368

Maaten, L. d., & Hinton, G. (2008). Visualizing data using t-sne. *Journal of Machine Learning Research*, *9*(Nov), 2579–2605.

Maestre, M. M., Vicente, M., Lloret, E., & Cueto, A. S. (2022). Extracting Narrative Patterns in Different Textual Genres: A Multilevel Feature Discourse Analysis. Information.

Maggs, D. & Robinson, J. (2020). Sustainability in an imaginary world: art and the question of agency.

Malkov, Y. A., & Yashunin, D. A. (2020). Efficient and Robust Approximate Nearest Neighbor Search Using Hierarchical Navigable Small World Graphs. *IEEE Transactions on Pattern Analysis and Machine Intelligence*, *42*(4), 824–836. DOI: 10.1109/TPAMI.2018.2889473 PMID: 30602420

Manning, C., & Schutze, H. (1999). *Foundations of statistical natural language processing*. MIT press.

Marambe, K. N., Edussuriya, D. H., & Dayaratne, K. (2012). Attitudes of Sri Lankan Medical Students toward Learning Communication Skills. *Education for Health*, *25*(3), 165–171. DOI: 10.4103/1357-6283.109796 PMID: 23823636

Mars, M. (2022). From word embeddings to pre-trained language models: A state-of-the-art walkthrough. Applied Sciences.

Martin, J. H. (2009). *Speech and language processing: An introduction to natural language processing, computational linguistics, and speech recognition.* Pearson/Prentice Hall.

Mattupalli, C., Seethepalli, A., York, L. M., & Young, C. A. (2019). Digital Imaging to Evaluate Root System Architectural Changes Associated with Soil Biotic Factors. *Phytobiomes Journal, 3*(2), 102–111. DOI: 10.1094/PBIOMES-12-18-0062-R

McEachan, R., Taylor, N., Harrison, R., Lawton, R., Gardner, P., & Conner, M. (2016). Meta-analysis of the Reasoned Action Approach (RAA) to understanding health behaviours. *Annals of Behavioral Medicine, 50*(4), 592–612. DOI: 10.1007/s12160-016-9798-4 PMID: 27169555

McManus, M., & McManus, M. (2020). The Emergence of Post-modern Culture in Neoliberal Society. The Rise of Post-Modern Conservatism: Neoliberalism, Post-Modern Culture, and Reactionary Politics, 45-110.

Meng, S., Wang, H., Shi, Y., & Gao, G. (2022). Improving automobile insurance claims frequency prediction with telematics car driving data. *ASTIN Bulletin, 52*(2), 363–391. DOI: 10.1017/asb.2021.35

Meskó, B. & Topol, E. J. (2023). The imperative for regulatory oversight of large language models (or generative AI) in healthcare. NPJ Digital Medicine.

Messer, U. (2024). Co-creating art with generative artificial intelligence: Implications for artworks and artists. Computers in Human Behavior: Artificial Humans.

Migicovsky, Z., Li, M., Chitwood, D. H., & Myles, S. (2018). Morphometrics Reveals Complex and Heritable Apple Leaf Shapes. *Frontiers in Plant Science, 8*, 2185. Advance online publication. DOI: 10.3389/fpls.2017.02185 PMID: 29354142

Mikalef, P., Conboy, K., Lundström, J. E., & Popovič, A. (2022). Thinking responsibly about responsible AI and 'the dark side'of AI. *European Journal of Information Systems, 31*(3), 257–268. DOI: 10.1080/0960085X.2022.2026621

Miyato, T., & Koyama, M. (2018). cGANs with projection discriminator. *arXiv, 26*(3), 180-189.

Mohamed, E. S., Belal, A. A., Abd-Elmabod, S. K., El-Shirbeny, M. A., Gad, A., & Zahran, M. B. (2021). Smart farming for improving agricultural management. *The Egyptian Journal of Remote Sensing and Space Sciences, 24*(3), 971–981. DOI: 10.1016/j.ejrs.2021.08.007

Molli, L. (2022). Just a pale shadow? The characterization of Briseis in Homer's Iliad. *Acta Antiqua Academiae Scientiarum Hungaricae*, *61*(1), 1–9. DOI: 10.1556/068.2021.00001

Moosavi, S., & Ramnath, R. (2023). Context-aware driver risk prediction with telematics data. *Accident; Analysis and Prevention*, *192*, 107269. DOI: 10.1016/j.aap.2023.107269 PMID: 37696064

Morgan, J., Halton, M., Qiao, Y., & Breslin, J. G. (2021). Industry 4.0 smart reconfigurable manufacturing machines. Journal of Manufacturing Systems.

Mudumba, B., & Kabir, M. F. (2024). Mine-first association rule mining: An integration of independent frequent patterns in distributed environments. Decision Analytics Journal, 100434.

Mumtaz, S., & Zahra, T. (2016). Role-play as a learning modality in Pakistan. *The Clinical Teacher*, *13*(2), 124–129. DOI: 10.1111/tct.12406 PMID: 26084372

Muneer, S., Farooq, U., Athar, A., Ahsan Raza, M., Ghazal, T. M., & Sakib, S. (2024). A Critical Review of Artificial Intelligence Based Approaches in Intrusion Detection: A Comprehensive Analysis. *Journal of Engineering*, *2024*(1), 3909173. DOI: 10.1155/2024/3909173

Murray, S., Malambo, L., Popescu, S., Cope, D., Anderson, S., Chang, A., & Penna Cruzato, N. (2019, June). G2F Maize UAV Data, College Station, Texas 2017. *G2F Maize UAV Data, College Station, Texas 2017*. DOI: 10.25739/4ext-5e97

Myers, D., Mohawesh, R., Chellaboina, V. I., Sathvik, A. L., Venkatesh, P., Ho, Y. H., Henshaw, H., Alhawawreh, M., Berdik, D., & Jararweh, Y. (2024). Foundation and large language models: Fundamentals, challenges, opportunities, and social impacts. *Cluster Computing*, *27*(1), 1–26. DOI: 10.1007/s10586-023-04203-7

Nascimento, B., Ribeiro, M., Silva, L., Capobiango, N., & Silva, M. (2022). A soybean seedlings dataset for soil condition and genotype classification. *2022 35th SIBGRAPI Conference on Graphics, Patterns and Images (SIBGRAPI), 1*, 85-90. DOI: 10.1109/SIBGRAPI55357.2022.9991792

Nenkova, A., & McKeown, K. (2011). Automatic summarization. Foundations and Trends® in Information Retrieval, 5(2–3), 103-233.

Ng, D. T. K., Luo, W., Chan, H. M. Y., & Chu, S. K. W. (2022). Using digital story writing as a pedagogy to develop AI literacy among primary students. *Computers and Education: Artificial Intelligence*, *3*, 100054. DOI: 10.1016/j.caeai.2022.100054

Nielsen, W. C. (2022). Motherless creations: Fictions of artificial life, 1650-1890.

Nogueira, R., & Cho, K. (2019). *Passage Re-ranking with BERT* (Version 5). DOI: 10.48550/ARXIV.1901.04085

Nogueira, M. R., Menezes, P., & Maçãs de Carvalho, J. (2024). Exploring the impact of machine learning on dance performance: A systematic review. *International Journal of Performance Arts and Digital Media, 20*(1), 1–50. DOI: 10.1080/14794713.2024.2338927

Nurmamatovich, T. I., & Azizjon o'g, N. A. Z. (2024). Neural network clustering methods. *American Journal of Open University Education, 1*(1), 16–18.

Obiedat, A. Z. (2022). Modern Virtuous Ethics: Knowing the Good and Doing the Right in Scientific Humanism. In *Modernity and the Ideals of Arab-Islamic and Western-Scientific Philosophy: The Worldviews of Mario Bunge and Taha Abd al-Rahman* (pp. 241–283). Springer International Publishing. DOI: 10.1007/978-3-030-94265-6_8

Oksanen, A., Cvetkovic, A., Akin, N., Latikka, R., Bergdahl, J., Chen, Y., & Savela, N. (2023). Artificial intelligence in fine arts: A systematic review of empirical research. Computers in Human Behavior: Artificial Humans, 100004.

Omia, E., Bae, H., Park, E., Kim, M. S., Baek, I., Kabenge, I., & Cho, B. K. (2023, January). Remote Sensing in Field Crop Monitoring: A Comprehensive Review of Sensor Systems, Data Analyses and Recent Advances. *Remote Sensing (Basel), 15*(2), 354. Advance online publication. DOI: 10.3390/rs15020354

Oraby, S., Bhuiyan, M., Gundecha, P., Mahmud, J., & Akkiraju, R. (2019). Modeling and computational characterization of twitter customer service conversations. [TiiS]. *ACM Transactions on Interactive Intelligent Systems, 9*(2-3), 1–28. DOI: 10.1145/3213014

Outcomes for graduates. Tomorrow's Doctor's. (2015). GMC. https://www.gmc-uk.org/static/documents/content/Outcomes_for_graduates_Dec_16.pdf

Paaß, G., & Giesselbach, S. (2023). Improving pre-trained language models. In Foundation Models for Natural Language Processing: Pre-trained Language Models Integrating Media (pp. 79-159). Cham: Springer International Publishing.

Pablos, A. B. (2024). Deleuze on Habit: Cognitive Science Beyond Prediction. *Journal of Archaeological Method and Theory.*

Pang, B., & Lee, L. (2008). Opinion mining and sentiment analysis. Foundations and Trends® in information retrieval, 2(1–2), 1-135.

Papadakis, S. (2022). Apps to promote computational thinking and coding skills to young age children: A pedagogical challenge for the 21st century learners. Educational Process: International Journal (EDUPIJ).

Park, J. S., O'Brien, J. C., Cai, C. J., Morris, M. R., Liang, P., & Bernstein, M. S. (2023). *Generative Agents: Interactive Simulacra of Human Behavior* (Version 2). arXiv. DOI: 10.1145/3586183.3606763

Park, J., Ko, E. Y., Park, Y. S., Yim, J., & Kim, J. (2024, March). DynamicLabels: Supporting Informed Construction of Machine Learning Label Sets with Crowd Feedback. In *Proceedings of the 29th International Conference on Intelligent User Interfaces* (pp. 209-228). DOI: 10.1145/3640543.3645157

Parsa, S., Debnath, B., Khan, M. A., & Amir Ghalamzan, E. (2023). Autonomous Strawberry Picking Robotic System (Robofruit). DOI: 10.48550/ARXIV.2301.03947

Pataranutaporn, P., Danry, V., Leong, J., Punpongsanon, P., Novy, D., Maes, P., & Sra, M. (2021). AI-generated characters for supporting personalized learning and well-being. *Nature Machine Intelligence*, *3*(12), 1013–1022. DOI: 10.1038/s42256-021-00417-9

Patel, A. A. (2019). *Hands-on unsupervised learning using Python: how to build applied machine learning solutions from unlabeled data*. O'Reilly Media.

Peng, J., Rezaei, E. E., Zhu, W., Wang, D., Li, H., Yang, B., & Sun, Z. (2022, November). Plant Density Estimation Using UAV Imagery and Deep Learning. *Remote Sensing (Basel)*, *14*(23), 5923. DOI: 10.3390/rs14235923

Pesantez-Narvaez, J., Guillen, M., & Alcañiz, M. (2019). Predicting motor insurance claims using telematics data—XGBoost versus logistic regression. *Risks*, *7*(2), 70. DOI: 10.3390/risks7020070

Pescapè, A. (n.d.). Exploring the Current State and Future Potential of Generative Artificial Intelligence Using a Generative Artificial Intelligence. Mind.

Peteinatos, G. G., Reichel, P., Karouta, J., Andújar, D., & Gerhards, R. (2020, December). Weed Identification in Maize, Sunflower, and Potatoes with the Aid of Convolutional Neural Networks. *Remote Sensing (Basel)*, *12*(24), 1–22. DOI: 10.3390/rs12244185

Pinheiro, S., Mota, N. B., Sigman, M., Fernández-Slezak, D., Guerreiro, A., Tófoli, L. F., Cecchi, G., Copelli, M., & Ribeiro, S. (2020). The history of writing reflects the effects of education on discourse structure: Implications for literacy, orality, psychosis and the axial age. *Trends in Neuroscience and Education*, *21*, 100142. DOI: 10.1016/j.tine.2020.100142 PMID: 33303107

Pinto, J., Powell, S., Peterson, R., Rosalen, D., & Fernandes, O. (2020, November). Detection of defoliation injury in peanut with hyperspectral proximal remote sensing. *Remote Sensing (Basel), 12*(22), 1–16. DOI: 10.3390/rs12223828

Podlecki, A. J. (2021). *One Homer, or Two?* Some Suggested Stylistic Separators in the Homeric Poems. Mouseion.

Porteous, J., Ferreira, J. F., Lindsay, A., & Cavazza, M. (2021). Automated narrative planning model extension. *Autonomous Agents and Multi-Agent Systems, 35*(2), 19. DOI: 10.1007/s10458-021-09501-1

Pound, M. P., Atkinson, J. A., Wells, D. M., Pridmore, T. P., & French, A. P. (2017). Deep Learning for Multi-task Plant Phenotyping. *2017 IEEE International Conference on Computer Vision Workshops (ICCVW)*, (pp. 2055-2063). DOI: 10.1109/ICCVW.2017.241

Pritoni, M., Paine, D., Fierro, G., Mosiman, C., Poplawski, M., Saha, A., Bender, J., & Granderson, J. (2021). Metadata schemas and ontologies for building energy applications: A critical review and use case analysis. *Energies, 14*(7), 2024. DOI: 10.3390/en14072024

Quaglia, G., Visconte, C., Scimmi, L. S., Melchiorre, M., Cavallone, P., & Pastorelli, S. (2020, March). Design of a UGV powered by solar energy for precision agriculture. *Robotics (Basel, Switzerland), 9*(1), 13. Advance online publication. DOI: 10.3390/robotics9010013

Quan, L., Feng, H., Lv, Y., Wang, Q., Zhang, C., Liu, J., & Yuan, Z. (2019, August). Maize seedling detection under different growth stages and complex field environments based on an improved Faster R–CNN. *Biosystems Engineering, 184*, 1–23. DOI: 10.1016/j.biosystemseng.2019.05.002

Radford, A., Kim, J. W., Hallacy, C., Ramesh, A., Goh, G., Agarwal, S., Sastry, G., Askell, A., Mishkin, P., Clark, J., Krueger, G., & Sutskever, I. (2021). *Learning Transferable Visual Models From Natural Language Supervision* (No. arXiv:2103.00020). arXiv. http://arxiv.org/abs/2103.00020

Radford, A., Narasimhan, K., Salimans, T., & Sutskever, I. (2018). Improving language understanding by generative pre-training.

Radford, A., Metz, L., & Chintala, S. (2015). Unsupervised representation learning with deep convolutional generative adversarial networks. arXiv:1511.06434.

Rajakannan, R. & Rukmini, S. (2021). Reading Paradigms of Digital Narratives: Reception of Hypertext Fictions and Its Implications. Journal of Narrative and Language Studies.

Ramamoorthy, P., Samiappan, S., Wubben, M. J., Brooks, J. P., Shrestha, A., Panda, R. M., Reddy, K. R., & Bheemanahalli, R. (2022, August). Hyperspectral Reflectance and Machine Learning Approaches for the Detection of Drought and Root–Knot Nematode Infestation in Cotton. *Remote Sensing (Basel), 14*(16), 4021. Advance online publication. DOI: 10.3390/rs14164021

Rani, S., Jining, D., Shah, D., Xaba, S., & Shoukat, K. (2024). Examining the impacts of artificial intelligence technology and computing on digital art: A case study of Edmond de Belamy and its aesthetic values and techniques. *AI & Society*. Advance online publication. DOI: 10.1007/s00146-024-01996-y

Rasti, S., Bleakley, C. J., Silvestre, G. C., Holden, N. M., Langton, D., & O'Hare, G. M. (2021, March). Crop growth stage estimation prior to canopy closure using deep learning algorithms. *Neural Computing & Applications, 33*(5), 1733–1743. DOI: 10.1007/s00521-020-05064-6

Ratnayake, M. N., Amarathunga, D. C., Zaman, A., Dyer, A. G., & Dorin, A. (2022, May). Spatial Monitoring and Insect Behavioural Analysis Using Computer Vision for Precision Pollination. *International Journal of Computer Vision*. Advance online publication. DOI: 10.1007/s11263-022-01715-4

Ray, P. P. (2023). ChatGPT: A comprehensive review on background, applications, key challenges, bias, ethics, limitations and future scope. Internet of Things and Cyber-Physical Systems.

Reddy, S. (2024). Generative AI in healthcare: an implementation science informed translational path on application, integration and governance. Implementation Science.

Reedha, R., Dericquebourg, E., Canals, R., & Hafiane, A. (2022, February). Transformer Neural Network for Weed and Crop Classification of High Resolution UAV Images. *Remote Sensing (Basel), 14*(3), 592. Advance online publication. DOI: 10.3390/rs14030592

Rees, C., Sheard, C., & Davies, S. (2002). The development of a scale to measure medical students' attitudes towards communication skills learning: The Communication Skills Attitude Scale (CSAS). *Medical Education, 36*(2), 141–147. DOI: 10.1046/j.1365-2923.2002.01072.x PMID: 11869441

Ribeiro, M. T., Singh, S., & Guestrin, C. (2016, August). " Why should i trust you?" Explaining the predictions of any classifier. In *Proceedings of the 22nd ACM SIGKDD international conference on knowledge discovery and data mining* (pp. 1135-1144). DOI: 10.18653/v1/N16-3020

Ris-Ala, R. (2023). *Fundamentals of reinforcement learning*. Springer. DOI: 10.1007/978-3-031-37345-9

Rodriguez, P., Velazquez, D., Cucurull, G., Gonfaus, J. M., Roca, F. X., & Gonzalez, J. (2019). Pay attention to the activations: A modular attention mechanism for fine-grained image recognition. *IEEE Transactions on Multimedia*, *22*(2), 502–514. DOI: 10.1109/TMM.2019.2928494

Romero, C., & Ventura, S. (2020). Educational data mining and learning analytics: An updated survey. *Wiley Interdisciplinary Reviews. Data Mining and Knowledge Discovery*, *10*(3), e1355. DOI: 10.1002/widm.1355

Romero-Frías, E., & Barbecho, L. B. (2023). Digital Humanities Labs: Spaces for Innovation to Reconnect the Humanities With Society. In Digital Humanities and Laboratories (pp. 253-269). Routledge.

Roos, M. & Reccius, M. (2024). Narratives in economics. Journal of Economic Surveys.

Rosário, A. T. (2024). *Generative ai and generative pre-trained transformer applications: Challenges and opportunities*. Making Art With Generative AI Tools. DOI: 10.4018/979-8-3693-1950-5.ch003

Roth, R. E. (2021). Cartographic design as visual storytelling: synthesis and review of map-based narratives, genres, and tropes. The Cartographic Journal.

Roumeliotis, K. I. & Tselikas, N. D. (2023). Chatgpt and open-ai models: A preliminary review. Future Internet.

Roy, P., Ghosh, S., Podder, A., & Sarkar, S. K. (2025a). Opportunities and Challenges of Artificial Intelligence (AI) in the Banking and Finance Sector. Shaping Cutting-Edge Technologies and Applications for Digital Banking and Financial Services, 120.

Roy, P., Pandit, R., & Naskar, S. K. (2025b). Innovative Approaches to Problem-Solving Through Educational Technology Integration. In J. Zhang, W. Wan Yahaya, M. Sanmugam, & D. Lim (Eds.), Integrating Technology in Problem-Solving Educational Practices (pp. 375-402). IGI Global Scientific Publishing. DOI: 10.4018/979-8-3693-6745-2.ch016

Rubinstein, Y. (2020). Uneasy listening: Towards a Hauntology of AI-generated music. Resonance: The Journal of Sound and Culture.

Sadeghi-Tehran, P., Virlet, N., & Hawkesford, M. J. (2021, March). A neural network method for classification of sunlit and shaded components of wheat canopies in the field using high-resolution hyperspectral imagery. *Remote Sensing (Basel), 13*(5), 1–17. DOI: 10.3390/rs13050898

Safavi, G., & Ghazinoory, S. (2024). Creative bits: Challenges of applying industry 4.0 in digital creative industries. *Multimedia Tools and Applications*. Advance online publication. DOI: 10.1007/s11042-024-19701-y

Safely, A. C. (2023). Advanced Applications of Generative AI and Natural Language Processing Models. Advanced Applications of Generative AI and Natural Language Processing Models, 69.

Sahoo, T., Mondal, A., Roy, P., & Podder, A. (2024). Artificial Intelligence and Its Application in Engineering: A Comprehensive Review. In El Kacimi, Y., & Alaoui, K. (Eds.), *Emerging Engineering Technologies and Industrial Applications* (pp. 1–20). IGI Global Scientific Publishing. DOI: 10.4018/979-8-3693-1335-0.ch001

Salazar-Gomez, A., Darbyshire, M., Gao, J., Sklar, E. I., & Parsons, S. (2022). Beyond mAP: Towards practical object detection for weed spraying in precision agriculture. *2022 IEEE/RSJ International Conference on Intelligent Robots and Systems (IROS)*, (pp. 9232-9238). DOI: 10.1109/IROS47612.2022.9982139

Santos, O., & Radanliev, P. (2024). *Beyond the algorithm: AI, security, privacy, and ethics*. Addison-Wesley.

Sartori, L. & Bocca, G. (2023). Minding the gap (s): public perceptions of AI and socio-technical imaginaries. AI & Society.

Sartori, L. & Theodorou, A. (2022). A sociotechnical perspective for the future of AI: narratives, inequalities, and human control. Ethics and Information Technology.

Saxena, D., & Cao, J. (2021). Generative adversarial networks (GANs) challenges, solutions, and future directions. *ACM Computing Surveys, 54*(3), 1–42. DOI: 10.1145/3446374

Scharr, H., Minervini, M., Fischbach, A., & Tsaftaris, S. (2014, July). Annotated Image Datasets of Rosette Plants. *Annotated Image Datasets of Rosette Plants*. Retrieved from https://juser.fz-juelich.de/record/154525/files/FZJ-2014-03837.pdf

Sebastiani, F. (2002). Machine learning in automated text categorization. *ACM Computing Surveys, 34*(1), 1–47. DOI: 10.1145/505282.505283

Seethepalli, A., Guo, H., Liu, X., Griffiths, M., Almtarfi, H., Li, Z., Liu, S., Zare, A., Fritschi, F. B., Blancaflor, E. B., Ma, X.-F., & York, L. M. (2020). RhizoVision Crown: An Integrated Hardware and Software Platform for Root Crown Phenotyping. *Plant Phenomics (Washington, D.C.), 2020*, 3074916. Advance online publication. DOI: 10.34133/2020/3074916 PMID: 33313547

Sellenthin, A. L. (2012). Students' attitudes towards learning communication skills: Correlating attitudes, demographic and metacognitive variables. *International Journal of Medical Education*, *3*, 201–208. DOI: 10.5116/ijme.5066.cef9

Shah. (2016). Teaching of Urdu: Problems and Prospects.

Shankar, P. (2024). Dwelling and landscape setting: Continuity of cultural ideas in the dwellings of Udaipur. Potency of the Vernacular Settlements.

Shankar, R. P., Dubey, A. K., Mishra, P., Deshpande, V. Y., Chandrasekhar, T. S., & Shivananda, P. G. (2006). Student attitudes towards communication skills training in a medical college in Western Nepal. *Education for Health (Abingdon)*, *19*(1), 71–84. DOI: 10.1080/13576280500534693 PMID: 16531304

Sharma, R. & Gupta, H. (2024). Leveraging cognitive digital twins in industry 5.0 for achieving sustainable development goal 9: An exploration of inclusive and sustainable industrialization strategies. Journal of Cleaner Production.

Sharma, R., Saxena, K., & Rana, A. (2021). Unsupervised learning in accordance with new aspects of artificial intelligence. Machine learning approach for cloud data analytics in IoT, 429-459.

Sheikh, S. (2020). Understanding the role of artificial intelligence and its future social impact.

Shorten, C., & Khoshgoftaar, T. M. (2019). A survey on Image Data Augmentation for Deep Learning. *Journal of Big Data*, *6*(1), 60. DOI: 10.1186/s40537-019-0197-0

Siegmann, B., Alonso, L., Celesti, M., Cogliati, S., Colombo, R., Damm, A., Douglas, S., Guanter, L., Hanuš, J., Kataja, K., Kraska, T., Matveeva, M., Moreno, J., Muller, O., Pikl, M., Pinto, F., Quirós Vargas, J., Rademske, P., Rodriguez-Morene, F., & Rascher, U. (2019, December). The high-performance airborne imaging spectrometer HyPlant-from raw images to top-of-canopy reflectance and fluorescence products: Introduction of an automatized processing chain. *Remote Sensing (Basel)*, *11*(23), 2760. Advance online publication. DOI: 10.3390/rs11232760

Sillett, M. (2020). Folklore and new Media Communications: An Exploration of Journey to the West, Its Modern Orality and Traditional Storytelling in Contemporary Online Spaces. canterbury.ac.uk

Silver, D., Schrittwieser, J., Simonyan, K., Antonoglou, I., Huang, A., Guez, A., Hubert, T., Baker, L., Lai, M., Bolton, A., Chen, Y., Lillicrap, T., Hui, F., Sifre, L., Van Den Driessche, G., Graepel, T., & Hassabis, D. (2017). Mastering the game of Go without human knowledge. *Nature*, *550*(7676), 354–359. DOI: 10.1038/nature24270 PMID: 29052630

Simpson, J., Furnace, J., Crosby, J., Cumming, A., Evans, P., Friedman, M., David, B., Harden, R., Lloyd, D., & McKenzie, H. (2002). The Scottish Doctor –learning outcomes for the medical undergraduate in Scotland: A foundation for competent and reflective practice. *Medical Teacher*, *24*(2), 136–143. DOI: 10.1080/01421590220120713 PMID: 12098432

Siro, C., Aliannejadi, M., & De Rijke, M. (2024). Understanding and Predicting User Satisfaction with Conversational Recommender Systems. *ACM Transactions on Information Systems*, *42*(2), 1–37. DOI: 10.1145/3624989

Škola, F., Rizvić, S., Cozza, M., Barbieri, L., Bruno, F., Skarlatos, D., & Liarokapis, F. (2020). Virtual reality with 360-video storytelling in cultural heritage: Study of presence, engagement, and immersion. *Sensors (Basel)*, *20*(20), 5851. DOI: 10.3390/s20205851 PMID: 33081154

Smith, B. & Monforte, J. (2020). Stories, new materialism and pluralism: Understanding, practising and pushing the boundaries of narrative analysis. Methods in Psychology.

Spennemann, D. H. R. (2023). ChatGPT and the generation of digitally born "knowledge": How does a generative AI language model interpret cultural heritage values?. Knowledge.

Srivastava, N., Hinton, G., Krizhevsky, A., Sutskever, I., & Salakhutdinov, R. (2014). Dropout: A Simple Way to Prevent Neural Networks from Overfitting. *Journal of Machine Learning Research*, *15*, 1929–1958.

Steffen, T. & Bjoraker, W. (2020). The return of oral hermeneutics: As good today as it was for the Hebrew Bible and first-century Christianity.

Stengel-Eskin, E., Murray, K., Zhang, S., White, A. S., & Van Durme, B. (2021). Joint Universal Syntactic and Semantic Parsing. *Transactions of the Association for Computational Linguistics*, *9*, 756–773. DOI: 10.1162/tacl_a_00396

Sterledev, R., Sterledeva, T., & Abramenko, V. (2021, October). Artificial intelligence as the possible third front of humanity. In *International Perm Forum Science and Global Challenges of the 21st Century* (pp. 819-826). Cham: Springer International Publishing.

Stewart, M. (1995). Effective physician-patient communication and health outcomes: A review. *Canadian Medical Association Journal, 152*, 1423–1433. PMID: 7728691

Sufi, F. (2024). Generative pre-trained transformer (GPT) in research: A systematic review on data augmentation. Information.

Sun, K., Luo, X., & Luo, M. Y. (2022, July). A survey of pretrained language models. In *International Conference on Knowledge Science, Engineering and Management* (pp. 442-456). Cham: Springer International Publishing.

Sun, S., Bi, J., Guillen, M., & Pérez-Marín, A. M. (2020). Assessing driving risk using internet of vehicles data: An analysis based on generalized linear models. *Sensors (Basel), 20*(9), 2712. DOI: 10.3390/s20092712 PMID: 32397508

Szegedy, C., Vanhoucke, V., Ioffe, S., & Shlens, J. (2016). *Wojna, ZB*. Rethinking the Inception Architecture for Computer Vision., DOI: 10.1109/CVPR.2016.308

Taeihagh, A. (2021). Governance of artificial intelligence. Policy and Society.

Tamblyn, R., Abrahamowicz, M., Dauphinee, D., Wenghofer, E., Jacques, A., Klass, D., Smee, S., Blackmore, D., Winslade, N., Girard, N., Du Berger, R., Bartman, I., Buckeridge, D. L., & Hanley, J. A. (2007). Physician scores on a national clinical skills examination as predictors of complaints to medical regulatory authorities. *Journal of the American Medical Association, 298*(9), 993–1001. DOI: 10.1001/jama.298.9.993 PMID: 17785644

Tanabe, R., Matsui, T., & Tanaka, T. S. (2023, February). Winter wheat yield prediction using convolutional neural networks and UAV-based multispectral imagery. *Field Crops Research, 291*, 108786. Advance online publication. DOI: 10.1016/j.fcr.2022.108786

Terentev, A., Dolzhenko, V., Fedotov, A., & Eremenko, D. (2022). Current state of hyperspectral remote sensing for early plant disease detection: A review. *Sensors (Basel), 22*(3), 757. DOI: 10.3390/s22030757 PMID: 35161504

Timilsina S, Karki S, & Singh JP. (2019). Attitudes Of Recently Admitted Undergraduate Medical Students Towards Learning Communication-Skills: A Cross-Sectional Study From Chitwan Medical College. Adv Med Educ Pract., 10, 963-969. DOI: 10.2147/AMEP.S229951

Topaz, M., Lai, K., Dhopeshwarkar, N., Seger, D. L., Sa'adon, R., Goss, F., Rozenblum, R., & Zhou, L. (2016). Clinicians' reports in electronic health records versus patients' concerns in social media: A pilot study of adverse drug reactions of aspirin and atorvastatin. *Drug Safety, 39*(3), 241–250. DOI: 10.1007/s40264-015-0381-x PMID: 26715498

Tortorella, G. L., Fogliatto, F. S., Cauchick-Miguel, P. A., Kurnia, S., & Jurburg, D. (2021). Integration of industry 4.0 technologies into total productive maintenance practices. *International Journal of Production Economics, 240,* 108224. DOI: 10.1016/j.ijpe.2021.108224

Totschnig, W. (2020). Fully autonomous AI. Science and Engineering Ethics.

Tran, Tran, Nguyen, Nguyen, & Cheung. (2021). On Data Augmentation for GAN Training. IEEE Transactions on Image Processing. .DOI: 10.1109/TIP.2021.3049346

Triantafillou, E., Zhu, T., Dumoulin, V., Lamblin, P., Evci, U., Xu, K., . . . Larochelle, H. (2019). Meta-dataset: A dataset of datasets for learning to learn from few examples. arXiv preprint arXiv:1903.03096.

Trichopoulos, G., Alexandridis, G., & Caridakis, G. (2023). A survey on computational and emergent digital storytelling. Heritage.

Turing, A. M. (1950). Computing Machinery and Intelligence. *Mind, LIX*(236), 433–460. DOI: 10.1093/mind/LIX.236.433

Turing, A. M. (2009). *Computing machinery and intelligence.* Springer Netherlands. DOI: 10.1007/978-1-4020-6710-5_3

Tu, Y.-H., Johansen, K., Phinn, S., & Robson, A. (2019, January). Measuring Canopy Structure and Condition Using Multi-Spectral UAS Imagery in a Horticultural Environment. *Remote Sensing (Basel), 11*(3), 269. DOI: 10.3390/rs11030269

Ugwuoke, E., & Onu, J. (2023). A Comparative Structuralist Analysis of Two Igbo folktales. Sprin Journal of Arts *Humanities and Social Sciences, 2*(05), 31–44.

Usama, M., Qadir, J., Raza, A., Arif, H., Yau, K. L. A., Elkhatib, Y., Hussain, A., & Al-Fuqaha, A. (2019). Unsupervised machine learning for networking: Techniques, applications and research challenges. *IEEE Access : Practical Innovations, Open Solutions, 7,* 65579–65615. DOI: 10.1109/ACCESS.2019.2916648

Vaswani, A., Shazeer, N., Parmar, N., Uszkoreit, J., Jones, L., Gomez, A. N., & Polosukhin, I. (2017). Attention is all you need. *Advances in Neural Information Processing Systems,* 30.

Veley, K. M., Berry, J. C., Fentress, S. J., Schachtman, D. P., Baxter, I., & Bart, R. (2017). High-throughput profiling and analysis of plant responses over time to abiotic stress. *Plant Direct, 1*(4), e00023. DOI: 10.1002/pld3.23 PMID: 31245669

Vélez, S., Ariza-Sentís, M., & Valente, J. (2023). Dataset on unmanned aerial vehicle multispectral images acquired over a vineyard affected by Botrytis cinerea in northern Spain. *Data in Brief, 46,* 108876. DOI: 10.1016/j.dib.2022.108876 PMID: 36660442

Verbelen, R., Antonio, K., & Claeskens, G. (2018). Unravelling the predictive power of telematics data in car insurance pricing. *Applied Statistics*, *67*(5), 1275–1304. DOI: 10.1111/rssc.12283

Vincent, R. R., Sakthivel, E., Kumari, M., Nisha, F., & Rohini, A. (2024). Machine Learning for Geospatial Analysis: Enhancing Spatial Understanding and Decision-Making. In Ethics, Machine Learning, and Python in Geospatial Analysis (pp. 168-195). IGI Global.

Viswanath, Y., Jamthe, S., Lokiah, S., & Bianchini, E. (2024). Machine unlearning for generative AI. Journal of AI. *Robotics & Workplace Automation*, *3*(1), 37–46. DOI: 10.69554/KZRS2422

von Davier, M. (2023). Training Optimus Prime, MD: A Case Study of Automated Item Generation Using Artificial Intelligence–From Fine-Tuned GPT2 to GPT3 and Beyond. In Advancing Natural Language Processing in Educational Assessment (pp. 90-106). Routledge.

Waardenburg, L. & Huysman, M. (2022). From coexistence to co-creation: Blurring boundaries in the age of AI. Information and Organization.

Waldron, A. (2022). Queer Screams: A History of LGBTQ+ Survival Through the Lens of American Horror Cinema.

Walters, R., & Novak, M. (2021). *Cyber security, artificial intelligence, data protection & the law*. Springer. DOI: 10.1007/978-981-16-1665-5

Wamwea, C. M., Muema, B. K., & Mung'atu, J. K. (2015). Modelling a pay-as-you-drive insurance pricing structure using a generalized linear model: Case study of a company in Kiambu. *American Journal of Theoretical and Applied Statistics*, *4*(6), 527–533. DOI: 10.11648/j.ajtas.20150406.23

Wang, X., Wei, J., Schuurmans, D., Le, Q., Chi, E., Narang, S., Chowdhery, A., & Zhou, D. (2023). *Self-Consistency Improves Chain of Thought Reasoning in Language Models* (No. arXiv:2203.11171). arXiv. http://arxiv.org/abs/2203.11171

Wang, Y., Yang, L., Chen, H., Hussain, A., Ma, C., & Al-gabri, M. (2022). Mushroom-YOLO: A deep learning algorithm for mushroom growth recognition based on improved YOLOv5 in agriculture 4.0. *2022 IEEE 20th International Conference on Industrial Informatics (INDIN)* (pp. 239-244). DOI: 10.1109/INDIN51773.2022.9976155

Wang, H., Can, D., Kazemzadeh, A., Bar, F., & Narayanan, S. (2012, July). A system for real-time twitter sentiment analysis of 2012 us presidential election cycle. In *Proceedings of the ACL 2012 system demonstrations* (pp. 115-120).

Wang, J., Li, X., Guo, T., Dzievit, M. J., Yu, X., Liu, P., Price, K. P., & Yu, J. (2021, November). Genetic dissection of seasonal vegetation index dynamics in maize through aerial based high-throughput phenotyping. *The Plant Genome*, *14*(3), e20155. Advance online publication. DOI: 10.1002/tpg2.20155 PMID: 34596348

Wang, L., Zeng, Y., & Chen, T. (2015, February). Back propagation neural network with adaptive differential evolution algorithm for time series forecasting. *Expert Systems with Applications*, *42*(2), 855–863. DOI: 10.1016/j.eswa.2014.08.018

Wang, X., Oxholm, G., Zhang, D., & Wang, Y. F. (2017). Multimodal transfer: A hierarchical deep convolutional neural network for fast artistic style transfer. In *Proceedings of the IEEE conference on computer vision and pattern recognition* (pp. 5239-5247). DOI: 10.1109/CVPR.2017.759

Wasserman, R. (2021). Ancient and contemporary industries based on alkali and alkali-earth salts and hydroxides: the historical and technological. Ionic Liquids: Thermophysical Properties and Applications, 123.

Watson, D. S. (2023). On the philosophy of unsupervised learning. *Philosophy & Technology*, *36*(2), 28. DOI: 10.1007/s13347-023-00635-6

Weaver, W. (1949). In Locke, W. N., & Donald Booth, A. (Eds.), *Translation in Machine Translation of Languages: Fourteen Essays. Machine Translation of Languages: Fourteen Essays* (pp. 15–23). MIT Press.

Wei, J., Wang, X., Schuurmans, D., Bosma, M., Ichter, B., Xia, F., Chi, E., Le, Q., & Zhou, D. (2022). *Chain-of-Thought Prompting Elicits Reasoning in Large Language Models* (Version 6). arXiv. DOI: 10.48550/ARXIV.2201.11903

Wei, J., Wang, X., Schuurmans, D., Bosma, M., Ichter, B., Xia, F., Chi, E., Le, Q., & Zhou, D. (2023). *Chain-of-Thought Prompting Elicits Reasoning in Large Language Models* (No. arXiv:2201.11903). arXiv. http://arxiv.org/abs/2201.11903

Wei, L., Wang, K., Lu, Q., Liang, Y., Li, H., Wang, Z., Wang, R., & Cao, L. (2021, August). Crops fine classification in airborne hyperspectral imagery based on multi-feature fusion and deep learning. *Remote Sensing (Basel)*, *13*(15), 2917. Advance online publication. DOI: 10.3390/rs13152917

Widyahening, I. S. (2011) Negative attitudes of fi rst year medical students of University of Indonesia towards communication skills learning. *Proceedings of the 8th Asia Pacifi c Medical Education Conference.*

Wienrich, C. & Latoschik, M. E. (2021). extended artificial intelligence: New prospects of human-ai interaction research. Frontiers in Virtual Reality.

Wijmans, E., Datta, S., Maksymets, O., Das, A., Gkioxari, G., Lee, S., & Batra, D. (2019). Embodied question answering in photorealistic environments with point cloud perception. In *Proceedings of the IEEE/CVF Conference on Computer Vision and Pattern Recognition* (pp. 6659-6668). DOI: 10.1109/CVPR.2019.00682

Williams, S., Weinman, J., & Dale, J. (1998). Doctor-patient communication and patient satisfaction: A review. *Family Practice, 15*(5), 480–492. DOI: 10.1093/fampra/15.5.480 PMID: 9848436

Wilmers, N. (2024). Generative AI and the Future of Inequality.

Wilson, A. A., Nehme, A., Dhyani, A., & Mahbub, K. (2024). A Comparison of Generalised Linear Modelling with Machine Learning Approaches for Predicting Loss Cost in Motor Insurance. *Risks, 12*(4), 62. DOI: 10.3390/risks12040062

World Health Organization. (1995). The five-star doctor: An asset to health care reform? https://www.who.int/hrh/en/HRDJ_1_1_02.pdf

Wu, J., Wen, S., Lan, Y., Yin, X., Zhang, J., & Ge, Y. (2022, December). Estimation of cotton canopy parameters based on unmanned aerial vehicle (UAV) oblique photography. *Plant Methods, 18*(1), 129. Advance online publication. DOI: 10.1186/s13007-022-00966-z PMID: 36482426

Xie, S. (2024). Estimating Risk Relativity of Driving Records using Generalized Additive Models: A Statistical Approach for Auto Insurance Rate Regulation. *Asia-Pacific Journal of Risk and Insurance, 18*(1), 55–86. DOI: 10.1515/apjri-2023-0032

Xu, B., Yang, A., Lin, J., Wang, Q., Zhou, C., Zhang, Y., & Mao, Z. (2023). *ExpertPrompting: Instructing Large Language Models to be Distinguished Experts* (No. arXiv:2305.14688). arXiv. http://arxiv.org/abs/2305.14688

Xu, J., Zhang, Z., & Hu, X. (2023). Extracting semantic knowledge from gans with unsupervised learning. *IEEE Transactions on Pattern Analysis and Machine Intelligence, 45*(8), 9654–9668. DOI: 10.1109/TPAMI.2023.3262140 PMID: 37030793

Yadav, P. K., Thomasson, J. A., Searcy, S. W., Hardin, R. G., Braga-Neto, U., Popescu, S. C., Martin, D. E., Rodriguez, R., Meza, K., Enciso, J., Diaz, J. S., & Wang, T. (2022). Assessing the performance of YOLOv5 algorithm for detecting volunteer cotton plants in corn fields at three different growth stages. *Artificial Intelligence in Agriculture, 6*, 292–303. DOI: 10.1016/j.aiia.2022.11.005

Yang, W., Yang, C., Hao, Z., Xie, C., & Li, M. (2019). Diagnosis of Plant Cold Damage Based on Hyperspectral Imaging and Convolutional Neural Network. *IEEE Access : Practical Innovations, Open Solutions, 7*, 118239–118248. DOI: 10.1109/ACCESS.2019.2936892

Yao, S., Zhao, J., Yu, D., Du, N., Shafran, I., Narasimhan, K., & Cao, Y. (2023). *ReAct: Synergizing Reasoning and Acting in Language Models* (No. arXiv:2210.03629). arXiv. http://arxiv.org/abs/2210.03629

Yeo, E., Pilson, A., Rutter, N., & Hasan, E. (2023). We Need to be as a Group: Using and Evaluating the Listening Guide in Feminist Collaborative Autoethnography With an Affective 'Fifth Listen' as a Tool to (re) construct Identities. *International Journal of Qualitative Methods, 22*. DOI: 10.1177/16094069231180166

Yigitcanlar, T., Desouza, K. C., Butler, L., & Roozkhosh, F. (2020). Contributions and risks of artificial intelligence (AI) in building smarter cities: Insights from a systematic review of the literature. Energies.

Young, M. (2022). "The Tablets I Spoke about Are Good to Preserve until Far-off Days": An Overview on the Creation and Evolution of Canons in Babylonia and Assyria from the .... Canonisation as Innovation.

Young, T., Hazarika, D., Poria, S., & Cambria, E. (2018). Recent trends in deep learning based natural language processing. IEEE Computational Intelligence Magazine, 13(3), 55-75.

Yuan, B., He, Y., Davis, J., Zhang, T., Dao, T., Chen, B., . . . Zhang, C. (2022). Decentralized training of foundation models in heterogeneous environments. Advances in Neural Information Processing Systems, 35, 25464-25477.

Yuan, C., & Moghaddam, M. (2020). Attribute-aware generative design with generative adversarial networks. *IEEE Access : Practical Innovations, Open Solutions, 8*(1), 190710–190721. DOI: 10.1109/ACCESS.2020.3032280

Yue, J., Yang, H., Yang, G., Fu, Y., Wang, H., & Zhou, C. (2023, February). Estimating vertically growing crop above-ground biomass based on UAV remote sensing. *Computers and Electronics in Agriculture, 205*, 107627. DOI: 10.1016/j.compag.2023.107627

Yu, H., & Guo, Y. (2023, June). Generative artificial intelligence empowers educational reform: Current status, issues, and prospects. *Frontiers in Education, 8*, 1183162. DOI: 10.3389/feduc.2023.1183162

Yu, H., & Zhang, X. (2020). Synthesis of Prostate MR Images for Classification Using Capsule Network-Based GAN Model. *Sensors (Basel), 20*(20), 5736. DOI: 10.3390/s20205736 PMID: 33050243

Yu, S., Xie, L., & Huang, Q. (2023, April). Inception convolutional vision transformers for plant disease identification. *Internet of Things : Engineering Cyber Physical Human Systems, 21*, 100650. DOI: 10.1016/j.iot.2022.100650

Yu, X., & Gen, M. (2010). *Introduction to evolutionary algorithms*. Springer Science & Business Media. DOI: 10.1007/978-1-84996-129-5

Zhang, Y., & Chen, D. Z. (2023, October). GPT4MIA: Utilizing Generative Pre-trained Transformer (GPT-3) as a Plug-and-Play Transductive Model for Medical Image Analysis. In International Conference on Medical Image Computing and Computer-Assisted Intervention (pp. 151-160). Cham: Springer Nature Switzerland. DOI: 10.1007/978-3-031-47401-9_15

Zhang, B., Zhu, J., & Su, H. (2023). Toward the third generation artificial intelligence. *Science China. Information Sciences*.

Zhang, H., Wang, L., Tian, T., & Yin, J. (2021, March). A review of unmanned aerial vehicle low-altitude remote sensing (Uav-lars) use in agricultural monitoring in china. *Remote Sensing (Basel)*, *13*(6), 1221. Advance online publication. DOI: 10.3390/rs13061221

Zhang, J., Chang, J., Danescu-Niculescu-Mizil, C., Dixon, L., Hua, Y., Taraborelli, D., & Thain, N. (2018). Conversations Gone Awry: Detecting Early Signs of Conversational Failure. *Proceedings of the 56th Annual Meeting of the Association for Computational Linguistics(*Volume 1*: Long Papers)*, 1350–1361. DOI: 10.18653/v1/P18-1125

Zhang, Y., Fei, H., Li, D., & Li, P. (2022). PromptGen: Automatically Generate Prompts using Generative Models. *Findings of the Association for Computational Linguistics: NAACL, 2022*, 30–37. DOI: 10.18653/v1/2022.findings-naacl.3

Zhang, Y., Huang, S., Zhou, G., Hu, Y., & Li, L. (2023, February). Identification of tomato leaf diseases based on multi-channel automatic orientation recurrent attention network. *Computers and Electronics in Agriculture*, *205*, 107605. DOI: 10.1016/j.compag.2022.107605

Zhao, W. X., Liu, J., Ren, R., & Wen, J.-R. (2024). Dense Text Retrieval Based on Pretrained Language Models: A Survey. *ACM Transactions on Information Systems*, *42*(4), 1–60. DOI: 10.1145/3637870

Zhavoronkov, A., Ivanenkov, Y. A., Aliper, A., Veselov, M. S., Aladinskiy, V. A., Aladinskaya, A. V., Terentiev, V. A., Polykovskiy, D. A., Kuznetsov, M. D., Asadulaev, A., Volkov, Y., Zholus, A., Shayakhmetov, R. R., Zhebrak, A., Minaeva, L. I., Zagribelnyy, B. A., Lee, L. H., Soll, R., Madge, D., & Aspuru-Guzik, A. (2019). Deep learning enables rapid identification of potent DDR1 kinase inhibitors. *Nature Biotechnology*, *37*(9), 1038–1040. DOI: 10.1038/s41587-019-0224-x PMID: 31477924

Zhong, Y., Hu, X., Luo, C., Wang, X., Zhao, J., & Zhang, L. (2020). WHU-Hi: UAV-borne hyperspectral with high spatial resolution (H2) benchmark datasets and classifier for precise crop identification based on deep convolutional neural network with CRF. *Remote Sensing of Environment*, *250*, 112012. DOI: 10.1016/j.rse.2020.112012

Zhou, Y., Geng, X., Shen, T., Tao, C., Long, G., Lou, J.-G., & Shen, J. (2023). *Thread of Thought Unraveling Chaotic Contexts* (No. arXiv:2311.08734). arXiv. http://arxiv.org/abs/2311.08734

Zhu, Liu, & Qin. (2017). Data Augmentation in Classification using GAN.

Zhu, Liu, Li, Wan, & Qin. (2018). Emotion Classification with Data Augmentation Using Generative Adversarial Networks. DOI: 10.1007/978-3-319-93040-428

Zwolińska-Ligaj, M. A. & Guzal-Dec, D. J. (2024). Rural Area Resilience during the COVID-19 Pandemic as Exemplified by Urban–Rural Communes in Poland. Sustainability.

About the Contributors

Rajkumar Kannan works in the Department of Computer Science since June 1993. He has founded the Department of Data Science and serves as HoD since its inception in 2019. Besides he is the Dean, Deanery International Relations at Bishop Heber College (Autonomous), Tiruchirappalli. Previously, Rajkumar worked for King Faisal University, Kingdom of Saudi Arabia in the Faculty of Computer Science and Information Technology where he taught ABET (USA) accredited BS and MS Computer Science as well as BS and MS Computer Information Systems Programmes. He received the BSc Computer Science and MSc Computer Science degrees in the year 1991 and 1993 from Bishop Heber College (Autonomous), Tiruchirappalli. He had also received his MPhil Computer Science from then Regional Engineering College, Tiruchirappalli. Rajkumar graduated his PhD degree in Computer Applications from National Institute of Technology - Tiruchirappalli, India, in the year 2007. Rajkumar visited many countries including UK, USA, Germany, Japan, Slovakia, Thailand, Austria, Malaysia, Indonesia and all Gulf countries in pursuance of teaching and research activities. His research primarily lies at the confluence of Artificial Intelligence, Data Science, Multimedia and Web Retrieval, Collective and collaborative Intelligence. Rajkumar has published several high impact papers in refereed journals from IEEE, Springer, Elsevier, World Scientific, Taylor and Francis and international conferences. He serves as a referee to journals, including IEEE Trans. MM, IEEE Trans. HMS, IEEE Trans. BME, ACM Trans. MCCA, Springer MTAP and Springer JMUI. Rajkumar is also a Technical Program Committee member of several international conferences and keynote speaker to several reputed events. He is the author of a widely followed book titled, Java Programming, published by Pearson and has edited a volume for Springer Verlag (LNCS 6411) - Germany. Rajkumar has edited a book for IGI Global - USA titled, Managing and Processing Big Data in Cloud Computing. Rajkumar is a senior member of ACM - USA and a life member of CSI - India and ISTE - India. More details can be found at https://in.linkedin.com/in/rajkumarkannan19.

Muneer Ahmad's academic journey is marked by a series of impressive accomplishments. He embarked on his educational pursuits by attaining Master's degrees in Mathematics (1999) and Computer Science (2002) from Punjab University and Islamia University, Pakistan, respectively. His quest for knowledge led him to further heights as he pursued an MPhil (MS, 2007) degree in Computer Science from COMSATS University, Pakistan. The pinnacle of his academic endeavors was reached with a Ph.D. (2015) from Universiti Teknologi PETRONAS, Malaysia. His doctoral research centered around the intricate domain of DNA signal processing, specifically focusing on "Enhancing protein-coding regions identification in Eukaryotic DNA splicing by proposing new fuzzy logic-based methods." Dr. Muneer Ahmad's scholarly contributions extend beyond his educational pursuits. He has authored an impressive portfolio of over 100 research articles, which are published in esteemed journals indexed in WoS and Scopus, along with various conference articles and book chapters. His intellectual curiosity has driven him to delve into a diverse array of research projects, totaling more than a dozen, carried out in Malaysia and Saudi Arabia. These endeavors have resulted in the successful acquisition of research grants amounting to approximately 500,000 MYR/SAR. As an academic mentor, Dr. Muneer's influence extends far and wide. He has overseen the guidance of more than 50 students, spanning Bachelor's, Master's, and Ph.D. levels, in the fields of Computer Science and Data Science. His commitment to fostering the next generation of scholars is evident through his supervisory role. Dr. Muneer's research interests encompass the dynamic realm of data science. His expertise lies in applied machine learning applications within diverse domains such as pattern recognition, image processing, signal analysis, e-commerce, cybersecurity, edge computing, and cloud computing. He has undertaken the exploration of machine learning, deep learning, and data-driven methodologies to propose finely-tuned solutions across various facets of computing. The overarching objective of Dr. Muneer's research endeavors is to catalyze advancements that resonate within the realms of industry 4.0 applications. With a steadfast commitment to developing enhanced and innovative solutions, he seeks to contribute substantial value to the evolving landscape of technology and industry.

***

Andi Asrifan, S.Pd, M.Pd, a distinguished figure in the realm of education, particularly in English Language Education, has made significant contributions through his extensive research, teaching, and leadership roles. As the Head of the Institute for Cooperation and International Affairs at Universitas Muhammadiyah Sidenreng Rappang, Dr. Asrifan's academic journey is marked by a rich tapestry of achievements, including a Doctor of Education in English Language Education.

His work spans various facets of education, language, and technology, reflecting the diverse topics covered in his publications and research endeavors. These include, but are not limited to, the impact of the COVID-19 pandemic on educational practices, methodologies in English as a Foreign Language (EFL) classrooms, and the integration of technology in teaching and learning processes. Dr. Asrifan's commitment to advancing educational standards and practices is further evidenced by his active participation in international conferences, webinars, and workshops across countries like India, the Philippines, and Pakistan. These events, organized by various institutions and associations, underscore his role as a global educator and thought leader. His dedication to professional development is also highlighted through his involvement in numerous courses and certifications in personal branding, public speaking, and literacy teaching. Moreover, Dr. Asrifan's leadership extends beyond academia into organizational and educational development, where he has served in various capacities, including as an external examiner for Ph.D. dissertations and a reviewer for scientific journals. His accolades, memberships in professional organizations, and roles as an ambassador for international associations speak volumes of his influence and commitment to fostering educational excellence and sustainable development goals globally.

Sadia Aziz is an experienced academic and researcher specializing in Computer Networks, Cybersecurity, and Wireless Communications. She has over 18 years of teaching experience across various cultural settings, including Australia, Saudi Arabia, Pakistan, and China. Dr. Aziz has contributed significantly to curriculum development, online learning innovations, and supervising postgraduate research, with her research interests encompassing mobile ad hoc networks, IoT, and distributed systems.

Muhammad Jawad Bashir is a dedicated researcher specializing in precision agriculture and computer vision. He completed his Bachelor's degree in 2019 and his Master's degree in 2020, focusing on crop disease detection and smart pesticide management in Mungbean crops. With extensive research experience in smart farming, he worked as a Research Assistant at the NUST-Coventry Internet of Things Lab at SEECS-NUST. His work utilizes UAVs, multispectral imagery, and computer vision to advance agricultural practices.

Aamna Bhatti received her B.S. degree in Electrical Engineering from UET Taxila, Pakistan, her M.Sc. degree in Information Technology from Quaid-i-Azam University, Islamabad, Pakistan, and her MS degree in Computer Science from the NUST, Islamabad, Pakistan. Her key research interests include deep learning, computer vision, and machine learning.

Muh. Fadli Hasa, S.Kom., M.Kom., born on June 16, 1996, in Akkotengen Village, Sajoanging District, Wajo Regency, South Sulawesi Province, has been passionate about technology and information since a young age. This interest led him to pursue a Bachelor's degree in Informatics Engineering at Muhammadiyah University of Sorong, graduating in 2019. To further his knowledge, he earned a Master's degree in Computer Science from Ahmad Dahlan University in 2020. After completing his master's studies, Fadli returned to his alma mater, Muhammadiyah University of Sorong, as a lecturer in the Informatics Engineering program. Since 2021, he has dedicated himself to educating students, helping them develop their potential and preparing them for the complexities of the professional world. Besides teaching, he is actively involved in research and scientific publications, believing that sharing knowledge and experience fosters a better, globally competitive generation.

Qazi Mudassar Ilyas received his M.Sc. in Computer Science from the University of Agriculture, Faisalabad, Pakistan, in 2000 and his Ph.D. in Information and Communication Engineering from the Huazhong University of Science and Technology, China, in 2005. He has served several educational institutions in Pakistan, including the Ghulam Ishaq Institute, Topi, the University of Punjab, Lahore, and the COMSATS Institute of Information Technology, Abbottabad. Currently, he is working as an Associate Professor at King Faisal University, Saudi Arabia. His research interests include machine learning, knowledge management, and information retrieval.

Mohsen Mahmoudi-Dehaki is an Assistant Professor of TEFL at the Islamic Azad University of Najafabad, Iran. With over a decade of experience teaching undergraduate and postgraduate students, he has established himself as a respected educator and scholar. His research has been widely published in national and international journals, solidifying his reputation as a prominent voice in the field. Dr. Mahmoudi-Dehaki serves as a peer reviewer for several esteemed scientific journals, including RELP, ensuring the highest standards of academic rigor and integrity. His academic achievements include winning the prestigious first place in the English Writing Award in Iran, a distinction earned among all university students from state universities and institutes of higher education. His paper "COVID-19 Lingo or Covidipedia" has garnered significant attention, with over 70,000 visits, making it the most visited paper in Iranian scientific journals. This remarkable achievement underscores his significant impact on the academic community. Dr. Mahmoudi-Dehaki's research and teaching interests span a diverse range of novel branches in applied linguistics, including psycho/cognitive/neurocognitive/forensic/ jury/sociocultural/ecological, and clinical linguistics. He is also well-versed in educational technology, educational psychology, and psychometrics, demonstrating his versatility and breadth of expertise in the interdisciplinary fields of education and linguistics.

Rafia Mumtaz (Senior Member, IEEE) received a Ph.D. degree in remote sensing and satellite image processing from the University of Surrey, U.K., in 2010. She is currently a Professor and the Director of the NUST Coventry Internet of Things (IoT) Lab, NUST-SEECS. She was a recipient of several national and international research grants worth PKR 174 million. She was awarded the NUST-SEECS Best Researcher Award in 2018, the Women of Wonder Award in 2021, and the University Best Teacher Award in 2022.

Sadaf Mumtaz received her PhD in 2010 from the University of Liverpool, UK specializing in Physiology related to the Medical field. She was the recipient of a '10% overseas scholarship award' from the Higher Education Commission of Pakistan in 2006 for her doctoral studies. Currently, she is working as Professor of Physiology & Director ORIC Rawalpindi Medical University, Rawalpindi, Pakistan. Previously she worked at the NUST School of Health Sciences (NSHS) as a Professor and Head of Physiology department. She also worked as a 'Research Fellow' in 2012 at the University of Liverpool, UK, and was awarded a Commonwealth Postdoctoral Academic Fellowship for the UK. During this time, she has produced internationally acclaimed research publications focusing on pathophysiological mechanisms in overweight and obese pregnant women. Additionally, she has served at the College of Medicine, Imam Abdul Rehman Bin Faisal University, Dammam, KSA as an Assistant Professor in Physiology for three years, winning a research grant on 'Alternative treatment of obesity-related complications' and produced educational research articles based on the medicine curriculum acquired from the University of Monash, Australia. Her research interest specifically includes climate-induced respiratory, cardiovascular, and neurological ailments, novel designing of Nano formulations for diabetic neuropathy, obesity-related metabolic disorders, neurological and breast cancers, and artificial intelligence-based designing of medical devices with the incorporation of concepts of telemedicine.

Nasim Nasr-Esfahani, PhD, is an Assistant Professor of TEFL at the Islamic Azad University of Isfahan (Khorasgan), Iran. She earned her PhD in TEFL at the Islamic Azad University of Isfahan, Khorasgan. She has over two decades of experience teaching undergraduate and postgraduate students in Iran. Her publications have appeared in leading international journals, such as the Australian Journal of Teacher Education. She serves as a reviewer and article editor of RELP Journal. Her areas of research and teaching interests are dynamic and evolving and span language education, generative artificial intelligence (GenAI) in education, critical thinking skills, oral and written communication skills, student engagement, advancing equity in education, brain-based teaching and learning, neurolinguistics, psycholinguistics as well as teaching and research methodologies.

Rajat Pandit is an accomplished academician and researcher specializing in Computer Science. He has made significant contributions to the fields of Natural Language Processing (NLP), Machine Learning, and Mobile Computing. With a Ph.D. from West Bengal State University, his doctoral research focused on computational semantics in Bengali, establishing his expertise in low-resource languages. Currently an Assistant Professor at West Bengal State University. He has over two decades of teaching and research experience. His research interests encompass Machine Translation, Sentiment Analysis, Text Summarization, Semantic Similarity, and Speech Processing. He has authored three edited books, two book chapters, and 23 journal publications, many of which are indexed in SCIE and other reputed platforms. Dr Pandit is actively involved in academic and administrative roles, serving on various committees at his university and contributing as a visiting faculty, external examiner, and syllabus committee member for other institutions. He is also recognized for his invited talks on topics like Machine Learning, Big Data, and IoT. A dedicated mentor, he supervises Ph.D. research and continuously contributes to advancing knowledge in computational sciences.

Akshay Bhuvaneswari Ramakrishnan is currently working with Hitachi Energy as a data engineer. With a strong passion for machine learning and AI, Akshay possesses extensive experience and expertise in these cutting-edge technologies.As an Intel innovator and ambassador, Akshay has demonstrated his prowess by emerging victorious in numerous hackathons and serving as a mentor for startups. His commitment to knowledge sharing is evident through his role as a speaker, having conducted over 50 sessions on Data Science and successfully trained more than 5000 students across India.Akshay's dedication to staying at the forefront of the field is underscored by his certification as an Intel Certified MLOps Professional. Furthermore, his research contributions are noteworthy, with 2 international conference papers, 1 sci paper, 3 Scopus papers, and 4 book chapters and a book to his credit.

Piyal Roy is an accomplished academician in the field of Computer Science & Engineering. He has completed his BSc in Computer Science, MSc in Computer Science and MTech in Computer Science & Engineering. Currently, he is working as an Assistant Professor at Computer Science & Engineering department at Brainware University, India.

Srijanani S. is a student who is pursuing B.E Computer Science and Engineering in Velammal Engineering College .Srijanani is an accomplished web developer with a strong passion for creating dynamic and user-friendly websites. Her academic background provided a solid foundation in programming, web development, and software engineering. Her journey is marked by valuable experiences, diverse internships, and notable participation in hackathons. Srijanani' s idea of blood warmer system for blood transfusion using Hardware and IOT secured best place in Hackathon organised in Velammal Engineering College. Her significant contribution in designing of Health Monitoring System for detecting sudden abnormalities using IOT has been shortlisted for the Smart India Hackathon. Srijanani has enriched her professional portfolio with internships at four different companies, each offering unique challenges and learning opportunities. Srijanani's technical skill set includes proficiency in HTML, CSS, JavaScript, and various JavaScript frameworks such as React and Angular. She is also well-versed in back-end technologies like Node.js and Express, as well as database management systems like MongoDB and SQL. Her ability to adapt to new technologies and frameworks quickly makes her a versatile developer.

Noor Sajjad is an Electrical Engineer specializing in AI and Autonomous Systems, currently pursuing a master's at NUST. With extensive experience in AI algorithms for IoT devices and precision agriculture, she has contributed to various innovative projects. Her achievements include winning first prize at the National Artificial Intelligence Forum 2021. She is working as a Research Assistant at NCIL, SEECS NUST.

Syafryadin is a lecturer of English postgraduate Program, Faculty of teacher Training and Education, University of Bengkulu. He was born in Kendari, on June 18 1988. His research interests are English Language Teaching, speaking, ICT and material development. He has been invited speaker in national and international conferences. He has published many papers in national accredited and international reputable journals.

Index

Y

www.ingramcontent.com/pod-product-compliance
Lightning Source LLC
LaVergne TN
LVHW081346300926
849161LV00008B/2084
* 9 7 9 8 3 6 9 3 6 2 5 5 6 *